Positive Psychology
in Racial and Ethnic Groups

CULTURAL, RACIAL, AND ETHNIC PSYCHOLOGY BOOK SERIES

Qualitative Strategies for Ethnocultural Research
Edited by Donna K. Nagata, Laura Kohn-Wood, and Lisa A. Suzuki

Positive Psychology in Racial and Ethnic Groups: Theory, Research, and Practice
Edited by Edward C. Chang, Christina A. Downey, Jameson K. Hirsch, and Natalie J. Lin

Positive Psychology

in Racial and Ethnic Groups

THEORY,
RESEARCH,
AND
PRACTICE

Edited by **Edward C. Chang, Christina A. Downey,
Jameson K. Hirsch, and Natalie J. Lin**

American Psychological Association • Washington, DC

Published by
American Psychological Association
750 First Street, NE
Washington, DC 20002-4242
www.apa.org

To order
APA Order Department
P.O. Box 92984
Washington, DC 20090-2984
Tel: (800) 374-2721; Direct: (202) 336-5510
Fax: (202) 336-5502; TDD/TTY: (202) 336-6123
Online: www.apa.org/pubs/books/
E-mail: order@apa.org

In the U.K., Europe, Africa, and the Middle East, copies may be ordered from
American Psychological Association
3 Henrietta Street
Covent Garden, London
WC2E 8LU England

Typeset in Goudy by Circle Graphics, Inc., Columbia, MD

Printer: Bang Printing, Brainerd, MN
Cover Designer: Mercury Publishing Services, Rockville, MD

The opinions and statements published are the responsibility of the authors, and such opinions and statements do not necessarily represent the policies of the American Psychological Association.

Library of Congress Cataloging-in-Publication Data

Names: Chang, Edward C. (Edward Chin-Ho), editor.
Title: Positive psychology in racial and ethnic groups : theory, research, and practice / edited by Edward C. Chang, Christina A. Downey, Jameson K. Hirsch, Natalie J. Lin.
Description: First edition. | Washington, DC : American Psychological Association, [2016] | Series: Cultural, racial, and ethnic psychology book series | Includes bibliographical references and index.
Identifiers: LCCN 2015025892 | ISBN 9781433821486 | ISBN 1433821486
Subjects: LCSH: Cultural psychiatry. | Positive psychology—Cross-cultural studies. | Minorities—Mental health. | Ethnopsychology.
Classification: LCC RC455.4.E8 P67 2016 | DDC 362.2—dc23 LC record available at http://lccn.loc.gov/2015025892

British Library Cataloguing-in-Publication Data

A CIP record is available from the British Library.

Printed in the United States of America
First Edition

http://dx.doi.org/10.1037/14799-000

CONTENTS

Contributors .... *ix*

Series Foreword .... *xi*
Frederick T. L. Leong

I. Introduction 1

Chapter 1.   Positive Psychology in Racial and Ethnic Groups:
             A Second Call to Action! 3
             Edward C. Chang, Christina A. Downey,
             Jameson K. Hirsch, and Natalie J. Lin

Chapter 2.   Positive Psychology in the Context of Race
             and Ethnicity 13
             Elizabeth L. Jeglic, Regina Miranda,
             and Lillian Polanco-Roman

II. Theory and Research 35

Chapter 3.   Positive Psychology in Asian Americans:
Theory and Research 37
Lucy Zhang Bencharit and Jeanne L. Tsai

Chapter 4.   Latina/os—Drive, Community, and Spirituality:
The Strength Within (*SOMOS Latina/os—
Ganas, Comunidad, y El Espíritu: La Fuerza
Que Llevamos Por Dentro*) 61
Jeanett Castellanos and Alberta M. Gloria

Chapter 5.   Positive Psychology in African Americans 83
*Jacqueline S. Mattis, Nyasha Grayman Simpson,
Wizdom Powell, Riana Elyse Anderson,
Lawanna R. Kimbro, and Jacob H. Mattis*

Chapter 6.   Positive Psychology in American Indians 109
*Gayle Skawennio Morse, Julie Guay McIntyre,
and Jeff King*

III. Assessment 129

Chapter 7.   Positive Psychology Assessment in Asian Americans 131
*Elizabeth A. Yu, Edward C. Chang, Hongfei Yang,
and Tina Yu*

Chapter 8.   Positive Psychology Assessment
Among Latinos 151
Rosemary Gonzalez and Amado M. Padilla

Chapter 9.   Positive Psychology Assessment
in African Americans 171
Laura P. Kohn-Wood and Alvin Thomas

Chapter 10.   Positive Psychology Assessment
in American Indians 195
Jeff King

IV. Practice 215

Chapter 11.   Social Connectedness Can Lead to Happiness:
Positive Psychology and Asian Americans 217
Michi Fu and Shannen Vong

Chapter 12.   Positive Psychology Practice With Latin Americans 235
               Marisa J. Perera, Elizabeth A. Yu, Shao Wei Chia,
               Tina Yu, and Christina A. Downey

Chapter 13.   Positive Psychology Practice With African
               Americans: Mental Health Challenges
               and Treatment 259
               Sussie Eshun and Esther Mortimer Packer

Chapter 14.   Positive Psychology Practice With
               Native Americans 281
               Michael T. Garrett, J. T. Garrett, Russ Curtis,
               Mark Parrish, Tarrell Awe Agahe Portman,
               Lisa Grayshield, and Cyrus Williams

V. Conclusion 305

Chapter 15.   Challenges and Prospects for Positive Psychology
               Research, Theory, Assessment, and Practice in a
               Multiracial and Multiethnic World 307
               Christina A. Downey, Edward C. Chang,
               Jameson K. Hirsch, and Natalie J. Lin

Index 323

About the Editors 337

CONTRIBUTORS

Riana Elyse Anderson, MA, Predoctoral Fellow, Yale University School of
    Medicine, New Haven, CT
Lucy Zhang Bencharit, MA, Doctoral Candidate, Stanford University,
    Stanford, CA
Jeanett Castellanos, PhD, University of California–Irvine
Edward C. Chang, PhD, University of Michigan, Ann Arbor
Shao Wei Chia, BA Degree Candidate, University of Michigan, Ann Arbor
Russ Curtis, PhD, Western Carolina University, Cullowhee, NC
Christina A. Downey, PhD, Indiana University, Kokomo
Sussie Eshun, PhD, East Stroudsburg University, East Stroudsburg, PA
Michi Fu, PhD, Alliant International University, Los Angeles, CA
J. T. Garrett, EdD, MPH, Director of Public Health and Human Services,
    Eastern Band of Cherokee Indians, Cherokee, NC
Michael T. Garrett, PhD, Broward County Public Schools, Ft. Lauderdale, FL
Alberta M. Gloria, PhD, University of Wisconsin–Madison
Rosemary Gonzalez, PhD, California State University, Northridge
Lisa Grayshield, PhD, New Mexico State University, Las Cruces
Jameson K. Hirsch, PhD, East Tennessee State University, Johnson City
Elizabeth L. Jeglic, PhD, John Jay College of Criminal Justice, New York, NY

Lawanna R. Kimbro, Esq., MPA, MA, Doctoral Candidate, The New School for Public Management, New York, NY

Jeff King, PhD, Western Washington University, Bellingham

Laura P. Kohn-Wood, PhD, University of Miami, Miami, FL

Frederick T. L. Leong, PhD, Michigan State University, East Lansing

Natalie J. Lin, MHSA, Kaiser Permanente, Pasadena, CA

Jacob H. Mattis, High School Diploma Candidate, East Brunswick High School, East Brunswick, NJ

Jacqueline S. Mattis, PhD, University of Michigan, Ann Arbor

Julie Guay McIntyre, PhD, The Sage Colleges, Troy, NY

Regina Miranda, PhD, Hunter College, City University of New York, New York

Gayle Skawennio Morse, PhD, The Sage Colleges, Troy, NY

Esther Mortimer Packer, Doctoral Candidate, Walden University, Minneapolis, MN

Amado M. Padilla, PhD, Stanford University, Stanford, CA

Mark Parrish, PhD, LPC, University of West Georgia, Carrollton

Marisa J. Perera, MS, Doctoral Candidate, University of Miami, Miami, FL

Lillian Polanco-Roman, MA, Doctoral Candidate, The Graduate Center, City University of New York, New York

Tarrell Awe Agahe Portman, PhD, Winona State University, Winona, MN

Wizdom Powell, PhD, MPH, University of North Carolina, Chapel Hill

Nyasha Grayman Simpson, PhD, Goucher College, Baltimore, MD

Alvin Thomas, PhD, Palo Alto University, Palo Alto, CA

Jeanne L. Tsai, PhD, Stanford University, Stanford, CA

Shannen Vong, MA, Doctoral Candidate, Alliant International University, Los Angeles, CA

Cyrus Williams, PhD, Regent University, Virginia Beach, VA

Hongfei Yang, PhD, Zhejiang University, Hangzhou City, Zhejiang, People's Republic of China

Elizabeth A. Yu, BA, Doctoral Candidate, University of Michigan, Ann Arbor

Tina Yu, BA Degree Candidate, University of Michigan, Ann Arbor

SERIES FOREWORD

As series editor of the American Psychological Association's (APA) Division 45 Cultural, Racial, and Ethnic Psychology Book Series, it is my pleasure to introduce the second volume in the series. Chang, Downey, Hirsch, and Lin's edited volume, *Positive Psychology in Racial and Ethnic Groups: Theory, Research, and Practice* coincided with a recent positive development with Division 45—the Society for the Psychological Study of Ethnic Minority Issues. After many years of deliberation, the Division finally decided to institute a name change that more accurately reflects the scope of our coverage by substituting the terms *race* and *culture* for *minority*. The new name of APA Division 45 is the Society for the Psychological Study of Culture, Ethnicity, and Race. The decision to remove the term was based in part on the fact that many states in the United States will soon become minority-majority states. More important, many in the Division felt that the term *minority* had considerable negative connotations. Therefore, it is quite timely that the appearance of this volume parallels the name change in the Division to move toward a more positive framing of our mission and focus.

The impetus for the series came from my presidential theme for Division 45, which focused on "Strengthening Our Science to Improve Our

Practice." Given the increasing attention to racial and ethnic minority issues within the discipline of psychology, I argued that we needed to both generate more research and get the existing research known. From the *Supplement* to the *Surgeon General's Report on Mental Health* to the *Unequal Treatment* report from the Institute of Medicine—both of which documented extensive racial and ethnic disparities in our health care system—the complex of culture, race, and ethnicity was becoming a major challenge in both research and practice within the field of psychology.[1]

To meet that challenge, Division 45 acquired its own journal devoted to ethnic minority issues in psychology (*Cultural Diversity and Ethnic Minority Psychology*). At the same time, a series of handbooks on the topic were published, including Bernal, Trimble, Burlew, and Leong's *Handbook of Racial and Ethnic Minority Psychology*.[2] Yet we felt that more coverage of this subdiscipline was imperative—coverage that would match the substantive direction of the handbooks but would come from a variety of research and practice perspectives. Hence, the Division 45 book series was launched.

The Cultural, Racial, and Ethnic Psychology Book Series was designed to advance our theories, research, and practice regarding this increasingly crucial subdiscipline. It will focus on, but not be limited to, the major racial and ethnic groups in the United States (i.e., African Americans, Hispanic Americans, Asian Americans, and American Indians) and will include books that examine a single racial or ethnic group as well as books that undertake a comparative approach. The series will also address the full spectrum of related methodological, substantive, and theoretical issues, including topics in behavioral neuroscience, cognitive and developmental psychology, and personality and social psychology. Other volumes in the series will be devoted to cross-disciplinary explorations in the applied realms of clinical psychology and counseling as well as educational, community, and industrial-organizational psychology. Our goal is to commission state-of-the art volumes in cultural, racial, and ethnic psychology that will be of interest to both practitioners and researchers.

For many psychologists, the development of positive psychology has usually been associated with the leadership of Martin Seligman, who in 1998 during his APA presidency advocated for increased attention to "positive psychology" as opposed to the deficit focus dominant within the field. Yet, as Leong and Wong pointed out,

---

[1]U.S. Department of Health and Human Services. (2001). *Mental health: Culture, race, and ethnicity, a supplement to Mental health: A report of the Surgeon General*. Washington, DC; Smedley, B. D., Stith, A. Y., & Nelson, A. R. (Eds.). (2003). *Unequal treatment: Confronting racial and ethnic disparities in health care*. Washington, DC: National Academies Press.

[2]Bernal, G., Trimble, J. E., Burlew, A. K., & Leong, F. T. L. (2002). *Handbook of racial and ethnic minority psychology*. Thousand Oaks, CA: Sage.

There has been considerable attention paid to the healthy, as opposed to the pathological side, of the human experience by psychologists in the last 5 decades. One stream of this early research and theoretical work is under the rubric of the Competence model. Dating back to Robert White's (1959) competence model, there have been various attempts to promote the competence model as a major organizing framework for psychology. (p. 124[3])

In fact, George Albee's chapter in *Competence and Coping During Adulthood* was entitled, "A Competency Model Must Replace the Defect Model," which is the underlying message in the positive psychology movement being spearheaded by Martin Seligman.[4] A decade later Sternberg and Kolligian continued to explore the concept of competence and its relevance for psychology in their volume entitled, *Competence Considered*.[5] The establishment of a field is usually heralded by the publication of an encyclopedia, and it was no different in this instance with the appearance of the *Encyclopedia of Positive Psychology*.[6] Therefore, I am very happy to be able to introduce this volume, which represents the continuing development of the field, namely, an analysis of positive psychology in racial and ethnic groups.

Let me end by thanking the members of the editorial board who do the work of recruiting and reviewing proposals for the series: Guillermo Bernal, University of Puerto Rico, Rio Piedras Campus; Beth Boyd, University of South Dakota; Lillian Comas-Diaz, private practice, Washington, DC; Sandra Graham, UCLA; Gordon Nagayama Hall, University of Oregon; Helen Neville, University of Illinois at Champaign–Urbana; Teresa LaFromboise, Stanford University; Richard Lee, University of Minnesota; Robert M. Sellers, University of Michigan; Stanley Sue, Palo Alto University; Joseph Trimble, Western Washington University; and Michael Zarate, University of Texas at El Paso. They represent leading scholars in psychology who have graciously donated their time to help advance the field.

—Frederick T. L. Leong
Series Editor

[3]Leong, F. T. L., & Wong, P. T. P. (2003). Optimal human functioning from cross-cultural perspectives: Cultural competence as an organizing framework. In W. B. Walsh (Ed.), *Counseling psychology and optimal human functioning*. (pp. 123–150). Mahwah, NJ: Erlbaum.
[4]Albee, G. W. (1980). A competency model must replace the defect model. In L. A. Bond, & J. C. Rosen (Eds.), *Competence and coping during adulthood*. Hanover, NH: University Press of New England.
[5]Sternberg, R. J., & Kolligian, J. (1990). *Competence considered*. New Haven, CT: Yale University Press.
[6]Lopez, S. (2009). *The encyclopedia of positive psychology*. New York, NY: Wiley-Blackwell.

I
INTRODUCTION

1

POSITIVE PSYCHOLOGY IN RACIAL AND ETHNIC GROUPS: A SECOND CALL TO ACTION!

EDWARD C. CHANG, CHRISTINA A. DOWNEY,
JAMESON K. HIRSCH, AND NATALIE J. LIN

In 1999, renowned psychologist Martin Seligman invited several rising junior researchers to join him and a few senior colleagues in Akumal, Mexico, to engage in conversation about a new scientific discipline devoted to understanding and applying knowledge about positive psychological phenomena. The first author was one of those fortunate to have been selected to participate in what was the "first conference" on positive psychology, a key moment in this discipline's development. Seligman's aim was for us to collectively outline the theoretical contours and scope of action of the new field of positive psychology (Seligman & Csikszentmihalyi, 2000). To put it simply, *positive psychology* can be defined as the application of scientific methods to identifying key antecedents, correlates, and consequences associated with living a good, full, and meaningful life. Thus, for example, positive psychology would be distinct from traditional positive philosophies that also focused on good living

http://dx.doi.org/10.1037/14799-001
Positive Psychology in Racial and Ethnic Groups: Theory, Research, and Practice, E. C. Chang, C. A. Downey, J. K. Hirsch, and N. J. Lin (Editors)

(e.g., Aristotle's *Nicomachean Ethics*, trans. 1925; Plato's *The Republic*, trans. 1948). For several days and nights in Akumal, we shared our hopeful thoughts of what a positive psychology could be. During these exciting, sometimes intense conversations under the hot Mexican sun, it was never questioned that positive psychology was going to be a good thing for the field of psychology and, more important, a good thing for the world. Now, more than 15 years later, it is clear that the fruits of those early discussions have had a strong impact on the field.

For example, highly regarded institutions of higher learning in the United States, including Harvard University, the University of Chicago, and the University of Michigan, were quick to begin offering formal courses on positive psychology to students. Likewise, the Positive Psychology Center was officially established at the University of Pennsylvania in 2003, and soon students could enroll in a Master of Applied Positive Psychology program. Moreover, new journals were developed to encourage and support the anticipated growth of high-quality research and theory associated with the new field of positive psychology (e.g., *The Journal of Positive Psychology, Journal of Happiness Studies*). Even long-established journals (e.g., *American Psychologist, Journal of Social and Clinical Psychology*) provided increasingly greater coverage to positive psychological topics like optimism, happiness, subjective well-being, and character strengths (e.g., McCullough & Snyder, 2000; Seligman & Csikszentmihalyi, 2000). Peterson and Seligman (2004) published *Character Strengths and Virtues: A Handbook and Classification*, a monumental work represented a compelling and comprehensive alternative to the *Diagnostic and Statistical Manual of Mental Disorders* (DSM) published by the American Psychiatric Association. Whereas the DSM focused on presenting a "negative" classification system of pathologies that compromised functioning and well-being, Peterson and Seligman's "positive" classification system focused on identifying globally recognized character strengths and virtues that made people happy, strong, and resilient. These are but some of the many examples of how positive psychology has found and maintained a niche in empirical and applied psychology.

Yet, despite the steady growth and progress that has been made in the field of positive psychology (Downey & Chang, 2014), we believe positive psychologists have not yet fully addressed two pressing and related challenges. First, positive psychologists have continued to take an essentialist view of human behavior by not carefully considering variations in what positive psychology may mean for individuals of different racial and ethnic backgrounds. Although the Peterson and Seligman (2004) volume did reference works from around the globe and across historical eras in its assemblage of virtues, there was simply no way for this one work to depict such variation in depth. Many committed researchers have continued to explore these issues (several of whom contributed chapters to the present volume), but there is much ground yet to cover. Second, and relatedly, the field of positive psychology has been slow to identify and validate positive psychological interventions that are designed to be culturally sensitive or meaningful to diverse groups. Such customization of technique would clearly be possible only with a sound understanding of how positive psychology manifests in diverse groups; it also requires knowing how one intervenes to maximize outcomes across these groups.

POSITIVE PSYCHOLOGISTS AND THE STUDY OF WEIRD AND MOSTLY WHITE INDIVIDUALS

Nearly three decades ago, Sears (1986) described a fundamental and ubiquitous problem in psychological research: Convenience sampling results in knowledge based largely on the study of young adults, most often college students. Years later, Graham (1992) expanded on this pressing concern by noting that studies in psychology are not only based on the narrow demographic of college students, but are usually based even more specifically on White middle-class college students. Because of such concerns, new journals were developed to expand and communicate research and scholarship on racial and ethnic minorities (e.g., *Asian American Journal of Psychology*, *Cultural Diversity and Ethnic Minority Research*, *Journal of Latina/o Psychology*). Yet, such efforts themselves have been insufficient in fostering a professional culture that is mindful of diversity; the fact remains that psychological studies published in most mainstream journals have been, and continue to be, limited in their focus on issues of diversity. Indeed, in a critical appraisal of findings obtained from psychological research studies conducted around the world, Henrich, Heine, and Norenzayan (2010) more recently argued that behavioral scientists have been making broad claims about human behavior that are based on a small and exceptional group of individuals: those characterized by being Western, educated, industrialized, rich, and democratic (what these authors referred to as WEIRD). What makes their analysis particularly important is that findings based on studies of individuals with WEIRD characteristics often differ markedly from those obtained from non-WEIRD people, with non-WEIRD people more often showing the statistically normative patterns of behavior. For example, although positive self-views or self-enhancement has long been considered in the West to reflect a fundamental aspect of being human (e.g., Maslow, 1962; Rogers, 1961), Henrich et al. noted that findings across studies involving non-Westerners typically show reduced levels of self-enhancement compared to Westerners; when studies included East Asians, researchers noted a "reversal" of self-appraisal tendencies. Specifically, East Asians, compared with Westerners, have been found to report self-effacing rather than self-enhancing tendencies (Chang, 2007; Chang & Fabian, 2012). Such an example probably represents just one of a great many psychological phenomena that are assumed in mainstream psychology to be universal in nature, until investigations of diverse populations reveal otherwise. Thus, when one examines the predominant journals in psychology over the past several decades and finds that most of them continue to focus on studies of a very select group of privileged individuals of White or European descent (e.g., Hartmann et al., 2013; Nagayama Hall & Maramba, 2001), it becomes not only a pressing scientific problem (e.g., low external validity) but also a challenging social problem (e.g., bias, invisibility, discrimination; Sue, 1999).

ON MAKING EVERYONE HAPPY LIKE US: ARE WE DESCRIBING OR PRESCRIBING POSITIVE PSYCHOLOGY TO THE WORLD?

According to Prilleltensky (1989), a central problem among social scientists is that they often portray themselves as impartial observers whose primary objective is to describe accurately the complex operations of human behavior and then disseminate such insights to the general public. Yet, what may be initially proffered as a purely descriptive finding often can easily turn into an unintended and culturally dangerous prescriptive act. Consider the case of emotional intelligence (Grewal & Salovey, 2005). *Emotional intelligence* refers to the ability to appreciate one's own feelings and those of others, to discriminate between them, and to use this understanding to guide one's subsequent thoughts and actions (Mayer, Salovey, & Caruso, 2008). Findings from studies based on Westerners have pointed to the positive value of possessing high emotional intelligence (for reviews, see Mayer et al., 2008; Salovey & Grewal, 2005), linking greater emotional intelligence in adults to greater positive outcomes (e.g., leadership, achieving business goals) and to lesser negative outcomes (e.g., stress, deviant behavior, drug use). That is, individuals with high emotional intelligence tend to be happy and successful people. Do these findings imply that everyone requires emotional intelligence training? From a scientific standpoint, the pattern noted above provides no evidence for the usefulness or appropriateness of increasing emotional intelligence in non-Westerners. However, in the absence of alternative competing theories of happiness and success, it is not surprising that the theory of emotional intelligence easily stands out; as a result, individuals may mistakenly take past (descriptive) findings on emotional intelligence to represent a clear and compelling (prescriptive) path for achieving future happiness and success. Consequentially, it is perhaps not too shocking to find that the fruits of Western studies conducted on emotional intelligence have culminated in the application of emotional training programs to facilitate happiness and success among non-Western individuals living on the other side of the world (Tatlow, 2014).

Perhaps, in the same way that Watters (2010) contended that American psychiatry, and the various industries associated with it, have worked to make everyone "crazy like us," so too one might argue that Western positive psychology has resulted in a global campaign to make everyone "happy like us." Such an effort, however, seems to be predicated on the notion that there are universal human processes that positively motivate us affectively, behaviorally, and cognitively. As a result, little attention has previously been placed on trying to identify useful assessment tools that may help scientists and practitioners to develop ethnically, racially, and culturally meaningful models of positive psychology theory and practice. In one of the few studies examining the cross-cultural validity of emotional intelligence measures, for example, factor structure, item loadings, and correlates of emotional intelligence differed in several ways between German (Western) and Indian (non-Western) samples (Sharma, Deller, Biswal, & Mandal, 2009). The authors speculated that such differences were driven by underlying cultural norms regarding individualism, collectivism, and social interaction. It is for this reason that unlike past works (Chang & Downey, 2012), we devote attention in this volume to the importance of culturally sensitive positive psychological assessments in bridging the link between positive psychology theory, research, and practice in diverse groups. We believe that assessment tools that reflect the questions we seek to examine, and often determine the answers we ultimately obtain, represent a critical point of intersectionality that can allow scientists and practitioners a means for not only testing the value of presumed universal positive psychology models in diverse groups (a top–down approach) but also for potentially identifying more nuanced models that also reflect the positive ways of living embodied by different racial and ethnic groups (a bottom–up approach; Betancourt & López, 1993).

OVERVIEW OF THIS VOLUME

This volume has five major sections. Part I focuses on a broad introduction to positive psychology and situates it within the context of race and ethnicity. In Chapter 2, Jeglic, Miranda, and Polanco-Roman offer a thoughtful and thorough discussion of positive psychology in the context of race, ethnicity, and culture. These authors contend that although positive psychology may have emerged with an emphasis on identifying universal strengths (e.g., optimism, self-esteem), findings from recent studies involving diverse racial, ethnic, and cultural groups point to a compelling need to also consider culture-specific strengths (e.g., ethnic identity, biculturalism).

Part II focuses on reviewing positive psychology theory and research in various racial and ethnic groups. In Chapter 3, Zhang Bencharit and Tsai provide a critical appraisal of positive psychology theory and research involving Asian Americans. These authors explore important considerations that need to be taken into account when we seek to conceptualize and study optimal functioning in Asian Americans. For example, they draw implications from findings of cultural differences in notions of the self: The presumed universal benefits of being optimistic, and universal costs of being pessimistic, may not apply as well to Asian Americans as it does to European Americans. In Chapter 4, Castellanos and Gloria provide a compelling emic-based model of positive psychology for Latina/os. Drawing on a growing body of Latina/o research and scholarship, these authors argue for the repositioning of earlier misguided pathological models of Latina/o culture, to highlight the growing need to consider and appreciate strength-based models that holistically encompass the interconnectedness between mind, body, and spirit within Latina/o culture. In Chapter 5, Mattis, Grayman Simpson, Powell, Anderson, Kimbro, and Mattis provide a thoughtful and thorough discussion of positive psychological development for understanding African Americans. Appreciating the ahistorical and acontextual nature of current models that have dominated the field of positive psychology, these authors borrow insights garnered from multiple sources of research and scholarship, from cultural studies to anthropology, to help us articulate the potential for developing an African-centered positive psychology. In Chapter 6, Morse, McIntyre, and King make a compelling case for the positive inclusion of American Indian and Alaskan Native (AI/AN) people. Specifically, these authors challenge past theory and research that has tended to focus on weaknesses among the diverse AI/AN people and reframe the ways in which they have managed to exert resilience and grow in the face of adversity.

Part III focuses on positive psychology assessment in different racial and ethnic groups. In Chapter 7, Yu, Chang, Yang, and Yu provide a useful review of some of the many common and culture-specific assessment tools that have been used to study positive psychological processes in Asians and Asian Americans. These authors argue that despite the value obtained from existing tools, it will be important to continue to identify and develop culturally informed instruments that better tap into the wide range of psychological processes that are relevant to Asian Americans. In Chapter 8, Gonzalez and Padilla provide a thoughtful review of key measures that have been used to study psychological strengths in Latina/os. These authors point to the need not only for more authentic and culturally informed assessment tools but also for more informed approaches to assessment. For example, in contrast to using conventional approaches whereby a researcher typically conducts an interview on or with a subject, the authors discuss the value of approaches that are more collaborative in nature, and thus, affirming the values of family and community commonly supported within Latina/o culture. Chapter 9, by Kohn-Wood and Thomas, focuses on positive psychological tools that can help us assess for the many strengths embodied among African Americans. Their careful review underscores the potential value of using existing tools to measure strengths like hope and coping among African Americans, but they also raise concerns about the scarcity of positive psychology assessment tools; available tools remain limited in tapping into the wide range of strengths manifested by African Americans. In Chapter 10, King provides a cogent discussion of the context of assessment within AI/AN people, beginning with an acknowledgement that in order to understand how to meaningfully assess positive psychological dimensions among AI/AN people, we must begin with a historically informed appreciation of the rich range of beliefs, customs, and lifeways of AI/AN people living within their communities. The author points out, for example, that contrary to some of the common assumptions held within mainstream positive psychology, Native values do not assert that one must experience positive emotions in order to live well.

Part IV focuses on positive psychology interventions in working with different racial and ethnic groups. In Chapter 11, Fu and Vong focus attention on the ways in which happiness may be fostered within the Asian American context. Following a review of existing work on positive psychology in Asian Americans, these authors offer an integrative model of positive practice in working with Asian Americans that centers on the cultivation of Asian strengths such as gratitude and a careful consideration of other therapeutic factors when working with Asian Americans (e.g., level of acculturation). In Chapter 12, Perera, Yu, Chia, Yu, and Downey review important psychological concepts and ideas that are likely to play a central role in articulating culturally meaningful positive practices when working with Latina/os. These authors suggest that apart from leveraging the power of culturally embodied concepts like *familismo*, there is a need to carefully consider how other concepts like *fatalismo* may also impact the facilitation of positive practice when working with Latina/os. In Chapter 13, Eshun and Packer discuss ways in which Africentric cultural values (e.g., unity, collective responsibility, faith) can and should be used to inform positive practice in working with African Americans. However, they caution that such efforts made by practitioners when working with African Americans must also be informed by an appreciation of the rich and often challenging historical, spiritual, and cultural context within which African Americans lead their lives. In the final chapter in Part III (Chapter 14), Garrett, Garrett, Curtis, Parrish, Portman, Grayshield, and Williams provide a critical discussion of the value of positive practice in working with Native Americans. Borrowing from research on positive practice, the authors begin with an appreciation for the potential utility of applying aspects of established positive techniques (e.g., identifying signature strengths within the individual, mindful and communal ways of knowing) when working with Native Americans. To build more meaningful approaches, however, they point to situating the individual in a broader context of Native American life (e.g., family, tribe, spiritual belief system). Thus, positive practice in working with Native Americans must respect the intricate and complex ways in which the self holds multiple identities and boundaries at any given time.

In the final chapter in the volume, we discuss what the future may hold in developing a meaningful and useful positive psychology that is inclusive to diverse racial and ethnic groups. We summarize several major themes emerging across the present volume, including the recurrent identification of resilience as a culturally relevant positive psychological phenomenon. We proceed to offer a critical examination of the concept of resilience in past research, noting problems with how resilience has been defined at various times as an individual trait, a characteristic of one's environment, or a transactional process involving personal traits and associated coping approaches. We then introduce a two-dimensional model of experiences of adversity, focusing on safe versus risky coping with adversity, and positive versus negative life outcomes, which when combined may or may not lead to what can be considered resilience in various individuals and groups.

FINAL THOUGHTS

More than a decade ago, the first call to establish positive psychology was made. Since then, great advances have been made toward developing the field of positive psychology, but these have largely been based on a narrow group of individuals, namely, White Americans. With the many thoughtful contributions offered in this volume, we hope to inspire, if not declare, a second call to action for scientists and practitioners alike to foster the development and maturity of not one, but many positive psychologies that capture both the common and distinct aspects of the diverse racial and ethnic groups that make up our rich and ever-changing society. As editors of this volume, we adamantly believe that for positive psychology to grow, it must be psychology that is positive for all.

REFERENCES

Betancourt, H., & López, S. R. (1993). The study of culture, ethnicity, and race in American psychology. *American Psychologist, 48,* 629–637. http://dx.doi. org/10.1037/0003-066X.48.6.629

Chang, E. C. (2007). Introduction to self-criticism and self-enhancement: Views from ancient Greece to the modern world. In E. C. Chang (Ed.), *Self-criticism and self-enhancement: Theory, research, and clinical implications* (pp. 3–15). Washington, DC: American Psychological Association.

Chang, E. C., & Downey, C. A. (Eds.). (2012). *Handbook of race and development in mental health*. New York, NY: Springer. http://dx.doi.org/10.1007/978-1-4614-0424-8

Chang, E. C., & Fabian, C. G. (2012). Introduction to adult psychopathology in Asians: From nomothetic to idiographic approaches. In E. C. Chang (Ed.), *Handbook of adult psychopathology in Asians: Diagnosis, etiology, and treatment* (pp. 1–11). New York, NY: Oxford University Press.

Downey, C. A., & Chang, E. C. (2014). Positive psychology: Current knowledge, multicultural and ethical considerations, and the future of the movement. In F. T. L. Leong, L. Comas-Diaz, G. C. Nagayama Hall, V. McLoyd, & J. E. Trimble (Eds.), *APA handbook on multicultural psychology: Vol. 2. Applications and training* (pp. 133–149). Washington, DC: American Psychological Association.

Graham, S. (1992). "Most of the subjects were White and middle class": Trends in published research on African Americans in selected APA journals, 1970–1989. *American Psychologist, 47*, 629–639. http://dx.doi.org/10.1037/0003-066X.47.5.629

Grewal, D., & Salovey, P. (2005). Feeling smart: The science of emotional intelligence. *American Scientist, 93*, 330–339. http://dx.doi.org/10.1511/2005.54.969

Hartmann, W. E., Kim, E. S., Kim, J. H. J., Nguyen, T. U., Wendt, D. C., Nagata, D. K., & Gone, J. P. (2013). In search of cultural diversity, revisited: Recent publication trends in cross-cultural and ethnic minority psychology. *Review of General Psychology, 17*, 243–254. http://dx.doi.org/10.1037/a0032260

Henrich, J., Heine, S. J., & Norenzayan, A. (2010). The weirdest people in the world? *Behavioral and Brain Sciences, 33*, 61–83. http://dx.doi.org/10.1017/S0140525X0999152X

Maslow, A. (1962). *Toward a psychology of being*. New York, NY: Van Nostrand. http://dx.doi.org/10.1037/10793-000

Mayer, J. D., Salovey, P., & Caruso, D. R. (2008). Emotional intelligence: New ability or eclectic traits? *American Psychologist, 63*, 503–517. http://dx.doi.org/10.1037/0003-066X.63.6.503

McCullough, M. E., & Snyder, C. R. (2000). Classical sources of human strength: Revisiting an old home and building a new one. *Journal of Social and Clinical Psychology, 19*, 1–10. http://dx.doi.org/10.1521/jscp.2000.19.1.1

Nagayama Hall, G. C., & Maramba, G. G. (2001). In search of cultural diversity: Recent literature in cross-cultural and ethnic minority psychology. *Cultural Diversity and Ethnic Minority Psychology, 7*, 12–26. http://dx.doi.org/10.1037/1099-9809.7.1.12

Peterson, C., & Seligman, M. E. P. (2004). *Character strengths and virtues: A handbook and classification*. Washington, DC: American Psychological Association.

Prilleltensky, I. (1989). Psychology and the status quo. *American Psychologist, 44*, 795–802.

Rogers, C. (1961). *On becoming a person*. Boston, MA: Houghton Mifflin.

Salovey, P., & Grewal, D. (2005). The science of emotional intelligence. *Current Directions in Psychological Science, 14*, 281–285. http://dx.doi.org/10.1111/j.0963-7214.2005.00381.x

Sears, D. O. (1986). College sophomores in the laboratory: Influences of a narrow data base on social psychology's view of human nature. *Journal of Personality and Social Psychology, 51*, 515–530. http://dx.doi.org/10.1037/0022-3514.51.3.515

Seligman, M. E. P., & Csikszentmihalyi, M. (2000). Positive psychology. An introduction. *American Psychologist, 55*, 5–14. http://dx.doi.org/10.1037/0003-066X.55.1.5

Sharma, S., Deller, J., Biswal, R., & Mandal, M. K. (2009). Emotional intelligence factorial structure and construct validity across cultures. *International Journal of Cross Cultural Management, 9*, 217–236. http://dx.doi.org/10.1177/1470595809335725

Sue, S. (1999). Science, ethnicity, and bias: Where have we gone wrong? *American Psychologist, 54*, 1070–1077. http://dx.doi.org/10.1037/0003-066X.54.12.1070

Tatlow, D. K. (2014, May 7). More hugs please, we're Chinese. *The New York Times*. Retrieved from http://sinosphere.blogs.nytimes.com/2014/05/07/more-hugs-please-were-chinese/?_php=true&_type=blogs&_php=true&_type=blogs&_r=1

Watters, E. (2010). *Crazy like us: The globalization of the American psyche*. New York, NY: Free Press.

2

POSITIVE PSYCHOLOGY IN THE CONTEXT OF RACE AND ETHNICITY

ELIZABETH L. JEGLIC, REGINA MIRANDA,
AND LILLIAN POLANCO-ROMAN

The population of the United States is becoming increasingly racially and ethnically diverse. Although the U.S. population has historically been majority White with a small Black minority, it has been estimated that by the year 2050, more than 50% of the U.S. population will consist of an ethnic minority (Passel & Cohn, 2008). These differences in the racial and ethnic composition of the United States are due largely to changes in immigration patterns and increased birth rates among minority populations (Shrestha & Heisler, 2011). Consequently, it is important to understand how culture affects psychological well-being. This is especially salient because individuals from different ethnic and racial backgrounds may possess unique cultural rules and norms that influence what is considered a personal strength. Currently, we know very little about how strengths are construed cross-culturally. This chapter reviews the research on diversity as it applies to the theory and application of positive psychology, highlighting

http://dx.doi.org/10.1037/14799-002
Positive Psychology in Racial and Ethnic Groups: Theory, Research, and Practice, E. C. Chang, C. A. Downey, J. K. Hirsch, and N. J. Lin (Editors)

the debate within the field and proposing avenues through which strengths-based approaches can contribute to the development of culturally competent treatments and assessments.

THE CHANGING FACE OF THE U.S. POPULATION

The United States is a nation founded on immigration. In the last 60 years, the U.S. population has doubled from 152 million to 309 million inhabitants (U.S. Census Bureau, 2010). A large proportion of this increase can be attributed to immigration; approximately one million immigrants per year have come to the United States over the past two decades (U.S. Department of Homeland Security, 2009). Historically, the majority of immigrants to the United States have come from Western Europe, but in 2009 the top immigrant source countries were Mexico, China, the Philippines, India, Dominican Republic, Cuba, and Vietnam (U.S. Department of Homeland Security, 2009). The Pew Hispanic Center estimated that 11.1 million unauthorized foreigners currently live in America, the majority of whom identify themselves as Hispanic (Passel & Cohn, 2010). The birthrate among minority groups has also been higher than that of Whites in the United States. According to the 2010 U.S. Census, slightly more than one third of Americans identify themselves as belonging to a minority group, but they gave birth to slightly more than half the children born in the preceding 12 months (U.S. Census Bureau, 2010).

The changing racial and ethnic composition is accompanied by changes in the psychological needs of the U.S. population as well. The majority of psychological treatments and assessments were developed for application with White Westerners. However, a considerable amount of research suggests that ethnic and racial disparities exist within the mental health system, and policymakers have made it a priority to address and overcome these disparities by calling attention to the fundamental role of race, ethnicity, and culture in the provision of mental health services (American Psychological Association [APA], 2003; U.S. Department of Health and Human Services, 2001).

ROLE OF POSITIVE PSYCHOLOGY IN A CHANGING CULTURE

Traditionally, the field of psychology has been grounded in Western middle class values and assumptions, viewing deviations from the norm as abnormal and pathological. Consequently, much of the research on assessment and treatment of mental health conditions has also been derived from this perspective. However, with the changing cultural landscape, population norms are shifting, so these approaches need to be reevaluated and reconsidered. Research needs to be conducted to better understand the interface between culture, race, and ethnicity, and psychological well-being, so that this knowledge may be integrated into a new set of culturally relevant findings that guide the theory and practice of psychology. In short, there has been a call to view individuals more holistically, within their cultural context (APA, 2003).

As noted in the opening chapter of this volume, the field of positive psychology was introduced in 2000 by Martin Seligman and Mihaly Csikszentmihalyi, in an effort to shift away from the disease or deficit model of human functioning that has dominated the field of psychology since World War II. Instead of emphasizing psychopathology, positive psychology focuses on human prospering and helping individuals live happier lives (Seligman & Csikszentmihalyi, 2000). This new field of psychology emerged at a pivotal time, as the discipline of psychology also recognized that current psychological approaches were not adequately addressing the needs of racial and ethnic minorities and that, in many cases, we were failing to understand culture-specific strengths. In recognition of this bias in the mental health system, the APA (2003) called for cultural competence in the practice of psychology. With its strength-based approach and its reliance on empiricism and objectivity, positive psychology was ideally suited to address these disparities and to lead psychology in the 21st century.

However, despite the initial intuitive appeal of the movement, many contend that the theory behind positive psychology is premised on a Western ideology and value system and that it is ethnocentric; it does not take into account the cultural context of the ever-increasing diversity of the population (Ahuvia, 2001; Bacigalupe, 2001; Brand, 2001; Christopher & Hickinbottom, 2008; Compton, 2001; Walsh, 2001). On the other hand, proponents of positive psychology argue that its goals transcend culture and that it is universal, but they also assert that these traits and characteristics must be understood within the context of culture (Seligman & Csikszentmihalyi, 2000).

Within positive psychology, areas such as optimism, subjective well-being, and self-esteem have been investigated across race and ethnicity. Furthermore, culture-specific traits such as ethnic identity, familism, and spiritual/religious belief have all been cited as strengths under this paradigm. In this chapter, we further explore the research and debate in these areas.

OPTIMISM AND CULTURE

What people expect about their futures has clearly been demonstrated to be associated with their physical and mental well-being (Carver, Scheier, & Segerstrom, 2010; Rasmussen, Scheier, & Greenhouse, 2009). Optimism about the future is the expectation that one will experience positive future events (Carver et al., 2010; Peterson & Chang, 2003) and has long been found to be associated with a number of important outcomes, including improved coping with stress (see Carver et al., 2010, for a review; Nes & Segerstrom, 2006) and better physical health over time (Rasmussen et al., 2009). Given evidence that the unique stressors faced by racial and ethnic minorities (e.g., discrimination) are associated with poorer health outcomes (Williams, Neighbors, & Jackson, 2003), understanding racial and ethnic differences in risk and resilience associated with such outcomes necessitates the study of cultural differences in optimism, its effects on coping, and its relation to health outcomes.

Available studies suggest little cultural variability in levels of optimism, though optimism appears to vary with other cultural dimensions such as individualism (see Fischer & Chalmers, 2008, for a meta-analysis). Most of the research on the effects of optimism on health outcomes has been derived from studies of individuals of European background (see Carver et al., 2010, for a review). However, a considerable amount of the available research on cultural differences in optimism has compared optimism among Asian (particularly East Asian), Asian American, and European American adults (Chang, Chang, & Sanna, 2009), with the assumption that optimism varies depending on the degree to which a culture values individualism or independence over collectivism or interdependence (Hofstede, 1980; Markus & Kitayama, 1991). This research suggests that compared with European Americans, Asian and Asian American individuals report comparable levels of optimism but higher levels of pessimism (the expectation that negative future events will occur; Chang, 1996a, 1996b), than do European Americans, with some exceptions (Chang, Sanna, & Yang, 2003).

Additional research suggests that European Americans tend to have an optimistic bias for positive and negative events—meaning that they tend to more often expect that positive events will happen to themselves rather than to another person and that negative events are more likely to happen to another person rather than to themselves (Chang & Asakawa, 2003). In contrast, the evidence is mixed among Asian individuals (see Heine & Hamamura, 2007, for a meta-analysis). For instance, one study that compared Japanese individuals with European American individuals found that Japanese individuals had a pessimistic bias toward positive and negative events; they were more likely to expect that negative events are more likely to happen to themselves than to others, whereas positive events are more likely to happen to others than to themselves. In contrast, European American individuals had an optimistic bias toward negative events (i.e., more often expected that negative events would happen to others than to themselves) but not for positive events (Chang, Asakawa, & Sanna,

2001). However, when individuals were asked to make ratings about themselves compared with a sibling, Japanese participants showed a pessimistic bias toward negative events but not toward positive events, whereas European Americans showed an optimistic bias toward both positive and negative events (Chang & Asakawa, 2003). Thus, the pessimistic bias observed among Asian individuals may be specific to expecting negative future outcomes but not to expecting fewer positive outcomes.

It has been suggested that the optimistic bias found among European Americans may reflect an emphasis on individualism and the saliency of self-enhancement motives, whereas the pessimistic bias found among Asian individuals may reflect an emphasis on collectivism, where criticism of self in the service of a group would be valued (Kitayama, Markus, Matsumoto, & Norasakkunkit, 1997). There is evidence of cultural variation in the effects of optimism and pessimism on psychological functioning. Whereas pessimism tends to be associated with poorer psychological functioning among European Americans, including maladaptive coping, it is associated with active coping and not associated with poor psychological outcomes among Asian individuals (Chang, 1996a). One explanation for this difference is that among Asian individuals, pessimism may motivate self-improvement (Chang et al., 2009). Thus, pessimism may not be detrimental to well-being among Asian individuals as it is among European Americans. Consistent with this idea, there is evidence that among Asian individuals, optimism is a better predictor of psychological functioning than is pessimism; the opposite is the case for European Americans (Chang, 1996a).

Although the majority of research examining cultural variability in the effects of optimism on psychological functioning has compared European American with Asian individuals, there is some evidence of cross-cultural differences when comparing Americans with Black Africans. Comparison of college students from Ghana to American college students found that Ghanaian students were more optimistic, less hopeless, and endorsed lower levels of suicidal ideation compared with American college students (Eshun, 1999). Hope, which has been described as an optimistic, goal-oriented attitude about the future, also appears to reflect cultural differences. For example, Chang, Yu, Kahle, Jeglic, and Hirsch (2013) found that low levels of hope were a significant predictor of hopelessness and suicide behavior among Latinos, and Davidson et al. (2010) found lack of hope to predict suicide ideation among African American students; however, this relationship was not evidenced among a sample of primarily European American students (Davidson et al., 2009). Thus, additional research is needed to understand the unique experiences among members of racial and ethnic minority groups that may affect levels of hope and optimism and psychological functioning.

SUBJECTIVE WELL-BEING

Just as there is evidence of cultural variability in the effects of optimism on physical and mental health-related outcomes, there is evidence of cultural differences in people's overall satisfaction with their lives—that is, in their subjective well-being. *Subjective well-being* refers to people's cognitive and affective evaluation of their lives, including how satisfied they are, overall, with their lives, satisfaction with specific life domains, and the experience of positive affect and low negative affect (Diener, 2000). There are well-established variations in well-being across nations (Diener, 2000; Diener, Diener, & Diener, 1995) that reflect differences in cultural values and needs (Diener, Oishi, & Lucas, 2003; Diener, Suh, Lucas, & Smith, 1999; Oishi, Diener, Lucas, & Suh, 1999). For instance, cross-national studies suggest that income is positively associated with life satisfaction (Diener et al., 1995; Diener, Sandvik, Seidlitz, & Diener, 1993), but this relationship varies with factors such as poverty level and by how much people's needs and values are met (Oishi et al., 1999). Oishi et al.'s (1999) study of responses from more than 54,000 adults, ages 18 and over, from 39 countries found a stronger relationship between increases in income and life satisfaction among poorer countries compared with wealthier nations, whereas there was a stronger relationship between satisfaction with home life and overall life satisfaction among wealthier nations than among poorer countries. Furthermore, surveys of more than 6,000 college students from 39 countries found that the relationship between how satisfied people were with themselves and overall life satisfaction varied by a country's degree of individualism versus collectivism. Specifically, people's satisfaction with themselves was more strongly associated with their overall life satisfaction in individualistic countries than in collectivistic countries (Oishi et al., 1999). Cross-national data also suggest that culture can increase the positive effects of certain personality variables (e.g., extraversion) on self-esteem when there is a match between people's personalities and the personalities of others in their culture (Fulmer et al., 2010). Thus, subjective well-being is affected by individual differences, cultural values, and the match between individuals and their culture.

Thus far, research on well-being has focused on personality variables (e.g., dispositional optimism and hope) and cross-cultural values (e.g., individualism–collectivism) that differentially affect subjective well-being (Diener et al., 2003). However, there has been limited research addressing the unique experiences of racial and ethnic minority groups that affect their well-being. One such experience warranting further research is that of racial discrimination. Previous population-based studies suggest that discrimination is associated with poorer physical and mental health, including lower levels of happiness, life satisfaction, and self-esteem and more symptoms of depression, anxiety, and substance use (see Williams et al., 2003, for a review). However, research aimed at understanding how, and under which circumstances, perceived discrimination affects well-being is limited. One study of a community sample of 139 African American adults found evidence that attributing previous negative events and hypothetical future outcomes to prejudice had both a direct negative impact on well-being but also an indirect positive impact on well-being through identification with a minority group. That is, although attributing events to prejudice was associated with lower overall well-being, it was also associated with stronger minority group identification. Stronger identification with a minority group was, in turn, associated with increased well-being (Branscombe, Schmitt, & Harvey, 1999). Additional research is necessary to determine whether there is variability in how different racial and ethnic minority groups cope with culturally related stressors, such as discrimination, and how the development of a strong ethnic identification may be protective against the negative impact of culturally related stressors on well-being.

SELF-ESTEEM

How people view themselves affects their psychological functioning (Taylor & Brown, 1988, 1994). Social psychology researchers have long held that people are motivated to maintain positive views of themselves and that they do so by enhancing positive information and minimizing negative information about the self. That is, they demonstrate self-enhancement biases (Sedikides, Gaertner, & Toguchi, 2003; Taylor & Brown, 1988, 1994). Research with East Asian cultures, however, suggests that this need for positive self-regard varies by culture (Heine, Lehman, Markus, & Kitayama, 1999) and that variations may arise from differences in the attributes found to be important by different cultures (Sedikides et al., 2003; Sedikides, Gaertner, & Vevea, 2005). Examinations of self-reported levels of self-esteem across cultures suggest that positive self-evaluations are, on average, universal (Schmitt & Allik, 2005) and that self-esteem is positively associated with well-being across cultures (Diener & Diener, 1995). However, the relationship between self-esteem and well-being has been found to be moderated by other variables, such as degree of individualism, in that the relationship between self-esteem and well-being tends to be stronger in individualistic than in collectivistic countries (Diener & Diener, 1995). At the same time, there is evidence that individuals from both Eastern and Western cultures engage in self-enhancement, but that they do so in different ways. Whereas Westerners do so by focusing on characteristics of themselves that are consistent with the cultural value of individualism, Easterners do so by focusing on characteristics of themselves that are consistent with the value of collectivism (Sedikides et al., 2003, 2005).

CULTURE-SPECIFIC STRENGTHS

Although Seligman and Csikszentmihalyi (2000) identified traits or characteristics that they believed transcended culture, there are specific strengths that may be unique to racial, cultural, and ethnic minorities. Despite the many challenges that racial and ethnic minorities confront in response to a compromised social status, a strong body of literature demonstrates that they draw upon certain culture-specific strengths that promote psychological well-being. These include ethnic identity, biculturalism, familism, and religiosity/spirituality.

Ethnic Identity

There is compelling evidence that a strong ethnic identity is advantageous for ethnic minority individuals (for a review, see Umaña-Taylor, 2011). Distinct from ethnicity, *ethnic identity* is a multidimensional social construct that is characterized by the meaning an individual ascribes to his or her ethnic group affiliation, a meaning that develops over time through a process of exploration and a sense of belonging to the respective ethnic group (Phinney & Ong, 2007). This framework is largely grounded in Tajfel and Turner's (1986) social identity theory, which suggests that intergroup relations spur a group identity to foster a sense of belonging and positive self-concept. Erikson's (1968) identity development theory, which proposes that identity development is a critical milestone across the lifespan, particularly during adolescence, also contributed to the understanding of the development of ethnic identity. Phinney (1990) expanded on these theories to suggest that a strong ethnic identity allows ethnic minorities to develop a positive self-regard in light of their lower social status to ward off the detrimental effects of discriminatory experiences.

An ethnic identity is most salient in a heterogeneous environment arising from the interaction of multiple ethnic groups. It is a response to differentiation between distinct groups, in part to counteract the negative attitudes inherent in stereotypes or discrimination, experiences that are common among ethnic minorities (Phinney & Ong, 2007). To combat the detrimental effects of these negative experiences, individuals explore what belonging to their ethnic group means to their self-concept by examining their own attitudes about their group. This exploration evolves into a sense of belonging or attachment to other people within their ethnic group, providing some degree of social support and positive self-regard. A large body of empirical evidence supports this idea: Ethnic identity has been consistently associated with well-being and psychosocial functioning among ethnic minorities (for a review, see Smith & Silva, 2011). In their meta-analytic review of more than 180 studies, Smith and Silva (2011) found that a stronger ethnic identity was associated with greater self-esteem and improved well-being. This effect, moderate in size, was most pronounced among adolescents and young adults.

Biculturalism

The advantages of an ethnic identity are well documented. However, recent research suggests that a bicultural identity or biculturalism is also advantageous, because it has been strongly linked to psychological adjustment (for a review, see Nguyen & Benet-Martínez, 2013). *Biculturalism* is the ability to competently navigate two cultural environments, which often entails maintaining beliefs and customs of a heritage culture while adopting those of the mainstream culture (Berry, 2003; LaFromboise, Coleman, & Gerton, 1993). A meta-analysis of more than 140 articles found that a strong cultural identity, mainstream or ethnic, is strongly related to adjustment (i.e., positive mood and self-esteem) but that this pattern was more pronounced among bicultural individuals (for a review, see Nguyen & Benet-Martínez, 2013). This finding is contrary to earlier theories (Gordon, 1964) that suggested that identifying with more than one culture promoted identity confusion, marginalization, and stress. The literature on ethnic identity has contributed substantially to our understanding of biculturalism, with both of these constructs emerging from the process of acculturation. Berry (2003) suggested that the consistent exposure to a novel cultural environment engenders numerous acculturation strategies, one of which is integration, that is, active participation in the heritage culture as well as the mainstream culture.

Although acculturation was originally described as a unidirectional trajectory whereby individuals, over time, relinquish their heritage cultural identity and adopt a mainstream cultural identity (Gordon, 1964), social scientists are now suggesting that cultural identities are not mutually exclusive. It is possible to simultaneously identify with two cultures, that is, to integrate more than one cultural identity or develop a bicultural identity (Berry, 2003; LaFromboise et al., 1993; Schwartz, Unger, Zamboanga, & Szapocznik, 2010). There is growing empirical evidence demonstrating that a bicultural identity may promote psychological adjustment through positive mood and high self-esteem (for a review, see Nguyen & Benet-Martínez, 2013). Various explanations have been given for the adaptive effect of biculturalism, one of which is that it facilitates problem solving by expanding an individual's repertoire of perspectives and behaviors (Berry, 2003), thus promoting a greater range of coping strategies. Another possible explanation is that biculturalism fosters cognitive flexibility through cultural frame switching, or alternating between cognitive schemas that are culturally bound (Hong, Morris, Chiu, & Benet-Martínez, 2000). A larger social network—and consequently, greater social support—has also been implicated in biculturalism (Mok, Morris, Benet-Martínez, & Karakitapoglu-Aygun, 2007). More specifically, bicultural individuals may develop a network of friends within their heritage group as well as a network of friends within the mainstream group, expanding their resources for social support.

Familism

A cultural value system wherein family relations are held in the highest regard is common among ethnic minority populations (Schwartz, Weisskirch, et al., 2010). For instance, *familism*, sometimes referred to as *familialism* or *familismo*, is regarded as a cultural phenomenon among Hispanic populations in which family relations are paramount (Sabogal, Marín, Otero-Sabogal, Marín, & Perez-Stable, 1987). Thus, behaviors and attitudes are centered on family relations, which often consist of an extended network beyond the nuclear family (Vega, 1990). The collectivistic need of the family supersedes individualistic need. Steidel and Contreras (2003) suggested that attitudinal familism comprises four domains: subjugation of the self (i.e., personal sacrifices for the betterment of the family), support (i.e., the perception of emotional or social support from family members), interconnectedness (i.e., a strong attachment to the family), and honor (i.e., a duty to protect the family and its name).

These attitudes are expressed through behaviors such as maintaining frequent contact with and residing in close proximity to family members (Sabogal et al., 1987). Although behaviors may decrease over time as future generations become more acculturated, these attitudes remain consistent (Sabogal et al., 1987; Steidel & Contreras, 2003). Similar family-oriented values have been observed in other ethnic minority populations. Traditional Asian and Asian American families are patriarchal, maintaining a hierarchical structure in which there is loyalty to authority figures and respect for elders. A view of the family as a collective and filial piety, or the view that one must respect one's family, is common among Asians and Asian Americans (Schwartz, Weisskirch, et al., 2010). Among African Americans, communalism, or a sense of community and kinship, is evidenced (Schwartz, Weisskirch, et al., 2010). Empirical evidence suggests that these family-oriented values promote positive psychological functioning among ethnic minorities. For example, Schwartz, Weisskirch, et al. (2010) found that family-oriented values were positively associated with self-esteem, well-being, meaning in life, life satisfaction, and happiness.

Religiosity/Spirituality

One of the earliest accounts of a culture-specific strength cited as promoting mental health is religiosity. For example, Durkheim (1897/1951) concluded that the low suicide rates among Catholics, compared with Protestants, was due to more social control and increased attachment to their community. Contemporary theories suggest that well-being is not linked to religious affiliation or involvement, but rather to how integrated religion is in a person's life (Pargament, 2002). This may explain why religiosity is a common culture-specific strength among ethnic minorities (Pargament, 2002; Tabak & Mickelson, 2009), one that is associated with improved mental health (Larson & Larson, 2003). In a longitudinal study with a nationally representative sample of adults in the United States, Tabak and Mickelson (2009) found that African American and Hispanic individuals were more likely to attend religious services than were non-Hispanic Whites. They also found that people who reported attending religious services either very frequently or not frequently at all also reported the highest psychological distress, and this relationship was stronger among African American and Hispanic individuals than non-Hispanic White individuals. Although religiosity is centered on a religious institution and affiliation with a specific doctrine, and spirituality is considered to encompass private thoughts and beliefs, the extant literature suggests that both are characterized by thoughts, feelings, and behaviors grounded in belief in a higher power (Larson & Larson, 2003; Miller & Thoresen, 2003). Researchers have identified some explanatory mechanisms in the relation between religiosity/spirituality and mental health. These include the deterrence of risky behaviors such as substance use, fostering positive self-perception and emotions, the availability of resources such as social support from clergy or congregation members, and encouragement of use of religious or spiritual coping strategies such as well-meaning appraisals and forgiveness (Ellison & Levin, 1998; Pargament, 2002).

DEBATE WITHIN THE FIELD

Since its inception, positive psychology has been lauded for its emphasis on human strength and resilience. However, positive psychology has not escaped controversy. Critics have argued that positive psychology is ethnocentric and based on Western cultural norms. Meanwhile, proponents of positive psychology have divided into two camps: those who believe in cultural transcendence and those who support cultural integration. Those perspectives, along with a more in-depth description of the culturally based critiques of positive psychology, are summarized in this section.

Cultural Transcendence

Advocates contend that positive psychology transcends race, culture, and ethnicity and is, in essence, culture free (Seligman & Csikszentmihalyi, 2000). Seligman and Csikszentmihalyi (2000) argued that "our common humanity is strong enough to suggest psychological goals to strive for that cut across social divides" (p. 90). They have further asserted that, above all, positive psychology is a science and, consequently, its methods "transcend particular cultures and politics and approach universality" (p. 5). Positive psychologists believe that by using objective empirical methodology to derive their science, they are overcoming deficits of other models of human prosperity, such as humanistic psychology (Seligman & Csikszentmihalyi 2000).

Peterson and Seligman (2003) further expanded on this perspective by establishing 24 character strengths (which they termed the Values in Action [VIA] Classification of Strengths) that they claim are present in all societies and are valued as positive by all cultural groups. These include humor, curiosity, open-mindedness, vitality, love, kindness, and fairness. These character strengths have been assessed by researchers and affirmed in populations across the globe (Biswas-Diener & Diener, 2006; Biswas-Diener, Vittersø, & Diener, 2005). Peterson and Seligman further identified six omnipresent virtues—courage, justice, humanity, temperance, wisdom, and transcendence—which they believe are universal, thus providing a "non-arbitrary basis for focusing on certain virtues rather than others" (p. 51).

Cultural Integration

An alternative to the culture-free perspective of positive psychology is that of cultural integration. In 2003, the APA published a series of guidelines for multicultural training, practice, and research. This was followed in 2008 by a task force report highlighting how the APA itself was incorporating the understanding of group differences into its own practices. Supporters of a culturally embedded approach felt that, despite appearances of objectivity, researchers could not separate their inquiries from their own cultural framework or those of their participants and that it was, thus, imperative to understand behaviors within the cultural context in which they exist.

Cultural integrationists contend that although a set of universal positive characteristics might exist across cultures, these characteristics might manifest themselves differently and hold different meanings for each culture. Leu, Wang, and Koo (2011) studied the role of positive emotions across three groups (European Americans, Asian Americans, and immigrant Asians) and found that positive emotions were associated with depressive symptoms in the Asian and European American samples but not the immigrant Asian sample, and they attributed this to the role of positive emotions in Western and Eastern cultures. Leu et al. argued that in Western cultures, positive emotions are associated with individual success, self-esteem, and good health, whereas in Eastern cultures positive emotions are more ambiguous: they could signify jealousy and disharmony in social relationships. Thus, in Eastern cultures, the aim is toward moderation of positive emotions as opposed to maximizing them, which is the goal of Western cultures. This example highlights the importance of cultural integration in the study and practice of positive psychology.

Ethnocentric and Western-Based Criticism

Critics have argued that positive psychology is based upon an individualistic framework rooted in Western culture (Ahuvia, 2001; Bacigalupe, 2001; Brand, 2001; Christopher & Hickinbottom, 2008; Compton, 2001; Walsh, 2001). According to Christopher, Richardson, and Slife (2008), positive psychology is ethnocentric and does not take into account the fact that human behavior is culture-bound. Christopher and colleagues have argued that the emphasis on individual autonomy and fulfillment are constructs that are valued in American society, but they pointed out that more than 70% of the world's population belongs to a collectivist culture in which the social environment of individuals plays an integral role in their psychological well-being (Christopher & Hickinbottom, 2008; Christopher et al., 2008; Held, 2002).

The basis of positive psychology is the development of the self. However, the self has different meanings across cultures. In Western culture, the self is independent and autonomous, whereas in collectivist cultures the self is viewed as interdependent and dutiful (Kubokawa & Ottaway, 2009). Accordingly, in Western cultures, the attainment of individualism is seen as the pathway to happiness and success, and dependence on others would be viewed as a barrier to achieving this goal (Christopher & Hickinbottom, 2008).

Values and emotions differ cross-culturally as well. For example, in Western culture achieving happiness is the ultimate goal, but in collectivist cultures, adhering to social expectations and obeying one's elders are most valued (Ahuvia, 2001). Furthermore, Christopher and Hickinbottom (2008) argued that what are viewed as positive and negative emotions may also vary cross-culturally. In Western culture, self-criticism is a negative emotion or trait that is often viewed as inhibiting potential success. However, in non-Western cultures, self-criticism may be viewed as a means to strengthen character and fall in line with societal expectations and, thus, may have positive connotations (Heine et al., 2001; Kubokawa & Ottaway, 2009). Peterson and Seligman (2003) claimed that their subset of character strengths (VIA Classification of Strengths) are universally held values that transcend culture. However, Christopher and Hickinbottom (2008) contended that these values may exist cross-culturally but that the meaning and understanding of these values differs. Thus, by only highlighting what is similar between cultures, Peterson and Seligman did not understand the significance of the value within its cultural context.

ROLE OF STRENGTHS-BASED APPROACHES IN THE DEVELOPMENT OF CULTURAL COMPETENCE

With growing disparities in mental health treatment and assessment services provided to racial and ethnic minorities in the United States, the APA (2003) affirmed that clinicians must be culturally competent in order to practice psychology. One way to achieve better mental health outcomes among racial and ethnic minorities is to understand how their cultural backgrounds and diversity contribute to psychological well-being. For example, it is imperative to understand that strengths may look different cross-culturally and that they may be influenced by different worldviews.

The mental health system in the United States has traditionally been monocultural, and this approach has often not recognized the role of diversity in the expression of mental health problems. In many instances, those whose beliefs differed from the "Western norm" were viewed to be abnormal, and ethnically expressed, culturally appropriate behaviors became pathologized (APA, 2003). This failure to understand cultural norms caused a distrust of the mental health system among clients from racial and ethnic minority groups (APA, 2003). However, with its focus on universal strengths, positive psychology may be well-suited to address these concerns. It is likely not a coincidence that positive psychology gained prominence during a period of transition where the status quo was no longer sufficient. With increasing research attention on the relationship between culturally based strengths and psychological well-being, positive psychology is ideally suited to establish itself as the pillar on which culturally competent treatment and assessment are based.

SUMMARY AND CONCLUSIONS

With globalization and immigration, the world is becoming increasingly ethnically and racially diverse. Consequently the field of psychology has recognized that change is required in order to adequately address the needs of the changing population. Within this context, positive psychology has emerged as a new psychological science. With a focus on positive emotions and growth, as opposed to psychopathology and disease, its arrival was embraced and well-suited for cultural integration and the development of culture competence in the practice of psychology. Universal characteristics such as optimism, subjective well-being, and self-esteem have been investigated across race and ethnicity and play a central role in the theory and practice of positive psychology. Furthermore, culture-specific traits such as ethnic identity, familism, and spiritual/religious beliefs are strengths that can be easily integrated within the positive psychology framework. This new model was greeted with enthusiasm as well as criticism for its ethnocentricism and roots within Western ideology. Critics argued that positive psychologists premised the framework on individualism and the pursuit of happiness, both Western values. However, more than two thirds of the world's population belongs to a collectivist culture where these characteristics are antithetical to their belief system. Proponents of positive psychology are divided as well. One camp claims that positive psychology is culture-free and that strengths and virtues transcend culture, whereas the other camp believes that adaptive traits and characteristics can only be understood through a cultural lens and that, although there may be commonalities cross-culturally, focus must be more aligned with the strengths, values, and virtues of each individual culture.

As a science grounded in empiricism, positive psychology is poised to make a difference in the approach to psychological health during a pivotal period of societal ethnic transition. Its emphasis on strengths makes it appropriate for integration with a multicultural perspective. Although many of the values touted as universal by positive psychologists may be present cross-culturally, it is detrimental to the field to deny the cultural milieu within which these values are expressed. Moving forward, positive psychology should embrace culture and examine how race and ethnicity affect the expression of its values, virtues, traits, and characteristics.

REFERENCES

Ahuvia, A. (2001). Well-being in cultures of choice: A cross-cultural perspective. *American Psychologist, 56*, 77–78. http://dx.doi.org/10.1037/0003-066X.56.1.77

American Psychological Association. (2003). Guidelines on multicultural education, training, research, practice, and organizational change for psychologists. *American Psychologist, 58*, 377–402.

American Psychological Association. (2008). *Report of the Task Force on the Implementation of the Multicultural Guidelines.* Washington, DC: Author. Retrieved from http://www.apa.org/pi/

Bacigalupe, G. (2001). Is positive psychology only white psychology? *American Psychologist, 56*, 82–83. http://dx.doi.org/10.1037/0003-066X.56.1.82b

Berry, J. W. (2003). Conceptual approaches to acculturation. In K. M. Chun, P. B. Organista, & G. Marin (Eds.), *Acculturation: Advances in theory, measurement,* and *applied research* (pp. 17–37). Washington, DC: American Psychological Association. http://dx.doi.org/10.1037/10472-004

Biswas-Diener, R., & Diener, E. (2006). The subjective well-being of the homeless, and lessons for happiness. *Social Indicators Research, 76,* 185–205. http://dx.doi.org/10.1007/s11205-005-8671-9

Biswas-Diener, R., Vitterso, J., & Diener, E. (2005). Most people are pretty happy, but there is cultural variation: The Inughuit, the Amish, and the Maasai. *Journal of Happiness Studies, 6,* 205–226. http://dx.doi.org/10.1007/s10902-005-5683-8

Brand, J. L. (2001). God is a Libertarian? *American Psychologist, 56,* 78–79. http://dx.doi.org/10.1037/0003-066X.56.1.78b

Branscombe, N. R., Schmitt, M. T., & Harvey, R. D. (1999). Perceiving pervasive discrimination among African Americans: Implications for group identification and well-being. *Journal of Personality and Social Psychology, 77,* 135–149. http://dx.doi.org/10.1037/0022-3514.77.1.135

Carver, C. S., Scheier, M. F., & Segerstrom, S. C. (2010). Optimism. *Clinical Psychology Review, 30,* 879–889. http://dx.doi.org/10.1016/j.cpr.2010.01.006

Chang, E. C. (1996a). Cultural differences in optimism, pessimism, and coping: Predictors of subsequent adjustment in Asian American and Caucasian American college students. *Journal of Counseling Psychology, 43,* 113–123. http://dx.doi.org/10.1037/0022-0167.43.1.113

Chang, E. C. (1996b). Evidence for the cultural specificity of pessimism in Asians vs Caucasians: A test of a general negativity hypothesis. *Personality and Individual Differences, 21,* 819–822. http://dx.doi.org/10.1016/0191-8869(96)00110-9

Chang, E. C., & Asakawa, K. (2003). Cultural variations on optimistic and pessimistic bias for self versus a sibling: Is there evidence for self-enhancement in the west and for self-criticism in the east when the referent group is specified? *Journal of Personality and Social Psychology, 84,* 569–581.

Chang, E. C., Asakawa, K., & Sanna, L. J. (2001). Cultural variations in optimistic and pessimistic bias: Do Easterners really expect the worst and Westerners really expect the best when predicting future life events? *Journal of Personality and Social Psychology, 81,* 476–491. http://dx.doi.org/10.1037/0022-3514.81.3.476

Chang, E. C., Chang, R., & Sanna, L. J. (2009). Optimism, pessimism, and motivation: Relations to adjustment. *Social and Personality Psychology Compass, 3,* 494–506. http://dx.doi.org/10.1111/j.1751-9004.2009.00190.x

Chang, E. C., Sanna, L. J., & Yang, K.-M. (2003). Optimism, pessimism, affectivity, and psychological adjustment in US and Korea: A test of a mediation model. *Personality and Individual Differences, 34,* 1195–1208. http://dx.doi.org/10.1016/S0191-8869(02)00109-5

Chang, E. C., Yu, E. A., Kahle, E. R., Jeglic, E. L., & Hirsch, J. K. (2013). Is doubling up on positive future cognitions associated with reduced suicidal risk in Latinos?: A look at hope and positive problem orientation. *Cognitive Therapy and Research, 37,* 1285–1293. http://dx.doi.org/10.1007/s10608-013-9572-x

Christopher, J. C., & Hickinbottom, S. (2008). Positive psychology, ethnocentrism, and the disguised ideology of individualism. *Theory & Psychology, 18,* 563–589. http://dx.doi.org/10.1177/0959354308093396

Christopher, J. C., Richardson, F. C., & Slife, B. S. (2008). Thinking through positive psychology. *Theory & Psychology, 18,* 555–561. http://dx.doi.org/10.1177/0959354308093395

Compton, W. C. (2001). The values problem in subjective well-being. *American Psychologist, 56,* 84. http://dx.doi.org/10.1037/0003-066X.56.1.84a

Davidson, C. L., Wingate, L. R., Rasmussen, K. A., & Slish, M. L. (2009). Hope as a predictor of interpersonal suicide risk. *Suicide and Life-Threatening Behavior, 39,* 499–507. http://dx.doi.org/10.1521/suli.2009.39.5.499

Davidson, C. L., Wingate, L. R., Slish, M. L., & Rasmussen, K. A. (2010). The great black hope: Hope and its relation to suicide risk among African Americans. *Suicide and Life-Threatening Behavior, 40,* 170–180. http://dx.doi.org/10.1521/suli.2010.40.2.170

Diener, E. (2000). Subjective well-being. The science of happiness and a proposal for a national index. *American Psychologist, 55,* 34–43. http://dx.doi.org/10.1037/0003-066X.55.1.34

Diener, E., & Diener, M. (1995). Cross-cultural correlates of life satisfaction and self-esteem. *Journal of Personality and Social Psychology, 68,* 653–663. http://dx.doi.org/10.1037/0022-3514.68.4.653

Diener, E., Diener, M., & Diener, C. (1995). Factors predicting the subjective well-being of nations. *Journal of Personality and Social Psychology, 69,* 851–864. http://dx.doi.org/10.1037/0022-3514.69.5.851

Diener, E., Oishi, S., & Lucas, R. E. (2003). Personality, culture, and subjective well-being: Emotional and cognitive evaluations of life. *Annual Review of Psychology, 54,* 403–425. http://dx.doi.org/10.1146/annurev.psych.54.101601.145056

Diener, E., Sandvik, E., Seidlitz, L., & Diener, M. (1993). The relationship between income and subjective well-being: Relative or absolute? *Social Indicators Research, 28,* 195–223. http://dx.doi.org/10.1007/BF01079018

Diener, E., Suh, E. M., Lucas, R. E., & Smith, H. L. (1999). Subjective well-being: Three decades of progress. *Psychological Bulletin, 125,* 276–302. http://dx.doi.org/10.1037/0033-2909.125.2.276

Durkheim, E. (1951). *Suicide: A study in sociology* (J. A. Spaulding & G. Simpson, Trans.). Glencoe, IL: The Free Press. (Original work published 1897)

Ellison, C. G., & Levin, J. S. (1998). The religion–health connection: Evidence, theory, and future directions. *Health Education & Behavior, 25,* 700–720. http://dx.doi.org/10.1177/109019819802500603

Erikson, E. H. (1968). *Identity: Youth and crisis.* New York, NY: Norton.

Eshun, S. (1999). Cultural variations in hopelessness, optimism, and suicidal ideation: A study of Ghana and U.S. college samples. *Cross-Cultural Research: The Journal of Comparative Social Science, 33,* 227–238. http://dx.doi.org/10.1177/106939719903300301

Fischer, R., & Chalmers, A. (2008). Is optimism universal? A meta-analytical investigation of optimism levels across 22 nations. *Personality and Individual Differences, 45,* 378–382. http://dx.doi.org/10.1016/j.paid.2008.05.008

Fulmer, C. A., Gelfand, M. J., Kruglanski, A. W., Kim-Prieto, C., Diener, E., Pierro, A., & Higgins, E. T. (2010). On "feeling right" in cultural contexts: How person–culture match affects self-esteem and subjective well-being. *Psychological Science, 21,* 1563–1569. http://dx.doi.org/10.1177/0956797610384742

Gordon, M. M. (1964). *Assimilation in American life.* New York, NY: Oxford University Press.

Heine, S. J., & Hamamura, T. (2007). In search of East Asian self-enhancement. *Personality and Social Psychology Review, 11,* 4–27. http://dx.doi.org/10.1177/1088868306294587

Heine, S. J., Kitayama, S., Lehman, D. R., Takata, T., Ide, E., Leung, C., & Matsumoto, H. (2001). Divergent consequences of success and failure in Japan and North America: An investigation of self-improving motivations and malleable selves. *Journal of Personality and Social Psychology, 81,* 599–615. http://dx.doi.org/10.1037/0022-3514.81.4.599

Heine, S. J., Lehman, D. R., Markus, H. R., & Kitayama, S. (1999). Is there a universal need for positive self-regard? *Psychological Review, 106,* 766–794. http://dx.doi.org/10.1037/0033-295X.106.4.766

Held, B. S. (2002). The tyranny of the positive attitude in America: Observation and speculation. *Journal of Clinical Psychology, 58,* 965–991. http://dx.doi.org/10.1002/jclp.10093

Hofstede, G. (1980). *Culture's consequences: International differences in work-related values.* Beverly Hills, CA: Sage.

Hong, Y. Y., Morris, M. W., Chiu, C. Y., & Benet-Martínez, V. (2000). Multicultural minds. A dynamic constructivist approach to culture and cognition. *American Psychologist, 55,* 709–720. http://dx.doi.org/10.1037/0003-066X.55.7.709

Kitayama, S., Markus, H. R., Matsumoto, H., & Norasakkunkit, V. (1997). Individual and collective processes in the construction of the self: Self-enhancement in the United States and self-criticism in Japan. *Journal of Personality and Social Psychology, 72,* 1245–1267. http://dx.doi.org/10.1037/0022-3514.72.6.1245

Kubokawa, A., & Ottaway, A. (2009). Positive psychology and cultural sensitivity: A review of the literature. *Graduate Journal of Counseling Psychology, 1*(2), Article 13.

LaFromboise, T., Coleman, H. L., & Gerton, J. (1993). Psychological impact of biculturalism: Evidence and theory. *Psychological Bulletin, 114,* 395–412. http://dx.doi.org/10.1037/0033-2909.114.3.395

Larson, D. B., & Larson, S. S. (2003). Spirituality's potential relevance to physical and emotional health: A brief review of quantitative research. *Journal of Psychology and Theology, 31,* 37–51.

Leu, J., Wang, J., & Koo, K. (2011). Are positive emotions just as "positive" across cultures? *Emotion, 11,* 994–999. http://dx.doi.org/10.1037/a0021332

Markus, H. R., & Kitayama, S. (1991). Culture and the self: Implications for cognition, motivation, and emotion. *Psychological Review, 98*, 224–253. http://dx.doi.org/10.1037/0033-295X.98.2.224.

Miller, W. R., & Thoresen, C. E. (2003). Spirituality, religion, and health. An emerging research field. *American Psychologist, 58*, 24–35.

Mok, A., Morris, M., Benet-Martínez, V., & Karakitapoglu-Aygun, Z. (2007). Embracing American culture: Structures of social identity and social networks among first-generation biculturals. *Journal of Cross-Cultural Psychology, 38*, 629–635. http://dx.doi.org/10.1177/0022022107305243

Nes, L. S., & Segerstrom, S. C. (2006). Dispositional optimism and coping: A meta-analytic review. *Personality and Social Psychology Review, 10*, 235–251. http://dx.doi.org/10.1207/s15327957pspr1003_3

Nguyen, A. M. D., & Benet-Martínez, V. (2013). Biculturalism and adjustment: A meta-analysis. *Journal of Cross-Cultural Psychology, 44*, 122–159. http://dx.doi.org/10.1177/0022022111435097

Oishi, S., Diener, E. F., Lucas, R. E., & Suh, E. M. (1999). Cross-cultural variations in predictors of life satisfaction: Perspectives from needs and values. *Personality and Social Psychology Bulletin, 25*, 980–990. http://dx.doi.org/10.1177/01461672992511006

Pargament, K. I. (2002). The bitter and the sweet: An evaluation of the costs and benefits of religiousness. *Psychological Inquiry, 13*, 168–181. http://dx.doi.org/10.1207/S15327965PLI1303_02

Passel, J. S., & Cohn, D. (2008). *U.S. population projections: 2005–2050*. Retrieved from http://www.pewhispanic.org/2008/02/11/us-population-projections-2005-2050/

Passel, J. S., & Cohn, D. (2010). *Unauthorized immigration flows are down sharply since mid-decade*. Washington, DC: Pew Hispanic Center.

Peterson, C., & Chang, E. C. (2003). Optimism and flourishing. In C. L. M. Keyes & J. Haidt (Eds.), *Flourishing: Positive psychology and the life well-lived* (pp. 55–79). Washington, DC: American Psychological Association.

Peterson, C., & Seligman, M. E. P. (2003). *The Values in Action (VIA) Classification of Strengths*. Washington, DC: American Psychological Association.

Phinney, J. S. (1990). Ethnic identity in adolescents and adults: Review of research. *Psychological Bulletin, 108*, 499–514. http://dx.doi.org/10.1037/0033-2909.108.3.499

Phinney, J. S., & Ong, A. D. (2007). Conceptualization and measurement of ethnic identity: Current status and future directions. *Journal of Counseling Psychology, 54*, 271–281. http://dx.doi.org/10.1037/0022-0167.54.3.271

Rasmussen, H. N., Scheier, M. F., & Greenhouse, J. B. (2009). Optimism and physical health: A meta-analytic review. *Annals of Behavioral Medicine, 37*, 239–256. http://dx.doi.org/10.1007/s12160-009-9111-x

Sabogal, F., Marín, G., Otero-Sabogal, R., Marín, B. V., & Perez-Stable, E. J. (1987). Hispanic familism and acculturation: What changes and what doesn't? *Hispanic Journal of Behavioral Sciences, 9*, 397–412. http://dx.doi.org/10.1177/07399863870094003

Schmitt, D. P., & Allik, J. (2005). Simultaneous administration of the Rosenberg Self-Esteem Scale in 53 nations: Exploring the universal and culture-specific features of global self-esteem. *Journal of Personality and Social Psychology, 89,* 623–642. http://dx.doi.org/10.1037/0022-3514.89.4.623

Schwartz, S. J., Unger, J. B., Zamboanga, B. L., & Szapocznik, J. (2010). Rethinking the concept of acculturation: Implications for theory and research. *American Psychologist, 65,* 237–251. http://dx.doi.org/10.1037/a0019330

Schwartz, S. J., Weisskirch, R. S., Hurley, E. A., Zamboanga, B. L., Park, I. J., Kim, S. Y., . . . Greene, A. D. (2010). Communalism, familism, and filial piety: Are they birds of a collectivist feather? *Cultural Diversity and Ethnic Minority Psychology, 16,* 548–560. http://dx.doi.org/10.1037/a0021370

Sedikides, C., Gaertner, L., & Toguchi, Y. (2003). Pancultural self-enhancement. *Journal of Personality and Social Psychology, 84,* 60–79. http://dx.doi.org/10.1037/0022-3514.84.1.60

Sedikides, C., Gaertner, L., & Vevea, J. L. (2005). Pancultural self-enhancement reloaded: A meta-analytic reply to Heine (2005). *Journal of Personality and Social Psychology, 89,* 539–551. http://dx.doi.org/10.1037/0022-3514.89.4.539

Seligman, M. E. P., & Csikszentmihalyi, M. (2000). Positive psychology: An introduction. *American Psychologist, 55,* 5–14. http://dx.doi.org/10.1037/0003-066X.55.1.5

Shrestha, L. B., & Heisler, E. J. (2011). *The changing demographic profile of the United States* (Congressional Research Service Report to Congress RL 32701). Retrieved from https://www.fas.org/sgp/crs/misc/RL32701.pdf

Smith, T. B., & Silva, L. (2011). Ethnic identity and personal well-being of people of color: A meta-analysis. *Journal of Counseling Psychology, 58,* 42–60. http://dx.doi.org/10.1037/a0021528

Steidel, A. G. L., & Contreras, J. M. (2003). A new Familism Scale for use with Latino populations. *Hispanic Journal of Behavioral Sciences, 25,* 312–330. http://dx.doi.org/10.1177/0739986303256912

Tabak, M. A., & Mickelson, K. D. (2009). Religious service attendance and distress: The moderating role of stressful life events and race/ethnicity. *Sociology of Religion, 70,* 49–64. http://dx.doi.org/10.1093/socrel/srp001

Tajfel, H., & Turner, J. C. (1986). The social identity theory of intergroup behavior. In S. Worchel & L. W. Austin (Eds.), *Psychology of intergroup relations* (pp. 7–24). Chicago, IL: Nelson-Hall.

Taylor, S. E., & Brown, J. D. (1988). Illusion and well-being: A social psychological perspective on mental health. *Psychological Bulletin, 103,* 193–210. http://dx.doi.org/10.1037/0033-2909.103.2.193

Taylor, S. E., & Brown, J. D. (1994). Positive illusions and well-being revisited: Separating fact from fiction. *Psychological Bulletin, 116,* 21–27. http://dx.doi.org/10.1037/0033-2909.116.1.21

Umaña-Taylor, A. J. (2011). Ethnic identity. In S. J. Schwartz, L. Luyckx, & V. L. Vignoles (Eds.), *Handbook of identity theory and research* (pp. 791–810). New York, NY: Springer. http://dx.doi.org/10.1007/978-1-4419-7988-9_33

U.S. Census Bureau. (2010). *Resident population*. Retrieved from http://www.census.gov/

U.S. Department of Health and Human Services. (2001). *Mental health: Culture, race, and ethnicity—A supplement to mental health: A report of the Surgeon General*. Rockville, MD: U.S. Department of Health and Human Services, Substance Abuse and Mental Health Services Administration, Center for Mental Health Services.

U.S. Department of Homeland Security. (2009). *Yearbook of immigration statistics 2009*. Retrieved from http://www.dhs.gov/yearbook-immigration-statistics

Vega, W. A. (1990). Hispanic families in the 1980s: A decade of research. *Journal of Marriage and the Family, 52*, 1015–1024. http://dx.doi.org/10.2307/353316

Walsh, R. (2001). Positive psychology: East and west. *American Psychologist, 56*, 83–84. http://dx.doi.org/10.1037/0003-066X.56.1.83

Williams, D. R., Neighbors, H. W., & Jackson, J. S. (2003). Racial/ethnic discrimination and health: Findings from community studies. *American Journal of Public Health, 93*, 200–208. http://dx.doi.org/10.2105/AJPH.93.2.200

II

THEORY AND RESEARCH

3

POSITIVE PSYCHOLOGY IN ASIAN AMERICANS: THEORY AND RESEARCH

LUCY ZHANG BENCHARIT AND JEANNE L. TSAI

Despite the tremendous advances that positive psychologists have made to our understanding of optimal human functioning, little attention has been paid to the role of culture in shaping these processes (Diener, 2000; Henrich, Heine, & Norenzayan, 2010; Tsai & Park, 2014). Yet, a growing body of empirical research demonstrates cultural variation in how people think, feel, and relate to others, suggesting that optimal functioning for Asian Americans and European Americans may differ in important ways. Thus, current ways of assessing and increasing well-being, which have been primarily developed in European American contexts, may be only partially applicable to Asian Americans. In this chapter, we review the research on positive affect, cognitions, and behaviors of Asian Americans and discuss implications for developing a positive psychology of Asian Americans.

We thank Lindsey Davis for her research assistance in the preparation of this chapter. We also thank members of the Stanford Culture and Emotion Laboratory and the Stanford Culture Co-laboratory for their valuable feedback on earlier versions of this chapter.

http://dx.doi.org/10.1037/14799-003
Positive Psychology in Racial and Ethnic Groups: Theory, Research, and Practice, E. C. Chang, C. A. Downey, J. K. Hirsch, and N. J. Lin (Editors)

OVERVIEW OF THE HISTORY AND DEMOGRAPHICS OF ASIAN AMERICANS

Asian Americans are an extremely diverse group: 21.9% of Asian Americans are of Chinese descent, 18.8% of Filipino descent, 17.5% of Indian descent, 10.2% of Vietnamese descent, 9.5% of Korean descent, and 7.1% of Japanese descent. The remaining 15% of Asian Americans include at least 16 other ethnic groups (i.e., Bangladeshi, Burmese, Cambodian, Hmong, Indonesian, Laotian, Taiwanese, Thai; U.S. Census Bureau, 2010). Despite tremendous variation in immigration histories and cultures of origin of Asian Americans, most research in psychology has focused on comparisons between East Asian (e.g., Chinese, Korean, Japanese) and European American groups. Because of this, much of the research we review here is based on these two groups.

Today, Asian Americans are the fastest-growing minority group in the United States, with 18.9 million documented residents. Asian American population growth is driven by international migration: 60% of Asian American population growth in 2012 was due to international migration; in comparison, 76% of Hispanic population growth in 2012 was due to actual births in the United States (U.S. Census Bureau, 2013). This suggests that Asian Americans may be even more influenced by their cultures of origin than other ethnic groups in the United States.

Asian Americans vary in the degree to which they are oriented to American culture and their cultures of origin (Abe-Kim, Okazaki, & Goto, 2001). Research on *acculturation* (i.e., the degree to which one adopts the values and practices of the host culture; B. S. K. Kim & Abreu, 2001; Suinn, 2010) in Asian Americans suggests that being oriented to American culture has both positive (e.g., decreased depression and anxiety; Yoon, Hacker, Hewitt, Abrams, & Cleary, 2012) and negative (e.g., increased stress due to acculturation; Ward & Kennedy, 1994) outcomes. Similarly, research conducted on *enculturation* (i.e., the degree to which one retains their culture of origin) suggests that being highly oriented to East Asian culture can lead to positive outcomes (e.g., higher educational achievement; Huntsinger, Jose, Larson, Balsink Krieg, & Shaligram, 2000; strong work and family values; Phinney, 1990) as well as negative ones (e.g., adjustment difficulties and psychological distress; Shim & Schwartz, 2007).

CULTURAL MODELS OF THE SELF

Although Asian Americans vary in their exposure to mainstream American and Asian cultures, by definition, they are directly or indirectly exposed to U.S. and Asian cultural ideas and practices, which vary in a number of ways. One fundamental difference between Western and East Asian cultures is the dominant model of the self and personhood (Markus & Kitayama, 1991). In Western cultures like the United States, the dominant model of the self is *independent*, autonomous, stable, and distinct from others; in East Asian cultures, however, the dominant model of the self is *inter-dependent*, fluid, contextual, and bound to others (Heine, Lehman, Markus, & Kitayama, 1999; Markus & Conner, 2013; Morling, Kitayama, & Miyamoto, 2002). As an illustration of these differences, Figure 3.1 shows the independent self as distinct from others (indicated by the solid line around the self and the distance between circles) and the interdependent self as connected to close others (indicated by the dotted line around the self and the overlap among circles; Markus & Conner, 2013; Markus & Kitayama, 1991). In contexts with independent views of the self, a good, well-adjusted, and happy person is one who asserts and expresses his or her desires, beliefs, and preferences; exerts influence over others; and acts consistently across situations. In contexts with interdependent views of the self, however, a good, well-adjusted, and happy person is one who adjusts his or her desires, beliefs, and preferences to fit in with others; accommodates others; and is responsive to situational demands (Cross, Morris, & Gore, 2002; Kanagawa, Cross, & Markus, 2001; Tsai, Knutson, & Fung, 2006; Tsai, Miao, Seppala, Fung, & Yeung, 2007).

Because they are exposed to both Western and East Asian cultures, Asian Americans may endorse both models of self. However, the ways in which these

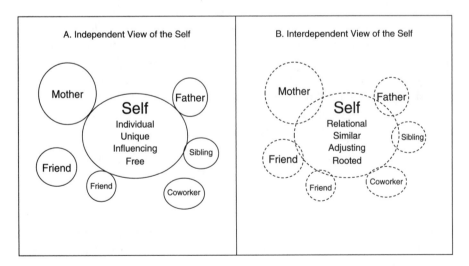

Figure 3.1. View of the self: A. Independent; B. Interdependent. Adapted from "Culture and the Self: Implications for Cognition, Emotion, and Motivation," by H. R. Markus and S. Kitayama, 1991, *Psychological Review*, 98, p. 226. Copyright 1991 by the American Psychological Association.

models are expressed may depend on the situation. Priming studies, in which one culture is made more salient than the other, suggest that Asian Americans who are highly oriented to both cultures behave in ways that are consistent with the culture being primed (Hong, Morris, Chiu, & Benet-Martínez, 2000). Most recently, Asian Americans' different models of self have been validated with neuroimaging data. Whereas European Americans show greater activation in areas that process self-relevant information (medial prefrontal cortex [MPFC]) in response to general self-descriptions (i.e., "In general, I am honest"), Japanese show greater MPFC activation in response to contextualized self-descriptions (i.e., "With my mother, I am honest"; Chiao et al., 2009). Asian Americans, who endorse both sets of values, show both patterns of MPFC activation depending on which culture is primed (Chiao et al., 2010).

VALUE OF POSITIVE PSYCHOLOGY FOR ASIAN AMERICANS

Positive psychology's goals of encouraging optimal human functioning, creating thriving individuals and communities, and helping people achieve their full potential (Seligman & Csikszentmihalyi, 2000) are relevant across cultures. However, most interventions designed to facilitate positive outcomes are based on European American views of optimal functioning, which may be less effective for individuals who are also influenced by East Asian ideas and practices. For instance, expressing gratitude, an increasingly popular way of enhancing well-being, seems to be more effective for European Americans[1] than South Koreans (Layous, Lee, Choi, & Lyubomirsky, 2013). Thus, understanding how culture shapes the meaning of optimal functioning should help researchers and practitioners develop more effective practices and interventions to improve the well-being of Asian Americans. Next, we review research on positive affect, cognitions, and behaviors of Asian Americans. We treat them as separate constructs for analytic purposes, but in fact positive affect, positive cognitions, and positive behaviors often co-occur.

THEORY AND RESEARCH ON POSITIVE AFFECT
OF ASIAN AMERICANS

One important contribution of positive psychology is its emphasis on positive affective states. Across cultures, affective states (i.e., feeling states that include emotions, attitudes, moods, and preferences) are organized in terms of

---

[1]When describing research findings in this chapter, we use the term *American* to describe people living in the United States. We use the terms *European American* and *Asian American* to describe specific ethnic groups living in the United States.

at least two dimensions: *valence* (positive to negative) and *arousal* (high to low; Barrett & Russell, 1999).

Relationship Between Positive and Negative States

In European American contexts, reports of positive and negative affective states are usually negatively correlated (i.e., less "mixed"); the more European Americans feel good, the less they feel bad. However, reports of positive and negative affective states are typically less negatively correlated (i.e., more "mixed") in East Asian contexts (Kööts, Realo, & Allik, 2012; Schimmack, Oishi, & Diener, 2002; Sims, Tsai, Wang, Fung, & Zhang, 2014). In other words, individuals in East Asian contexts are more likely to report feeling the good with the bad and the bad with the good than those in European American contexts. Furthermore, studies of Asian Canadians suggest that their experiences of positive and negative states depend on the cultural context they are in. Following situations in which they recently spoke English, Asian Canadians' positive and negative feelings resemble those of their European Canadian counterparts, and following situations in which they recently spoke an Asian language, Asian Canadians' positive and negative feelings resemble those of their East Asian counterparts (Perunovic, Heller, & Rafaeli, 2007).

Why do these differences exist? In European American contexts that promote independent selves, individuals are encouraged to stand out in a positive way. Maximizing the experience and expression of positive emotion (and dampening the experience and expression of negative emotion) is one way to achieve this. However, in East Asian contexts that promote interdependent selves, individuals are encouraged to fit in with others. Moderating experiences and expressions of positive and negative emotions makes it easier for individuals to adjust to others (Markus & Kitayama, 1991). Consistent with this idea, Sims and colleagues (2014) found that European Americans ideally want to feel positive states more and negative states less than their Chinese American counterparts do and that both groups want to feel positive states more and negative states less than their Hong Kong Chinese and Beijing Chinese counterparts do. Moreover, these cultural differences in ideal affect accounted for cultural differences in the experiences of mixed emotions. Thus, European American contexts teach people to value maximizing positive and minimizing negative emotions more than Asian American or East Asian contexts do, which influences how individuals experience positive relative to negative emotions.

Positive States That People Ideally Want to Feel

Although most people want to feel positively, cultures differ in the specific positive states they encourage. European Americans ideally want to feel high arousal positive states (i.e., excitement and elation) more than East Asians, and East Asians want to feel low arousal positive states (i.e., calm and serenity) more than European Americans (Tsai et al., 2006). Asian Americans value high arousal positive states more than their East Asian counterparts do, but they also value low arousal positive states more than their European American counterparts do (Tsai et al., 2006). These cultural differences emerge even after controlling for how much people actually feel these states (*actual affect*; Tsai et al., 2007).

These differences in ideal affect are again related to cultural differences in models of the self (Tsai et al., 2007). In contexts that have independent models of the self, individuals are encouraged to exert influence (i.e., shape their environments to be consistent with their own desires, needs, and preferences; Morling et al., 2002). Because influencing others requires action, and action requires increases in physiological arousal, individuals (and cultures) that value influence should also value high arousal positive states. In contexts that have interdependent models of the self, individuals are encouraged to adjust (i.e., change their own desires, needs, and preferences to be consistent with their environments; Morling et al., 2002). Because adjusting to others requires suspending action, and suspending action requires decreases in physiological arousal, individuals (and cultures) that value adjustment should also value low arousal states. In support of these predictions, correlational and experimental studies find that, across cultures, individuals whose goal it was to influence their partner preferred excited (vs. calm) states more than those whose goal it was to adjust to their partner (Tsai et al., 2006, 2007). These findings suggest that individuals value the affective states that are consistent with the larger interpersonal goals of their cultures.

Social Context of Emotions

Although people across contexts experience both socially engaging (e.g., feeling friendly, respectful) and disengaging (e.g., feeling proud, superior) emotions, culture influences how prevalent these emotions are and whether they are associated with general positive feelings. In Japan, socially engaging emotions are more prevalent than socially disengaging emotions, whereas the opposite is true in the United States (Kitayama, Markus, & Kurokawa, 2000). Furthermore, socially disengaging emotions are more strongly associated with general positive states (i.e., happy) for Americans than for Japanese, and socially engaging emotions are more strongly associated with general positive states for Japanese than Americans (Kitayama, Mesquita, & Karasawa, 2006). These differences are due to different models of the self in European American and East Asian contexts.

THEORY AND RESEARCH ON POSITIVE COGNITIONS
OF ASIAN AMERICANS

Several interventions that aim to increase well-being focus on changing people's cognitions, or ways of thinking about themselves and the worlds around them (i.e., cognitive behavior therapy, Fordyce happiness program; Sin & Lyubomirsky, 2009). However, as with positive affect, researchers have observed cultural differences in cognitive processes. In this section, we review two areas in which positive cognitions vary across European American and East Asian contexts.

Thinking About the Self (Self-Esteem)

High self-esteem (i.e., evaluation of one's own worth) is regarded as positive, desirable, and motivating in European American contexts (Baumeister, 1993; Fulmer et al., 2010). Significant research suggests that East Asians and Asian Americans report lower levels of self-esteem than European Americans and European Canadians (Yamaguchi et al., 2007) do. From a European American perspective, these differences suggest that East Asians and Asian Americans are more psychologically distressed than their European American counterparts; however, research suggests that having high self-esteem may not be as adaptive in East Asian cultures because it works against the goal of adjusting to and fitting in with others (Heine et al., 1999). Thus, having lower self-esteem may better facilitate interdependent goals in East Asian contexts.

Although Chinese individuals score lower than European Americans on overall self-reported self-esteem, these differences are driven by responses to the negative statements. Whereas Chinese individuals and European Americans equally endorsed positive statements like, "I take a positive attitude toward myself," Chinese were more likely than European Americans to endorse negative statements like, "At times I think I am no good at all." These findings have been replicated with measures of implicit self-esteem (i.e., the Implicit Association Test), suggesting that cultural differences are not just due to differences in self-presentation (Boucher, Peng, Shi, & Wang, 2009; Spencer-Rodgers, Boucher, Mori, Wang, & Peng, 2009). For Asian Americans, reports of self-esteem vary by cultural orientation (e.g., Chinese Americans highly affiliated with other Chinese report lower self-esteem; Tsai, Ying, & Lee, 2001) and social context (e.g., Asian American reports of self-esteem depend on the reference group against which individuals are comparing themselves; Yamaguchi et al., 2007).

Thinking About the World (Dialecticism and Optimism/Pessimism)

Dialectical thinking includes the beliefs that (a) the universe is always changing in dynamic and unpredictable ways (i.e., theory of change), (b) contradictory statements can both be true (i.e., theory of contradiction), and (c) everything exists as part of a whole and cannot be understood absent of a larger context (i.e., holism). Dialectical ways of thinking are higher among East Asians and Asian Americans than European Americans (Nisbett, Peng, Choi, & Norenzayan, 2001; Peng & Nisbett, 1999). These differences in dialecticism have implications for how individuals process and recall information and make inferences. For instance, when asked to look at an image with focal and background features (e.g., a fish in water with background bubbles and plants), Americans attended more to focal objects (e.g., fish) than to background features (e.g., water color, bubbles, plants), whereas Japanese did the reverse (Masuda & Nisbett, 2001; Miyamoto, Nisbett, & Masuda, 2006). Moreover, whereas Japanese better recognized focal objects when paired with their original backgrounds, Americans recognized focal objects regardless of the background. These findings also extend to emotional processing: Japanese are more likely to consider the emotions of the people surrounding the central figure than are Americans (Masuda, Gonzalez, Kwan, & Nisbett, 2008).

Dialecticism also highlights differences between Americans and East Asians in the types of predictions they make about the future. For instance, when given a sequence of numbers (e.g., 200, 300, 400, 500, ___), Americans were more likely to predict that the fifth data point was consistent with the trend (e.g., increase in number). However, Chinese more often predicted that the fifth data point was inconsistent with the trend (e.g., decrease in number). Americans were more likely to continue the trend if it was in the positive direction than if it was in the negative direction, an interesting finding that is consistent with Americans' desire to maximize the positive (Ji, Nisbett, & Su, 2001).

Another difference in the cognitive processes of East Asians and European Americans is their levels of optimism and pessimism. Among European Americans, *optimism* (i.e., expecting future positive outcomes) is linked to numerous positive outcomes related to coping, adjustment, and mental health (Norem & Chang, 2002), whereas *pessimism* (i.e., expecting negative outcomes) is related to negative outcomes, including problem avoidance, depression, and social withdrawal (Chang, 1996; Long & Sangster, 1993). The benefits of being optimistic and the costs of being pessimistic, however, may be less applicable to Asian Americans. Although Asian Americans and European Americans do not differ in their levels of optimism, the former are significantly more pessimistic than the latter;

however, pessimism is a stronger predictor of depression for European Americans than it is for Asian Americans (Chang, 1996). Thus, expecting negative outcomes may have different implications for psychological functioning for European Americans and Asian Americans.

Cultural differences in outcomes related to optimism and pessimism are a product of different models of self. In independent contexts, where individuals are encouraged to maximize positive and minimize negative cognitions and emotions, pessimism is more detrimental to psychological functioning. In interdependent cultures, where individuals are encouraged to moderate positive and negative cognitions and emotions, pessimism exacts a lesser cost.

THEORY AND RESEARCH ON POSITIVE BEHAVIORS OF ASIAN AMERICANS

Differences in affective and cognitive processes between Asian Americans and European Americans have implications for the specific behaviors that the two groups view as positive and optimal. In this section, we provide examples of behaviors that have different meanings in Asian American and European American settings.

Interactions With the Environment (Authenticity, Choice)

One difference between European Americans and East Asians is the emphasis placed on *authenticity*, or the degree to which one is consistent in personality, thoughts, and behaviors across situations, despite external pressure to change. For European Americans, greater authenticity is associated with better psychological adjustment (Donahue, Robins, Roberts, & John, 1993; Swann, De la Ronde, & Hixon, 1994); however, less of an association is observed for Asian Americans and East Asians (English & Chen, 2011). Compared with European Americans, East Asians are less disturbed by inconsistencies between public and private thoughts and actions and less critical of others' incongruent behaviors (Kashima, Siegal, Tanaka, & Kashima, 1992). Furthermore, Koreans spontaneously describe themselves as inconsistent in their personality traits (Choi & Choi, 2002) and as "two-faced" (Suh, 2002), suggesting that flexibility, not authenticity, is considered normative and positive in Korean culture. These cultural differences also influence social judgments: European Americans tend to attribute people's behavior to their personality traits (vs. situational circumstances) more than East Asians do (Choi, Nisbett, & Norenzayan, 1999; Morris, Nisbett, & Peng, 1995).

Individuals in European American contexts value making autonomous choices; they are more likely to construe daily actions as self-choices and are faster at making self-choices compared with individuals in Indian contexts, who less often construe actions as choices and are slower at making self-choices (Savani, Markus, & Conner, 2008; Savani, Markus, Naidu, Kumar, & Berlia, 2010). Moreover, individuals from European American contexts enjoy objects they have chosen for themselves more than those they have not chosen, and they are willing to pay more for an object they choose for themselves than one they do not. Indians do not show the same bias for objects they have chosen (Savani et al., 2008). In addition, European American children perform better on, spend more time doing, and enjoy self-selected tasks more than tasks that were selected for them, but the opposite is true for Asian American children (Chen & Stevenson, 1995; Fu & Markus, 2014; Iyengar & Lepper, 1999). Different models of self can explain these differences in the value of choice. In European American contexts, choice for oneself is highly valued because it reinforces the importance of individual traits and preferences. However, in Asian contexts, personal choice may be less valued because it reduces the importance of social norms and prevents people from adjusting to the preferences of others.

In addition, there are cultural differences in how individuals make choices; European Americans more often make personal choices for themselves (i.e., choices based on individual preferences) by choosing the item they rate highest among similar items (e.g., several different CDs; Kitayama, Snibbe, Markus, & Suzuki, 2004). In contrast, Indians and Japanese less often make personal choices, as they are less likely than European Americans to choose products they rate highest for themselves (Savani et al., 2008). Similarly, European Americans often strive to be unique in their choices and preferences, whereas East Asians often strive to conform to the norms of the group. For instance, when given the option to choose one pen from five similar pens (four of the same color, one of a different color), European Americans more often choose the minority pen color. East Asians, however, more often choose the majority pen color (H. S. Kim & Markus, 1999). Whereas in European American contexts, choice behaviors express one's independence and personal preferences, in Asian cultures, choice behaviors appear to express one's interdependence and group preferences.

Interactions With Others (Self-Presentation, Emotion Regulation, Interpersonal Relationships)

The way in which individuals present themselves to others reflects cultural differences in values. Considerable research suggests that in Western contexts, individuals are motivated to view and present themselves positively instead of negatively: European Americans recall information about successes more than about failures (Crary, 1966), evaluate themselves more positively than others evaluate them (Heine & Renshaw, 2002), and more strongly associate themselves with positive than negative words (Greenwald & Farnham, 2000). However, the opposite is true of East Asians and Asian Americans. Japanese students, for instance, not only rate themselves less positively than others rate them, but they are also more self-critical than European Americans (Heine & Lehman, 1999). In a meta-analysis of 91 cross-cultural comparisons, Westerners self-enhanced significantly more than East Asians, and Asian Americans scored somewhere between the two groups (Heine & Hamamura, 2007). Again, these differences stem from different models of self. Self-enhancement is more useful in European American contexts, which value influencing others and positively differentiating oneself from others; for Asian Americans and East Asians, by contrast, adjusting to others and minimizing differences to fit in with others are valued (Markus & Kitayama, 1991; Morling et al., 2002). Research suggests that Asian Americans, who are influenced by both cultures, alternate in the degree of self-enhancement depending on the culture being primed (Zusho, 2008).

Emotional behaviors also factor into self-presentation during interpersonal interactions. Emotional suppression (i.e., actively inhibiting emotional expressions) is associated with negative outcomes for European Americans, including avoidant attachment, reduced feelings of closeness, increased negative feelings about interpersonal interactions, depressive symptoms, and lower life satisfaction (Gross & John, 2003). However, emotional suppression is not associated with these negative outcomes for Asian Americans or East Asians, for whom suppression is a critical part of maintaining interpersonal harmony (English & John, 2013; Soto, Perez, Kim, Lee, & Minnick, 2011).

Cultural differences in models of self also influence what is expected and valued in interpersonal interactions and the ways in which they influence individual attitudes and behaviors. For example, employees in European American contexts show less deference and respect for authority, are more likely to see the self as equal to leaders, and focus more on personal goals (vs. duties and obligations) than employees in East Asian contexts (Farh, Hackett, & Liang, 2007). Indeed, a meta-analysis suggests that perceived employee–supervisor relationship quality (known as *leader–member exchange*) is more strongly related to job satisfaction and employee turnover in Western than in Eastern contexts (Rockstuhl, Dulebohn, Ang, & Shore, 2012). A poorer relationship between employer and employee (lower leader–member exchange) hurts employee performance across cultures, but it has a greater impact on employee satisfaction and the likelihood that employees stay in their jobs in Western contexts than in East Asian contexts. In East Asian contexts, identification with collective goals seems to be more important. Although few studies have examined these processes in Asian American employees, it is likely that they are influenced by a combination of these East Asian and Western values.

DEVELOPING A POSITIVE PSYCHOLOGY OF ASIAN AMERICANS

The work described here suggests that a positive psychology of Asian Americans may, in many ways, look different from a positive psychology of European Americans. For instance, instead of defining *well-being* as the presence of positive states and the absence of negative states, practitioners might consider the possibility that, for some Asian Americans, *well-being* is the presence of moderate levels of both positive and negative affect. In this section, we describe what a positive psychology of Asian Americans might look like and how it might be achieved.

Rethinking Optimal Functioning

As illustrated in Figure 3.2, a good, well-adjusted person in independent European American contexts (light gray circle on the right) is one who focuses on positive instead of negative emotions and experiences; values high arousal positive states such as excitement; experiences emotions that differentiate one from others; has positive feelings about the self; thinks in a linear, analytic way; attends to focal objects; is consistent in one's thoughts and behaviors across situations; has positive feelings about the self; is highly optimistic; makes choices that express one's uniqueness and personal preferences; and is not suppressing core elements of oneself, like emotional expressions. In contrast, a good, well-adjusted person in interdependent East Asian contexts (in Figure 3.2, dark gray circle on left) is one who maintains balance between positive and negative emotions and experiences; values low arousal positive states such as calm; experiences emotions that connect one with others; has positive and negative feelings about the self; thinks in a holistic way; attends to context; is responsive to the situation; suppresses emotional expressions to facilitate social harmony; and is tolerant of contradiction, change, and inconsistencies in the self and the world.

Because Asian Americans are exposed to both European American and East Asian cultural ideas and practices (as indicated by the medium gray middle circle in Figure 3.2), they often internalize both models of optimal functioning. For instance, because Asian Americans, like their Asian counterparts, recognize and value both positive and negative aspects of the situation, negative cognitions like pessimism and low self-esteem may be less useful when diagnosing depression or anxiety in Asian Americans. Similarly, counseling practices that emphasize replacing negative cognitions with more positive ones (e.g., cognitive reappraisal; Beck, 1976) may be less effective for Asian Americans. Thus, in both research and practice, psychologists should evaluate Asian Americans' affect, thoughts, and behaviors in the context of European American and East Asian models of optimal functioning.

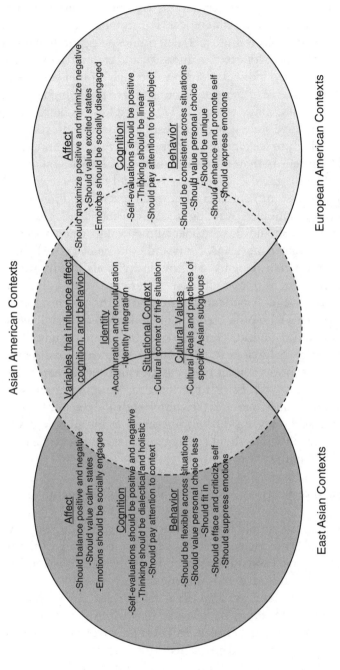

Asian American Contexts

European American Contexts

East Asian Contexts

Affect
-Should maximize positive and minimize negative
-Should value excited states
-Emotions should be socially disengaged

Cognition
-Self-evaluations should be positive
-Thinking should be linear
-Should pay attention to focal object

Behavior
-Should be consistent across situations
-Should value personal choice
-Should be unique
-Should enhance and promote self
-Should express emotions

Variables that influence affect, cognition, and behavior

Identity
-Acculturation and enculturation
-Identity integration

Situational Context
-Cultural context of the situation

Cultural Values
-Cultural ideals and practices of specific Asian subgroups

Affect
-Should balance positive and negative
-Should value calm states
-Emotions should be socially engaged

Cognition
-Self-evaluations should be positive and negative
-Thinking should be dialectical and holistic
-Should pay attention to context

Behavior
-Should be flexible across situations
-Should value personal choice less
-Should fit in
-Should efface and criticize self
-Should suppress emotions

Figure 3.2. Optimal functioning in East Asian, Asian American, and European American contexts.

Promoting Positive Outcomes in Ways That Are Culturally Meaningful

Practitioners who plan interventions to promote healthy behavior should also consider these cultural differences. For instance, *ideal affect* (i.e., emotions that people ideally want to feel) determines perceptions of how vigorous exercise is, preferences for exercise intensity, and emotional experiences after exercise. Specifically, individuals who value high arousal positive states are more likely to perceive exercise as vigorous and to prefer high intensity exercise (Hogan, Chim, Sims, & Tsai, 2012). Therefore, in cultures that value high arousal positive states (i.e., European American contexts), individuals may be more likely to seek intense exercises (e.g., running) and have a higher threshold for intensity than in cultures that value low arousal positive states (i.e., East Asian contexts). Practitioners should take these individual and cultural differences into consideration when recommending health-related behaviors (e.g., running vs. walking) to Asian Americans.

Practitioners should also consider cultural values when designing health messages for Asian Americans. Sims and colleagues (2014) showed that choosing a physician depends on how individuals ideally want to feel. Because highly enculturated Chinese Americans value calm states more than their European American counterparts, they were more likely to choose physicians who promoted a calm and relaxed lifestyle versus those who promoted a dynamic, vital lifestyle. In another study, East Asians increased health behaviors (e.g., flossing) following loss-framed health messages ("Floss now or suffer from cavities and gum disease") more than British participants did. British participants, however, increased flossing after promotion-framed messages ("Healthy teeth and gums only a floss away") more than East Asians did (Uskul, Sherman, & Fitzgibbon, 2009). Thus, counselors and clinicians should design and market mental health services in culturally congruent ways.

Developing Interventions That Are Culturally Consistent

Interventions should also be designed to consider Asian American cultural ideas and practices. For instance, Western models of coping herald forgiveness as a necessary and important element in relationship repair; researchers have found that forgiveness interventions are effective for treating depression and anxiety (Reed & Enright, 2006; Williamson & Gonzales, 2007). This may be because, in Western contexts, forgiveness is viewed as an individual choice. In contrast, in certain Asian contexts, forgiveness is often defined in terms of the situation, with some situations being more forgivable than others (Sandage, Hill, & Vang, 2003). Moreover, relationships of mutual obligation (more common in Asian contexts) often continue in the absence of forgiveness (McCullough, 2000). Thus, forgiveness interventions may be less effective for some Asian American groups.

Another example is related to social support, a coping mechanism related to increased well-being and decreased stress (Taylor, 2007). Despite having social networks that are equally supportive as European Americans, Asian Americans are less likely to explicitly ask for support or help from social networks during stressful times because they do not want to burden others (H. S. Kim, Sherman, & Taylor, 2008; S. Kim, Gonzales, Stroh, & Wang, 2006; Sasaki & Kim, 2011). Instead, Asian Americans benefit more from *implicit social support* (the knowledge that one has support). In fact, Asian Americans show decreased stress responses (i.e., cortisol levels) when they are simply asked to think about groups that they feel close to before completing a stressful task (Taylor, Welch, Kim, & Sherman, 2007). In contrast, European Americans more often seek and benefit most from explicit social support (H. S. Kim et al., 2008). These findings suggest that one way clinicians can decrease stress and facilitate well-being among Asian Americans is to focus less on talking through problems and more on thinking about close others.

A major source of reduced happiness and well-being and increased depression and anxiety in Asian Americans is *acculturation gap distress* (conflicts that arise from unequal rates of acculturation between parents and children; Phinney, 2003). When children acculturate faster than parents (i.e., become more American than parents), changes in language, values, and behaviors may increase familial tension. One way to reduce acculturation gap distress is family therapy, with a focus on cultural competence (Phinney, 2010). For example, practitioners might identify one or more domains in which conflicts occur (e.g., interpersonal relationship, academic achievement, leisure time), isolate behaviors and values that contribute to conflict, and then encourage parents and children to share their cultural perspectives with each other to increase intergenerational understanding (Ying, 1999).

Acculturation and identity research suggests that Asian American bicultural individuals (those who identify highly with both American and Asian cultures) have better outcomes compared with other identification profiles (Yoon et al., 2012). This may be because bicultural individuals are more familiar with the values and practices of both cultures and are, thus, better equipped to navigate both European American and Asian cultural contexts (Hong et al., 2000). It may also be because bicultural individuals have integrated their Asian and American identities and view these identities as compatible and connected as opposed to incompatible and separate (Haritatos & Benet-Martínez, 2002). These findings suggest that interventions should focus on increasing identification with and integration of

American and Asian cultures among Asian Americans, ideally at a young age. Recognizing cultural differences and promoting intergroup dialogue in schools or other institutions would facilitate this process.

Doing More Research on Asian American Contexts

Although more research has been conducted on Asian Americans than many other ethnic groups, unanswered questions remain. First, most current cross-cultural researchers have examined differences between European Americans and East Asian Americans. Much less work has focused on Filipino Americans and Indian Americans, who are increasing in number and who differ from Chinese, Japanese, and Korean Americans in their religious and cultural ideals and practices. Future research should focus on other Asian American groups to see how they compare with each other as well as with other ethnic groups in the United States.

Second, researchers should also consider how other social categories, like social class, interact with culture to shape affective, cognitive, and behavioral processes. Most findings on promoting positive outcomes, like much of psychological research, are based on middle class groups (Henrich et al., 2010; Markus & Conner, 2013). It is possible that in working class contexts, where resources are sparse, these cultural differences are even more pronounced as individuals struggle to meet basic needs.

Another important research direction is to examine ways in which Asian American models of optimal functioning are fostered. For instance, East Asian parents often take an active role in helping children work to achieve high standards (Fiske, Kitayama, Markus, & Nisbett, 1998). Asian American children appear to be motivated by parental pressure, whereas parental pressure appears to undermine motivation among European American children (Fu & Markus, 2014). Thus, whereas discouraging parents from applying too much pressure on their children might be helpful in European American contexts, it might have unintended costs in Asian American contexts. More work should focus on the practices that foster different forms of optimal functioning in European American, Asian American, and East Asian contexts.

We have described Asian Americans as being influenced by both East Asian and European American contexts, but some experiences, ideas, and practices that are unique to Asian Americans. For instance, whereas enculturation and acculturation were more predictive of well-being for immigrant than American-born Asian Americans, discrimination was more predictive of well-being for American-born than immigrant Asian Americans (Ying, Lee, & Tsai, 2000). More research is needed to focus on these aspects of being Asian American and the implications they have for optimal functioning.

REFERENCES

Abe-Kim, J., Okazaki, S., & Goto, S. G. (2001). Unidimensional versus multi-dimensional approaches to the assessment of acculturation for Asian American populations. *Cultural Diversity and Ethnic Minority Psychology, 7*, 232–246.

Barrett, L. F., & Russell, J. A. (1999). Structure of current affect. *Current Directions in Psychological Science, 8*, 10–14. http://dx.doi.org/10.1111/1467-8721.00003

Baumeister, R. (Ed.). (1993). *Self-esteem: The puzzle of low self-regard.* New York, NY: Plenum. http://dx.doi.org/10.1007/978-1-4684-8956-9

Beck, A. T. (1976). *Cognitive therapy and the emotional disorders.* New York, NY: International University Press.

Boucher, H. C., Peng, K., Shi, J., & Wang, L. (2009). Culture and implicit self-esteem Chinese are "good" and "bad" at the same time. *Journal of Cross-Cultural Psychology, 40*, 24–45. http://dx.doi.org/10.1177/0022022108326195

Chang, E. (1996). Cultural differences in optimism, pessimism, and coping: Predictors of subsequent adjustment in Asian American and Caucasian American college students. *Journal of Counseling Psychology, 43*, 113–123. http://dx.doi.org/10.1037/0022-0167.43.1.113

Chen, C., & Stevenson, H. W. (1995). Motivation and mathematics achievement: A comparative study of Asian-American, Caucasian-American, and east Asian high school students. *Child Development, 66*, 1215–1234. http://dx.doi.org/10.2307/1131808

Chiao, J. Y., Harada, T., Komeda, H., Li, Z., Mano, Y., Saito, D., . . . Iidaka, T. (2009). Neural basis of individualistic and collectivistic views of self. *Human Brain Mapping, 30*, 2813–2820. http://dx.doi.org/10.1002/hbm.20707

Chiao, J. Y., Harada, T., Komeda, H., Li, Z., Mano, Y., Saito, D., . . . Iidaka, T. (2010). Dynamic cultural influences on neural representations of the self. *Journal of Cognitive Neuroscience, 22*(1), 1–11. http://dx.doi.org/10.1162/jocn.2009.21192

Choi, I., & Choi, Y. (2002). Culture and self-concept flexibility. *Personality and Social Psychology Bulletin, 28*, 1508–1517. http://dx.doi.org/10.1177/014616702237578

Choi, I., Nisbett, R. E., & Norenzayan, A. (1999). Causal attribution across cultures: Variation and universality. *Psychological Bulletin, 125*, 47–63. http://dx.doi.org/10.1037/0033-2909.125.1.47

Crary, W. G. (1966). Reactions to incongruent self-experiences. *Journal of Consulting Psychology, 30*, 246–252. http://dx.doi.org/10.1037/h0023347

Cross, S. E., Morris, M. L., & Gore, J. S. (2002). Thinking about oneself and others: The relational-interdependent self-construal and social cognition. *Journal of Personality and Social Psychology, 82*, 399–418. http://dx.doi.org/10.1037/0022-3514.82.3.399

Diener, E. (2000). Subjective well-being. The science of happiness and a proposal for a national index. *American Psychologist, 55*, 34–43. http://dx.doi.org/10.1037/0003-066X.55.1.34

Donahue, E. M., Robins, R. W., Roberts, B. W., & John, O. P. (1993). The divided self: Concurrent and longitudinal effects of psychological adjustment and social roles on self-concept differentiation. *Journal of Personality and Social Psychology, 64,* 834–846. http://dx.doi.org/10.1037/0022-3514.64.5.834

English, T., & Chen, S. (2011). Self-concept consistency and culture: The differential impact of two forms of consistency. *Personality and Social Psychology Bulletin, 37,* 838–849. http://dx.doi.org/10.1177/0146167211400621

English, T., & John, O. P. (2013). Understanding the social effects of emotion regulation: The mediating role of authenticity for individual differences in suppression. *Emotion, 13,* 314–329. http://dx.doi.org/10.1037/a0029847

Farh, J.-L., Hackett, R. D., & Liang, J. (2007). Individual-level cultural values as moderators of perceived organizational support-employee outcome relationships in China: Comparing the effects of power distance and traditionality. *Academy of Management Journal, 50,* 715–729. http://dx.doi.org/10.5465/AMJ.2007.25530866

Fiske, A., Kitayama, S., Markus, H., & Nisbett, R. E. (1998). The cultural matrix of social psychology. In D. T. Gilbert, S. T. Fiske, & G. Lindzey (Eds.), *The handbook of social psychology: Vols. 1 and 2* (4th ed., pp. 915–981). New York, NY: Oxford University Press.

Fu, A. S., & Markus, H. R. (2014). My mother and me: Why tiger mothers motivate Asian Americans but not European Americans. *Personality and Social Psychology Bulletin, 40,* 739–749. http://dx.doi.org/10.1177/0146167214524992

Fulmer, C. A., Gelfand, M. J., Kruglanski, A. W., Kim-Prieto, C., Diener, E., Pierro, A., & Higgins, E. T. (2010). On "feeling right" in cultural contexts: How person-culture match affects self-esteem and subjective well-being. *Psychological Science, 21,* 1563–1569. http://dx.doi.org/10.1177/0956797610384742

Greenwald, A. G., & Farnham, S. D. (2000). Using the implicit association test to measure self-esteem and self-concept. *Journal of Personality and Social Psychology, 79,* 1022–1038. http://dx.doi.org/10.1037/0022-3514.79.6.1022

Gross, J. J., & John, O. P. (2003). Individual differences in two emotion regulation processes: Implications for affect, relationships, and well-being. *Journal of Personality and Social Psychology, 85,* 348–362. http://dx.doi.org/10.1037/0022-3514.85.2.348

Haritatos, J., & Benet-Martínez, V. (2002). Bicultural identities: The interface of cultural, personality, and socio-cognitive processes. *Journal of Research in Personality, 36,* 598–606. http://dx.doi.org/10.1016/S0092-6566(02)00510-X

Heine, S. J., & Hamamura, T. (2007). In search of East Asian self-enhancement. *Personality and Social Psychology Review, 11*(1), 4–27. http://dx.doi.org/10.1177/1088868306294587

Heine, S. J., & Lehman, D. R. (1999). Culture, self-discrepancies, and self-satisfaction. *Personality and Social Psychology Bulletin, 25,* 915–925. http://dx.doi.org/10.1177/01461672992511001

Heine, S. J., Lehman, D. R., Markus, H. R., & Kitayama, S. (1999). Is there a universal need for positive self-regard? *Psychological Review, 106*, 766–794. http://dx.doi.org/10.1037/0033-295X.106.4.766

Heine, S. J., & Renshaw, K. (2002). Interjudge agreement, self-enhancement, and linking: Cross-cultural divergences. *Personality and Social Psychology Bulletin, 28*, 578–587. http://dx.doi.org/10.1177/0146167202288002

Henrich, J., Heine, S. J., & Norenzayan, A. (2010). The weirdest people in the world? *Behavioral and Brain Sciences, 33*(2-3), 61–83. http://dx.doi.org/10.1017/S0140525X0999152X

Hogan, C. L., Chim, L., Sims, T., & Tsai, J. L. (2012, January). *Do you want to "feel the burn"? Ideal affect and exercise perceptions, decisions, and experiences.* Poster presented at the 13th Annual Meeting of the Society for Personality and Social Psychology, San Diego, CA.

Hong, Y. Y., Morris, M. W., Chiu, C. Y., & Benet-Martínez, V. (2000). Multicultural minds. A dynamic constructivist approach to culture and cognition. *American Psychologist, 55*, 709–720. http://dx.doi.org/10.1037/0003-066X.55.7.709

Huntsinger, C. S., Jose, P. E., Larson, S. L., Balsink Krieg, D., & Shaligram, C. (2000). Mathematics, vocabulary, and reading development in Chinese American and European American children over the primary school years. *Journal of Educational Psychology, 92*, 745–760. http://dx.doi.org/10.1037/0022-0663.92.4.745

Iyengar, S. S., & Lepper, M. R. (1999). Rethinking the value of choice: A cultural perspective on intrinsic motivation. *Journal of Personality and Social Psychology, 76*, 349–366. http://dx.doi.org/10.1037/0022-3514.76.3.349

Ji, L. J., Nisbett, R. E., & Su, Y. (2001). Culture, change, and prediction. *Psychological Science, 12*, 450–456. http://dx.doi.org/10.1111/1467-9280.00384

Kanagawa, C., Cross, S. E., & Markus, H. R. (2001). "Who am I?" The cultural psychology of the conceptual self. *Personality and Social Psychology Bulletin, 27*(1), 90–103. http://dx.doi.org/10.1177/0146167201271008

Kashima, Y., Siegal, M., Tanaka, K., & Kashima, E. S. (1992). Do people believe behaviors are consistent with attitudes? Towards a cultural psychology of attribution processes. *British Journal of Social Psychology, 31*, 111–124. http://dx.doi.org/10.1111/j.2044-8309.1992.tb00959.x

Kim, B. S. K., & Abreu, J. M. (2001). Acculturation measurement: Theory, current instruments, and future directions. In J. G. Ponterotto, J. M. Casa, L. Suzuki, & C. M. Alexander (Eds.), *Handbook of multicultural counseling* (2d ed., pp. 394–424). Thousand Oaks, CA: Sage.

Kim, H. S., & Markus, H. R. (1999). Deviance or uniqueness, harmony or conformity? A cultural analysis. *Journal of Personality and Social Psychology, 77*, 785–800. http://dx.doi.org/10.1037/0022-3514.77.4.785

Kim, H. S., Sherman, D. K., & Taylor, S. E. (2008). Culture and social support. *American Psychologist, 63*, 518–526. http://dx.doi.org/10.1037/0003-066X

Kim, S., Gonzales, N. A., Stroh, K., & Wang, J. (2006). Parent–child cultural marginalization and depressive symptoms in Asian American family members. *Journal of Community Psychology*, *34*, 167–182. http://dx.doi.org/10.1002/jcop.20089

Kitayama, S., Markus, H. R., & Kurokawa, M. (2000). Culture, emotion, and well-being: Good feelings in Japan and the United States. *Cognition and Emotion*, *14*(1), 93–124. http://dx.doi.org/10.1080/026999300379003

Kitayama, S., Mesquita, B., & Karasawa, M. (2006). Cultural affordances and emotional experience: Socially engaging and disengaging emotions in Japan and the United States. *Journal of Personality and Social Psychology*, *91*, 890–903. http://dx.doi.org/10.1037/0022-3514.91.5.890

Kitayama, S., Snibbe, A. C., Markus, H. R., & Suzuki, T. (2004). Is there any "free" choice? Self and dissonance in two cultures. *Psychological Science*, *15*, 527–533. http://dx.doi.org/10.1111/j.0956-7976.2004.00714.x

Kööts, L., Realo, A., & Allik, J. (2012). Relationship between linguistic antonyms in momentary and retrospective ratings of happiness and sadness. *Journal of Individual Differences*, *33*(1), 43–53. http://dx.doi.org/10.1027/1614-0001/a000061

Layous, K., Lee, H., Choi, I., & Lyubomirsky, S. (2013). Culture matters when designing a successful happiness-increasing activity: A comparison of the United States and South Korea. *Journal of Cross-Cultural Psychology*, *44*, 1294–1303. http://dx.doi.org/10.1177/0022022113487591

Long, B. C., & Sangster, J. I. (1993). Dispositional optimism/pessimism and coping strategies: Predictors of psychosocial adjustment of rheumatoid and osteoarthritis patients. *Journal of Applied Social Psychology*, *23*, 1069–1091. http://dx.doi.org/10.1111/j.1559-1816.1993.tb01022.x

Markus, H. R., & Conner, A. (2013). *Clash! 8 cultural conflicts that make us who we are*. New York, NY: Penguin.

Markus, H. R., & Kitayama, S. (1991). Culture and the self: Implications for cognition, emotion, and motivation. *Psychological Review*, *98*, 224–253. http://dx.doi.org/10.1037/0033-295X.98.2.224

Masuda, T., Gonzalez, R., Kwan, L., & Nisbett, R. E. (2008). Culture and aesthetic preference: Comparing the attention to context of East Asians and Americans. *Personality and Social Psychology Bulletin*, *34*, 1260–1275. http://dx.doi.org/10.1177/0146167208320555

Masuda, T., & Nisbett, R. E. (2001). Attending holistically versus analytically: Comparing the context sensitivity of Japanese and Americans. *Journal of Personality and Social Psychology*, *81*, 922–934. http://dx.doi.org/10.1037/0022-3514.81.5.922

McCullough, M. E. (2000). Forgiveness as human strength: Theory, measurement, and links to well-being. *Journal of Social and Clinical Psychology*, *19*, 43–55. http://dx.doi.org/10.1521/jscp.2000.19.1.43

Miyamoto, Y., Nisbett, R. E., & Masuda, T. (2006). Culture and the physical environment. Holistic versus analytic perceptual affordances. *Psychological Science*, *17*, 113–119. http://dx.doi.org/10.1111/j.1467-9280.2006.01673.x

Morling, B., Kitayama, S., & Miyamoto, Y. (2002). Cultural practices emphasize influence in the United States and adjustment in Japan. *Personality and Social Psychology Bulletin*, *28*, 311–323. http://dx.doi.org/10.1177/0146167202286003

Morris, M. W., Nisbett, R. E., & Peng, K. (1995). Causality across domains and cultures. In D. Sperber, D. Premack, & A. J. Premack (Eds.), *Causal cognition: A multidisciplinary debate* (pp. 577–614). New York, NY: Oxford University Press.

Nisbett, R. E., Peng, K., Choi, I., & Norenzayan, A. (2001). Culture and systems of thought: Holistic versus analytic cognition. *Psychological Review*, *108*, 291–310. http://dx.doi.org/10.1037/0033-295X.108.2.291

Norem, J. K., & Chang, E. C. (2002). The positive psychology of negative thinking. *Journal of Clinical Psychology*, *58*, 993–1001. http://dx.doi.org/10.1002/jclp.10094

Peng, K., & Nisbett, R. E. (1999). Culture, dialectics, and reasoning about contradiction. *American Psychologist*, *54*, 741–754. http://dx.doi.org/10.1037/0003-066X.54.9.741

Perunovic, W. Q., Heller, D., & Rafaeli, E. (2007). Within-person changes in the structure of emotion: The role of cultural identification and language. *Psychological Science*, *18*, 607–613. http://dx.doi.org/10.1111/j.1467-9280.2007.01947.x

Phinney, J. S. (1990). Ethnic identity in adolescents and adults: Review of research. *Psychological Bulletin*, *108*, 499–514. http://dx.doi.org/10.1037/0033-2909.108.3.499

Phinney, J. S. (2003). Ethnic identity and acculturation. In K. Chun, P. Organista, & G. Marin (Eds.), *Acculturation: Advances in theory, measurement, and applied research* (pp. 63–81). Washington, DC: American Psychological Association. http://dx.doi.org/10.1037/10472-006

Phinney, J. S. (2010). Increasing our understanding of the acculturation gap: A way forward. *Human Development*, *53*, 350–355. http://dx.doi.org/10.1159/000323301

Reed, G. L., & Enright, R. D. (2006). The effects of forgiveness therapy on depression, anxiety, and posttraumatic stress for women after spousal emotional abuse. *Journal of Consulting and Clinical Psychology*, *74*, 920–929. http://dx.doi.org/10.1037/0022-006X.74.5.920

Rockstuhl, T., Dulebohn, J. H., Ang, S., & Shore, L. M. (2012). Leader-member exchange (LMX) and culture: A meta-analysis of correlates of LMX across 23 countries. *Journal of Applied Psychology*, *97*, 1097–1130. http://dx.doi.org/10.1037/a0029978

Sandage, S. J., Hill, P. C., & Vang, H. C. (2003). Toward a multicultural positive psychology: Indigenous forgiveness and Hmong culture. *The Counseling Psychologist*, *31*, 564–592. http://dx.doi.org/10.1177/0011000003256350

Sasaki, J. Y., & Kim, H. S. (2011). At the intersection of culture and religion: A cultural analysis of religion's implications for secondary control and social affiliation.

Journal of Personality and Social Psychology, 101, 401–414. http://dx.doi.org/10.1037/a0021849

Savani, K., Markus, H. R., & Conner, A. L. (2008). Let your preference be your guide? Preferences and choices are more tightly linked for North Americans than for Indians. *Journal of Personality and Social Psychology, 95,* 861–876. http://dx.doi.org/10.1037/a0011618

Savani, K., Markus, H. R., Naidu, N. V. R., Kumar, S., & Berlia, N. (2010). What counts as a choice? U.S. Americans are more likely than Indians to construe actions as choices. *Psychological Science, 21,* 391–398. http://dx.doi.org/10.1177/0956797609359908

Schimmack, U., Oishi, S., & Diener, E. (2002). Cultural influences on the relation between pleasant emotions and unpleasant emotions Asian dialectic philosophies or individualism-collectivism? *Cognition and Emotion, 16,* 705–719. http://dx.doi.org/10.1080/02699930143000590

Seligman, M. E. P., & Csikszentmihalyi, M. (2000). Positive psychology. An introduction. *American Psychologist, 55,* 5–14. http://dx.doi.org/10.1037/0003-066X.55.1.5

Shim, Y. R., & Schwartz, R. C. (2007). The relationship between degree of acculturation and adjustment difficulties among Korean immigrants living in a Western society. *British Journal of Guidance & Counselling, 35,* 409–426. http://dx.doi.org/10.1080/03069880701593516

Sims, T., Tsai, J. L., Wang, I., Fung, H. H., & Zhang, X. (2014). *Wanting to maximize the positive and minimize the negative: Implications for affective experience in American and Chinese contexts.* Manuscript in preparation.

Sin, N. L., & Lyubomirsky, S. (2009). Enhancing well-being and alleviating depressive symptoms with positive psychology interventions: A practice-friendly meta-analysis. *Journal of Clinical Psychology, 65,* 467–487. http://dx.doi.org/10.1002/jclp.20593

Soto, J. A., Perez, C. R., Kim, Y. H., Lee, E. A., & Minnick, M. R. (2011). Is expressive suppression always associated with poorer psychological functioning? A cross-cultural comparison between European Americans and Hong Kong Chinese. *Emotion, 11,* 1450–1455. http://dx.doi.org/10.1037/a0023340

Spencer-Rodgers, J., Boucher, H. C., Mori, S. C., Wang, L., & Peng, K. (2009). The dialectical self-concept: Contradiction, change, and holism in East Asian cultures. *Personality and Social Psychology Bulletin, 35*(1), 29–44. http://dx.doi.org/10.1177/0146167208325772

Suh, E. M. (2002). Culture, identity consistency, and subjective well-being. *Journal of Personality and Social Psychology, 83,* 1378–1391. http://dx.doi.org/10.1037/0022-3514.83.6.1378

Suinn, R. M. (2010). Reviewing acculturation and Asian Americans: How acculturation affects health, adjustment, school achievement, and counseling. *Asian American Journal of Psychology, 1*(1), 5–17. http://dx.doi.org/10.1037/a0018798

Swann, W. B., Jr., De la Ronde, C., & Hixon, J. G. (1994). Authenticity and positivity strivings in marriage and courtship. *Journal of Personality and Social Psychology, 66,* 857–869. http://dx.doi.org/10.1037/0022-3514.66.5.857

Taylor, S. E. (2007). Social support. In H. S. Friedman & R. C. Silver (Eds.), *Foundations of health psychology* (pp. 145–171). New York, NY: Oxford University Press.

Taylor, S. E., Welch, W. T., Kim, H. S., & Sherman, D. K. (2007). Cultural differences in the impact of social support on psychological and biological stress responses. *Psychological Science, 18,* 831–837. http://dx.doi.org/10.1111/j.1467-9280.2007.01987.x

Tsai, J. L., Knutson, B., & Fung, H. H. (2006). Cultural variation in affect valuation. *Journal of Personality and Social Psychology, 90,* 288–307. http://dx.doi.org/10.1037/0022-3514.90.2.288

Tsai, J. L., Miao, F. F., Seppala, E., Fung, H. H., & Yeung, D. Y. (2007). Influence and adjustment goals: Sources of cultural differences in ideal affect. *Journal of Personality and Social Psychology, 92,* 1102–1117. http://dx.doi.org/10.1037/0022-3514.92.6.1102

Tsai, J. L., & Park, B. K. (2014). The cultural shaping of happiness: The role of ideal affect. In J. Moskowitz & J. Gruber (Eds.), *The light and dark sides of positive emotion* (pp. 345–362). New York, NY: Oxford University Press. http://dx.doi.org/10.1093/acprof:oso/9780199926725.003.0019

Tsai, J. L., Ying, Y. W., & Lee, P. A. (2001). Cultural predictors of self-esteem: A study of Chinese American female and male young adults. *Cultural Diversity and Ethnic Minority Psychology, 7,* 284–297. http://dx.doi.org/10.1037/1099-9809.7.3.284

U.S. Census Bureau. (2010). *Asian alone or in combination with one or more other races, and with one or more Asian categories for selected groups.* Retrieved from http://factfinder2.census.gov/faces/tableservices/jsf/pages/productview.xhtml?pid=DEC_10_SF1_PCT7&prodType=table

U.S. Census Bureau. (2013). *Asian fastest-growing race or ethnic group in 2012, Census Bureau Reports.* Retrieved from http://www.census.gov/newsroom/press-releases/2013/cb13-112.html

Uskul, A. K., Sherman, D. K., & Fitzgibbon, J. (2009). The cultural congruency effect: Culture, regulatory focus, and the effectiveness of gain- vs. loss-framed health messages. *Journal of Experimental Social Psychology, 45,* 535–541. http://dx.doi.org/10.1016/j.jesp.2008.12.005

Ward, C., & Kennedy, A. (1994). Acculturation strategies, psychological adjustment, and sociocultural competence during cross-cultural transitions. *International Journal of Intercultural Relations, 18,* 329–343. http://dx.doi.org/10.1016/0147-1767(94)90036-1

Williamson, I., & Gonzalez, M. H. (2007). The subjective experience of forgiveness: Positive construals of the forgiveness experience. *Journal of Social and Clinical Psychology, 26,* 407–446. http://dx.doi.org/10.1521/jscp.2007.26.4.407

Yamaguchi, S., Greenwald, A. G., Banaji, M. R., Murakami, F., Chen, D., Shiomura, K., . . . Krendl, A. (2007). Apparent universality of positive implicit self-esteem. *Psychological Science, 18,* 498–500. http://dx.doi.org/10.1111/j.1467-9280.2007.01928.x

Ying, Y. W. (1999). Strengthening intergenerational/intercultural ties in migrant families: A new intervention for parents. *Journal of Community Psychology, 27,* 89–96. http://dx.doi.org/10.1002/(SICI)1520-6629(199901)27:1<89::AID-JCOP6>3.0.CO;2-O

Ying, Y. W., Lee, P. A., & Tsai, J. L. (2000). Cultural orientation and racial discrimination: Predictors of coherence in Chinese American young adults. *Journal of Community Psychology, 28,* 427–441. http://dx.doi.org/10.1002/1520-6629(200007)28:4<427::AID-JCOP5>3.0.CO;2-F

Yoon, E., Hacker, J., Hewitt, A., Abrams, M., & Cleary, S. (2012). Social connectedness, discrimination, and social status as mediators of acculturation/enculturation and well-being. *Journal of Counseling Psychology, 59*(1), 86–96. http://dx.doi.org/10.1037/a0025366

Zusho, A. (2008). Cultural variation in the motivational standards of self-enhancement and self-criticism among bicultural Asian American and Anglo American students. *International Journal of Psychology, 43,* 904–911. http://dx.doi.org/10.1080/00207590701838121

4

LATINA/OS—DRIVE, COMMUNITY, AND SPIRITUALITY: THE STRENGTH WITHIN (SOMOS LATINA/OS—GANAS, COMUNIDAD, Y EL ESPÍRITU: LA FUERZA QUE LLEVAMOS POR DENTRO)

JEANETT CASTELLANOS AND ALBERTA M. GLORIA

The eagle danced in the sky and the woman looked up to see bright-ness and great light. She listened to the wind, felt the softness of the clouds against her cheek and tasted the sweetness of the nectar of the earth. She understood change was coming and new horizons were at the onset of her days. She was patient in looking forward to the future—the positive that was coming, and she gave thanks for the past, the pain, and lessons of those chal-lenges. Ancient knowledge reminded her that the sun leads while the moon supports, the water nurtures and the wind caresses and holds. She hears in her ear, be still daughter, we are coming—to aid, to be, to lead . . . be still, we are near.

The prose poem in the preceding paragraph suggests that resilience, the power of family and past ancestors, positive affect, hope, and cultural values (e.g., *familismo*/familism, *comunidad*/community, *respeto*/respect) play different roles in life depending on one's experiences, exposure to hardship, and tools

http://dx.doi.org/10.1037/14799-004
Positive Psychology in Racial and Ethnic Groups: Theory, Research, and Practice, E. C. Chang, C. A. Downey, J. K. Hirsch, and N. J. Lin (Editors)

gained along the path to navigate challenges. To familiarize the reader with Latina/o cultural values, practices, and means of living in positivity, we begin with a brief historical overview and a description of Latina/os' value system. Then we address the (re)positioning of positive psychology for Latina/os: We offer a paradigm shift and a reorientation to understand psychological processes of wellness from an emic or "Latina/o-centric" or *Latinidad* (meaning of being Latina/o) perspective. The chapter emphasizes Latina/o "processes" (e.g., deep-structure meanings and manifestation of cultural values and beliefs) versus "characteristics" (e.g., surface level descriptions and labels; Laird, 1998) as a means for understanding wellness and positive functioning for Latina/os.

DEMOGRAPHICS AND TERMINOLOGY

By 2050, it is expected that 130 million Latina/os will be living in the United States (U.S. Census Bureau, 2010). Latina/os have multiethnic backgrounds and ethnicities reflecting their countries of origin: Mexicanos (31.7 million), Puerto Ricans (4.6 million), Cubans (1.7 million), Salvadorians (1.6 million), Dominicans (1.4 million), Guatemalans (1 million), and "all others" (8.1 million; U.S. Census Bureau, 2010).

Generational differences, educational attainment, labor force participation, and occupation were examined to help determine the group's resources, social capital, upward mobility, and social influence in the broader society. Given the varied reasons for continued migration (e.g., political turmoil, economic and educational advancement, geography), Latina/os continue to be primarily first-generation immigrants (62%); approximately 19% are second-generation and 19% are third-generation. In addition, 37.8% do not have a high school diploma, 62.2% have a high school diploma or its equivalent, and only 13% have a bachelor's degree or higher (U.S. Census Bureau, 2010). Latina/os constitute a large percentage (15%) of the labor force, with Latino males making up 59% of that percentage (U.S. Department of Labor, 2012).

Latina/os have a long history in the United States: *Mexicanos* have been in the United States for more than 200 years (Acuña, 2010), but Latina/os' diversity and continued migration to the United States have created an array of different experiences (Aguirre & Turner, 2011) and thus, identities. The multitude of unique realities and experiences for the different groups (e.g., native born in the United States vs. refugees) creates a diversity of identities for Latina/os (Gloria & Castellanos, 2012). Differences arise in Latino groups depending on their country of origin (e.g., Mexico vs. a Central American country) and their immigrant status (e.g., first or second generation), yet they share a collective identity (Alexander, Eyerman, Giesen, & Smelser, 2004) and are united by cultural values and beliefs as well as shared economic, cultural, and political histories (Avila-Saavedra, 2008). In this chapter, we use *Latina/o* to denote a Latina/o ethnic consciousness (F. M. Padilla, 1985, 1997), keeping in mind the roles of history, gender, and sociocultural and sociopolitical systems and processes that encompass multiple dimensions of identity (Gloria & Castellanos, 2012).

In this chapter, we elucidate the various positive processes and practices of the group, and in this connection it is imperative to address the role of acculturation. *Acculturation* is the multidimensional process (Alamilla, Kim, & Lam, 2010) of adjusting to a new or host culture while maintaining and navigating one's own native values, practices, and beliefs. Latina/os adjust and acclimate to the United States in varying degrees that cannot be separated from their ethnicity, immigrant generation, socioeconomic status, and language proficiency (Gamst et al., 2002). The process of individual adaptation is both cultural and psychological (Hurtado & Cervantez, 2009) and has been described as "assimilation, integration, or biculturality, separation or maintenance of traditionality, and marginalization or peripheral status in both cultures" (Gamst et al., 2002, p. 480). This series of processes can moderate good health and well-being and occur concurrently with a person's cultural self-identification (i.e., the process of ethnic identity; see Gonzalez, Fabrett, & Knight, 2009; Quintana & Scull, 2009). As Latina/os work toward wellness, adjustment, and well-being, they negotiate their identities and work toward being culturally grounded (Gloria & Castellanos, 2012). Many Latina/os keep *cultura* (culture) at the center of their processes as a means for navigating identity and life challenges.

POSITIONING POSITIVE PSYCHOLOGY FOR LATINA/OS— BRINGING *LATINIDAD* TO THE FOREGROUND

As recently as the 1980s, the behaviors, values, and beliefs of many Latina/os were described as "non-normative," "deviant," or even "pathological" (Niemann, 2004). Such labels not only discount the core values and processes within Latina/o culture but also effectively call into question the ability of Latinos to claim wellness. Research on Latina/o psychology has brought to light the undergirding strengths and deep-structure meanings of different Latina/o values as they translate into attitudes, actions, and behaviors (McNeill et al., 2001). In particular, the emic-focused Latina/o norms have been (re)claimed and (re)positioned as healthful, helpful, strength-based, and positive (Santiago-Rivera, Arredondo, & Gallardo-Cooper, 2002). Much like the early work of George I. Sánchez's (A. M. Padilla, 1984), who argued that the testing and assessment of Mexican children in public schools was invalid unless it was conducted in their primary language (i.e., Spanish), the values and worldviews of Latina/os must be understood in context in order for them to hold relevance and meaning and to be understood as strengths.

The (re)positioning of Latina/o values and worldview must be accompanied by an end to cultural or individual blaming. Instead, seeking to understand the meaning and root of Latina/o interactions and processes situates the values as strengths for individuals, groups, and communities. The values may not intuitively have meaning or may not be understood easily by individuals who have different worldviews. For example, one of many often-cited descriptions or portrayals of Latina women has been that of passive, weak, or submissive "creatures" who are unable to act or think for themselves (Gloria & Castellanos, 2012). Such a depiction of Latinas has been harmful; by negatively describing them, it dehumanizes them as women and discounts and disparages different ways of being and engaging interpersonally. Individualists might regard them as sacrificing their individual needs to group needs or losing themselves to the family; others might recognize that Latinas find core strength and a foundation for self-care and wellness in the family, from which many Latinas find meaning and draw strength (Comas-Díaz, 1989; Gloria & Castellanos, 2012; Gloria & Segura-Herrera, 2004).

The ability to act and enact Latina/o values in a way that fulfills one's cultural and spiritual *patrón* (Gloria & Castellanos, 2012) is perceived as strength and in effect as positive functioning. It is from one's *patrón* or cultural and spiritual blueprint that Latina/os can draw strength and meaning from those beliefs, processes, and values, which have been transmitted across time (from generation to generation) and have allowed for survival, growth, and a sense of meaning. Similar to A. M. Padilla's (1995) notion of finding and making meaning for oneself, it is this same process of identifying deep value strengths and positive processes from the transmission of *patrónes* that Latina/os carry and find connection to something larger than themselves as a means for wellness.

CONEXIONES CULTURALES: INTERCONNECTIONS OF MIND, BODY, SPIRIT, AND LATINA/O VALUES

Stemming from a core Mestizo tenet is the belief of many Latina/os that we are all part of an open system (Ramírez, 1991). The notion of being interconnected to environments and to one another extends to an individual's own processes, whereby one's mental, physical, and spiritual processes and entities are interconnected. This is a discussion that has only more recently been considered an important tenet for understanding individual processes within etic notions of psychology; it has a long-standing history within the beliefs and traditional practices of many ethnocultural and indigenous

Latina/o communities (McNeill & Cervantes, 2008) and emic psychologies (Ramírez, 1991, 1998).

To understand the various processes Latina/os engage for wellness and a positive state of mind, one might begin with the core processes of inner strength and will (see *Fortaleza and Voluntad*/Strength and Will processes in Gloria & Castellanos, 2012). Latina/os utilize a mind–body–spirit paradigm to navigate life challenges, engage with the environment, and sustain wellness (Cervantes, 2010). Education, family, community, and environment are the foundation of good life adjustment, achievement through self-challenge, and development (Ramírez, 1998).

Numerous works that examine the role of Latina/o consciousness and self-reflection call attention to the Mayan belief *Tu eres mi otro yo* (You are my other self), which come from the Nahual (Mayan) language, *In Lak'ech Ala K'in* (Cervantes, 2010). The saying captures the belief that Latina/os have a collective identity grounded in community (Ramírez, 1991, 1998); they are frequently socialized to develop a strong responsibility for and a loyalty to others. As a group, Latina/os build strong communities through active participation, socialization of youth to be part of the larger group, and centrality of elders as valued members of the group to maintain cultural groundedness (Santiago-Rivera et al., 2002).

Embedded within the collective identity are one's family identity, *familismo*, and a role and function within *comunidad* (Gloria & Castellanos, 2009). Perhaps most salient to Latina/o core cultural values are the values of family and community. Review of any scholarly writing about Latina/os identifies *familia* and the importance of relational connections (i.e., *comunidad*) as critical and salient processes from which all values and beliefs emerge (Gloria & Castellanos, 2009). For example, the role of family has been written about extensively (e.g., *Counseling Latinos and la Familia: A Practical Guide* by Santiago-Rivera et al., 2002), and academic articles identify family and its processes as the central and driving force behind all cultural values for Latina/os. These processes of many Latina/o families have been negatively portrayed within the psychological and educational literatures over the past several decades. For example, Santiago-Rivera et al. (2002) observed that "diagnostic labels such as enmeshed and codependent have been widely used to describe Latino families" (p. 43). The authors noted that when the familial behaviors and processes are taken out of context or viewed from a different cultural value (e.g., individualist perspective), negative notions or pathological perspectives are attributed to Latina/o interactions and approaches. Indeed, Latina/o familial values and processes are "quite normal when viewed with a cultural lens" (Santiago-Rivera et al., 2002, p. 43).

Familismo is the "preference for maintaining a close connection to family" (Santiago-Rivera et al., 2002, p. 42), centralizing solidarity, interdependence, and reciprocity (Gloria & Castellanos, 2009). Family, the foundational structure of Latina/o culture (Lopez, 2006), is the main resource for the group (Falicov, 1998). As a result, the notion of placing "family first" is a common collective approach that affects the person's well-being (Santiago-Rivera et al., 2002). The family is the primary system that provides physical, emotional, and social support for many Latina/os (Gloria & Castellanos, 2009).

It is through the process of developing and implementing a sense of *familismo* that caring for and having responsibility to the family create and maintain a larger sense of *comunidad*. Family is frequently physically manifested through extended kinship systems that include nuclear, extended, and nonrelated family members and that create a sense of wellness. Both nuclear and extended family members are considered part of the collective family identity (Smith-Morris, Morales-Campos, Alvarez, & Turner, 2013), and often family and subsequent community are further extended with a system of *compadrazgo* (i.e., coparentage).

The process and the responsibility of *compadrazgo*, or coparentage, of children are manifested within families and communities through the appointment of additional sets of parents or *padrinos* (godfathers) and *madrinas* (godmothers). Seeded in interpersonal connections, supportive relationships, and shared responsibility for the well-being of the group (family and community), the practice assigns *padrinos* and *madrinas* to care for offspring (Gill-Hopple & Brage-Hudson, 2012; Gloria & Castellanos, 2009). The care of others occurs at different life events, such as baptisms, coming of age ceremonies, or weddings, at which coparents (either fictive or nonfictive/biological) take on the responsibilities of spiritual, physical, and even economic welfare of children. The ritual of coparenting or "sponsorship" (Mintz & Wolf, 1950) involves taking on a responsibility of a lifelong relationship that ties together and expands the family and community. It is from these interconnections that many Latina/os have a positive notion of self.

Many Latina/os find in these dimensioned and multiple connections of family and community a source of strength and value of interconnection and interdependence (Gloria & Castellanos, 2012). The interactions emphasize connection, respect, sincerity, and genuineness (Garza & Watts, 2010), and they illuminate the importance of social connections and social resilience. Core to the notion of interconnection and value of the group, it is important to note the undergirding strength and value for Latina/o families to withstand change and "reconfigure" in order to flexibly integrate new members into the group or family (e.g., elders, children, visitors, close friends; Gloria & Castellanos, 2009). Strength and continuity are often seeded in the notion of being part of some larger process and interconnection beyond oneself.

Latina/os draw from a wealth of indigenous teachings and influences. They practice a traditional belief system fused with Catholic ideology, which offers a deep archetypal structure of coping processes embedded with spiritual values and beliefs (Cervantes, 2010; Cervantes & Ramirez, 1992). A body of literature supports the idea that religion holds great meaning and is a major part of Latina/o culture (from Evangelism to Catholicism to *Espiritismo* or *Santeria*; see Baez & Hernandez, 2001). The religious practices and daily prayers, engaging incantations, creating altars, and attending mass or other activities (Caplan et al., 2011) reflect the use of varying means of finding a space to attain tranquility, congruity, and understanding of life processes.

Rooted in the core of connection and community are the notions of universal energies and interconnections within the open system (Ramírez, 1991). As such, spirituality is also a keystone of Latina/o beliefs for personal transformation and a strength-based approach that connects individuals, communities, and life experiences to life meaning. *Spirituality* is defined as a practice associated with operating from a higher power, a sacred subjective experience embedded in sacredness, and an energy center that facilitates personal transformation (Walsh, 1999). It is communal, grounded in gender equality, and has teaching elements offering Latina/os a positive outcome from their adversities (Comas-Díaz, 2006; Ramírez, 1983). *Curanderismo*, a healing system that encompasses various folk practices and traditions (see Harris, Velásquez, White, & Renteria, 2004), is an example of spiritual complementary beliefs that center on Latina/os views of wellness, energetic forces and exchanges, and cosmic influences. Some Latina/os believe the imbalance of energies can lead to syndromes that are culturally based (e.g., *susto*/fright, *empacho*/indigestion, *mal de ojo*/evil eye, *envidia*/jealousy) and that can affect their lives, exchanges, and overall wellness (Ortiz, Davis, & McNeill, 2008). These beliefs are examples of Latina/os' traditional understandings of the interconnectedness between people, their bodies, and the universe.

Although much has been written on the effect of *curanderismo* on well-being and mental health processes, little has been written on the role of energy, Toltec beliefs (Nelson, 2003), shamanic practices (Glass-Coffin, 2010), and well-being. Toltec teachings position the importance of personal power, nature, awareness of self-reflection, and intention (Sanchez, 1996) that exist within indigenous practices representing a collective Latina/o ethnic consciousness wherein values, beliefs, and practices overlap. The teachings also empower the person, offering the possibility of transformative realities while underscoring the duality of the material and spiritual worlds. They emphasize the principle that individuals are multidimensional as mortals and unidimensional in spirit, which is ultimately the sharing of one reality and vision (Nelson, 2003). Honoring the connection of spirit and universe as shared through ancestral teachings and *patrones* (cultural and spiritual blueprints), the chapter's opening paragraph brings out the connections between energy, intention, and nature.

By the late 1990s, approximately 300 articles had been published on shamanism and psychotherapy (Gagan, 1998); however, the focus on the individual processes that clients engage to gain personal freedom and transformation has been substantially more limited. Mackinnon (2012) called for the integration of shamanism and spirituality into the basis of therapeutic practice as a "quest for connection, meaning, wholeness and belonging and the expansion of our consciousness" (p. 16). Whether drawing from indigenous (Mackinnon, 2012) or ancestral teachings (Gloria & Castellanos, 2012), Latina/os' beliefs encompass the principles of harmony, spirituality, respect for the universe, values, and the importance of ancestors (Comas-Díaz, 2006). Moreover, there is a strong emphasis on the connection between person and spirit (Cervantes, 2010; Comas-Díaz, 2006; Ramírez, 1998) creating a unique consciousness and collective unconsciousness, which feeds Latina/os' interpretation of life situations and positions.

In creating a framework for which positive psychology can be applied to Latina/os, Cervantes (2010) wrote that the mind–body–spirit paradigm is centered in shifting energy (Gallo, 2005) and that indigenous beliefs infuse "spirit energy and cosmic forces" (Cervantes, 2010, p. 528), directly and indirectly affecting Latina/os' psychological, healing, and wellness processes. Cervantes proposed a model of *Mestizo* spirituality that integrates indigenous beliefs and principles (e.g., the earth is a living system for which one has roles, responsibilities, and interrelationships) with the centrality of one's spiritual journey as a means for healing and wellness. Similarly, Gloria and Castellanos (2012) highlighted the synergetic ability and shamanic-like practices for Latinas to convert difficulties into manageable processes, promoting their healing and well-being: "Latinas often gravitate to the teachings of their mothers and grandmothers, who often provide insight into family interactions, how to navigate differences, and shift energies" (p. 175). Navigating their dualities, Latinas shape-shift as they interpret energy bodies, account for old traditions, and transform the present to persist (Gloria & Castellanos, 2012). The ancestral teachings of previous generations are subconsciously embedded or imprinted in Latina/o spiritual *patrónes* or blueprints. Lightheartedness and laughter, and the ability to digress and regress through time and space— recalling past teachings and pulling strength and power from the sacrifices of communal energy shared through past generations and spiritual and tribal blueprints, engenders positive functioning and wellness in Latina/os (Gloria & Castellanos, 2012; Perkins, 1997).

Taking an emic approach is unlike traditional models of help. This strength-based approach centralizes the role and value of harmony between the physical, mental, social, and spiritual. Moreover, it emphasizes the affect and behaviors/practices of the individual in the context of what she/he values and believes. Although presented as separate processes for the purposes of this chapter, many of the core Latina/o values are affectively, cognitively, and behaviorally intertwined processes (Garza & Watts, 2010; Ortiz, 2009). There is inherent overlap and interconnection of processes, which is consistent with the notion of *conexiones culturales* or interplay of mind, body, and spirit as a means for positive functioning for many Latina/os.

FACILITATING POSITIVE AFFECT IN LATINA/OS

As family and community are central to Latina/os lives, determining how to ensure the continuity and interconnection of the individuals to the groups and within relationships is key. Centered within the familial and community exchanges is the emotional interaction or process of engaging *personalismo* with others. *Personalismo* is a cultural script and social orientation according to which Latina/os place the emphasis of interaction on the person, holding people as more important than tasks or events and time (Ortiz, 2009). In doing so, the emphasis of interactions is on the importance of creating strong and substantial relationships (Marín & Marín, 1991). The relationships are expected to be warm; genuinely affectionate and caring (*cariño*); and steeped in respectful (*respeto*), harmonious, and personable interactions (*simpatía*; Ortiz, 2009; Santiago-Rivera et al., 2002). Although relationships are known to be key to positive functioning, these specific interactions simultaneously express culture in everyday interactions that engage positive functioning. For example, one way in which positive engagements occur is through the process of *haciendo tiempo* (making time). Making relationships of central importance involves creating or making time with others. Engaging in the process of *haciendo tiempo* is different from the commonly known process of making time for someone or something (i.e., scheduling time out of one's day). Instead, the process of *hacienda tiempo* emphasizes the energetic exchange and interconnections that come from being in relationship with others (Gloria & Castellanos, 2012). The process of establishing and nurturing a substantive relationship, whether with family members or individuals in the community, is paramount to engagement.

The process of congruent self-expression of one's core feelings has been consistently linked to affect for many Latina/os (Santiago-Rivera & Altarriba, 2002; Santiago-Rivera, Altarriba, Poll, Gonzalez-Miller, & Cragun, 2009). Specifically, self-expression in one's native language, whether English, Spanish, or "Spanglish" (i.e., a complex and nuanced combination of Spanish and English; Ardila, 2005), can readily increase positive functioning. Although Spanish language ability differs based on a host of factors (e.g., ethnicity, generation, context, historical oppression, socioeconomic standing), nearly half of all Latina/os are bilingual (e.g., speaking English well to very well and speaking Spanish at home; Saenz, 2010).

Notwithstanding the variation in the ability to speak Spanish, Latino/as strongly prefer to speak Spanish at home as well as outside the home when the setting allows (e.g., store or business; Santiago-Rivera et al., 2002). Engaging in one's native, colearned, or even second language (Spanish) may permit a more natural or freer expression of ideas and feelings. Santiago-Rivera and Altarriba (2002) argued that Spanish–English bilingual Latina/os "represent emotional words differently in their two languages and typically associate these words with a broader range of emotions in their first language" (p. 33). In particular, speaking in Spanish has been linked to comfort and willingness to discuss personal or intimate matters (Gloria, Ruiz, & Castillo, 2004) and is preferred for emotion-oriented conversations (Echeverry, 1997; Santiago-Rivera et al., 2009). Speaking in Spanish is frequently considered a primary process to maintain cultural tradition and identity (Santiago-Rivera & Altarriba, 2002; Santiago-Rivera et al., 2009) and as a result is linked to a sense of wellness and positive functioning.

Another process that facilitates positive emotions for Latina/os is that of giving blessings or *dando bendiciónes*. It is linked to the notion of protection by a higher power and engaged in by individuals who have stature, presence, and *respeto* (respect) within the family and community. Giving one's blessing for mundane actions to life choices promotes a sense of wellness for those who receive the approval or blessing. For example, grandparents or parents often provide children a blessing of protection when they leave the house at the start of the day or even for life decisions (e.g., going away for college; Orozco, 2003). Latina/os derive from *bendiciónes* a sense of confidence and wellness; they feel supported and approved by their family and/or community.

Likewise, the process of *aceptación* (acceptance) allows for a sense of positive functioning. The idea that ambiguity and uncertainty are central elements of the life process often manifests in accepting circumstances as a given, considering them ordained by a higher source (Bermúdez, Kirkpatrick, Hecker, & Torres-Robles, 2010) and is often linked to religious beliefs (Hovey & Morales, 2006). For example, *fatalismo* (fatalism) has been addressed in the psychological literature, which describes Latina/os as pessimistic and in effect "holds a negative connotation and reflects a deficit model of Latino culture" (Flórez et al., 2009, p. 292). In contrast, Falicov (1998) called for a "resource-oriented" view of *fatalismo* instead of a "deficit model," which disempowers and limits individuals' possible outlooks. Examined through a Latina/o-specific cultural lens, the ability to accept situations or losses that are beyond one's control (Falicov, 1998), to "take things as they come," or to view one's process as *destino* (destiny) is a way by which positive functioning can occur when challenges or difficulties arise. Flórez et al. (2009) described destiny as a complex combination of internal (personal actions) and external forces (those beyond one's control) that determine or shape one's life.

For Latina/os, having a sense of *el destino*, which is intertwined with the belief that there is a "divine providence governing the world" (Bermúdez et al., 2010, p. 159), can be a strength to manage life circumstances beyond one's personal agency or intervention (Comas-Díaz, 1993) as they coexist with, find acceptance of, and/or make peace with a concern that is externally induced (Falicov, 1998).

Reconfiguring or reframing the subsequent meaning of a difficult situation, concern, or event can serve as positive functioning and a source of strength for Latina/os. In addition to the process of cognitive reframing, in which "barriers are viewed as challenges" (Gomez et al., 2001, p. 296), the integration of destiny and reframing is evident in the common saying *Si Dios quiere* (If God wills/allows) in response to mundane daily events (e.g., returning for a visit next weekend) or life crises (e.g., surviving an illness). Use of such a statement reflects the understanding that individuals do not have full control over their lives (Falicov, 1998). For example, despite having a blessing for protection when traveling, it comes with the understanding that a safe journey or arrival occurs only *si Dios así lo ha querido* (if God has so willed it).

FACILITATING POSITIVE BEHAVIORS IN LATINA/OS

Consistent within the plethora of ethnic identity literature for Latina/os, the process of identity involves the degree to which individuals understand and hold important values, attitudes, and behaviors as manifested through different customs and traditions (Gonzalez et al., 2009; Quintana & Scull, 2009). Part of the enculturation process for Latina/os by one's family and cultural community is the importance of being *bien educada/o* (well-educated) as reflected by one's implementing "culturally appropriate manners" (Ortiz, 2009, p. 177). *Being well-educated* refers to knowing the values and appropriate ways to behave in different social situations. It is the responsibility of Latina/o families to educate or socialize family members to engage core values, to provide children with a "sense of moral, social, and personal responsibility" (Valenzuela, 1999, p. 23). For example, socializing one's children to greet individuals with appropriate respect and dignity reflects on the adults/ parents for having taught or transmitted the importance of relationships and the processes by which relationships should be navigated (e.g., with respect and dignity and according to a hierarchy). Expressing gratitude to family is central to continued positive functioning.

For many Latina/os, most interactions revolve around their families, and so it is not surprising that family is frequently credited as the reason individuals strive for (or achieve) success (Castellanos & Gloria, 2008). Latina/os express gratitude to loved ones and families in a variety of ways.

For example, maintaining *altares* (altars) for loved ones in homes serves to help them "cope with bereavement and grief, help [individuals] remember their loved ones, memorialize the living, unify families, help families and couples learn to work collaboratively, and strengthen blended families" (Bermúdez & Bermúdez, 2002, p. 329). Similarly, a public expression of gratitude and naming the centrality of one's family are common, as was evident in Sonia Sotomayor's response to President Obama when nominated to the United States Supreme Court:

> I stand on the shoulders of countless people, yet there is one extra-ordinary person who is my life aspiration—that person is my mother, Celina Sotomayor. My mother has devoted her life to my brother and me . . . she worked often two jobs to help support us after Dad died. I have often said that I am all I am because of her, and I am only half the woman she is. (The White House, Office of the Press Secretary, 2009)

In maintaining positive actions and staying the course to one's goals, another core process central to positive functioning for many Latina/os is having *ganas* or feelings of motivation, drive to persist toward goals, or desire to succeed (Easley, Bianco, & Leech, 2012). The "will or determination to achieve" (p. 115) is a core process for many Latina/os who are seeking positive functioning, such as educational advancement (Contreras, 2011). Perhaps one of the most famous contemporary U.S. Latino heroes and civil rights activist was Cesar Chavez, who for many Latina/os has provided a voice of hope for all Latina/os who face injustice or challenge. This activist for farm worker and labor movement rights said, "We draw our strength from the very despair in which we have been forced to live. We shall endure" (Chavez, 1966, p. 66). He was expressing the conviction that individuals can and will succeed despite life's hardships (e.g., oppressive employment contexts, stressful immigration experiences, social injustices, lack of access) or daily life events (e.g., having to take two buses to go the grocery store because of a lack of personal transportation), a conviction that gave rise to a common rally cry for United Farm Workers of America members that resonated with many Latina/os: *¡Si se puede!*® (Yes we can) Having the will to take action to succeed is a critical ingredient to engage behaviors that focus on goals of success, and ultimately on well-being and functioning.

FACILITATING POSITIVE COGNITIONS IN LATINA/OS

For Latina/os, subjective and objective well-being (Eid & Larsen, 2008) goes beyond material, virtue, and earnings ratios; family, community, and spirituality are the main sources of well-being (Comas-Díaz, 2006). Based on a strength-based approach, paralleling the work of early psychology researchers, well-being is measured through everyday life, connection, and positive exchanges (Gloria & Castellanos, 2009; Gloria, Castellanos, Scull, & Villegas, 2009; see also Ponterotto & Casas, 1991) and can be highly influenced by the interpretations of Latina/os, who might have religion and spirituality at the core of their values and practices (Cervantes, 2010).

In aligning the new modern positive psychology models (Peterson & Seligman, 2004) of meaning and happiness for different cultural communities, it is critical that the emic meaning of existentialism and happiness is considered. By taking an emic or culture-specific understanding of wellness or positive functioning, the assessment and interpretation then take a strength-based and positive approach. For Latina/os in particular, one would do well to address the role of ancestry, culture, indigenous learnings, and cultural metaphors in Latina/o culture and healing (Aviera, 1996). For example, Zuniga (1991) contended that *dichos* or *refranes* (sayings or proverbs) can be used to guide, teach, and share principles of personal growth, development, and wellness. Similarly, *dichos* can engender feelings of belonging or be used to gain insight through the cognitive reframing of concerns (Flores-Torres & Ramirez, 2006; see also Aviera, 1996; Zuniga, 1991).

Dichos underscore lessons or teachings from the Latina/o culture. These sayings help Latina/os express perspectives on life experiences, help pass down cultural values, facilitate the verbalization of coping, and provide *aliento* (support) toward resilience. Families and communities can build on sayings and proverbs (e.g., Wanting is being able to; ¡*Si se puede!*® [Yes, it can be done: United Farm Workers of America]). The messages that underscore the ability to endure and be resilient (Zuniga, 1991) and reinforce Latina/o values of *esperanza* (hope) and *aguantarse* (enduring challenge). This reframing strength-based approach allows for positive reframing or different perspective taking.

Some examples of these cultural proverbs include *El que no ariezga no gana ni pierde* (Nothing ventured, nothing gained), *Camaron que se duerme se lo lleva la corriente* (The shrimp that falls asleep is swept away by the current), and *Dios aprieta pero no ahorca* (When God shuts a door, He always opens a window). These three proverbs remind Latina/os that one must take risks for a gain and keep consistently moving toward goals and that when things become too challenging, God will be compassionate and clear their pathway. These proverbs call attention to the roles of resistance and perseverance, diligence, withstanding challenge (i.e., *aguantarse*), and envisioning a positive outcome. Two other values highlight the role of a collective identity in the process of coping: *Somos un solo pueblo* (We are one community) and *Haz un bien y no mires a quien* (Do good and don't look to whom). Through these *dichos*, generations are able to pass down the value of communal responsibility, group care, and service. Two final examples underscore the role of resources and security:

Mas vale un pajaro en mano que cien volando (A bird in the hand is worth two in the bush) and *El que a buen árbol se arrima, buena sombra le cobija* (He who gets closest to a good tree gets good shade). These sayings remind Latina/os of the importance of attaining success in increments, with measure and caution. They also reinforce the importance of having a positive environment that supports the individual's efforts toward success and wellness.

As Latinas/os journey through their lives, *dichos* can be used as mechanisms of healing to show what is possible and to reveal truth and learn from the collective unconsciousness. These messages help reveal simple truths and allow Latina/os to revisit the training in values received during their upbringing and facilitate a form of storytelling, emotional disclosure (Zuniga, 1991), cultural teachings, reflection, and self-transformation toward wellness.

EXPLICANDO EL BIEN ESTAR: MENTE SALUDABLE, FUERZA INTERNA Y VOLUNTAD PARA LATINA/OS (EXPLAINING WELL-BEING: HEALTHY MINDS, INNER STRENGTH, AND WILL FOR LATINA/OS)

Implications for training and research as well as policy and guidelines emerge from the previous discussion of Latina/o well-being (*bien estar*) and positive functioning. Inner strengths, will, and resilience are rooted in deep-structure culture and meaning, which add a nuanced complexity of the multidimensional realities that warrant exploration and continued attention within scholarly inquiry, culturally emphasized training, and subsequent policy and practices. Toltec principles and masteries offer a collective Latina/o ethnic consciousness for wellness (Nelson, 2003). In this section, we explain well-being through the framework of awareness, transformation, and intent.

Awareness

Awareness is the active engagement that allows for the observation and naming of processes that assist in the creation of wellness. Awareness of the self in process or context, or about other in relation to past, present, or future, is a critical process for many Latina/os' survival and management of dualities (Anzaldúa, 1987). For example, naming life's challenges and using a platform from which one can learn (e.g., using *dichos* to manage and overcome difficulties; understanding one's role, function, and connection within family) serve as entryways into a *conciencía* (consciousness) of wellness. Indeed, the importance of such consciousness subsequently calls for trainers, clinicians, and researchers to centralize cultural self-awareness within curricula, practice, and scholarly inquiry. As a starting point, individuals must take stock of their understanding of culture (White & Henderson, 2008); exposure to cultural differences; and perspectives of different worldviews, values, and beliefs. The process and meaning of wellness is best understood within the context of past exchanges and the role of oppression, discrimination, and marginalization of Latina/os.

Similarly, scholarly inquiry should be considered and taught by connecting theory and practice while underscoring social advocacy for Latina/os. By focusing on the value of community and action research, researchers can gain narratives (i.e., life stories) and better understand fundamental information (e.g., cultural values, beliefs, coping processes) needed to implement a culturally grounded perspective to develop strength-based research questions addressing Latina/o mental health, coping, and well-being. For example, implementing a mixed-methods design of interacting with the community and learning community challenges, social issues, and unique ethnic specific resilience beliefs and practices will help researchers better understand the process, value, and meaning of well-being for Latina/o communities.

Transformation

Transformation is the process of "unfaltering," or removal of the filters through which life experiences or processes are understood; it ranges from reclaiming the positive aspects and accurately understanding cultural values to the ability and "flexibility to reconfigure" (Gloria & Castellanos, in press) in response to political, economic, educational, or historical events. It is through the re-storying (i.e., the retelling and one's re-interpretation of life experiences) of narratives that one finds strength and wellness—a process that is centered in survival and meaning-making of experiences. As a result, trainers, supervisors, and researchers must hold others and themselves accountable to perform at minimal competency with Latina/os to integrate holistic and comprehensive services for transformation.

As the field of psychology seeks to validate and test traditional and evolving theories of well-being (Eid & Larsen, 2008; Peterson & Seligman, 2004), it is critical to consider emic theories or frameworks that will generate a culturally inclusive examination of Latina/os and psychology (Arredondo, 2004; Cervantes, 2010; Gloria & Castellanos, 2012; Ramírez, 1998; Segura-Herrera, 2008). How are the phenomenological processes accounted for in the design, and do the measures encompass Latina/o group values, beliefs, and practices that allow transformation? Scholars and trainers must capture the scope of Latina/o realities (e.g., life challenges and social struggles), coping processes (e.g., *aguantarse*), and values (e.g., *familismo*/family, *comunidad*/community) in the context of re-storying and un-filtering the notions of individual and collective well-being.

Intent

According to Toltec principles (Nelson, 2003), the process of intent is different from intention: *Intention* is in effect the plan to do something, whereas *intent* includes the strength of conscious resolve and will to manifest or engage change. Intent drives our energies such that we create a certainty of belief that no other reality or process can exist. Latina/os use intent to align with others—families, communities, and even with the Divine (higher power)—to create a sense of wellness. Because cultural values such as engaging notions of *fatalismo* or *compadrazgo* are steeped in intent, the provision of clinical services for Latina/o clients requires nuanced training. Only a few programs across the nation claim to have a specific Latina/o training emphasis, so faculty and supervisors must take action to provide culturally integrative programs. In particular, the intent must address students' cognitive and behavioral processes for culturally relevant conceptualization, assessment, and service with Latina/o clients. Likewise, researchers must recognize their intent and social responsibility to assess properly all groups in the process of studying a phenomenon (Knight, Roosa, & Umana-Taylor, 2009). To fully examine the multidimensionality of Latina/os (e.g., identity, gender, sex), research questions must be dimensionalized to include psychological (e.g., self-power), social (e.g., community), and cultural (e.g., spirituality) processes within the context or setting of the individual to engage wellness (Castellanos & Gloria, 2008).

CONCLUSION

The (re)positioning of positive psychology for Latina/os requires a paradigm shift and a reorientation to understand psychological processes of wellness from a strength-based Latina/o centered perspective. Moreover, accessing deep-structure meanings of cultural values and beliefs enables behavioral, affective, and cognitive processes of Latina/o wellness and positive functioning that are culturally centered and meaningful.

REFERENCES

Acuña, R. F. (2010). *Occupied America: A history of Chicanos*. New York, NY: Harper & Row.

Aguirre, A., Jr., & Turner, J. H. (2011). *American ethnicity: The dynamics and consequences of discrimination* (7th ed.). New York, NY: McGraw Hill.

Alamilla, S. G., Kim, B. S. K., & Lam, N. A. (2010). Acculturation, enculturation, perceived racism, minority status stressors, and psychological symptomatology among Latino/as. *Hispanic Journal of Behavioral Sciences, 32*, 55–76. http://dx. doi.org/10.1177/0739986309352770

Alexander, J. C., Eyerman, R., Giesen, B., & Smelser, N. J. (2004). *Cultural trauma and collective identity.* Berkeley: University of California Press. http://dx.doi.org/ 10.1525/california/9780520235946.001.0001

Anzaldúa, G. (1987). *Borderlands/La frontera.* San Francisco: Spinsters/Aunt Lute Book.

Ardila, A. (2005). Spanglish: An Anglicized Spanish dialect. *Hispanic Journal of Behavioral Sciences, 27*, 60–81. http://dx.doi.org/10.1177/0739986304272358

Arredondo, P. (2004). Psychotherapy with Chicanas. In R. J. Velasquez, L. M. Arellano, & B. W. McNeill (Eds.), *The handbook of Chicana/o psychology and mental health* (pp. 231–250). Mahwah, NJ: Lawrence Erlbaum.

Aviera, A. (1996). "*Dichos*" therapy group: A therapeutic use of Spanish language proverbs with hospitalized Spanish-speaking psychiatric patients. *Cultural Diversity and Mental Health, 2*, 73–87. http://dx.doi.org/10.1037/1099-9809.2.2.73

Avila-Saavedra, G. (2008). *The Latino trend identity, influence and transformations in U.S. television* (Doctoral dissertation). Temple University, Philadelphia, PA.

Baez, A., & Hernandez, D. (2001). Complementary spiritual beliefs in the Latino community: The interface with psychotherapy. *American Journal of Orthopsychiatry, 71*, 408–415. http://dx.doi.org/10.1037/0002-9432.71.4.408

Bermúdez, J. M., & Bermúdez, S. (2002). Altar-making with Latino families: A narrative therapy perspective. *Journal of Family Psychotherapy, 13*, 329–347. http:// dx.doi.org/10.1300/J085v13n03_06

Bermúdez, J. M., Kirkpatrick, D. R., Hecker, L., & Torres-Robles, C. (2010). Describing Latino families and their help-seeking attitudes: Challenging the family therapy literature. *Contemporary Family Therapy, 32*, 155–172. http://dx.doi.org/ 10.1007/s10591-009-9110-x

Caplan, S., Paris, M., Whittemore, R., Desai, M., Dixon, J., Alvidrez, J., . . . Schaill, L. (2011). Correlates of religious, supernatural and psychosocial causal beliefs about depression among Latino immigrants in primary care. *Mental Health, Religion & Culture, 14*, 589–611. http://dx.doi.org/10.1080/13674676.2010.497810

Castellanos, J., & Gloria, A. M. (2008). *Rese un Ave Maria y ensendi una velita:* The use of spirituality and religion as a means of coping with educational experiences for Latina/o college students. In B. McNeill & J. Cervantes (Eds.), *Latina/o healing practices: Mestizo and Indigenous perspectives* (pp. 195–219). New York, NY: Routledge.

Cervantes, J. M. (2010). Mestizo spirituality: Toward an integrated approach to psychotherapy for Latina/os. *Psychotherapy: Theory, Research, Practice, Training, 47*, 527–539. http://dx.doi.org/10.1037/a0022078

Cervantes, J. M., & Ramirez, O. (1992). Spirituality and family dynamics in psychotherapy with Latino children. In L. Vargas & J. Koss-Chioino (Eds.), *Working with culture: Psychotherapeutic interventions with ethnic minority children and adolescents* (pp. 103–128). San Francisco, CA: Jossey-Bass.

Chavez, C. (1966). *The plan of Delano*. Retrieved from http://chavez.cde.ca.gov/ModelCurriculum/teachers/Lessons/resources/documents/plan_of_delano.pdf

Comas-Díaz, L. (1989). Culturally relevant issues and treatment implications for Hispanics. In D. R. Koslow & E. Salett (Eds.), *Crossing cultures in mental health* (pp. 31–48). Washington, DC: Society for International Education Training and Research.

Comas-Díaz, L. (1993). Hispanic Latino communities: Psychological implications. In D. R. Atkinson, G. Morten, & D. W. Sue (Eds.), *Counseling American minorities: A cross-cultural perspective* (pp. 245–263). Madison, WI: Brown & Benchmark.

Comas-Díaz, L. (2006). Latino healing: The integration of ethnic psychology into psychotherapy. *Psychotherapy: Theory, Research, Practice, Training, 43*, 436–453. http://dx.doi.org/10.1037/0033-3204.43.4.436

Contreras, F. (2011). *Achieving equity for Latino students: Expanding the pathway to higher education through public policy*. New York, NY: Teacher College Press.

Easley, N., Jr., Bianco, M., & Leech, N. (2012). *Ganas:* A qualitative study examining Mexican heritage student's motivation to succeed in higher education. *Journal of Hispanic Higher Education, 11*, 164–178. http://dx.doi.org/10.1177/1538192712440175

Echeverry, J. J. (1997). Treatment barriers: Accessing and accepting professional help. In J. G. Garcia & M. C. Zea (Eds.), *Psychological intervention and research with Latino populations* (pp. 94–107). Boston, MA: Allyn and Bacon.

Eid, M., & Larsen, R. (2008). *The science of subjective-well-being*. New York, NY: Guilford Press.

Falicov, C. J. (1998). *Latino families in therapy: A guide to multicultural practice*. New York, NY: Guilford Press.

Flores-Torres, L. L., & Ramirez, S. Z. (2006). Indigenous treatments: *Dichos.* In Y. Jackson (Ed.), *Encyclopedia of multicultural psychology* (pp. 250–251). Thousand Oaks, CA: Sage. http://dx.doi.org/10.4135/9781412952668.n126

Flórez, K. R., Aguirre, A. N., Viladrich, A., Céspedes, A., De La Cruz, A. A., & Abraído-Lanza, A. F. (2009). Fatalism or destiny? A qualitative study and interpretative framework on Dominican women's breast cancer beliefs. *Journal of Immigrant and Minority Health, 11*, 291–301. http://dx.doi.org/10.1007/s10903-008-9118-6

Gagan, J. M. (1998). *Journeying: Where shamanism and psychology meet*. Santa Fe, NM: Rio Champa.

Gallo, F. P. (2005). *Energy psychology: Explorations at the interface of energy, cognition, behavior, and health* (2d ed.). Boca Raton, FL: CRC Press.

Gamst, G., Dana, R. H., Der-Karabetian, A., Aragon, M., Arellano, L. M., & Kramer, T. (2002). Effects of Latino acculturation and ethnic identity on mental health outcomes. *Hispanic Journal of Behavioral Sciences, 24*, 479–504. http://dx.doi.org/10.1177/0739986302238216

Garza, Y., & Watts, R. E. (2010). Filial therapy and Hispanic values: Common ground for culturally sensitive helping. *Journal of Counseling & Development*, 88(1), 108–113. http://dx.doi.org/10.1002/j.1556-6678.2010.tb00157.x

Gill-Hopple, K., & Brage-Hudson, D. (2012). *Compadrazgo:* A literature review. *Journal of Transcultural Nursing*, 23, 117–123. http://dx.doi.org/10.1177/1043659611433870

Glass-Coffin, B. (2010). Shamanism and San Pedro through time: Some notes on the archaeology, history, and continued use of an entheogen in northern Peru. *Anthropology of Consciousness*, 21, 58–82.

Gloria, A. M., & Castellanos, J. (2009). Latinas/os and their communities. In Council of National Psychological Associations for the Advancement of Ethnic Minority Interests (Ed.), *Psychology education and training from culture-specific and multiracial perspectives: Critical issues and recommendations* (pp. 12–18). Washington, DC: American Psychological Association.

Gloria, A. M., & Castellanos, J. (2012). *Realidades culturales y identidades dimensionadas:* The complexities of Latina diversities. In C. Enns & E. Williams (Eds.), *Handbook of feminist multicultural counseling psychology* (pp. 169–182). New York, NY: Oxford University Press. http://dx.doi.org/10.1093/oxfordhb/9780199744220.013.0009

Gloria, A. M., & Castellanos, J. (in press). *Latinas poderosas:* Shaping mujerismo to manifest sacred spaces for healing and well-being. In T. Bryant-Davis & L. Comas-Diaz (Eds.), *Womanist and mujerista psychologies: Voices of fire, acts of courage*. Washington, DC: American Psychological Association.

Gloria, A. M., Castellanos, J., Scull, N. S., & Villegas, F. J. (2009). Psychological coping and well-being of male Latino undergraduates: *Sobreviviendo la universidad. Hispanic Journal of Behavioral Sciences*, 31, 317–339. http://dx.doi.org/10.1177/0739986309336845

Gloria, A. M., Ruiz, E. L., & Castillo, E. M. (2004). Counseling Latinos and Latinas: A psychosociocultural approach. In T. Smith (Ed.), *Practicing multiculturalism: Affirming diversity in counseling and psychology* (pp. 167–184). Boston, MA: Allyn and Bacon.

Gloria, A. M., & Segura-Herrera, T. (2004). *Somos!* Latinos and Latinas in the U.S. In D. Atkinson, G. Morton, & D. W. Sue (Eds.), *Counseling American minorities: A cross-cultural perspective* (6th ed., pp. 279–299). New York, NY: McGraw Hill.

Gomez, M. J., Fassinger, R. E., Prosser, J., Cooke, K., Mejia, J., & Luna, J. (2001). *Voces abriendo caminos* (Voices forging paths): A qualitative study of the career development of notable Latinas. *Journal of Counseling Psychology*, 48, 286–300. http://dx.doi.org/10.1037/0022-0167.48.3.286

Gonzalez, N. A., Fabrett, F. C., & Knight, G. P. (2009). Acculturation, enculturation, and the psychosocial adaptation of Latino youth. In F. A. Villarruel, G. Carlo, J. M. Grau, M. Azmitia, N. J. Cabrera, & T. J. Chahin (Eds.), *Handbook of U.S. Latino psychology: Developmental and community-based perspectives* (pp. 115–134). Thousand Oaks, CA: Sage.

Harris, M., Velásquez, R. J., White, J., & Renteria, T. (2004). Folk healing and *curanderismo* within the contemporary Chicana/o community: Current status. In R. J. Velásquez, L. M. Arellano, & B. W. McNeill (Eds.), *The handbook of Chicana/o psychology and mental health* (pp. 111–125). Mahwah, NJ: Erlbaum.

Hovey, J., & Morales, L. (2006). Religious/spiritual beliefs: *Fatalismo*. In Y. Jackson (Ed.), *Encyclopedia of multicultural psychology* (pp. 410–411). Thousand Oaks, CA: Sage. http://dx.doi.org/10.4135/9781412952668.n181

Hurtado, A., & Cervantez, K. (2009). A view from within and from without: The development of Latina feminist psychology. In F. Villarruel, G. Carlo, J. Grau, M. Azmitia, N. Cabrera, & T. J. Chahin (Eds.), *Handbook of U.S. Latino psychology: Development and community-based perspectives* (pp. 171–190). Thousand Oaks, CA: Sage.

Knight, G. P., Roosa, M. W., & Umana-Taylor, A. (2009). *Studying ethnic minority and economically disadvantaged populations: Methodological challenges and practices.* Washington, DC: American Psychological Association. http://dx.doi.org/10.1037/11887-000

Laird, J. (1998). Theorizing culture: Narrative ideas and practice principles. In M. McGoldrick (Ed.), *Re-visioning family therapy: Race, color, and gender in clinical practice* (pp. 20–36). New York, NY: Guilford Press.

Lopez, T. (2006). Familismo. In Y. Jackson (Ed.), *Encyclopedia of multicultural psychology* (p. 211). Thousand Oaks, CA: Sage.

Mackinnon, C. (2012). *Shamanism and spirituality in therapeutic practice: An introduction.* London, England: Singing Dragon.

Marín, G., & Marín, B. V. (1991). *Research with Hispanic populations.* Newbury Park, CA: Sage.

McNeill, B. W., & Cervantes, J. M. (Eds.). (2008). *Latina/o healing practices: Mestizo and indigenous perspectives* (pp. 271–300). New York, NY: Routledge/Taylor & Francis Group.

McNeill, B. W., Prieto, L. R., Niemann, Y. F., Pizarro, M., Vera, E. M., & Gómez, S. P. (2001). Current directions in Chicana/o psychology. *The Counseling Psychologist, 29,* 5–17. http://dx.doi.org/10.1177/0011000001291001

Mintz, S. W., & Wolf, E. R. (1950). An analysis of ritual co-parenthood (*Compadrazgo*). *Southwestern Journal of Anthropology, 6,* 341–368.

Niemann, Y. F. (2004). Stereotypes of Chicanas and Chicanos: Impact on family functioning, individual expectations, goals, and behavior. In R. J. Velásquez, L. M. Arellano, & B. W. McNeill (Eds.), *The handbook of Chicana/o psychology and mental health* (pp. 61–82). Mahwah, NJ: Lawrence Erlbaum.

Nelson, M. C. (2003). *Toltec prophecies of Don Miguel Ruiz.* Tulsa, OK: Council Oak Books.

Orozco, V. (2003). Latinas and the undergraduate experience: ¡No estamos solas! In L. Jones & J. Castellanos (Eds.), *Majority in the minority: Expanding the representation of Latina/o faculty, administrators and students in higher education* (pp. 126–137). Sterling, VA: Stylus.

Ortiz, F. A. (2009). Personalismo. In M. A. de la Torre (Ed.), *Hispanic American religious cultures* (p. 177). Santa Barbara, CA: ABC: CLIO.

Ortiz, F. A., Davis, K. G., & McNeill, B. W. (2008). Curanderismo: Religious and spiritual worldviews and indigenous healing traditions. In B. W. McNeill & J. M. Cervantes (Eds.), *Latina/o healing practices: Mestizo and indigenous perspectives* (pp. 271–300). New York, NY: Routledge/Taylor & Francis Group.

Padilla, A. M. (1984). Synopsis of the history of Chicano psychology. In J. Martinez & R. Mendoza (Eds.), *Chicano psychology* (2nd ed., pp. 1–19). New York, NY: Academic Press. http://dx.doi.org/10.1016/B978-0-12-475660-1.50007-3

Padilla, A. M. (1995). Introduction to Hispanic psychology. In A. M. Padilla (Ed.), *Hispanic psychology: Critical issues in theory and research* (pp. xi–xxi). Thousand Oaks, CA: Sage. http://dx.doi.org/10.4135/9781483326801

Padilla, F. M. (1985). *Latino ethnic consciousness: The case of Mexican Americans and Puerto Ricans in Chicago*. Notre Dame, IN: University of Notre Dame Press.

Padilla, F. M. (1997). *The struggle of Latino/Latina university students: In search of a liberating education*. New York, NY: Routledge.

Perkins, J. (1997). *Shapeshifting: Shamanic techniques for global and personal transformation*. Rochester, VT: Destiny Books.

Peterson, C., & Seligman, M. E. P. (2004). *Character strengths and virtues: A handbook and classification*. Washington, DC: American Psychological Association and Oxford University Press.

Ponterotto, J., & Casas, J. M. (1991). *Handbook of racial/ethnic minority counseling research*. Springfield, IL: Charles C Thomas.

Quintana, S. M., & Scull, N. (2009). Latino ethnic identity. In F. A. Villarruel, G. Carlo, J. M. Grau, M. Azmitia, N. J. Cabrera, & T. J. Chahin (Eds.), *Handbook of U.S. Latino psychology: Development and community-based perspectives* (pp. 81–98). Thousand Oaks, CA: Sage.

Ramírez, M., III. (1983). *Psychology of the Americas: Mestizo perspectives on personality and mental health*. New York, NY: Pergamon Press. http://dx.doi.org/10.1016/B978-0-08-026311-3.50007-0

Ramírez, M., III. (1991). *Psychotherapy and counseling with minorities: A cognitive approach to individual and cultural differences*. New York, NY: Pergamon Press.

Ramírez, M. (1998). *Multicultural/multiracial psychology: Mestizo perspectives in personality and mental health*. Lanham, MD: Rowman & Littlefield.

Saenz, R. (2010). Latinos in the United States 2010. *Population Bulletin Update*. Washington, DC: Population Reference Bureau.

Sanchez, V. (1996). *Toltecs of the new millennium*. Santa Fe, NM: Bear and Company.

Santiago-Rivera, A. L., & Altarriba, J. (2002). The role of language in therapy with the Spanish-English bilingual client. *Professional Psychology: Research and Practice, 33*, 30–38. http://dx.doi.org/10.1037/0735-7028.33.1.30

Santiago-Rivera, A. L., Altarriba, J., Poll, N., Gonzalez-Miller, N., & Cragun, C. (2009). Therapists' views on working with bilingual Spanish-English speaking clients: A qualitative investigation. *Professional Psychology: Research and Practice, 40*, 436–443. http://dx.doi.org/10.1037/a0015933

Santiago-Rivera, A. L., Arredondo, P., & Gallardo-Cooper, M. (Eds.). (2002). *Counseling Latinos and la familia: A practical guide*. Thousand Oaks, CA: Sage.

Segura-Herrera, T. (2008). *An examination of psychological well-being for Latina/o college students*. The University of Wisconsin-Madison. Retrieved from http://search.proquest.com/docview/304451582 (UMI Number 3327990)

Smith-Morris, C., Morales-Campos, D., Alvarez, E. A. C., & Turner, M. (2013). An anthropology of *familismo:* On narratives and description of Mexican/ immigrants. *Hispanic Journal of Behavioral Sciences, 35*(1), 35–60. http://dx.doi.org/10.1177/0739986312459508

The White House, Office of the Press Secretary. (2009). *Remarks by the President in nominating Judge Sonia Sotomayor to the United States Supreme Court*. Retrieved from http://www.whitehouse.gov/the_press_office/Remarks-by-the-President-in-Nominating-Judge-Sonia-Sotomayor-to-the-United-States-Supreme-Court

U.S. Census Bureau. (2010). *The Hispanic population: 2010*. Retrieved from http://www.census.gov/prod/cen2010/briefs/c2010br-04.pdf

U.S. Department of Labor. (2012, April). *The Latino labor force at a glance* [Electronic version]. Washington, DC: Author. Retrieved from http://www.dol.gov/_sec/media/reports/HispanicLaborForce/HispanicLaborForce.pdf

Valenzuela, A. (1999). *Subtractive schooling*. Albany: SUNY Press.

Walsh, R. (1999). *Essential spirituality*. New York, NY: John Wiley & Sons.

White, J. L., & Henderson, S. (2008). *Building multicultural competency: Development, training, and practice*. Lanham, MD: Rowman & Littlefield.

Zuniga, M. E. (1991). "Dichos" as metaphorical tools for resistant Latino clients. *Psychotherapy: Theory, Research, Practice, Training, 28*, 480–483. http://dx.doi.org/10.1037/0033-3204.28.3.480

5

POSITIVE PSYCHOLOGY IN AFRICAN AMERICANS

JACQUELINE S. MATTIS, NYASHA GRAYMAN SIMPSON,
WIZDOM POWELL, RIANA ELYSE ANDERSON,
LAWANNA R. KIMBRO, AND JACOB H. MATTIS

The extant literature on the positive psychological development of African Americans is sparse, and the literature that does exist is generally ahistorical and acontextual. In our overview of scholarship on positive outcomes among African Americans, we take an interdisciplinary approach combining perspectives from cultural studies, gender studies, sociology, anthropology, and political science. We seek to account for how culture and sociopolitical context may change the way that we understand virtues and strengths. We conclude by noting the need for a positive psychology that imagines positive constructs not exclusively as elements of personal character but as cultural, historical, and sociopolitical constructs that are deployed in complex ways by African Americans.

http://dx.doi.org/10.1037/14799-005
Positive Psychology in Racial and Ethnic Groups: Theory, Research, and Practice, E. C. Chang, C. A. Downey, J. K. Hirsch, and N. J. Lin (Editors)

OVERVIEW OF HISTORY AND DEMOGRAPHICS
OF AFRICAN AMERICANS

People of African descent had an established presence in ancient and pre-Columbian America (Van Sertima, 1976). However, the presence of Africans in post-Columbian America occurred as a consequence of the trans-Atlantic slave trade, characterized by the involuntary capture, trade, and transport of human beings from the African continent (usually West Africa) to the Caribbean and the Americas. This Middle Passage left in its wake the chaotic disruption and decimation of families; numerous ethnocultural communities on the African continent; and the deaths of untold numbers of men, women, and children, who were held in captivity in slave ports and later transported en masse as cargo on slave ships across the Atlantic Ocean.

America's system of chattel slavery has been sanitized and historically reenvisioned as little more than an unfortunate, albeit profoundly profitable, economic system rooted in exploitative labor of people of African descent. However, that sanitized history masks centuries of rape, lynching, burnings, beating, deliberate mutilation, physical branding, medical experimentation, psychological torture, family disruption, humiliation, and routine dehumanization (Foner, 2006; Thomas, 1999). People of African descent were bred like cattle, sold, hunted, traded as merchandise, willed as property from one generation to another, and accessed by courts as property for the settlement of the debts of the White men, women, and families who claimed ownership of them (Bell, 2013; Tadman, 1989). With the de facto end of slavery, African Americans transitioned into a postemancipation era marked by the continuation of brutal and dehumanizing conditions, poverty, residential segregation, economic exploitation, violence, the absence of civil rights, marginalization, and the relative absence of institutions dedicated to advancing the health and welfare of people of African descent.

According to the 2010 U.S. Census, approximately 42 million people residing in the United States (14% of the population) identify as people of Black/African American ancestry. National vital statistics demonstrate the complex pattern of achievements and ongoing struggles of the African American community, who continue to lag behind their White counterparts on important indices of quality of life, morbidity, and mortality. However, positive group-level changes have taken place over the years: In 1970, 4.4% of African Americans held college or professional degrees, and by 2010 about 19.8% had degrees (U.S. Census Bureau, 2012b). In 1980, 32.5% of African Americans lived at or below the national poverty line, and by 2009 that number fell to 25.8%. The average life expectancy for African Americans in 1970 was 64.1 years, but by 2010 it had increased to 73.8 years and, by 2020, to 76.1 years (U.S. Census Bureau, 2012a). Positive psychology provides a lens through which to understand the progress of African Americans.

FOUNDATIONAL RESEARCH: AFRICAN-CENTERED POSITIVE PSYCHOLOGY

What is the value of a positive psychological approach to the lives of African Americans? On its face this question seems both strange and simplistic. However, its meaning and relevance become clear when one considers three key points. First, in empirical research, "African American" identity(ies) often are flattened and robbed of nuance. Within-group differences in ethnic origins, regional identities, sexual and gender identities, class backgrounds, physical ability status, values, ideologies, and lived experience often are obscured as people are lumped under the common category "Black/African American." Second, social science literature has been preoccupied with pathos and negative life outcomes among African Americans. Research on the lives of African Americans is almost irrevocably linked to concepts of distress and "risk." The field has not imagined African Americans as people who experience joys, desires, passion, and growth or who make love or compassionate sacrifices for others. A third point centers on the way in which positive psychological constructs are often studied. Empirical work in the area of positive psychology is often ahistorical, apolitical, acultural, acontextual, and divorced from the forces that operate in everyday life. An African American positive psychology that does not acknowledge the complexity of what it means to be African American can seem both impractical and naive to those whose mission is to engage in ecologically valid empirical work that has translational and transformative value. As such, we review a broad swath of literature on the optimal development of people of African descent, highlighting how constructs function within the context of cultural, social, or sociopolitical experiences.

Over the past 40 years, scholars have examined the cultural orientations, values, ideologies, behavioral patterns, styles, and preferences that are defining features of African American culture, to discern what it means for African Americans to develop and to live optimally (Caldwell-Colbert, Parks, & Eshun, 2009). Operating at the zenith of the Civil Rights and post–Civil Rights eras when there was intentional concern for asserting the rights to liberty, dignity, and the full recognition of the humanity of people of African descent, scholars sought to study the lives of African Americans beyond the constraints of a social science that represented African American people as deficient, marginal, morally bankrupt, and crippled by pathos. Some scholars looked to African philosophical systems as a start point for scripting a healthier view of the cosmology of individuals in the African diaspora, a body of scholarship dubbed "Afri-centric" or "African-centered" scholarship. In articulating the foundational principles of Africentric psychology, Nobles (2013) asserted,

> Relying on the principles of harmony within the universe as a natural order of existence, African-centered psychology recognizes (a) the Spirit that permeates everything, (b) the idea that everything in the universe is interconnected, (c) the value that the collective is the most salient element of existence, and (d) the idea that communal self-knowledge is the key to mental health. African psychology is ultimately concerned with understanding the systems of meaning of human Beingness, the features of human functioning, and the restoration of the normal/natural order of human development. (pp. 292–293)

Those four points served as centerpieces for an African-centered optimal psychology.

> [Optimal psychology] embraces an ontological premise emphasizing unity consciousness (all is Spirit) and yielding an episteme in which self-knowledge is assumed as the basis of all knowledge and the sense of self endorsed is multidimensional, inclusive of those having gone before or ancestors, future generations, community, and all of nature. (Myers, 2013, p. 258)

The effort to name and examine optimal African American psychological functioning was ultimately distilled to a focus on seven core principles: (a) unity of the family, community, nation, and race; (b) self-determination including the African American people's right to define, name, and speak for themselves; (c) collective work and responsibility focused on communal problem-solving; (d) cooperative economics to build businesses profiting the community and world; (e) a sense of purpose and engagement in purposeful living; (f) creativity with an eye toward building community aesthetic and creative traditions; and (g) faith and intentional belief in the community, family, and leaders and in the possibilities that struggle leads to positive change (Caldwell-Colbert et al., 2009; Grills & Longshore, 1996).

A related stream of scholarship posits a cultural ethos that defines and guides the positive social behavior and development of people of African descent. That "Afrocultural ethos" includes *communalism* (belief in social interdependence of people and an orientation toward the social world rather than material objects); *psychological and behavioral verve* (preference for vibrancy, activity, stimulation, and variation in cognitive tasks and social interactions); *affect* (emotional expressiveness and responsiveness); *movement* (expression through bodily movement, rhythms, dance); *spirituality* (shared sacred essence in all things); *orality* (capacity to impart and extract knowledge from word-of-mouth communications such as storytelling, joke telling); *harmony* (minimization of competition); and *expressive individualism* (tendency to privilege autonomy and a view of oneself as the author of one's own existence and accomplishments, as well as to judge one's worth through material objects; Boykin, Jagers, Ellison, & Albury, 1997; Jagers, Smith, Mock, & Dill, 1997).

Since the mid-1990s or so, a separate and distinct stream of scholarship not rooted in African philosophy or cosmology has emerged, focused on identifying developmental and psychosocial tasks and competencies that reflect optimal functioning in the lived experience of contemporary African Americans. This second stream of work covers an array of topics, primary among them being racial identity and spirituality. We reach within and across disciplines to summarize the state of knowledge about the positive psychological development of African Americans.

THEORY AND RESEARCH ON POSITIVE AFFECT IN AFRICAN AMERICANS

We begin the dialogue with a brief exploration of two concepts, *mattering* and *love*, that although critical to dialogue about positive development, have received limited empirical attention in research on African American life.

Mattering

In contexts in which individuals are treated without respect or dignity, the concept of *mattering* has particular cache. Tucker, Dixon, and Griddine (2010) noted: "Individuals who perceive that they are noticed by, important to, and cared for by others experience mattering in their relationships" (p. 135). Tucker et al. observed that African American boys who believed that they mattered to teachers, peers, and others in school were more academically motivated and focused on academic success. Furthermore, membership in a religious organization and religious service attendance were associated with a greater sense of mattering (Lewis & Taylor, 2009). Lewis and Taylor (2009) reasoned that the religiosity–mattering link (and the link between these constructs and outcomes such as hope and resilience) results from believing in a loving and caring God and belonging to religious organizations that provide support and connectedness.

Love

Related to the concept of mattering is the concept of *love*, on which little research has been conducted among African Americans. In one study, among married African Americans, spouses who were egalitarian in management of household tasks, who spent equal amounts of time with their children, and who had equal knowledge about children's daily activities reported a greater degree of love for one another (Stanik, McHale, & Crouter, 2013). Researchers (Collins & Champion, 2011; Tyson, 2012) have examined the process by which young, unmarried African Americans come to understand how to negotiate the challenges of emotional and physical intimacy with their partners, and they found that African Americans were searching for unconditional support; trying to defy stereotypes about African American partnerships; attempting to avoid relationship mistakes made by their parents; wanting to emulate the love they witnessed in their parents' relationships; and making efforts to behave with integrity (e.g., by being faithful) in their relationships with partners. In a study of African American lesbians, Mays, Cochran, and Rhue (1993) highlighted the challenges of forging romantic relationships in the context of homophobic discrimination within the African American community, noting that African American lesbians whose partners were White also had to contend with racism within their relationships with White female partners. Taken together, these studies highlight the reality that, for African Americans, love and other forms of positive affect are informed by subjective and interpersonal factors as well as by broader socio-ecological and sociopolitical factors.

THEORY AND RESEARCH ON POSITIVE BEHAVIORS IN AFRICAN AMERICANS

Data on advances made by African Americans, including educational and professional attainment, as well as data demonstrating improvements in the mortality of the community as a whole demonstrates a critical capacity of African American people to survive and thrive even in the context of adversity. These data point to the need for attention to resilience as a core strength.

Resilience in African American Families

Little has been written about resilience in African American families (Boyd-Franklin & Karger, 2012; Hollingsworth, 2013). *Resilience*, defined as the "dynamic process encompassing positive adaptation within the context of significant adversity" (Luthar, Cicchetti, & Becker, 2000, p. 543), is posited as a psychological construct largely responsible for the well-being of youth and adults who would otherwise be expected to perform poorly when experiencing risk factors. Three elements tie together most definitions and models of resilience. First, resilience is often only viewed through the lens of hardship. Second, families are considered buoyant and have the ability to bounce up. Third, resilience is a strengths-based construct (Walsh, 2003).

Bowman (2013) advanced an *adversity paradox*: People can grow stronger by confronting adversity, particularly with strong support systems. Indeed, McAdams, Reynolds, Lewis, Patten, and Bowman (2001) posited that resiliency comes from universal protective strengths as well as protective sociocultural factors (e.g., racial identity, racial socialization) that can reinforce personal strengths despite chronic environmental risks. Building on Bowman's work, Gregory (2002) identified a range of processes associated with resilience in African American families, including positive outlook, transcendence, and spirituality, making meaning of adversity, connectedness, open emotional expression, expression of empathy, compassion, forgiveness, use of remembering, use of rituals, the experience of gratitude and humility, and the experience of dreams and clairvoyant experiences. Bagley and Carroll (1998) identified several variables describing resilient African American families, including immediate family and extended family support, community participation, self-esteem in family members, an oral tradition, racial awareness, an attitude of challenge, proactive behavior, and compromise. Baldwin (1981) added to this list: being aware of and recognizing their African history and identity, prioritizing ideologies and activities that seek African American survival, prioritizing activities that facilitate self-knowledge and affirmation, and having a posture of resolute resistance toward forces that threaten the survival of African American people generally.

Recent work on family resilience has emphasized that the shift from understanding factors supporting resilience to understanding resilient processes is crucial to determining how children succeed despite adversity (Luthar et al., 2000). Yet, few theoretical models explain how protective factors translate into resilient processes for African Americans, particularly in contexts within which they live. This represents an important area for future work.

Civic Engagement, Volunteerism, and Altruistic Care

Ever since the days of slavery, African Americans have launched ideological, moral, spiritual, social, and political opposition to slavery and other forms of injustice. As a result of that activism, America's opportunity structure has opened substantially. However, institutional, community-level, and interpersonal racism continue to thrive and to create and sustain conditions (e.g., mass incarceration, failing schools, limited access to quality health care) that are inimical to the health and well-being of African Americans (Alexander, 2012; Thompson, 2013).

One way of responding to the awareness of unfairness and injustice has been to become involved in actions that promote care and that seek to instill justice. The literature on African American civic engagement, justice orientation, and altruistic care suggests that, rather than thwarting African American people's decisions to become civically engaged, exposure to racism is related to an increased likelihood of adults' involvement in political and social justice activities (Mattis, Beckham, et al., 2004).

Contextual factors such as whether the setting is religious or secular, and the racial composition of the setting, have implications for African American volunteering and civic involvement (Musick, Wilson, & Bynum, 2000). African Americans are especially likely to volunteer at their place of worship (Farmer & Piotrkowski, 2009), and African Americans attending majority African American churches are more likely to be asked to volunteer and to volunteer more hours per month than those attending churches where African Americans are in the minority (Smith, Fabricatore, & Peyrot, 1999). The willingness of African American young adults to engage in volunteer work or political action is related to their level of optimism, perceptions of community functioning (e.g., perceived neighborhood disorder), perceptions of trust and cooperation among residents, and beliefs about whether political actions can yield positive community outcomes (e.g., keep neighborhood children safe; Chung & Probert, 2011).

In an ethnographic study of altruism, Mattis et al. (2009) identified several motives for altruistic engagement. *Need-based motives* indicated that people behave altruistically when they become aware through direct or indirect contact of the needs of others. Here, compassion, empathy, and perspective-taking help to sensitize prospective actors to the needs of others. Some individuals behave altruistically because of the norms they have internalized. These include ideological norms (i.e., religious or spiritual norms related to selfless giving); norms rooted in personality, character, or calling (i.e., norms related to people's sense of who they are); and relationally derived norms (e.g., norms developed over a lifetime of receiving or witnessing acts of giving). Mattis and colleagues found that models of altruism had a different impact depending on whether those models were proximal (e.g., family members) or distal (e.g., strangers). Family models helped to catalyze an altruistic identity in people (i.e., a sense of "I am a part of a legacy of people who are giving") whereas stranger altruism stimulated social capital (e.g., social trust, connectedness). In addition to needs and norms, altruism was motivated by two *moral motives*: an orientation towards humanism, and a conviction about the worth of specific individuals or groups. Finally, individuals behaved altruistically because of *sociopolitical motives*. Here, peoples' own experience with poverty, marginality, and discrimination promoted altruism.

Altruism also is shaped by the interplay between social identities and the contexts in which they operate (Mattis et al., 2008). Different combinations of social identities create different patterns of vulnerability and shape ideas about who is most in need or most deserving of help. These factors informed the kinds of help that individuals were likely to receive or extend to others. Mattis et al. (2008) noted that altruists in low-income, urban communities sometimes find themselves in the morally difficult position of having to lie, steal, or break rules in order to care for others. For example, young, urban-residing African American men were particularly likely to be victims of violence at the hands of peers and police. In order to protect them, community members sometimes had to lie in order to get often unresponsive police departments to respond to the needs of these young men.

THEORY AND RESEARCH ON POSITIVE COGNITIONS IN AFRICAN AMERICANS

A broad view of positive African American development requires attention to research and conceptual work on the positive behaviors as well as research and conceptual work on positive cognitions. We attend here to the positive implications of making meaning of the world through constructing the self as a racialized being, through religion and spirituality, and through contemplations on justice and fairness. We also explore research on the exercise of creativity, humor, and purpose in terms of their relevance to a discussion of positive African American development.

Racial Identity

In an effort to more effectively represent the complex needs, experiences, strengths, and perspectives of African Americans, social scientists within the African American community have called for greater attention to the diversity of this community. The demographic profile of today's African Americans has been transformed by (a) forcible and voluntary movement of individuals within and out of Africa to North America, the Caribbean, Europe, South and Central America, Asia, and the Pacific Isles; (b) voluntary and involuntary miscegenation; (c) differential patterns of access to opportunities and resources; and (d) differential patterns of achievement. Despite the complex profile of the community, within-group ethnic diversity continues to be obscured in the service of articulating a digestibly familiar but highly essentialized image of what it means to be African American. The call for attention to the diversity of the African American community compels us to ask, "Who are the African Americans?" Gomez (1998) suggested that

African Americans are an imagined community, a creation and recreation of transcontinental racialist thinking which, by 1830, had firmly taken root within the United States. Before this time, a large subset of we who now call ourselves African Americans were ethnic Igbo, Akan, Bantu, and Bambara.

Figures from the most recent U.S. census highlight the diversity in the present population of African Americans. Of the U.S. population, 13% self-identifies as "Black or African American alone"; 1% self-identifies as "Black in combination" with one or more other races (e.g., White, Native American/Alaska Native, Asian). Of the total "Black or African American alone" population, approximately 8% are foreign born, mostly coming from Jamaica, Haiti, Trinidad and Tobago, Nigeria, Ethiopia, and Ghana; 3% report being of Hispanic, Latino, or Spanish heritage, with 1% of that population being foreign born (Grieco, 2010). Sociological research further complicates these data by demonstrating that many first and second generation immigrants identify as Black and that people vary with regard to the contexts under which they will identify as American, Caribbean, or Black (Butterfield, 2004).

In sociopolitical contexts in which being African American signals opportunities for being surveilled, dehumanized, treated with disrespect, excluded from opportunities for advancement, and (in extreme cases) physically harmed, constructing a healthy racial identity emerges as an important positive developmental outcome (Neblett, Smalls, Ford, Nguyên, & Sellers, 2009; Sellers, Rowley, Chavous, Shelton, & Smith, 1997). Sellers and colleagues delineated several dimensions of racial identity important for African Americans: (a) centrality of race, that is, extent to which race is a core part of an individual's self-concept; (b) positive regard, the extent to which individuals hold positive feelings and judgments about their race; and (c) nationalist, assimilationist, humanist, and oppressed minority ideological stances. These dimensions of racial identity are related to a range of outcomes including, but not limited to, better mental health and effectively negotiating life stress including the stress of racial discrimination (Caldwell, Zimmerman, Bernat, Sellers, & Notaro, 2002; Neblett, Shelton, & Sellers, 2004) and involvement in prosocial action (White-Johnson, 2012).

Racial Socialization and Self-Regulation

Racial socialization (i.e., process by which children develop the perspective of their ethnic group) may be one of the most practical ethnic-specific mechanisms for helping youth to develop a positive racial identity (Neblett et al., 2009) and for developing resilience to discrimination (Caldwell-Colbert et al., 2009; Stevenson, Davis, & Abdul-Kabir, 2001). Cultural socialization occurs as families and communities provide children with guidance and support and offer a historical and cultural map of the African American experience that describes how people have survived many adverse conditions and that reminds young people that despite social barriers they are able to excel and prosper. Parents who promote racial socialization typically espouse four dimensions: pride, preparation for bias and discrimination, promotion of mistrust, and egalitarianism (Hughes et al., 2006). A history of encounters with racism and systemic barriers (McLoyd, 1990) may explain parents' emphasis on mistrust and preparation for bias messages (Stevenson et al., 2001).

Another element of racial socialization is a focus on *self-regulation*, which is the ability to motivate, direct, and reflect on specific thoughts and behaviors (Zimmerman & Schunk, 2011) and the strategies individuals use to monitor and adjust their emotional and cognitive states to achieve internal goals and meet external expectations (Carver & Scheier, 1981). Self-regulation requires (a) setting clear standards or goals, (b) self-monitoring and evaluation to detect discrepancies between one's behavior and goals, (c) motivation and strength to change one's behavior, and (d) effective mechanisms for behavior change (Fitzsimons & Bargh, 2004; Schmeichel & Baumeister, 2004). Kliewer et al. (2004) proffered a model of resilience for African American children exposed to community violence, suggesting that self-regulation may mitigate the risk associated with exposure to violence by promoting adaptive coping.

Self-regulation theory has focused mainly on how this process occurs for individuals in their perception of a single event. Less is understood about how individuals manage the cumulative impact of chronic external stressors such as racism. Racial, as well as classed and gendered, identities have implications for how one is treated by public and private institutions (e.g., the extent to which one is treated with respect by authorities, educators, and police). As such, African Americans learn early in their socialization how to conduct themselves and regulate their behavior in the presence of individuals and systems that might be inimical to their well-being (e.g., law enforcement). In the frustrating advent of racial profiling and unjust harassment, many African American boys and men learn not put their hands in their pockets and to refrain from gesticulating or making furtive movements to reduce the chances that their behavior might be misinterpreted as aggression. In public settings and professional contexts, African American men and women often monitor and modify (i.e., regulate) their behaviors to minimize the likelihood of being labeled as aggressive, threatening, or unfriendly or to avoid unfair evaluations (Baumeister, Vohs, & Tice, 2007). The processes by which individuals learn these strategies, and the short- and long-term benefits and costs to health, professional development, and personal well-being for mastering or failing to master these processes, are unclear.

Arguably, one cultural value that is central in the racial socialization process is the value of communalism. Boykin et al. (1997) noted,

> Communalism denotes awareness of the fundamental interdependence of people. One's orientation is social rather than being directed toward objects. There is overriding importance attached to social bonds and social relationships. One acts in accordance with the notion that duty to one's social group is more important than individual rights and privileges. Hence, one's identity is tied to group membership rather than individual status and possessions. Sharing is promoted because it affirms the importance of social interconnectedness. Self-centeredness and individual greed are frowned upon. (p. 411)

In keeping with its conceptual framing, communalism has been shown to be positively correlated with moral reasoning skills in youths (Woods & Jagers, 2003). Among adults, it is correlated with community involvement (Grayman-Simpson & Mattis, 2013) and with the amount of time that individuals dedicate to volunteer work (Mattis, Beckham, et al., 2004).

Religion and Spirituality

Having withdrawn from White churches that often professed a faith that was contradicted by the involvement of Christians in unjust and violent subjugation of their African American brethren, African Americans established their own religious institutions founded in a new theology rooted in four core themes: hope, justice, love, and liberation (Cone, 1986).

Religion has been a central force in African American life. According to the most recent Pew study on religion and public life (Sahgal & Smith, 2009), African Americans are the most religious racial/ethnic group in the nation, with 88% reporting a certainty about God's existence. Findings from the National Survey of American Life revealed that 90.4% of African Americans report that prayer is important in their efforts to deal with stress, and approximately 90% report that they turn to God for strength, support, and guidance (Chatters, Taylor, Jackson, & Lincoln, 2008).

Religion influences meaning-making and coping among African American adults and youth. Young people who used religious coping strategies to manage adversity (i.e., who rely on their own skills but also turn to God for support) reported a greater number of reasons for living (Molock, Puri, Matlin, & Barksdale, 2006). Mattis (2002) asserted that religion and spirituality allow individuals (a) to confront and accept reality; (b) to gain the insight and courage needed to surrender adversity to God; (c) to acknowledge and transcend personal limitations; (d) to identify existential questions and life lessons to be learned from adversity; (e) to discern life purpose and destiny; (f) to shape character and behave in principled ways; (g) to achieve growth; and (h) to deepen trust in God and in transcendent sources of knowledge (e.g., power of prayer).

The study of African American religiosity and spirituality requires attention to individual faith as well as to the historical and contemporary role of religious institutions. The overwhelming majority of African Americans identify as Christian (U.S. Census Bureau, 2010), and the church is a principal site for spiritual development. However, since its inception, the reach of the church has extended well beyond traditional matters of spirit. The church historically has served as a place of refuge for those disenfranchised by political, educational, economic, and other systemic inequalities. African Americans turn to their churches and ministers for spiritual and social support; counseling; financial help; emergency assistance with food, clothing, and housing; legal support; childcare needs; and educational support (Chatters et al., 2011; Krause, 2012; Mattis et al., 2007). The church has also served as a site for organizing African American civic, political, and social justice activities (Lincoln & Mamiya, 1990; McKenzie, 2004). For this reason, church involvement is one of the most robust predictors of volunteerism for African Americans (Musick, Wilson, & Bynum, 2000; Smetana & Metzger, 2005). Even in light of these powerful positive functions of church and faith life, religious institutions remain complicated and sometimes painful spaces in which to operate, particularly for individuals whose identities mark them as outcasts in some communities of faith (e.g., lesbian, gay, bisexual, transgender, and queer individuals). How people wrestle constructively with theological conflict and with discrimination within religious environments requires attention.

Although religiosity and spirituality are often treated as elements of personal choice and as individual-level forces, anthropologists (e.g., Geertz, 1973) remind us that religions are cultural systems, and theologians remind us that faith is sociopolitically and sociohistorically situated (Raboteau, 1989). Theology research demonstrates that the psychology of religion has missed the audacious and powerful dismantling, deauthorizing, revisioning, improvisational, inventive processes by which African Americans inscribe and reify their dignity and humanity and assure their own well-being through religious faith (Dantley, 2010; Stewart, 1996). Theologians have argued that African American Christian theology and African American religious institutions were hewn in the context of slavery and the quest for human and civil rights and have been forged against a landscape of conditions that required the community to grapple with questions about evil, liberation, and the meaning and value of suffering (Raboteau, 1989). Raboteau (1989) and Dantley (2010) have noted that the musical traditions, ideologies, systems of meaning-making, and language that have evolved among religious African Americans provide clear evidence of a prophetic religious tradition that is rooted in themes of love, hope, compassion, freedom, and justice. These authors also suggested that African American religiosity is marked by a thematic focus on trust in God's improvisational power; ability to transform people, spaces, and negative conditions (i.e., to make a way out of no way); and a belief in His love, goodness, and forgiveness. Given these thematic foci in African American spirituality, we summarize empirical findings related to the topics of morality, justice, fairness, optimism, gratitude, creativity, humor and purpose.

Morality, Justice, and Fairness

Morality represents efforts to behave in accordance with right and excellent thought and action. Morality is informed by values, beliefs, lived experience, social context, and affect and the interaction among these. Moral and judicious thinking and action require that people weigh a range of personal, interpersonal, and communal needs and expectations including those that run counter to the values and expectations of the institutions or social contexts in which they operate.

Empirical studies of justice morality among African American adults have often relied on the Defining Issues Test (Rest, 1979), which assesses the degree to which one's moral thinking reflects postconventional moral standards reflected in the highest stages of moral development, according to Kohlberg's theory: Stage 5 (purported to privilege social arrangements, the will of the people, fairness and protection of basic human rights), and Stage 6 (reflects appeals to rational idealism consistent with classical Western philosophers). African American college students who complete the test demonstrate scores more consistent with those expected for junior high school or high school students (Dunston & Roberts, 1987; Moreland & Leach, 2001). Critiquing the cultural relevancy of Kohlberg's model, scholars have suggested that moral development within the African American community centers on processes more akin to Gilligan's ethic of care than to the ethic of justice outlined by Kohlberg. Knox and colleagues tested this assumption (Knox, Fagley, & Miller, 2004) using the Moral Orientation Scale (Yacker & Weinberg, 1990) and, contrary to expectations, African American college students had relatively low-care moral orientation scores. The equivocal findings of this body of work support Ward's (1991) argument for culturally grounded phenomenological studies of morality that can yield a meaningful theoretical frame for understanding African American moral orientation and African American ethics of care and that can elucidate the social-cognitive processes (e.g., cultural memory and consciousness) that support them (Grayman, 2009; Ward, 1991).

Discussions of morality cannot take place outside of discussions of concepts such as fairness, justice, and integrity. Here, the concept of *behavioral integrity*, or the perceived match between espoused and enacted values and the extent to which promises are seen as being kept, becomes especially relevant (Simons,

Friedman, Liu, & McLean Parks, 2007). Research on behavioral integrity suggests that African Americans are more "perceptually primed" (Fiske & Taylor, 1991) to detect violations of behavioral integrity (Simons et al., 2007), having substantial reasons, based on historical injustice, to be vigilant to hypocrisy by those in power and, thus, to be especially sensitive to word and action misalignments (Simons et al., 2007). Behavior integrity violations occur routinely in the criminal justice system where African Americans are victimized by disproportionate targeting and unfair treatment; racially skewed charging, prosecutory, and sentencing practices; and the failure of elected officials, judges, and policymakers to redress these inequities (Leadership Conference on Civil Rights, 2000). Such violations are also endemic in other contexts including the educational and health care systems (Harper & Davis, 2012).

The forced sterilization and coercive reproductive control of African American women by medical professionals (Roberts, 1997), and the Tuskegee syphilis experiment, have been identified as important contexts and sources of medical mistrust among African Americans (Gamble, 1997); this mistrust is exacerbated by their experience of disrespectful treatment by service providers, unequal access to first-rate medical treatments, and financial discrimination (Jacobs, Rolle, Ferrans, Whitaker, & Warnecke, 2006). Mistrust, rooted in unethical, unsatisfactory, and disrespectful treatment, has led many African Americans to avoid seeking formal care (Hammond, 2010). Although mistrust might be a negative, albeit justified, outcome, it is important to explore the extent to which wise and critical evaluations, and reasoned skepticism, emerge as healthy responses to unhealthy conditions.

African Americans are routinely called upon to make decisions about how to respond to violations of behavior integrity. For many, the perceptions and empirical evidence of formal institutions' past and current violation of behavior integrity have led to mistrust of these institutions. In the face of violations of integrity, individuals must decide when to name, challenge, forgive, or remain silent about such violations; must discern how to succeed despite such violations; must decide whether to behave with integrity despite a context that does not value integrity; and must be willing to endure the consequences of their choices (Hammond, Banks, & Mattis, 2006; Harper & Davis, 2012). Individuals must also develop the capacity to endure the hypocrisy of individuals and contexts that profess to be ethical even while they engage in practices that are immoral, illegal, or unjust.

Optimism and Gratitude

Optimism has emerged as an area of interest among scholars of African American well-being (Bediako & Neblett, 2011) and has been consistently associated with religiosity among African Americans (Mattis, Fontenot, &

Hatcher-Kay, 2003; Mattis, Fontenot, Hatcher-Kay, Grayman, & Beale, 2004; Utsey, Hook, Fischer, & Belvet, 2008). The foundations of this link are still a matter of speculation, but scholars assert that those who believe that they matter to and are loved by a compassionate, forgiving, and omnipotent God and those who have access to religious support (e.g., church support) may believe that life outcomes will be positive.

Related to optimism is the concept of gratitude. One of the core messages of Abrahamic religions involves trusting that God has a purpose and plan for each person's life and being grateful that we are beneficiaries of unearned love and grace. African Americans who believe that adversity is part of God's plan are more likely to feel grateful to God when adversity arises (Krause, 2012). Relative to other ethnic groups (i.e., Whites and Mexican Americans), African Americans report greater gratitude to God and that gratitude appears fueled by spiritual support from others, the religious meaning ascribed to life events, and self-knowledge. How religiously based feelings of gratitude inform other aspects of African American positive development (e.g., resilience, volunteerism, altruism) has yet to be explored.

Creativity, Humor, and Sense of Purpose

African Americans have developed myriad strategies to share knowledge, to highlight joys, and to cope with and traverse adversity. Key among these is the use of storytelling, humor, and the creative arts. Anthropologists, linguists, literary critics, musicologists, and cultural theorists have studied humor and creativity (Dance, 1978; Watkins, 1994); however, little attention has been paid to these topics in psychology. The research that does exist suggests that, even at young ages, African American children internalize some culturally determined narrative strategies associated with effective storytelling. Relative to White and Latino children, African American children embellish stories more by emphasizing fantasy and suspense and by including direct dialogue in the stories (a performative feature of storytelling believed to engage audiences; Gorman, Fiestas, Peña, & Clark, 2011).

Practitioners have begun to advocate for the use of humor and storytelling as culturally grounded practices that can deepen therapeutic work with African American adults (Vereen, Hill, & Butler, 2013). The relevance of these tools for therapy is evident from research on normative African American development that demonstrates that stories embedded in religious songs, including songs of praise and thanksgiving and songs of instruction, help African Americans to manage adversity (Hamilton, Sandelowski, Moore, Agarwal, & Koenig, 2013).

Another important discursive tool with implications for positive psychology is humor. Humor allows us to lift up and publicly name experiences or conditions as ludicrous, ironic, absurd, profane, confusing, tragic, tender, beautiful, or awe-inspiring. Humor and creativity both signal and imbue vitality (often in the form of pleasure and amusement) in social contexts. Humor can be used to single out people or conditions or to create an experience of solidarity by referencing common or defining cultural or communal experiences (e.g., as in the inside joke).

Gordon (1998) noted that "African American humor" is distinct from the humor of other cultural communities in the devices that it uses (e.g., satire, metaphor, double entendre, self-deprecation, improvisation, word play); the topics and conditions it takes up as its subject matter (e.g., class, gender, racial hegemony); and its intentions and outcomes (e.g., interrogate and dismantle the presumed authenticity of ideas about ontological Blackness). Humor and creativity are tied to wisdom traditions and truth-telling, because those who engage in these practices often have an acute and critical capacity to observe, interrogate, and critique the world and to convey nuanced and authentic ideas to others about structures of power, relational dynamics, and their impact on the human condition. For African Americans, humor and storytelling have provided a safe discursive space from which to display verbal and intellectual prowess, to critique systems and practices of power as well as particular power brokers, and to overtly or subversively articulate anger, emotional vulnerability, and wisdom safely (Gordon, 1998). Although African American storytelling and humor are varied, there are strategies that have been identified as emblematic in African American stories and humor (e.g., signifying, testifying). African Americans vary in their familiarity or comfort with these strategies of humor and storytelling. Furthermore, the social functions and roles of these strategies in promoting wisdom and in preserving mental health among African Americans have yet to be explored.

DEVELOPING A POSITIVE PSYCHOLOGY OF AFRICAN AMERICANS

What is the future of a positive psychology of African Americans? A meaningful dialogue about positive psychological development among African Americans requires examining the diversity of African Americans and the historical and contemporary context within which African Americans reside. In this regard, we cannot lose sight of the very real challenges, oppressions, limitations, and adverse conditions that African Americans face in a nation that continues to struggle with matters of race, class, and justice. In fact, we must seek to understand how African American people develop character strengths and virtues within contexts that might otherwise yield less positive outcomes, and we should address three key concerns: (a) the extent to which

African Americans are able to identify and use personal and ecological assets to mitigate negative forces (e.g., racial discrimination) and advance personal, familial, social, institutional, and societal goals; (b) the processes by which these outcomes are achieved; and (c) the virtues, character strengths, and areas of positive functioning that may be absent from the existing taxonomy of positives represented in the field but that may be especially relevant to the lives of African Americans.

REFERENCES

Alexander, M. (2012). *The new Jim Crow: Mass incarceration in the age of colorblindness*. New York, NY: New Press.

Bagley, C. A., & Carroll, J. (1998). Healing forces in African-American families. In H. I. McCubbin, E. A. Thompson, A. I. Thompson, & J. A. Futrell (Eds.), *Resiliency in African-American families* (pp. 117–142). Thousand Oaks, CA: Sage.

Baldwin, J. A. (1981). Notes on an Africentric theory of Black personality. *The Western Journal of Black Studies*, 5, 172–179.

Baumeister, R. F., Vohs, K. D., & Tice, D. M. (2007). The strength model of self-control. *Current Directions in Psychological Science*, 16, 351–355. http://dx.doi.org/10.1111/j.1467-8721.2007.00534.x

Bediako, S. M., & Neblett, E. W. (2011). Optimism and perceived stress in sickle-cell disease: The role of an Afrocultural social ethos. *Journal of Black Psychology*, 37, 234–253.

Bell, R. (2013). The great jugular vein of slavery: New histories of the domestic slave trade. *History Compass*, 11, 1150–1164. http://dx.doi.org/10.1111/hic3.12114

Bowman, P. J. (2013). A strengths-based social psychological approach to resiliency: Cultural diversity, ecological, and life span issues. In S. Prince-Embury & D. H. Saklofske (Eds.), Resilience in children, adolescents, and adults (pp. 299–324). New York, NY: Springer.

Boyd-Franklin, N., & Karger, M. (2012). *Intersections of race, class, and poverty: Challenges and resilience in African American families* (pp. 273–296). New York, NY: Guilford Press.

Boykin, A. W., Jagers, R. J., Ellison, C. M., & Albury, A. (1997). Communalism: Conceptualization and measurement of an Afrocultural social orientation. *Journal of Black Studies*, 27, 409–418. http://dx.doi.org/10.1177/002193479702700308

Butterfield, S. (2004). Challenging American conceptions of race and ethnicity: Second generation West Indian immigrants. *The International Journal of Sociology and Social Policy*, 24, 75–102. http://dx.doi.org/10.1108/01443330410791028

Caldwell, C. H., Zimmerman, M. A., Bernat, D. H., Sellers, R. M., & Notaro, P. C. (2002). Racial identity, maternal support, and psychological distress among

African American adolescents. *Child Development, 73*, 1322–1336. http://dx.doi.org/10.1111/1467-8624.00474

Caldwell-Colbert, A., Parks, F. M., & Eshun, S. (2009). Positive psychology: African American strengths, resilience, and protective factors. In H. A. Neville, B. M. Tynes, & S. O. Utsey (Eds.), *Positive psychology: African American strengths, resilience, and protective factors* (pp. 375–384). Thousand Oaks, CA: Sage.

Carver, C. S., & Scheier, M. F. (1981). The self-attention-induced feedback loop and social facilitation. *Journal of Experimental Social Psychology, 17*, 545–568. http://dx.doi.org/10.1016/0022-1031(81)90039-1

Chatters, L. M., Mattis, J. S., Woodward, A. T., Taylor, R. J., Neighbors, H. W., & Grayman, N. A. (2011). Use of ministers for a serious personal problem among African Americans: Findings from the national survey of American life. *American Journal of Orthopsychiatry, 81*, 118–127. http://dx.doi.org/10.1111/j.1939-0025.2010.01079.x

Chatters, L. M., Taylor, R. J., Jackson, J. S., & Lincoln, K. D. (2008). Religious coping among African Americans, Caribbean Blacks and Non-Hispanic Whites. *Journal of Community Psychology, 36*, 371–386. http://dx.doi.org/10.1002/jcop.20202

Chung, H. L., & Probert, S. (2011). Civic engagement in relation to outcome expectations among African American young adults. *Journal of Applied Developmental Psychology, 32*, 227–234. http://dx.doi.org/10.1016/j.appdev.2011.02.009

Collins, J. L., & Champion, J. D. (2011). An exploration of young ethnic minority males' beliefs about romantic relationships. *Issues in Mental Health Nursing, 32*, 146–157. http://dx.doi.org/10.3109/01612840.2010.538813

Cone, J. (1986). *Speaking the truth*. Grand Rapids, MI: William B. Eerdmans.

Dance, D. (1978). *Shuckin' and jivin': Folklore from contemporary African Americans*. Bloomington: Indiana University Press.

Dantley, M. E. (2010). Successful leadership in urban schools: Principals and critical spirituality, a new approach to reform. *The Journal of Negro Education, 79*, 214–219.

Dunston, P. J., & Roberts, A. (1987). The relationship of moral judgment and ego development to political-social values in Black college students. *Journal of Black Psychology, 13*(2), 43–49. http://dx.doi.org/10.1177/009579848701300202

Farmer, G. L., & Piotrkowski, C. S. (2009). African and European American women's volunteerism and activism: Similarities in volunteering and differences in activism. *Journal of Human Behavior in the Social Environment, 19*, 196–212. http://dx.doi.org/10.1080/10911350802687182

Fiske, S. T., & Taylor, S. E. (1991). *Social cognition* (2d ed.). New York, NY: McGraw-Hill.

Fitzsimons, G. M., & Bargh, J. A. (2004). Automatic self-regulation. In R. F. Baumeister & B. K. D. Vohs (Eds.), *Handbook of self-regulation* (pp. 151–170). New York, NY: Guilford Press.

Foner, E. (2006). *Forever free: The story of Emancipation and Reconstruction*. New York, NY: Vintage.

Gamble, V. N. (1997). The Tuskegee Syphilis Study and women's health. *Journal of the American Medical Women's Association, 52*, 195–196.

Geertz, C. (1973). *The interpretation of cultures*. New York, NY: Basic Books.

Gomez, M. A. (1998). *Exchanging our country marks: The transformation of African identities in the colonial and antebellum south*. Durham: University of North Carolina Press.

Gordon, D. B. (1998). Humor in African American discourse: Speaking of oppression. *Journal of Black Studies, 29*, 254–276. http://dx.doi.org/10.1177/002193479802900207

Gorman, B. K., Fiestas, C. E., Peña, E. D., & Clark, M. R. (2011). Creative and stylistic devices employed by children during a storybook narrative task: A cross-cultural study. *Language, Speech, and Hearing Services in Schools, 42*, 167–181. http://dx.doi.org/10.1044/0161-1461(2010/10-0052)

Grayman, N. (2009). "We who are dark . . .": The Black community according to Black adults in America. *Journal of Black Psychology, 35*, 433–455. http://dx.doi.org/10.1177/0095798408329943

Grayman-Simpson, N., & Mattis, J. S. (2013). "If it wasn't for the church . . .": Organizational religiosity and informal community helping among African American adults. *Journal of African American Studies, 17*, 243–252.

Gregory, W. H., Jr. (2002). *Resiliency in the Black family* (Doctoral dissertation). Fielding Graduate Institute, Santa Barbara, CA.

Grieco, E. M. (2010). *Race and Hispanic origin of the foreign-born population in the United States: 2007*. Retrieved from http://www.census.gov/prod/2010pubs/acs-11.pdf

Grills, C., & Longshore, D. (1996). Africentrism: Psychometric analyses of a self-report measure. *Journal of Black Psychology, 22*, 86–106. http://dx.doi.org/10.1177/00957984960221007

Hamilton, J. B., Sandelowski, M., Moore, A. D., Agarwal, M., & Koenig, H. G. (2013). "You need a song to bring you through": The use of religious songs to manage stressful life events. *The Gerontologist, 53*(1), 26–38. http://dx.doi.org/10.1093/geront/gns064

Hammond, W. P. (2010). Psychosocial correlates of medical mistrust among African American men. *American Journal of Community Psychology, 45*(1-2), 87–106. http://dx.doi.org/10.1007/s10464-009-9280-6

Hammond, W. P., Banks, K. H., & Mattis, J. (2006). Masculinity ideology and forgiveness of racial discrimination among African American men: Direct and interactive relationships. *Sex Roles, 55*, 679–692. http://dx.doi.org/10.1007/s11199-006-9123-y

Harper, S. R., & Davis, C. H. F., III. (2012, Winter–Spring). They (don't) care about education: A counter-narrative on Black male students' responses to inequitable schooling. *Educational Foundations*, 103–120.

Hollingsworth, L. D. (2013). Resilience in Black families. In D. S. Becvar (Ed.), *Handbook of family resilience* (pp. 229–243). New York, NY: Springer.

Hughes, D., Rodriguez, J., Smith, E. P., Johnson, D. J., Stevenson, H. C., & Spicer, P. (2006). Parents' ethnic-racial socialization practices: A review of research and directions for future study. *Developmental Psychology, 42,* 747–770. http://dx.doi.org/10.1037/0012-1649.42.5.747

Jacobs, E. A., Rolle, I., Ferrans, C. E., Whitaker, E. E., & Warnecke, R. B. (2006). Understanding African Americans' views of the trustworthiness of physicians. *Journal of General Internal Medicine, 21,* 642–647. http://dx.doi.org/10.1111/j.1525-1497.2006.00485.x

Jagers, R. J., Smith, P., Mock, L. O., & Dill, E. (1997). An Afrocultural social ethos: Component orientations and some social implications. *Journal of Black Psychology, 23,* 328–343. http://dx.doi.org/10.1177/00957984970234002

Kliewer, W., Cunningham, J. N., Diehl, R., Parrish, K. A., Walker, J. M., Atiyeh, C., . . . Mejia, R. (2004). Violence exposure and adjustment in inner-city youth: Child and caregiver emotion regulation skill, caregiver-child relationship quality, and neighborhood cohesion as protective factor. *Journal of Clinical Child and Adolescent Psychology, 33,* 477–487. http://dx.doi.org/10.1207/s15374424jccp3303_5

Knox, P. L., Fagley, N. S., & Miller, P. M. (2004). Care and justice moral orientations among African American college students. *Journal of Adult Development, 11*(1), 41–45. http://dx.doi.org/10.1023/B:JADE.0000012526.73211.cd

Krause, N. (2012). Feelings of gratitude toward God among older Whites, older African Americans, and older Mexican Americans. *Research on Aging, 34,* 156–173. http://dx.doi.org/10.1177/0164027511417884

Leadership Conference on Civil Rights (May 2000). *Justice on trial: Racial disparities in the American criminal justice system.* Retrieved from http://www.protectcivilrights.org/pdf/reports/justice.pdf

Lewis, R., & Taylor, J. (2009). The social significance of religious resources in the prediction of mattering to others: African American and White contrasts. *Sociological Spectrum, 29,* 273–294. http://dx.doi.org/10.1080/02732170802584484

Lincoln, C., & Mamiya, L. (1990). *The Black church in the African American experience.* Durham, NC: Duke University Press. http://dx.doi.org/10.1215/9780822381648

Luthar, S. S., Cicchetti, D., & Becker, B. (2000). The construct of resilience: A critical evaluation and guidelines for future work. *Child Development, 71,* 543–562. http://dx.doi.org/10.1111/1467-8624.00164

Mattis, J. S. (2002). Religion and spirituality in the meaning making and coping experiences of African American women: A qualitative analysis. *Psychology of Women Quarterly, 26,* 309–320. http://dx.doi.org/10.1111/1471-6402.t01-2-00070

Mattis, J. S., Beckham, W., Saunders, B., Williams, J., McAllister, D., Myers, V., . . . Dixon, C. (2004). Who will volunteer? Religiosity, everyday racism and social participation among African American men. *Journal of Adult Development, 11,* 261–272. http://dx.doi.org/10.1023/B:JADE.0000044529.92580.6d

Mattis, J. S., Fontenot, D., & Hatcher-Kay, C. (2003). Religiosity, racism and dispositional optimism among African Americans. *Personality and Individual Differences*, *34*, 1025–1038. http://dx.doi.org/10.1016/S0191-8869(02)00087-9

Mattis, J. S., Fontenot, D., Hatcher-Kay, C., Grayman, N., & Beale, R. (2004). Religiosity, optimism and pessimism among African Americans. *Journal of Black Psychology*, *30*, 187–207. http://dx.doi.org/10.1177/0095798403260730

Mattis, J. S., Grayman, N., Cowie, S., Winston, C., Watson, C., & Jackson, D. (2008). Intersectional identities and the politics of altruistic care in a low-income, urban community. *Sex Roles*, *59*, 418–428. http://dx.doi.org/10.1007/s11199-008-9426-2

Mattis, J. S., Mitchell, N., Zapata, A., Grayman, N. A., Taylor, R. J., Chatters, L. M., & Neighbors, H. W. (2007). Uses of ministerial support by African Americans: A focus group study. *American Journal of Orthopsychiatry*, *77*, 249–258. http://dx.doi.org/10.1037/0002-9432.77.2.249

Mattis, J. S., Powell Hammond, W., Grayman, N., Cowie, S., Bonacci, M., Brennan, W., & Massie, D. (2009). The social production of altruism: Motivations for caring action in a low-income community. *American Journal of Community Psychology*, *43*, 71–84. http://dx.doi.org/10.1007/s10464-008-9217-5

Mays, V. M., Cochran, S. D., & Rhue, S. (1993). The impact of perceived discrimination on the intimate relationships of black lesbians. *Journal of Homosexuality*, *25*(4), 1–14. http://dx.doi.org/10.1300/J082v25n04_01

McAdams, D. P., Reynolds, J., Lewis, M., Patten, A. H., & Bowman, P. J. (2001). When bad things turn good and good things turn bad: Sequences of redemption and contamination in life narrative and their relation to psychosocial adaptation in midlife adults and in students. *Personality and Social Psychology Bulletin*, *27*, 474–485. http://dx.doi.org/10.1177/0146167201274008

McKenzie, B. D. (2004). Religious social networks, indirect mobilization, and African-American political participation. *Political Research Quarterly*, *57*, 621–632. http://dx.doi.org/10.1177/106591290405700410

McLoyd, V. C. (1990). The impact of economic hardship on black families and children: Psychological distress, parenting, and socioemotional development. *Child Development*, *61*, 311–346. http://dx.doi.org/10.2307/1131096

Molock, S. D., Puri, R., Matlin, S., & Barksdale, C. (2006). Relationship between religious coping and suicidal behaviors among African American adults. *Journal of Black Psychology*, *32*, 366–389. http://dx.doi.org/10.1177/0095798406290466

Moreland, C., & Leach, M. M. (2001). The relationship between racial identity and moral development. *Journal of Black Psychology*, *27*, 255–271. http://dx.doi.org/10.1177/0095798401027003001

Musick, M., Wilson, J., & Bynum, W. (2000). Race and formal volunteering: The differential effects of class and religion. *Social Forces*, *78*, 1539–1570. http://dx.doi.org/10.1093/sf/78.4.1539

Myers, L. J. (2013). Restoration of spirit: An African-centered communal health model. *Journal of Black Psychology, 39,* 257–260. http://dx.doi.org/10.1177/0095798413478080

Neblett, E. W., Jr., Shelton, J. N., & Sellers, R. M. (2004). The role of racial identity in managing daily racial hassles. In G. Philogène (Ed.), *Racial identity in context: The legacy of Kenneth B. Clark* (pp. 77–90). Washington, DC: American Psychological Association.

Neblett, E. W., Jr., Smalls, C. P., Ford, K. R., Nguyên, H. X., & Sellers, R. M. (2009). Racial socialization and racial identity: African American parents' messages about race as precursors to identity. *Journal of Youth and Adolescence, 38,* 189–203. http://dx.doi.org/10.1007/s10964-008-9359-7

Nobles, W. W. (2013). Fundamental task and challenge of Black psychology. *Journal of Black Psychology, 39,* 292–299. http://dx.doi.org/10.1177/0095798413478072

Raboteau, A. J. (1989). Down at the cross: Afro-American spirituality. *U.S. Catholic Historian, 8*(1/2), 33–38.

Rest, J. (1979). *Development in judging moral issues.* Minneapolis: University of Minnesota Press.

Roberts, D. (1997). *Killing the Black body: Race, reproduction, and the meaning of liberty.* New York, NY: Pantheon Books.

Sahgal, N., & Smith, G. (2009). *A religious portrait of African-Americans.* Retrieved from http://www.pewforum.org/2009/01/30/a-religious-portrait-of-african-americans/

Schmeichel, B. J., & Baumeister, R. F. (2004). Self-regulatory strength. In R. F. Baumeister & K. D. Vohs (Eds.), *Handbook of self-regulation: Research, theory, and applications* (pp. 84–98). New York, NY: Guilford Press.

Sellers, R. M., Rowley, S. A., Chavous, T. M., Shelton, J. N., & Smith, M. A. (1997). Multidimensional Inventory of Black Identity: A preliminary investigation of reliability and construct validity. *Journal of Personality and Social Psychology, 73,* 805–815. http://dx.doi.org/10.1037/0022-3514.73.4.805

Simons, T., Friedman, R., Liu, L. A., & McLean Parks, J. (2007). Racial differences in sensitivity to behavioral integrity: Attitudinal consequences, in-group effects, and "trickle down" among Black and non-Black employees. *Journal of Applied Psychology, 92,* 650–665. http://dx.doi.org/10.1037/0021-9010.92.3.650

Smetana, J., & Metzger, A. (2005). Family and religious antecedents of civic involvement in middle class African American late adolescents. *Journal of Research on Adolescence, 15,* 325–352. http://dx.doi.org/10.1111/j.1532-7795.2005.00099.x

Smith, H. L., Fabricatore, A., & Peyrot, M. (1999). Religiosity and altruism among African American males: The Catholic experience. *Journal of Black Studies, 29,* 579–597. http://dx.doi.org/10.1177/002193479902900407

Stanik, C. E., McHale, S. M., & Crouter, A. C. (2013). Gender dynamics predict changes in marital love among African American couples. *Journal of Marriage and Family, 75,* 795–807. http://dx.doi.org/10.1111/jomf.12037

Stevenson, H. C., Davis, G., & Abdul-Kabir, S. (2001). *Stickin' to, watchin' over, and getting' with: An African American parent's guide to discipline*. San Francisco, CA: Jossey-Bass.

Stewart, C. F., III. (1996). *Street corner theology*. Nashville, TN: James Winston.

Tadman, M. (1989). *Speculators and slaves: Masters, traders, and slaves in the Old South*. Madison: University of Wisconsin Press.

Thomas, H. (1999). *The slave trade: The story of the Atlantic slave trade, 1440–1870*. New York, NY: Simon & Schuster.

Thompson, G. L. (2013). African American women and the US criminal justice system: A statistical survey. *The Journal of African American History, 98*, 291–303.

Tucker, C., Dixon, A., & Griddine, K. (2010). Academically successful African American male urban high school students' experiences of mattering to others at school. *Professional School Counseling, 14*, 135–145. http://dx.doi.org/10.5330/prsc.14.2.k215671rj018g134

Tyson, S. Y. (2012). Developmental and ethnic issues experienced by emerging adult African American women related to developing a mature love relationship. *Issues in Mental Health Nursing, 33*, 39–51. http://dx.doi.org/10.3109/01612840.2011.620681

U.S. Census Bureau. (2010). *Statistical abstracts of the United States*. Washington, DC: Author.

U.S. Census Bureau, Statistical Abstract of the United States. (2012a). *Table 104. Expectation of Life at Birth, 1970 to 2008, and Projections, 2010 to 2020*. Retrieved from http://www2.census.gov/library/publications/2011/compendia/statab/131ed/tables/vitstat.pdf

U.S. Census Bureau, Statistical Abstracts of the United States. (2012b). *Table 229 Educational Attainment by Race and Hispanic Origin: 1970 to 2010*. Retrieved from http://www2.census.gov/library/publications/2011/compendia/statab/131ed/tables/educ.pdf

Utsey, S., Hook, J., Fischer, N., & Belvet, B. (2008). Cultural orientation, ego resilience, and optimism as predictors of subjective well-being in African Americans. *The Journal of Positive Psychology, 3*, 202–210. http://dx.doi.org/10.1080/17439760801999610

Van Sertima, I. (1976). *They came before Columbus: The African presence in ancient America*. New York, NY: Random House.

Vereen, L. G., Hill, N. R., & Butler, S. K. (2013). The use of humor and storytelling with African American men: Innovative therapeutic strategies for success in counseling. *International Journal for the Advancement of Counselling, 35*, 57–63. http://dx.doi.org/10.1007/s10447-012-9165-5

Walsh, F. (2003). Family resilience: A framework for clinical practice. *Family Process, 42*(1), 1–18. http://dx.doi.org/10.1111/j.1545-5300.2003.00001.x

Ward, J. V. (1991). "Eyes in the back of your head": Moral themes in African American narratives of racial conflict. *Journal of Moral Education, 20*, 267–281. http://dx.doi.org/10.1080/0305724910200304

Watkins, M. (1994). *On the real side: Laughing, lying, and signifying—The underground tradition of African American humor that transformed American culture, from slavery to Richard Pryor.* New York, NY: Simon & Schuster.

White-Johnson, R. L. (2012). Prosocial involvement among African American young adults: Considering racial discrimination and racial identity. *Journal of Black Psychology, 38,* 313–341. http://dx.doi.org/10.1177/0095798411420429

Woods, L. N., & Jagers, R. J. (2003). Are cultural values predictors of moral reasoning in African American adolescents? *Journal of Black Psychology, 29,* 102–118. http://dx.doi.org/10.1177/0095798402239231

Yacker, N., & Weinberg, S. L. (1990). Care and justice moral orientation: A scale for its assessment. *Journal of Personality Assessment, 55,* 18–27.

Zimmerman, B. J., & Schunk, D. H. (2011). Self-regulated learning and performance: An introduction and an overview. In B. J. Zimmerman & D. H. Schunk (Eds.), *Handbook of self-regulation of learning and performance. Educational psychology handbook series* (pp. 1–12). New York, NY: Routledge/Taylor & Francis Group.

6

POSITIVE PSYCHOLOGY IN AMERICAN INDIANS

GAYLE SKAWENNIO MORSE, JULIE GUAY McINTYRE, AND JEFF KING

Much has been written about the plight of American Indians and Alaska Natives (AI/ANs). Even those not familiar with this literature are most likely aware of the high rates of alcoholism, poverty, and unemployment and their consequences for AI/AN children and adults. However, far less has been written about Native people's strength and resilience and how their worldview and traditional practices may be central to their psychological and physical health.

Positive psychology, health psychology, and Native American studies are somewhat disparate fields, and most readers may be more familiar with one than another. Beginning with his presidential address to the American Psychological Association in 1999, Seligman called for a refocusing in psychology from a maladjustment and pathology perspective to a more optimistic strength-based view (Fowler, Seligman, & Koocher, 1999). Thus, the subfield

http://dx.doi.org/10.1037/14799-006
Positive Psychology in Racial and Ethnic Groups: Theory, Research, and Practice, E. C. Chang, C. A. Downey, J. K. Hirsch, and N. J. Lin (Editors)

of positive psychology was born. Although much literature existed before this time in areas such as optimism and positive affect, the positive psychology movement integrated this work and sparked further interest. As Taylor and Sherman (2004) so aptly noted, "health psychology has been an arena in which the contributions of positive psychology have been evident, yielding insights that, in turn, have helped to refine the theories that gave birth to applications" (p. 305). A perusal of most health psychology textbooks quickly reveals that culture is relegated to a mere paragraph or feature box; AIs often are not mentioned at all. Indeed, the entire 2012 special issue of the flagship journal *Health Psychology* focused on ethnic disparities in health and made no mention of AIs.

This chapter brings together positive psychology and health psychology research findings as they relate to various types of coping strategies used by AI/AN people. Beginning with an overview of the history and demographics of AIs, and using Native American stories to illustrate central positive psychology themes, we explore potential pathways to psychological and physical health. We conclude with areas for future research.

OVERVIEW OF HISTORY AND DEMOGRAPHICS OF AMERICAN INDIANS AND ALASKA NATIVES

AIs have inhabited North America for thousands of years. They may often refer to themselves as *Native*; however, this can be complicated because many people born in the United States of European descent refer to themselves as native as well. Therefore, we refer to the people we discuss in this chapter as *American Indians* (AIs) and *Alaska Natives* (ANs) or the inclusive *AI/ANs*. Consistent with U.S. Census data and terminology, we refer to those of European ancestry as *White*.

According the U.S. Census Bureau (2012), there are currently 5,200,000 AI/ANs in the lower 48 states and Alaska—about 1.7% of the U.S. population at the time of the census. Often they are thought of as one vast homogeneous group, yet this highly heterogeneous culture incorporates more than 550 tribes and 300 language families (Black, 2012). One common way to understand this vast group is to categorize them into geographic regions. For example, tribes from similar regions such as Northeast Woodland, Northern Plains, Southwest, or Northwest Coast typically share common backgrounds and languages. However, substantial variation in language and cultural tradition is found even within these categories. Furthermore, not all AI/ANs identify with their AI status (Phinney, 1992); therefore, merely asking individuals to self-identify does not provide evidence of their level of ethnic group identification, cultural pride, or participation in cultural activities (Trimble, 1991; Trimble, Helms, & Root, 1991). At this time AI/ANs live in all areas across the United States. The nine largest populations are located in California, Oklahoma, Arizona, Texas, New York, New Mexico, Washington, North Carolina, and Florida (U.S. Census Bureau, 2012). Currently up to 67% of AI/ANs who solely identify as such live outside of AI/AN reservations or territories. For example, as part of the Indian Relocation Act of 1956, many AI/ANs were relocated to cities. In 2015, the cities with the five largest populations of AI/ANs are New York, New York; Phoenix, Arizona; Oklahoma City, Oklahoma; Anchorage, Alaska; and Tulsa, Oklahoma, all primarily due to the Indian Relocation Act of 1956.

Despite the wide distribution of AI/ANs, research including AI/ANs may be difficult to obtain for two primary reasons. First, the dispersion of AI/AN people in numerous small, isolated groups means that it might not be economically feasible to collect data from them. As a result, some groups are missed or even deliberately not included. Second, because there are so few AI/ANs in the United States relative to the general population, it is often difficult to accrue a large enough sample for meaningful conclusions to be made. For example, the National Health and Nutrition Examination Survey, a survey research program conducted by the National Center for Health Statistics, was designed to assess the health and nutritional status of adults and children in the United States. This study tracked changes over time and was one of the largest health questionnaires used in the United States, yet it did not have large enough numbers of AI/ANs to report significant findings on many of the measures (Barnes, Adams, & Powell-Grineer, 2010). However, other research indicated that even with the paucity of data on AI/ANs, the surprisingly consistent finding is that they show poorer health outcomes, such as higher rates of diabetes, smoking, and drinking; unmet medical needs (in particular, because of cost); and more psychological distress than any other group in the United States (Barnes et al., 2010). One positive exception is that the incidence of breast cancer for AI/AN women is the lowest of all groups (Centers for Disease Control and Prevention, 2014).

It is imperative that clinicians working with AI/ANs understand the unique strengths and belief systems of this population that support their lifeways and help them face the challenges in their lives. Available data show that AI/ANs experience higher rates of posttraumatic stress disorder, depression, and suicide than the general population (Beals et al., 2005). Those who have been resilient in the face of these challenges have used ceremony, sweat lodge, and wisdom gained through vision quests, sun dances, and other traditional practices that emphasize spiritual strength and endurance through hard times. The strength of the community also provides support and understanding within a shared worldview. In particular, it is important to understand the ubiquitous interconnectedness of the physical, mental, spiritual, and emotional realms for AI/ANs. The Medicine Wheel represents their circular thinking about the interconnectedness of the four sacred directions and the intertwining of affect, cognitions, behaviors, and spirituality. The Medicine Wheel goes from the East (Spiritual), to the South (Emotional), to the West (Physical), and to the North (Cognitions). The directions are seen as being so inextricably linked and interconnected that it is impossible to separate them (Bopp, Brown, & Lane, 1989). An understanding of the symbolism of the Medicine Wheel can help practitioners who work with AI/AN populations have a better grasp of the holistic view that many AI/AN people have of their health and thus develop better treatment plans.

In this chapter, we integrate research published in a wide range of disciplines that have considered the strategies AI/ANs use to cope with a variety of stressors, in particular, their resilience. We hope that this chapter gives readers a better understanding of the factors associated with their resilience and how Native culture contributes to that resilience. Resilience is often considered the "inner strength that helps individuals bounce back and carry on in the face of adversity" (Anisnabe Kekandzone, n.d.). We focus on several positive psychology themes that are most relevant to the worldview and traditions of AI/ANs. The application of positive psychology theory and research to the AI/AN literature highlights the difficulty of separating the four sacred directions: spiritual, physical, emotional, and cognitive.

VALUE OF POSITIVE PSYCHOLOGY FOR AMERICAN INDIANS AND ALASKA NATIVES

To provide a context for the challenges AI/ANs have faced in the past and continue to face today, much work has focused on the construct of historical trauma. Brave Heart (1999) defined *historical trauma* as a "collective psychological scar resulting from the experience of violence, land loss, culture, discrimination and marginalization" (p. 10) that resulted from European colonialism. Duran, Duran, Brave Heart, and Yellow Horse-Davis (1998) referred to historical trauma as "soul wound." Despite U.S. government efforts to wipe out any trace of traditional culture—efforts that have included such acts as genocide, eugenics, and compulsory boarding school attendance—AI/ANs continued to survive because they are resilient and persevering (Gonzales, Kertész, & Tayac, 2007; Whitbeck, Adams, Hoyt, & Chen, 2004). Although no discussion of Native peoples is complete without acknowledging the egregious horrors that they have endured, in this chapter we focus on what makes them resilient, what has sustained them through these periods of violence and colonialism. AI/ANs rely on their spiritual resources, their connection to family and community, their ubiquitous humor, the wisdom of their elders, and the teachings of the ancestors as means to persevere in the face of overwhelming oppression. Most of the time, they kept these things hidden from their oppressors. When their ceremonies were outlawed, they went underground with them. These resources have provided a strength that has helped them endure severe hardships.

THEORY AND RESEARCH ON POSITIVE OUTLOOK/AFFECT OF AMERICAN INDIANS AND ALASKA NATIVES

Positive psychology dimensions among AI/ANs are constructed very differently than they are in Western society. Whereas Western society starts with the individual for identity and well-being, AI/ANs start with the many relationships within the cultural collective ecosystem. Satisfaction with social relationships is a more important predictor of subjective well-being in collectivist cultures than in individualist cultures (Tam, Lau, & Jiang, 2012). In contrast, in individualist countries, self-esteem needs more strongly predict global life satisfaction (Oishi, Diener, Lucas, & Suh, 1999). In the AI/AN cultural worldview, well-being is viewed as keeping oneself and the community in balance and harmony. This balance is maintained within physical, mental, emotional, and relational well-being dimensions, and may often include balance with the land and all that is part of it. Well-being is intricately tied to community and belonging to part of something bigger than oneself. This worldview and its components are consistent with the core elements of positive psychology methodology, theory, and intervention. As Waller (2001) noted, culture fuels the relationship among the individual, community, and environment. Thus, we can infer that cultural components affect resilience. Indeed, research with AI/ANs has indicated that protective factors for positive outcomes include family, community, and culture (Brockmeier & Carbaugh, 2001). More specific cultural factors that promote resiliency include spirituality, family, respect for elders, ceremonial rituals, oral traditions, tribal identity, traditional healing practices, and other social support networks (Brockmeier & Carbaugh, 2001; LaFromboise, Hoyt, Oliver, & Whitbeck, 2006; Waller, 2001). This interactive perspective highlights how the AI/AN worldview is related to resilience, which has been critical in the survival of AI/ANs, and why it is important to understand this cultural context relative to positive psychology.

Meaning-Making, Connection to the Universe, and Well-Being

Address of Thanksgiving
   To be a human being is an honor, and we offer thanksgiving for all
the gifts of life.
   Mother Earth, we thank you for giving us everything we need. The
deep blue water, the soft green grass, the sweet colorful berries, the four-
legged brothers and sisters, the shady, leafy trees, the winged brothers and
sisters, the four direction winds, Grandfather Thunder, Elder Brother
Sun, Mother Earth, Grandmother Moon, the twinkling stars, and the
spirit protectors. (Swamp, 1995)

One strength of AI/AN peoples is their commitment to shared narrative, and how passing these narratives down through the generations furthers
a legacy of wisdom about living well. In fact, the AI/AN worldview may be
understood through stories from their oral tradition. One important Iroquois
statement is the daily Address of Thanksgiving, which speaks of the human
connection to nature and the world. Used in a variety of individual and group
contexts, these words serve as a powerful reminder of what life means.

In AI/AN culture stories may help explain the indigenous worldview
by highlighting symbolic meanings in everyday life; AI/ANs also build narratives or self-stories to define and help understand their lives. This is similar
to *meaning-making*, which is defined as a self-protective cognitive process by
which individuals use information based on their own experiences and biases
(Cacioppo, Hawkley, Rickett, & Masi, 2005). AI/AN narratives are significant bits and pieces from lived experience rather than objective, written facts,
and they can have a significant impact on well-being. Thus, they create both
lesson-laden stories and a deep sense of meaning (McLean, Pasupathi, &
Pals, 2007). For example, the Inuit story (that has various versions) of "The
Woman Who Would Not Take a Mate" tells of a woman who lost everything
by being dragged by polar bears into the sea. The fish ate her flesh, and only
a skeleton remained. She found her way to land but had no fire, no igloo
to protect her from the cold, no furs to sleep on or to keep her warm. Deep
within herself, she thought, "I guess I will just have to hope." After saying
this to herself, she caught sight of an igloo, where she took shelter. The story
goes on to show how she held on to hope despite the bleakness of her situation, yet in the end her flesh is restored, she is back in relationship, and she is
much wiser. There are many messages within this story, but the main theme
of hoping and remaining positive when there is absolutely nothing visible to
give you this hope is a powerful message about endurance.

A large body of work shows a relation between negative experience and
meaning-making (e.g., McAdams, 2006; McLean & Pratt, 2006; McLean &
Thorne, 2003; Pals, 2006; Thorne, 2004). Researchers have suggested that

when disruption occurs, people may be motivated to resolve the negativity or disruption by narrating the experience to gain insight. Furthermore, even talking or writing about negative events seems to be particularly beneficial not only to well-being (Lyubomirsky, Sousa, & Dickerhoof, 2006) but also to physical health outcomes (Pennebaker & Beall, 1986; Pennebaker, Kiecolt-Glaser, & Glaser, 1988; Pennebaker & Seagal, 1999). Most of the research on narratives and how they are shaped by culture has been conducted with Western European Americans. Brockmeier and Carbaugh (2001) found that AI/ANs narratives are based on a type of cultural discourse that includes history, identity, social drama, and lessons for managing intercultural dynamics, cultural preservation, and resistance. Furthermore, researchers suggest that the ancestral view of connectedness is more powerful than the more modern view of independent individualism (Cacioppo et al., 2005). For example, in the Mohawk ceremony, the opening address usually ends in *Onen ska'nikonra onton* or "Now there is one mind." This emphasizes the connectedness and unity of the Mohawk people in important matters (Porter, 2008).

Meaning-making can also help us understand the health beliefs of AI/ANs. AI/ANs traditionally believe that humans and the natural world are inextricably linked. Whereas the Western view is that humans are superior to creation, AI/ANs view themselves as equal to creation. *Mitakuye oyas'in!* ("all my relatives" or "we are all related") is a Lakota expression that exemplifies this, meaning that all aspects of nature are relatives and should be treated equally (Voss, Douville, Little Soldier, & Twiss, 1999). This primary view forms an integral part of AI/AN health beliefs. For example, Navajos call this worldview of everything in life being interconnected *hózhó*, meaning "walking in beauty." Sickness, according to this belief, results from the various influences becoming out of balance (Alvord & Van Pelt, 2000). The AI/AN worldview of interconnectedness of everything and being part of something bigger than oneself dovetails nicely with much of positive psychology theory (Wong, 2011). Furthermore, for many AI/AN cultures, the goal in life is not happiness but to live life well. The pursuit of happiness can lead to avoidant behavior, disappointment, frustration, and depression when difficult times occur (Mauss, Tamir, Anderson, & Savino, 2011). "To live life well" embodies these difficult experiences and encourages one to face them with courage and integrity. In the Mohawk belief system, people are taught to strive for *Skennen* (Peace based on social and political consciousness) and *Kariwiio* (Good Mind by eliminating prejudice, privilege, and superiority) with the outcome of *Kastasensera* (Strength; Santiago-Rivera, Skawennio Morse, Hunt, & Lickers, 1998). Tasunka Witko (Crazy Horse) was a holy man of the Lakota who is believed to have said, "Today is a good day to die," a statement that epitomizes this philosophy. It is a belief that one should never live a moment of one's life with any regrets or tasks left undone. Doing so would make today, regardless of circumstances, as good a day as any to die.

Humor and Well-Being

AI/ANs find meaning and foster community connectedness through humor, the ability to view an experience as amusing as a means of improving one's mood or to mask one's pain (Bryant-Davis, 2005). Humor plays many roles in AI/AN communities, such as connecting to community, indirect correction of unhealthy behaviors and attitudes, problem solving, emotion management, and spiritual exploration (M. T. Garrett, Garrett, Torres-Rivera, Wilbur, & Roberts-Wilbur, 2005). AI/ANs may also use humor a strategy for stepping back and looking at a problem in a different way in a community setting (M. T. Garrett et al., 2005; Hill, 2006). Humor serves as a powerful coping strategy for enhancing psychological well-being and various aspects of health (Bennett & Lengacher, 2006; Kuiper & Nicholl, 2004; Svebak, Kristoffersen, & Aasarod, 2006). As Mohawk Spiritual Leader Sakokwenionkwas explained,

> Whenever something traumatic or sad happens, we have to find something to laugh at. That's what will get us through. And the Indian people, we are professionals at making jokes about our own selves, at how crazy we are. It keeps us going. (Porter, 2008, p. 156)

M. T. Garrett et al. (2005) stated that Native humor is a spiritual tradition that is a powerful healing force. Indeed, Fredrickson (1998) suggested that humor might "undo" some of the ill effects of life stressors and build a stronger foundation for AI/ANs. M. T. Garrett et al. (2005) posited that Native forms of humor contributed significantly to surviving the horrors of the AI Holocaust, persecution, and oppression. In an interview, AI novelist Louise Erdrich stated, "It's impossible to write about Native life without humor—that's how people maintain sanity" (Bacon, 2001). As a cognitive problem-solving technique, humor ties together the constructs of spirituality, resilience, community connectedness, group identity, and emotional regulation. More specifically, humor may provide a means of working out feelings of sadness, happiness, joy, loss, and fear; the distress of tragedies; ways of connecting to community members; and ways to depower persecutors (Dean, 2003; M. T. Garrett et al., 2005).

Humor is such a core part of AI/AN daily life that it is even used in teaching life lessons. For example, humor can be used to manage behavior by reminding someone who appears arrogant to be humble (Wetsit, 1999). When a person displays arrogance or superiority, he or she is reminded to have humility and not to have too much pride (Karihiosta Thomas, personal communication, July 1992). A good example of this are the Koshares, the sacred clowns of the Pueblo, who often make fun of leaders in the community during feast days or other ceremonies, reminding all that no one is superior to another.

THEORY AND RESEARCH ON POSITIVE COGNITIONS OF AMERICAN INDIANS AND ALASKAN NATIVES

That is the hardest thing for Indians to do, or anybody that's colonized to do, is to get back their freedom, the real freedom to think, be thinkers again. (Sakokwenionkwas, in Porter, 2008)

Traditional Native practices and beliefs define the connection between humans and the natural world. They also fit within the positive psychology framework as ways to provide connectedness, meaning, and purpose to our human role in the world. Believing that one is connected to nature is associated with well-being, which is consistent with the AI/AN worldview of the deep human connection to the natural world (Howell, Dopko, Turowski, & Buro, 2011). The AI worldview of spirituality, existence, and community may also be understood through the lens of AI/AN creation stories. The Iroquois creation story "Woman Who Fell from the Sky" is replete with examples of community harmony, interaction with nature, persistence, and resilience. In this story, all the creatures in the world band together to save a woman who falls through a hole in the sky and together build the world as we now know it. Although each tribe has its own story of how humanity began, each story expresses the AI/AN way of thinking about spirituality, physical health, mental health, and emotions, all of which are community concerns.

As described by Keyes (2002), mental health is characterized by a subjective sense of well-being or optimism and positive feelings or emotions. For example, the broaden and build theory posits that positive emotions broaden awareness and build upon learning to build future emotional resources (Fredrickson, 1998). According to Fredrickson's undo hypothesis, the broadening effect of positive emotions could serve to undo the effects of negative emotions (Fredrickson et al., 2000). This research showed that the positive emotion of contentment undid the effects of the negative emotion of anxiety using cardiac reactivity as an outcome measure. In addition, a recent study with individuals in late adulthood found that happiness seemed to "undo" the negative effects of loneliness on activity level and mortality (Newall, Chipperfield, Bailis, & Stewart, 2013). Among Native American elders, optimism was related to better health outcomes (Ruthig & Allery, 2008). The researchers found that "health optimists" who rate their health positively, despite having objectively poor health had fewer difficulties with activities of daily living, got more exercise, were hospitalized less, and were more socially engaged than their "health pessimist" counterparts. Expanding upon the broaden and build theory, it is likely that Native people have long understood that humor—as a component of positive feelings—undoes some of the ill effects of life stressors and builds a stronger foundation for AI/ANs, as individuals and as communities.

More broadly, in Native communities the holistic view of health includes family and community support as part of the whole person, not as a separate entity. Walters, Simoni, and Evans-Campbell (2002) outlined an indigenist stress-coping model, which included family and community, spirituality and traditional practices, and attitudes about group identity. Data indicated that these more holistic and inclusive ways of coping might provide greater support for resilience in AI/AN communities (Mohatt, Fok, Burket, Henry, & Allen, 2011). Consistent with the core notions of the broaden and build theory, the AI/AN understanding of coping as an integral, holistic function anchored in community, family, spirituality, and traditional practices is supported by the coping and resilience research findings, which have indicated that children and women who experienced abuse in their lifetime had better outcomes when they experienced social support in coping with these abuses than those who had not received support (Walters et al., 2002).

As stated in the indigenist stress-coping model, spirituality within the AI/AN world is an integral part of resilience and coping and can be viewed as a belief or connection, as something that is an all-powerful force bigger than the self (LaFromboise et al., 2006; Walters et al., 2002). Shults and Sandage (2006) defined *spirituality* as "ways of relating to the sacred" (p. 161). "Spirituality is not just seen as at the core, but rather infused throughout all ways of life" (King & Trimble, 2013, p. 24). Spirituality is also distinct from religion, though it is a component of religion and often institutionalized into a form of religion (Graham, 2002). Verghese (2008) indicated that the lack of spirituality can be an important indicator of mental illness and affect regulation. However, even spirituality must not be seen as a single belief system; it varies as much as the different worldviews vary among the tribes. Furthermore, unlike the predominant Western worldview, there is no separation of the physical from the spiritual, mind, or body. Attaining and maintaining a sense of physical, emotional, and communal harmony is central in AI medicine. Today, most AI/ANs use a blend of Western biomedicine, traditional medicine, and spiritualism (Gurung, 2014). The goal of medicine is to bring the four major forces of mind, body, spirit, and context into balance (Hobfoll et al., 2002).

With respect to context, community is an important backdrop for understanding mental health. Community ties can be on reservation lands or in urban areas (U.S. Census Bureau, 2012). One example of community within an urban setting is the American Indian Community Center in New York City, where AI/ANs can find a local community that is supportive and embracing. It is a gathering place to connect with others; a link to useful resources; and a place to explore traditions, to heal, to laugh, and to be nurtured. It provides a community connection without which it might be difficult for individuals to survive far from home communities. Group activities similar to what might take place in the community center or at home on the "rez" emphasize harmony and cooperation, which represent the precedence of the group over the individual (J. T. Garrett & Garrett, 1994). This is very unlike Western views of "Man" as superior to all other beings. In the Native belief system, all people are part of creation, with the main purpose in life being "to care for mother earth and to serve others" (King & Trimble, 2013, p. 12). The connection to mother earth is seen in the Navajo tradition of mourners sprinkling dirt on the casket before burial.

Humility, Gratitude, and Well-Being

To serve others requires a certain amount of humility, an important value nurtured in AI/AN communities. Humility entails a lack of self-focus, an increased awareness, and an appreciation for others (Peterson & Seligman, 2004; Tangney, 2000). Another hallmark of humility is to see others as having the same value and importance as oneself (Peterson & Seligman, 2004; Tangney, 2000). Kruse, Chancellor, Ruberton, and Lyubomirsky (2014) noted that "humility may lead to happiness by making it easier for people to experience gratitude" (p. 11). The Iroquois prophet Seneca reputedly stated, "He who would do great things should not attempt them all alone" (Parker, 1913). Chancellor and Lyubomirsky (2013) suggested that humility may lead to genuine happiness because there is no need to bolster one's own ego or feel threatened by others' success.

All of these areas focus on the person within the community context and how the relationships with the family, community, and the environment all affect the individual's ability to overcome adversity and attain well-being. However, no discussion of how AI/ANs view mental health can be complete without understanding their specific worldview. The AI/AN worldview has been described as a relational one that acknowledges the interconnectedness of everything (Cross, 1997; M. T. Garrett et al., 2005). Mind, body, spirit, environment, universe, and community are all connected and necessary for well-being; it is existing in balance with these interconnected entities that supports resilience and health (King & Trimble, 2013). Thus, the healthy "individual" among many tribes is not viewed in isolation from family, community, or even the land. Among the Muscogee, for example, the words for a healthy individual are *Heyv este hermemahet omet, cemvnice tayet omes*, meaning, "This person is there, a person of good repute, around and available to help." Lakota terminology for well-being is *Tiwahe eyecinka egloiyapi nahan oyate op unpi kte*, meaning "The family moving forward interdependently while embracing the values of generosity and interdependence always with the community in mind." The Diné (Navajo) concept of *hózhó* is similar; it is a much deeper, transcendent word than *well-being*, not easily translatable in English. It implies a unity or balance at all levels of life, including people, community, animals, the spiritual, and the land. In Tewa (Pueblo), the term is *ta e go mah ana thla mah*, translated as "this person is of good demeanor, kind and empathetic to the people and generous to those in need, including the animals" (King, 2009, p. 48).

Positive Coping and Resilience

Resilience is a general term referring to a process of successful adaptation to adversity (Zautra, Hall, & Murray, 2010). Over the past few decades, there has been much debate about how to measure this construct and whether it is a personality trait or an interaction between the person and the environment. Early studies identified a number of factors that were associated with later resilience, and a "second wave of resilience work" focused more on processes variables and contextual issues that included the role of culture (Goldstein & Brooks, 2006, p. 25). In the literature on ethnic and cultural dimensions of resilience, there is little research on AI/ANs, with most focusing on the acculturation process of immigrants and refugees from various countries. Fleming and Ledogar (2008) discussed current definitions of *resilience* applied to Indigenous research: "adaptation despite high risk," "good development despite high risk," "competence under stress," "recovery from trauma," and "normal development under difficult conditions" (p. 8). A qualitative study of tribal college and university students in the Midwest who transferred to 4-year predominantly White colleges found that they were able to succeed despite a lack of community with other AI/AN faculty and students and in the face of ignorance and discrimination they had not encountered at their previous institutions (Makomenaw, 2012). Furthermore, they did not seek out non-Native faculty and peers and took it upon themselves to serve as AI educators. They felt they were making a contribution by educating others about their culture and dispelling myths that perpetuated stereotypes about their people.

Rather than looking at protective factors on an individual level, researchers have tried to understand resilience at the community level. Kirmayer, Sehdev, Whitley, Dandeneau, and Isaac (2009) noted that community resilience can be interpreted as either (a) how people overcome stress, trauma, and other life challenges by drawing from social networks and cultural resources embedded in communities or (b) the ways in which communities themselves exhibit resilience, responding to stresses and challenges in ways that tend to restore their functioning. Healy (2006) defined *cultural resilience* as "the capacity of a distinct community or cultural system to absorb disturbance and reorganize while undergoing change, so as to retain key elements of its structure and identity that preserve its distinctiveness" (p. 10). LaFromboise and colleagues (2006), for example, examined how healing, blessing, and purification ceremonies can counteract the negative experiences of people as a group. Among the challenges of the third wave of research will be to develop interventions and policies that are informed by these cultural, community-derived dimensions of resilience.

DEVELOPING A POSITIVE PSYCHOLOGY AND FUTURE DIRECTIONS FOR AMERICAN INDIANS/ALASKA NATIVES

AI/AN psychology has a great deal to offer positive psychology, and future directions of research in positive psychology would benefit from exploring AI/AN culture, traditions, and lifeways. For example, the emerging health psychology literature regarding AI/ANs, though still limited, has begun to define the strengths of AI/AN traditional health practices, which may lead to better health outcomes. These health practices include cultural values, elders, spiritual practices, and community support (J. T. Garrett & Garrett, 1994).

Research regarding the AI/AN protective factors for resilience might inform the positive psychology literature regarding the importance of cultural identity, traditional health practices, and community support. As Goldstein and Brooks (2006) asserted, the next phase of research on resilience should be the identification of associated cultural factors, which can include research on AI/ANs. Future research must examine the multidimensional nature of cultural identity to better understand how various domains of ethnic self-identification are correlated with well-being. This could further define these dimensions across cultures in terms of culture-specific factors. Trimble (1991) pointed out that most of the social and behavioral science research has grouped participants of different ethnic/racial groups together, thus relying on broad "ethnic glosses." These superficial categories tell little to nothing about the ways that individuals identify (or don't identify) with their cultural heritage and the concomitant outcomes.

As discussed in other chapters in this volume, culturally relevant assessment tools are paramount to collecting data useful for positive psychology theory. Psychometrically sound instruments that measure important positive psychology constructs could be developed further in AI/AN communities. For example, it might be very useful to create AI/AN norms for measures such as the Coping Humor Scale, which is designed to measure the use of humor in coping with life stress (Martin, 1996) or the Connectedness to Nature Scale, which purports to measure an individual's connection to nature (Perrin & Bebassum, 2009; see also Mayer & Frantz, 2004). It may be useful to implement these measures in AI/AN communities in which humor and man's connection to nature are considered important coping mechanisms and then compare the findings with those from other communities where these mechanisms are considered less important. Mohatt et al.'s (2011) assessment of awareness of connectedness as a culturally based protective factor could serve as a prototype for other tribal communities to assess culture-specific sources for resilience and positive coping.

It is clear that assessment must be culturally defined, or at least carefully scrutinized for its cultural applicability. Likewise, interventions must be culturally sensitive. This poses a particular challenge when, in most cases, a non-Native practitioner is likely to be the person working with the AI/AN population. For example, Ruthig and Allery (2008) recommended motivational interviewing as a way to increase health optimism and reduce health pessimism. *Motivational interviewing* is "a collaborative conversation style for strengthening a person's own motivation and commitment to change" (p. 12). Further research is needed on how this technique might be used in various settings to best help AI/ANs change unhealthy behaviors and beliefs. Using AI/AN perspectives that include family, community, notions of balance, connection, harmony, and land can improve upon existing assessment instruments and pave the way for new, creative, and holistic perspectives to be integrated into our ways of evaluation and assessing.

In summary, there is little research in the area of AI/AN culture and positive psychology. However, there are oral histories and traditional stories in AI/AN culture that suggest a positive approach to living, which is consistent with positive psychology theory. Further research would help practitioners understand the underpinnings of positive psychology constructs such as resilience in AI/AN communities.

REFERENCES

Alvord, L. A., & Van Pelt, E. C. (2000). *The scalpel and the silver bear: The first Navajo woman surgeon combines western medicine and traditional healing*. New York, NY: Bantam Books.

Anisnabe Kekandzone. (n.d.). *Building resilience in Aboriginal communities*. Retrieved from http://akneahr.ciet.org/publications/resilience/

Bacon, K. (2001, January). An emissary of the between-world. *The Atlantic*. Retrieved from http://www.theatlantic.com/past/docs/unbound/interviews/int2001-01-17.htm

Barnes, P. M., Adams, P. F., & Powell-Grineer, E. (2010). Health characteristics of the America Indian or Alaska Native adult population: United States, 2004–2008. *National Health Statistics Reports, 20*, 1–7. Retrieved from http://www.cdc.gov/nchs/data/nhsr/nhsr020.pdf

Beals, J., Novins, D. K., Whitesell, N. R., Spicer, P., Mitchell, C. M., & Manson, S. M. (2005). Prevalence of mental disorders and utilization of mental health services in two American Indian reservation populations: Mental health disparities in a national context. *The American Journal of Psychiatry, 162,* 1723–1733.

Bennett, M. P., & Lengacher, C. A. (2006). Humor and laughter may influence health: II. Complementary therapies and humor in a clinical population. *Evidence-based Complementary and Alternative Medicine, 3,* 187–190. http://dx.doi.org/10.1093/ecam/nel014

Black, M. S. (2012). Indian entities recognized and eligible to receive services from the Bureau of Indian Affairs. *Federal Register, 44,* 47868–47873.

Bopp, J. B. M., Brown, L., & Lane, P. (1989). *The sacred tree.* Alberta, Canada: The Four Worlds Development Project.

Brave Heart, M. Y. H. (1999). Gender differences in the historical trauma response among the Lakota. *Journal of Health and Social Policy, 10*(4), 1–21.

Brockmeier, J., & Carbaugh, D. A. (Eds.). (2001). *Narrative and identity: Studies in autobiography, self and culture.* Amherst, MA: John Benjamins.

Bryant-Davis, T. (2005). Coping strategies of African American adult survivors of childhood violence. *Professional Psychology: Research and Practice, 36,* 409–414.

Cacioppo, J. T., Hawkley, L. C., Rickett, E. M., & Masi, C. M. (2005). Sociality, spirituality, and meaning making: Chicago health, aging, and social relations study. *Review of General Psychology, 9,* 143–155. http://dx.doi.org/10.1037/1089-2680.9.2.143

Centers for Disease Control and Prevention. (2014). *Breast cancer rates by race and ethnicity.* Retrieved from http://www.cdc.gov/cancer/breast/statistics/race.htm

Chancellor, J., & Lyubomirsky, S. (2013). Humble beginnings: Current trends, state perspectives, and hallmarks of humility. *Social and Personality Psychology Compass, 7,* 819–833.

Cross, T. (1997). *Understanding the relational worldview in Indian families.* Retrieved from http://www.nicwa.org/services/techassist/worldview/worldview.htm

Dean, R. A. (2003). Native American humor: Implications for transcultural care. *Journal of Transcultural Nursing, 14*(1), 62–65.

Duran, E., Duran, B., Brave Heart, M. Y. H., & Yellow Horse-Davis, S. (1998). Healing the American Indian soul wound. In Y. Danieli (Ed.), *International handbook of multigenerational legacies of trauma* (pp. 341–354). New York, NY: Plenum Press.

Fleming, J., & Ledogar, R. J. (2008). Resilience, an evolving concept: A review of literature relevant to aboriginal research. *Pimatisiwin, 6*(2), 7–23.

Fowler, R. D., Seligman, M. E. P., & Koocher, G. P. (1999). The APA 1998 annual report. *American Psychologist, 54,* 537–568. http://dx.doi.org/10.1037/0003-066X.54.8.537

Fredrickson, B. L. (1998). What good are positive emotions? *Review of General Psychology, 2,* 300–319.

Fredrickson, B. L., Mancuso, R. A., Branigan, C., & Tugade, M. M. (2000). The undoing effect of positive emotions. *Motivation and Emotion, 24,* 237–258.

Garrett, J. T., & Garrett, M. W. (1994). The path of good medicine: Understanding and counseling Native American Indians. *Journal of Multicultural Counseling and Development, 22*(3), 134–144. http://dx.doi.org/10.1002/j.2161-1912.1994.tb00459.x

Garrett, M. T., Garrett, J. T., Torres-Rivera, E., Wilbur, M., & Roberts-Wilbur, J. (2005). Laughing it up: Native American humor as spiritual tradition. *Journal of Multicultural Counseling and Development, 33*, 194–204. http://dx.doi.org/10.1002/j.2161-1912.2005.tb00016.x

Goldstein, S., & Brooks, R. B. (2006). *Handbook of resilience in children.* New York, NY: Springer.

Gonzales, A., Kertész, J., & Tayac, G. (2007). Eugenics as Indian removal: Sociohistorical processes and the de(con)struction of American Indians in the southeast. *The Public Historian, 29*(3), 53–67. http://dx.doi.org/10.1525/tph.2007.29.3.53

Graham, T. L. C. (2002). Using reasons for living to connect to American Indian healing traditions. *Journal of Sociology and Social Welfare, 29*(1), 55–75.

Gurung, R. A. R. (2014). *Health psychology: A cultural approach.* Belmont, CA: Wadsworth, Cengage.

Healy S. (2006, June). *Cultural resilience, identity and the restructuring of political power in Bolivia.* Presented at the 11th Biennial Conference of the International Association for the Study of Common Property; Bali, Indonesia. Available at http://dlc.dlib.indiana.edu/dlc/handle/10535/1488

Hill, D. L. (2006). Sense of belonging as connectedness, American Indian worldview, and mental health. *Archives of Psychiatric Nursing, 20*(5), 210–216. http://dx.doi.org/10.1016/j.apnu.2006.04.003

Hobfoll, S. E. B., Bansal, A., Schurg, R., Young, S., Pierce, C. A., Hobfoll, I., & Johnson, R. (2002). The impact of perceived child physical and sexual abuse history on Native American women's psychological well-being and AIDS risk. *Journal of Consulting and Clinical Psychology, 70*, 252–257. http://dx.doi.org/10.1037/0022-006X.70.1.252

Howell, A. J., Dopko, R. L., Turowski, J. B., & Buro, K. (2011). The disposition to apologize. *Personality and Individual Differences, 51*, 509–514.

Indian Relocation Act of 1956, Pub. L. No. 959, 70 Stat. 986 (1956).

Keyes, C. L. (2002). The mental health continuum: From languishing to flourishing in life. *Journal of Health and Social Research, 43*, 207–222.

King, J. (2009). Psychotherapy within an American Indian perspective. In M. Gallardo & B. McNeill (Eds.), *Intersections of multiple identities: A casebook of evidence-based practices with diverse populations* (pp. 114–136). Mahwah, NJ: Erlbaum.

King, J., & Trimble, J. E. (2013). The spiritual and sacred among North American Indians and Alaska Natives: Mystery, wholeness, and connectedness in a relational world. In K. I. Pargement, J. Exline, J. Jones, A. Mahoney, & E. Shafranske (Eds.), *APA Handbook of psychology, religion, and spirituality* (Vol. 1, pp. 565–580). Washington, DC: American Psychological Association.

Kirmayer, L. J., Sehdev, M., Whitley, R., Dandeneau, S. F., & Isaac C. (2009). Community resilience: Models, metaphors and measures. *Journal de la santé autochtone*, 62–117.

Kruse, E., Chancellor, J., Ruberton, P. M., & Lyubomirsky, S. (2014). An upward spiral between gratitude and humility. *Social Psychological and Personality Science*, 5, 805–814. http://dx.doi.org/10.1177/1948550614534700

Kuiper, N. A., & Nicholl, S. (2004). Thoughts of feeling better? Sense of humor and physical health humor. *International Journal of Humor Research*, 17(1–2), 37–66. http://dx.doi.org/10.1515/humr.2004.007

LaFromboise, T. D., Hoyt, D. R., Oliver, L., & Whitbeck, L. B. (2006). Family, community, and school influences on resilience among American Indian adolescents in the upper midwest. *Journal of Community Psychology*, 34, 193–209. http://dx.doi.org/10.1002/jcop.20090

Lyubomirsky, S., Sousa, L., & Dickerhoof, R. (2006). The costs and benefits of writing, talking, and thinking about life's triumphs and defeats. *Journal of Personality and Social Psychology*, 90, 4, 692–708.

Makomenaw, M. V. (2012). Welcome to a new world: Experiences of American Indian tribal college and university transfer students at predominately White institutions. *International Journal of Qualitative Studies in Education*, 25, 855–866. http://dx.doi.org/10.1080/09518398.2012.720732

Martin, R. A. (1996). The situation humor response questionnaire and Coping Humor Scale: A decade of research findings. *International Journal of Humor Research*, 9, 251–272.

Mauss, I. B., Tamir, M., Anderson, C. L., & Savino, N. S. (2011). Can seeking happiness make people unhappy? Paradoxical effects of valuing happiness. *Emotion*, 11, 807–815.

Mayer, F. S., & Frantz, C. M. (2004). The connectedness to nature scale: A measure of individuals' feeling in community with nature. *Journal of Environmental Psychology*, 24, 503–515. http://dx.doi.org/10.1016/j.jenvp.2004.10.001

McAdams, D. P. (2006). *The redemptive self? Stories Americans live by*. New York, NY: Oxford University Press.

McLean, K. C., Pasupathi, M., & Pals, J. L. (2007). Selves creating stories creating selves: A process model of self development. *Personality and Social Psychology Review*, 11, 262–278.

McLean, K. C., & Pratt, M. W. (2006). Life's little (and big) lessons: Identity statuses and meaning-making in the turning point narratives of emerging adults. *Developmental Psychology*, 42, 714–722.

McLean, K. C., & Thorne, A. (2003). Adolescents' self-defining memories about relationships. *Developmental Psychology*, 39, 635–645.

Mohatt, N. V., Fok, C. C., Burket, R., Henry, D., & Allen, J. (2011). Assessment of awareness of connectedness as a culturally-based protective factor for Alaska native youth. *Cultural Diversity and Ethnic Minority Psychology*, 17, 444–455. http://dx.doi.org/10.1037/a0025456

Newall, N. E. G., Chipperfield, J. G., Bailis, D. S., & Stewart, T. L. (2013). Consequences of loneliness on physical activity and mortality in older adults and the power of positive emotions. *Health Psychology, 32,* 921–924.

Oishi, S., Diener, E., Lucas, R. E., & Suh, E. M. (1999). Cross-cultural variations in predictors of life satisfaction: Perspectives from needs and values. *Personality and Social Psychology Bulletin, 25,* 980–990.

Pals, J. L. (2006). The narrative identity processing of difficult life experiences: Pathways of personality development and positive self-transformation in adulthood. *Journal of Personality, 74,* 2–31.

Parker, A. C. (1913). *The code of Handsome Lake, the Seneca prophet.* Retrieved from http://www.sacred-texts.com/nam/iro/parker/index.htm

Pennebaker, J. W., & Beall, S. K. (1986). Confronting a traumatic event: Toward and understanding of inhibition and disease. *Journal of Abnormal Psychology, 95,* 274–281.

Pennebaker, J. W., Kiecolt-Glaser, J. K., & Glaser, R. (1988). Disclosure of traumas and immune function: Health implications for psychotherapy. *Journal of Consulting and Clinical Psychology, 56,* 239–245.

Pennebaker, J. W., & Seagal, J. D. (1999). Forming a story: The health benefits of narrative. *Journal of Clinical Psychology, 55,* 1243–1254.

Perrin, J. L., & Bebassum, V. A. (2009). The connectedness to nature scale: A measure of emotional connection to nature? *Journal of Environmental Psychology, 29,* 434–440.

Peterson, C., & Seligman, M. E. P. (2004). *Character strengths and virtues: A handbook and classification.* Washington, DC: American Psychological Association Press and Oxford University Press.

Phinney, J. S. (1992). The multigroup ethnic identity measure: A new scale for use with diverse groups. *Journal of Adolescent Research, 7,* 156–176. http://dx.doi.org/10.1177/074355489272003

Porter, T. (2008). *And grandma said: Iroquois traditions.* Bloomington, IN: XLibras.

Ruthig, J. C., & Allery, A. (2008). Native American elders' health congruence: The role of gender and corresponding functional well-being, hospital admissions, and social engagement. *Journal of Health Psychology, 13,* 1072–1081. http://dx.doi.org/10.1177/1359105308097972

Santiago-Rivera, A. L., Skawennio Morse, G. S., Hunt, A., & Lickers, H. (1998). Building a community-based research partnership: Lessons from the Mohawk Nation of Akwesasne. *Journal of Community Psychology, 26,* 163–174. http://dx.doi.org/10.1002/(SICI)1520-6629(199803)26:2<163::AID-JCOP5>3.0.CO;2-Y

Shults, F. L., & Sandage, S. J. (2006). *Transforming spirituality: Integrating theology and psychology.* Grand Rapids, MI: Baker Academic.

Svebak, S., Kristoffersen, B., & Aasarod, K. (2006). Sense of humor and survival among a county cohort of patients with end-state renal failure: A two year prospective study. *International Journal of Psychiatry Medicine, 36,* 269–281.

Swamp, J. (1995). *Giving thanks: A Native American good morning message*. New York, NY: Lee and Low Books.

Tam, K., Lau, H. P. B., & Jiang, D. (2012). Culture and subjective well-being: A dynamic constructivist view. *Journal of Cross-Cultural Psychology, 43*, 23–31.

Tangney, J. P (2000). Humility: Theoretical perspectives, empirical findings and directions for future research. *Journal of Social and Clinical Psychology, 19*, 70–82.

Taylor, S. E., & Sherman, D. K. (2004). Positive psychology and health psychology: A fruitful liaison. In P. A. Linley & S. Joseph (Eds.), *Positive psychology in practice* (pp. 305–316). Hoboken, NJ: Wiley.

Thorne, A. (2004). Putting the person into social identity. *Human Development, 253*, 1–5.

Trimble, J. E. (1991). Ethnic specification, validation prospects and the future of drug abuse research. *International Journal of the Addiction, 25, 149–169*.

Trimble, J. E., Helms, J. E., & Root, M. P. P. (1991). Social and psychological perspectives on ethnic and racial identity. In G. Bernal, J. E. Trimble, A. K. Burley, & F. T. L. Leong (Eds.), *Handbook of racial and ethnic minority psychology* (pp. 239–275). Thousand Oaks, CA: Sage.

U.S. Census Bureau. (2012). *The American Indian and Alaska native population: 2010*. Washington, DC: U.S. Department of Commerce.

Verghese, A. (2008). Spirituality and mental health. *Indian Journal of Psychiatry, 50*(4), 233–237.

Voss, R., Douville, V., Little Soldier, A., & Twiss, G. (1999). Tribal and shamanic-based social work practice: A Lakota perspective. *Social Work, 44*(3), 228–241.

Waller, M. A. (2001). Resilience in ecosystemic context: Evolution of the concept. *American Journal of Orthopsychiatry, 71*, 290–297. http://dx.doi.org/10.1037/0002-9432.71.3.290

Walters, K. L., Simoni, J. M., & Evans-Campbell, T. (2002). Substance use among American Indians and Alaska natives: Incorporating culture in an "indigenist" stress-coping paradigm. *Public Health Reports, 117*(Suppl. 1), S104–S117.

Wetsit, D. (1999). Effective counseling with American Indian students. In *Next steps: Research and practice to advance Indian education*. Retrieved from http://files.eric.ed.gov/fulltext/ED427910.pdf

Whitbeck, L. B., Adams, G. W., Hoyt, D. R., & Chen, X. (2004). Conceptualizing and measuring historical trauma among American Indian people. *American Journal of Community Psychology, 33*(3–4), 119–130. http://dx.doi.org/10.1023/B:AJCP.0000027000.77357.31

Wong, P. T. P. (2011). Positive psychology 2.0: Towards a balanced interactive model of the good life. *Canadian Psychology, 52*, 69–81.

Zautra, A. J., Hall, J. S., & Murray, K. E. (2010). Resilience: A new definition of health for people and communities. In J. W. Reich, A. J. Zautra, & J. S. Hall (Eds.), *Handbook of adult resilience* (pp. 3–29). New York, NY: Guilford Press.

III

ASSESSMENT

7

POSITIVE PSYCHOLOGY ASSESSMENT IN ASIAN AMERICANS

ELIZABETH A. YU, EDWARD C. CHANG, HONGFEI YANG, AND TINA YU

Asian Americans—who number about 14.6 million and constitute approximately 4% of the U.S. population—are a cultural group that continues to grow rapidly (Humes, Jones, & Ramirez, 2011). It is important to build on the limited literature on psychological problems in this group (Chang, 2012; Chang & Kwon, 2014) and to acknowledge and assess the many positive psychological strengths demonstrated by Asian Americans. Despite facing stressors such as acculturation and discrimination in American society (Alvarez, Juang, & Liang, 2006), Asian Americans have shown incredible signs of resilience in the face of adversity (Pan & Chan, 2007; Yee, DeBaryshe, Yuen, Kim, & McCubbin, 2007). According to Yee et al. (2007), *resilience* is the ability to achieve positive outcomes despite challenging situations by drawing upon resources (e.g., social support, family traditions). In this chapter, we focus on the identification and assessment of a number of positive affective, behavioral, and cognitive variables that contribute to resiliency in Asian Americans.

http://dx.doi.org/10.1037/14799-007
Positive Psychology in Racial and Ethnic Groups: Theory, Research, and Practice, E. C. Chang, C. A. Downey, J. K. Hirsch, and N. J. Lin (Editors)
Copyright © 2016 by the American Psychological Association. All rights reserved.

We address a number of universal positive strengths and pay special attention to indigenous strengths that have emerged through centuries of rich cultural heritage (e.g., philosophies, values). Given the collectivistic culture prevalent in most, if not all, Asian societies, we identify Asian positive strengths not only at the individual level but also at the familial and interpersonal levels. We also identify useful assessment tools for examining the positive psychological strengths of Asian Americans. However, it is important to note the need for further development of effective assessment measures for use in the Asian American population; thus, we conclude the chapter with a discussion of possible future directions for this area.

KEY MEASURES OF POSITIVE AFFECT IN ASIAN AMERICANS

A number of positive affects that apply universally to all groups, regardless of racial or ethnic background, have also been found to apply to Asian Americans. For example, in a broad sense, *positive affectivity*, which reflects how enthusiastic, active, and alert an individual feels (Watson, Clark, & Tellegen, 1988), is an important and universal emotional strength. One of the best-established measures of positive affect is the Positive Affectivity subscale of the Positive and Negative Affect Schedule (Watson et al., 1988), which consists of 10 items (e.g., "interested," "excited," "enthusiastic") for which respondents are asked to rate the way they feel, on average, for each item using a 5-point Likert-type scale ranging from 1 (*very slightly*) to 5 (*extremely*). Some researchers have argued that because of the Asian value of emotional self-control (B. K. Kim, Atkinson, & Yang, 1999; B. K. Kim, Li, & Ng, 2005), Asian Americans differ in their conceptualization of positive, as well as negative, affects compared with European Americans (Wirtz, Chiu, Diener, & Oishi, 2009). However, others have provided empirical evidence of few differences in mean levels, or the functionality, of positive affectivity between these groups (Chang, Tsai, & Sanna, 2010). For example, Chang et al. (2010) found no significant differences between the mean scores of positive affectivity between Asian Americans and European Americans, and they further found that for both groups, positive affectivity was significantly associated with less depressive symptoms and greater life satisfaction. Thus, positive affectivity can be considered to be an important positive affective strength in Asian Americans.

Happiness, or subjective well-being, is a goal of most, if not all, individuals and can be measured using the Subjective Happiness Scale (Lyubomirsky & Lepper, 1999). The Subjective Happiness Scale is a four-item measure of global subjective happiness. Individuals are asked to consider each item and rate where it most appropriately describes them on a 7-point Likert-type scale. For example, one item is "In general, I consider myself": 1 (*not a very happy person*) to 7 (*a very happy person*). W. Tsai, Chang, Sanna, and Herringshaw (2011) found no significant differences in mean scores of depressive symptoms when comparing happy Asian Americans to happy European Americans, supporting the notion that happiness is a universal positive affective strength across ethnic groups.

As with other racial and ethnic groups (e.g., Sprecher, Brooks, & Avogo, 2013), *self-esteem* is an important positive affect for Asian Americans (J. L. Tsai, Ying, & Lee, 2001) and is defined as a global feeling of self-worth (Bednar, Wells, & Peterson, 1989; Rosenberg, 1965). Having higher self-esteem (i.e., more positive regard for oneself) is related to more positive health outcomes (e.g., life satisfaction; Moksnes & Espnes, 2013) and fewer negative health outcomes (e.g., poor sleeping patterns, depression; Lemola, Räikkönen, Gomez, & Allemand, 2013; Orth & Robins, 2013) in most racial and ethnic groups, including Asian Americans (Kiang, Witkow, & Champagne, 2013). The Rosenberg Self-Esteem Scale (Rosenberg, 1965) is a widely used 10-item self-report assessment tool that measures self-esteem, including with Asian Americans (e.g., Kiang, Witkow, & Champagne, 2013; Shek & McEwen, 2012; Wei, Yeh, Chao, Carrera, & Su, 2013). Items assess how an individual generally feels about himself or herself (e.g., "On the whole, I am satisfied with myself," "I feel that I'm a person of worth, at least on an equal plane with others"). Respondents indicate their degree of agreement with each statement on a 4-point Likert-type scale, ranging from 1 (*strongly agree*) to 4 (*strongly disagree*).

In addition to individual self-esteem, *collective self-esteem* is an important marker of positive affectivity; it refers to the worth that an individual attributes to a group they belong to, such as their racial and ethnic group (E. Kim & Lee, 2011). Greater positive regard for one's racial/ethnic group is associated with greater positive health outcomes (e.g., psychological well-being; Crocker, Luhtanen, Blaine, & Brodnax, 1994). One measure of collective self-esteem commonly used with Asian American samples is the Collective Self-Esteem Scale (Luhtanen & Crocker, 1992), a 16-item scale assessing four types of group-focused self-esteem (i.e., membership esteem, private collective self-esteem, public collective self-esteem, and importance to identity). An example item measuring for membership esteem is "I am a worthy member of the social groups I belong to." An example of private collective self-esteem is "In general, I'm glad to be a member of the social groups I belong to." An example of public collective self-esteem is "Overall, my social groups are considered good by others." Finally, an example of importance to identity is "The social groups I belong to are an important reflection of who I am." Respondents indicate the extent to which they agree with each statement using a 7-point Likert-type scale ranging from 1 (*strongly disagree*) to 7 (*strongly agree*). This measure has also been modified to be more race specific by replacing *social group/s* with *race/ethnic group* in each of the items.

In addition to universally common positive affects, culture-specific values strongly influence positive strengths exhibited by Asians and Asian Americans. For example, although happiness is a prototypical example of a universal positive affect, peace of mind may be a better conceptualization of how Asians and Asian Americans understand, manifest, and experience positive affect. *Peace of mind* is defined as an internal state of peacefulness and harmony (Lee, Lin, Huang, & Fredrickson, 2013). The Peace of Mind Scale (Lee, Lin, et al., 2013) is a seven-item measure that assesses the sense of internal peace and ease in daily life (e.g., "My mind is free and at ease"). Items are rated using a 5-point Likert-type scale ranging from 1 (*not at all*) to 5 (*all the time*). Lee, Lin, et al. (2013) found peace of mind to be negatively related to depressive symptoms and positively related to satisfaction with life.

Harmony is an important cultural value of Asians and Asian Americans. Although *harmony* can be defined in many ways, it can be understood to refer to a sense of peace and contentment (Ip, 2014). According to Uba (1994), Asians and Asian Americans strive for the positive affect of harmony in everyday life, especially in relationships with others. Harmony, as an affect, can be measured with the Harmony subscale of the Cross-Cultural Personality Assessment Inventory-2 (Cheung, Cheung, & Zhang, 2004), a 14-item measure of one's inner peace of mind, contentment, and interpersonal harmony; items are scored as either true or false. An example item from the Harmony Scale is "I always try hard to get along well with others." Results of studies that have used this measure with Asians indicate that greater harmony is related to better life satisfaction (Ho, Cheung, & Cheung, 2008).

KEY MEASURES OF POSITIVE BEHAVIORS IN ASIAN AMERICANS

Positive behaviors are also central to the understanding and assessment of positive psychological functioning in Asian Americans. When studying individual positive behaviors, it is important to address coping strategies, especially in ethnic minority groups like Asian Americans, given that discrimination and acculturation can be robust stressors. *Coping* refers to the strategies one uses to manage both internal and external strains resulting from stressful situations, and although some aspects of coping are cognitive–emotional, behavioral strategies are important to understand (see Chang, Tugade, & Asakawa, 2006, for a review). Tobin, Holroyd, and Reynolds's (1984) Coping Strategies Inventory is a 72-item self-report measure that assesses coping strategies in response to a specific stressor. Respondents think of and write about a specific stressful episode and then rate each of the 72 items using a 5-point Likert-type scale ranging from a (*not at all*) to e (*very much*). This measure contains 14 subscales, eight of which are primary scales including problem solving, cognitive restructuring, social support, express emotions, problem avoidance, wishful thinking, and social withdrawal. For example, "I worked hard on solving the problems in the situation" is an item representative of the problem-solving factor. An interesting finding is that only two significant differences emerged when comparing coping strategies between Asian Americans and European Americans; Asian Americans scored significantly higher on problem avoidance and social withdrawal (Chang et al., 2006).

Personal growth initiative, defined as the active and intentional engagement in the process of self-change (Robitschek, 1998), is also worth noting. In Confucian culture, personal growth is traditionally perceived as intentional behaviors starting with self-cultivation, developing in family regulation and, finally, reaching the ideal level by devoting oneself to the world (Confucius, 2013). The Personal Growth Initiative Scale-II (PGIS-II; Robitschek et al., 2012) is a 16-item self-report measure rated on a 6-point Likert-type scale ranging from 0 (*definitely disagree*) to 5 (*definitely agree*). It comprises four subscales measuring readiness for change (four items, e.g., "I know when it's time to change specific things about myself"), planfulness (five items, e.g., "When I try to change myself, I make a realistic plan for my personal growth"), using resources (three items, e.g., "I ask for help when I try to change myself"), and intentional behavior (four items, e.g., "I actively work to improve myself"). *Readiness for change* taps one's preparedness for making specific self-changes. *Planfulness* taps one's ability to make effective plans to facilitate growth. *Using resources* taps one's ability to capitalize on available resources to facilitate positive personal growth. *Intentional behavior* taps the conscious pursuit of personal growth. Readiness and planfulness are believed to capture cognitive aspects of personal growth initiative, whereas using resources and intentional behavior are believed to capture behavioral aspects. Previous research (Yakunina, Weigold, & Weigold, 2013) with an international sample of students studying in the United States indicated that planfulness accounted for significant variance in adjustment, and higher levels of using resources buffered the effect of acculturative stress on adjustment. The cross-cultural utility of the PGIS-II has also been confirmed among Chinese university students (H. Yang & Chang, 2014). Consistent with previous findings, all four subscales of the Chinese translation of the PGIS-II were positively and significantly associated with positive psychological adjustment (viz., resilience and life satisfaction) and negatively related to poor psychological adjustment (viz., self-inferiority, Internet addiction, and depression). Finally, the four personal growth initiative dimensions, especially planfulness, accounted for additional unique variance in psychological adjustment beyond resilience. Consequently, the PGIS-II might be used as a valid measure for assessing personal growth initiative in Asian Americans.

The family system is also an important influence on developing and maintaining positive psychological strengths in Asians and Asian Americans (A. Wong, Wong, & Obeng, 2012). Indeed, Kawahara, Pal, and Chin (2013) argued that many common values endorsed by Asian American leaders (e.g., being humble, concern for others' well-being first, respect for elders, valuing education) stem from their upbringing and families; thus, it is not surprising to find that many positive behaviors exhibited by Asian Americans involve the family. For example, B. K. Kim et al. (2005) identified such values as bringing honor to the family through academic achievements and occupational success as an important Asian American value. Other sample items from this subscale of the Asian American Values Scale (the Family Recognition through Achievement subscale; B. K. Kim et al., 2005) include "Succeeding occupationally is an important way of making one's family proud," "One should go as far as one can academically and professionally on behalf of one's family," and "Getting into a good school reflects well on one's family." Individuals are asked to rate their level of agreement on a 7-point Likert-type scale ranging from 1 (*strongly disagree*) to 7 (*strongly agree*). Greater scores on the Family Recognition through Achievement subscale are related to higher levels of positive affect (Liao & Wei, 2014).

Filial piety is an important Asian cultural value that encompasses the behaviors involved with how children should honor, love, care for, respect, and obey their parents in order to demonstrate gratitude toward them (Yeh & Bedford, 2003). On the Filial Piety Scale (Yeh & Bedford, 2003), respondents indicate level of agreement with eight statements on a 5-point Likert-type scale ranging from 1 (*strongly disagree*) to 5 (*strongly agree*); example items include "Be grateful to your parents for raising you," "Hurry home upon the death of a parent," and "Compliment your parents when necessary to save face for them." Studies using the Filial Piety Scale found that greater filial piety is significantly predictive of greater academic motivation (Hui, Sun, Chow, & Chu, 2011).

Similar to filial piety, *family obligation* is a set of behaviors such as support and respect that children exhibit toward their family (Fuligni & Zhang, 2004). The Index of Family Obligation (Fuligni, Tseng, & Lam, 1999) is a 24-item measure that assesses attitudes and expectations toward providing one's family with support, assistance, or respect; sample items include "Help take care of brothers and sisters" and "Help your parents financially in the future." Respondents indicate the level of importance of each statement on a 5-point Likert-type scale ranging from 1 (*Not at all important*) to (*Very important*). Higher scores indicate greater family obligation. Using the Index of Family Obligation, Kiang, Andrews, Stein, Supple, and Gonzalez (2013) found that family obligation serves a protective role in the relationship between socioeconomic stress and academic adjustment in Asian Americans.

In addition to family, other interpersonal relationships are also important in understanding positive behaviors of Asians and Asian Americans. The concept of ren qing (人情) is important to Asian and specifically Chinese culture. Ren qing means relationship in Chinese, but it includes the implicit rules of interaction involving reciprocity, exchanging social favors, and exchanging affections (Cheung et al., 1996). The Ren Qing scale from the Cross-Cultural (Chinese) Personality Assessment Inventory (Cheung et al., 2004) is a 13-item, true–false measure that assesses adherence to the cultural norms of interaction (e.g., courteous rituals). An example item is "After I have been treated to a meal, I will try to return the favor as soon as possible." The value of ren qing is important in maintaining harmonious relationships because it works to maintain the social balance of exchanging goods, services, favors, and time, and is associated with greater life satisfaction and fewer negative life events (Ho et al., 2008).

Another important positive behavior in Asian (specifically Chinese) culture is guanxi use. Guanxi (关系) use can be defined as asking family, friends, and other social connections for specific assistance (e.g., doing favors, offering help, giving gifts), which helps maintain positive relationships (Taormina & Gao, 2010). Guanxi use is a two-part concept that involves both aspects of giving unsolicited favors as well as soliciting favors. The Guanxi Behaviors Scale (Taormina & Gao, 2010) is a 15-item measure that assesses three important aspects of guanxi: seeking networking help from one's family, actively helping friends, and doing favors for associates. Each subscale is made up of five items. Seeking (social networking) help from one's family is an important component of guanxi use because family is an important part of Asian culture and society, and the extent to which an individual asks for help from family members and others known to family members exemplifies greater guanxi use. An example item from the Guanxi subscale regarding seeking help from one's family subscale is "I can rely on my family's contacts for help when I ask for assistance." Additionally, actively helping friends is another important aspect of guanxi use. Next to family, friends are the next greatest source from whom assistance may be requested and, in turn, providing help to friends is regarded as an important aspect of guanxi behavior and in maintaining friendships. An example item from the Guanxi Friends subscale is "When my friends have difficulties, I try to help them." Finally, as noted above, ren qing is important for maintaining social connections, and individuals exchange favors to do so; thus, doing favors for others is an important aspect of guanxi. An example of the Guanxi Favors subscale is "My associates can rely on me to do favors for them." With regard to positive psychological functioning, guanxi use and behaviors, specifically guanxi favors, account for significant variance in life satisfaction (Taormina & Gao, 2010).

KEY MEASURES OF POSITIVE COGNITIONS
IN ASIAN AMERICANS

Positive cognitions are considered to be important predictors of psychological adjustment (Snyder, Sympsom, Michael, & Cheavens, 2001); indeed, previous research suggests that positive cognitions, such as hope and life satisfaction, are essential cognitive strengths of individuals from all cultural and ethnic backgrounds (Chang & Banks, 2007).

Hope is the belief that one can reach a goal and that one has the ability to generate many ways to reach that goal (Snyder et al., 1991). Greater hope is related to more positive outcomes and fewer negative outcomes (e.g., fewer symptoms of depression and anxiety, lower stress, greater life satisfaction, subjective well-being, and self-efficacy; Arnau, Rosen, Finch, Rhudy, & Fortunato, 2007; O'Sullivan, 2011; Werner, 2012). The Hope Scale (Snyder et al., 1991) is a 12-item measure of dispositional hope. Respondents are asked to rate how accurately each statement describes them using an 8-point Likert-type scale ranging from 1 (*definitely false*) to 8 (*definitely true*); a sample item is "My past experiences have prepared me well for my future."

Life satisfaction is another universal positive cognition that is worth considering among Asian Americans. Although life satisfaction may seem similar to happiness, it is actually quite different: *Happiness* reflects affective subjective well-being, whereas *life satisfaction* refers to the cognitive-judgmental processes of assessing one's quality of life (Diener, Emmons, Larsen, & Griffin, 1985). Diener et al.'s (1985) Satisfaction with Life Scale consists of five items (e.g., "In most ways my life is close to my ideal," "The conditions of my life are excellent"). Respondents rate their level of agreement on a 7-point Likert-type scale ranging from 1 (*strongly disagree*) to 7 (*strongly agree*). Some researchers of life satisfaction in Asian Americans have found that mean scores of life satisfaction are significantly lower compared with European American counterparts (Benet-Martínez & Karakitapogli-Aygün, 2003), yet others have found that mean levels do not differ (Arango-Lasprilla et al., 2009). Thus, although slight differences may (or may not) exist between Asian Americans and other ethnic groups, the extant literature suggests that life satisfaction remains an important positive cognitive judgment of well-being both universally and in Asian Americans specifically.

Other positive cognitions are more indigenous to Asians and may stem from classical Asian philosophies (e.g., Confucianism, Buddhism). Some of these cognitions include mindfulness, acceptance, traditionalism, face, and humility. *Mindfulness*, which originated from Eastern Buddhist culture, involves attentiveness toward the present moment (K. W. Brown & Ryan, 2003). Many measures of mindfulness exist, but perhaps the most widely used measure is K. W. Brown and Ryan's (2003) Mindful Attention Awareness

Scale, which consists of 15 brief statements describing mindless experiences (e.g., "I find it difficult to stay focused on what's happening in the present"). Respondents rate statements on a 6-point Likert-type scale ranging from 1 (*almost always*) to 6 (*almost never*); higher scores represent more mindfulness. Studies of the relationship between mindfulness and well-being in Asian Americans have found mindfulness to be significantly and negatively related to emotional distress (Masuda, Wendell, Chou, & Feinstein, 2010).

Like mindfulness, *acceptance* also stems from Eastern Buddhist philosophies (Hayes, 2002) and is defined as the willingness to experience unwanted events in order to pursue one's values and goals. One useful measure of acceptance is the Acceptance and Action Questionnaire-II (Bond et al., 2011), a seven-item measure that asks respondents to rate how true each statement is to them using a 7-point Likert-type scale ranging from 1 (*never true*) to 7 (*always true*). Example items include "It's OK if I remember something unpleasant," "I am in control of my life," and "My thoughts and feelings do not get in the way of how I want to live my life." Cook and Hayes (2010) found that Asian Americans scored higher in acceptance than European Americans, but they do not use acceptance-oriented coping methods as much as European Americans do. As expected, Cook and Hayes found that greater levels of acceptance were associated with positive psychological health.

Concern for face is also an important concept among Asians and Asian Americans (S. Sue & Morishima, 1982), representing concern for losing social integrity, especially within interpersonal relationships. Indeed, it serves as a motivational factor for avoiding conflict with others and maintaining interpersonal harmony. One important measure of concern for face is Zane's (1991) Loss of Face scale, consisting of 21 items assessing the extent to which respondents endorse concern for loss of face. Respondents are asked to consider and rate each statement, using a 7-point Likert-type scale ranging from 1 (*strongly disagree*) to 7 (*strongly agree*). Some example items are "Even when I know another person is at fault, I am careful not to criticize that person," "I will not complain publicly even when I have been treated unfairly," and "I say I may be in error before commenting on something." This is a useful tool in understanding the cultural value of protecting face in social situations for Asian Americans.

Finally, *humility* is an important Asian and Asian American value that promotes and maintains interpersonal harmony (B. K. Kim et al., 1999; B. K. Kim et al., 2005; Uba, 1994). Indeed, it has been noted to be an important quality of Asian American leaders (Kawahara et al., 2013; Lee, Haught, Chen, & Chan, 2013). Humility can be defined as acknowledging one's weaknesses, limited control, dependence on others, and value in others (S. L. Brown, Chopra, & Schiraldi, 2013). One notable measure of humility is the six-item Humility Subscale of the Asian American Values Scale (B. K. Kim et al., 2005), on which respondents rate their degree of agreement using a 7-point Likert-type scale ranging from 1 (*strongly disagree*) to 7 (*strongly agree*). Example items include "One should not sing one's own praises," "One should not openly talk about one's accomplishments," and "Being boastful should not be a sign of one's weakness and insecurity" (reverse coded). Another more recent measure of humility is the Humility Inventory (S. L. Brown et al., 2013), which conceptualizes humility as a multidimensional construct consisting of esteem for others, systemic perspective, and acceptance of fallibility. The Humility Inventory is a 15-item measure where respondents are asked to rate each item using a 5-point Likert-type scale ranging from *strongly disagree* to *strongly agree*. To represent esteem for others, an example item is "I believe most people are capable of great things." An example of systemic perspective is "I recognize I need help from other people." Finally, an example of acceptance of fallibility is "I readily admit when I am wrong." In previous research, adherence to Asian values, including humility, is related to better life satisfaction and greater positive affect in Asian students (Y. J. Wong, Ho, Li, Shin, & Tsai, 2011).

DEVELOPMENT OF POSITIVE PSYCHOLOGY ASSESSMENT TOOLS FOR ASIAN AMERICANS

As we have seen through our summary of useful positive psychology assessment tools that may be used with Asian Americans, some measures of positive strengths are universally valued in all or most cultures. However, many of the measures may not have been validated in Asian American samples and, thus, it is unclear whether they may be appropriate to use (Okazaki & Sue, 2000). In addition to assessment of universal strengths, there are many indigenous assessment tools that may be more useful for Asian and Asian American samples. It is important to recognize that although efforts to create useful assessments of positive psychological strengths for Asian Americans are increasing, many culturally relevant positive psychological strengths still lack assessment tools. For example, B. K. Kim et al. (1999, 2005) have noted that emotional regulation is an important Asian and Asian American value. Indeed, Uba (1994) observed that withholding the free expression of feelings is important for maintaining harmonious relationships with others. Thus, there are potentially many positive affects that would be difficult to measure because they may not be expressed overtly. Additionally, there are other positive Asian and Asian American strengths for which there are no ways to effectively translate to English in order to develop a positive psychology assessment measure. For example, the affect of *ren* (仁) is defined as a moral virtue consisting of the feeling a righteous person experiences when being altruistic (Wu, 2013), and it is an important topic in Confucian philosophy. However, because it is difficult to understand the meaning of *ren* in English, it is not surprising that there is not yet a useful tool to assess this virtue. Similarly, the affect of *ping chang xin* (平常心, common mind), is an important virtue originating from Taoist philosophy, but it is rarely measured in psychology (e.g., H. Yang, 2006). *Ping chang xin* is a belief that everything cannot be importunate and that one should let nature take its course. It refers to feeling calm when granted with favors as well as when subjected to humiliation. Importantly, *ping chang xin* encourages an individual to do what he or she ought to do and discourages an individual from doing what he/she should not do. Because keeping *ping chang xin* is such a popular strength within Chinese culture, it is worthy of empirical research in Chinese and Asian Americans. Additionally, a number of researchers have focused on racial microaggressions within Asian American communities and how that influences well-being (Ong, Burrow, Fuller-Rowell, Ja, & Sue, 2013; D. W. Sue, Bucceri, Lin, Nadal, & Torino, 2009). Accordingly, assessment tools for measuring racial microaggressions exist (e.g., Nadal, 2011). However, research on, and assessments of, the opposite (i.e., microfacilitation—individuals of the same background helping each other) do not exist. Indeed, studies have shown that social support is important in mitigating the negative effects of racial discriminations in Asian Americans (I. Kim, 2014; Wei et al., 2013). Thus, it may be important to further study and develop assessment tools for more focused supportive and facilitative efforts between Asian Americans.

Developing positive psychology assessment tools for use in Asian Americans may also be challenging because, as B. K. Kim et al. (2005) argued, Asian Americans may not adhere as strongly to indigenous values of their culture. Instead, Asian Americans often find themselves in the unique position of having to reconcile aspects of Asian culture and American culture (Uba, 1994). Thus, it is not always useful to strictly refer to Asian values and strengths or American values and strengths. Additionally, as a group distinct from Asian and American cultures, Asian American individuals may relate differently on this spectrum. Furthermore, the many Asian cultures (e.g., Chinese, Japanese, Korean, Southeast Asian, Filipino) vary in their values and traditions. Thus, Asian Americans should also not be considered a homogenous group. Unfortunately, even in Asia, there is a growing tendency for Asian psychologists to be more likely to study Western/American psychology than the indigenous psychologies of Asia (Smith, 1894/2003). Furthermore, even though some indigenous psychological tools have been developed to measure Asian strengths such as familism (K. S. Yang & Ye, 1997) and *ping chang xin* (H. Yang, 2006), studies on these processes have remained scarce. That said, in considering Asian American positive psychology assessment, it may prove valuable for future researchers to gain some understanding of indigenous Asian psychologies.

In addition to these considerations, researchers should seek to focus on specific Asian American groups to determine whether differences in ethnic ancestry contribute differentially to what each group considers to be meaningful positive values and strengths. Although some researchers have suggested that values acculturation does not occur as quickly as behavioral acculturation (e.g., B. S. Kim, Yang, Atkinson, Wolfe, & Hong, 2001), differences in acculturation level may also contribute to differences in what values and strengths are held by individuals, especially beyond third-generation Asian Americans (B. S. Kim et al., 2001). Thus, it may be important to study whether first-generation Asian Americans hold different positive psychological strengths than, for example, fifth-generation Asian Americans. Using behavioral acculturation measures such as the Suinn-Lew Asian Self-Identity Acculturation Scale (Suinn, Rickard-Figueroa, Lew, & Vigil, 1987) and values acculturation measures such as the Asian Values Scale (B. K. Kim et al., 1999) and Asian American Values Scale (B. K. Kim, Li, & Ng, 2005) may allow researchers to better account for acculturation when studying and developing future assessments of Asian American strengths.

Most of the available Asian American positive psychology assessments tap into strengths at the individual level. Thus, future research will benefit from studying positive psychology strengths at familial and interpersonal levels. For example, family growth initiative may be more important than personal growth initiative for Asians and Asian Americans, whereas personal growth initiative may be more important than family growth initiative for Europeans/European Americans. To test these hypotheses, the PGIS-II could be modified so that all items refer to family (e.g., "My family knows when it's time to change specific things about the family"). In the same way, some other individual strength assessments (e.g., Hope Scale, Satisfaction with Life Scale) might be adapted to measure family strengths (e.g., family hope, family satisfaction with life) or interpersonal strengths (e.g., interpersonal hope, interpersonal satisfaction with life). Additionally, future research may also benefit from examining the sources from which these positive psychology strengths are developed and maintained (e.g., from parental influence, peer influences, partner influences; Perera & Chang, 2015). Examining the foundation from which positive strengths in Asian Americans are developed may provide greater understanding for how these strengths work to promote better health and greater resilience. Having a greater understanding of these strengths may equip researchers to generate interventions to foster such positive strengths in Asian Americans, perhaps providing a means of both mitigating negative and promoting beneficial health outcomes. Alternatively, it would be important to understand when and how some universally presumed negative psychological weaknesses or risk factors may actually be associated with greater positive outcomes for Asian Americans (e.g., pessimism; Chang, 1996; Norem & Chang, 2002). Finally, future studies will need to use cross-cultural designs to examine the extent to which Asian American positive strengths, their sources, and intervention strategies are distinct or universal across different Asian and non-Asian American groups.

REFERENCES

Alvarez, A. N., Juang, L., & Liang, C. T. (2006). Asian Americans and racism: When bad things happen to "model minorities." *Cultural Diversity and Ethnic Minority Psychology, 12,* 477–492.

Arango-Lasprilla, J. C., Ketchum, J. M., Gary, K., Hart, T., Corrigan, J., Forster, L., & Mascialino, G. (2009). Race/ethnicity differences in satisfaction with life among persons with traumatic brain injury. *NeuroRehabilitation, 24,* 5–14.

Arnau, R. C., Rosen, D. H., Finch, J. F., Rhudy, J. L., & Fortunato, V. J. (2007). Longitudinal effects of hope on depression and anxiety: A latent variable analysis. *Journal of Personality, 75,* 43–64. http://dx.doi.org/10.1111/j.1467-6494.2006.00432.x

Bednar, R. L., Wells, M., & Peterson, S. R. (1989). *Self-esteem: Paradoxes and innovations in clinical theory and practice.* Washington, DC: American Psychological Association. http://dx.doi.org/10.1037/10068-000

Benet-Martínez, V., & Karakitapogli-Aygün, Z. (2003). The interplay of cultural syndromes and personality in predicting life satisfaction. *Journal of Cross-Cultural Psychology, 34,* 38–60. http://dx.doi.org/10.1177/0022022102239154

Bond, F. W., Hayes, S. C., Baer, R. A., Carpenter, K. M., Guenole, N., Orcutt, H. K., . . . Zettle, R. D. (2011). Preliminary psychometric properties of the Acceptance and Action Questionnaire-II: A revised measure of psychological inflexibility and experiential avoidance. *Behavior Therapy, 42,* 676–688. http://dx.doi.org/10.1016/j.beth.2011.03.007

Brown, K. W., & Ryan, R. M. (2003). The benefits of being present: Mindfulness and its role in psychological well-being. *Journal of Personality and Social Psychology, 84,* 822–848. http://dx.doi.org/10.1037/0022-3514.84.4.822

Brown, S. L., Chopra, P. K., & Schiraldi, G. R. (2013). Validation of the Humility Inventory (HI), a five-factor, self-report measure of humility. *The International Journal of Educational and Psychological Assessment, 12,* 57–77.

Chang, E. C. (1996). Cultural differences in optimism, pessimism, and coping: Predictors of subsequent adjustment in Asian American and Caucasian American college students. *Journal of Counseling Psychology, 43,* 113–123. http://dx.doi.org/10.1037/0022-0167.43.1.113

Chang, E. C. (Ed.). (2012). *Handbook of adult psychopathology in Asians: Diagnosis, etiology, and treatment.* New York, NY: Oxford University Press.

Chang, E. C., & Banks, K. H. (2007). The color and texture of hope: Some preliminary findings and implications for hope theory and counseling among diverse racial/ethnic groups. *Cultural Diversity and Ethnic Minority Psychology, 13*, 94–103. http://dx.doi.org/10.1037/1099-9809.13.2.94

Chang, E. C., & Kwon, P. (2014). Special issue on psychopathology in Asians and the *DSM–5*: Culture matters. *Asian Journal of Psychiatry, 7*, 66–67. http://dx.doi.org/10.1016/j.ajp.2013.12.001

Chang, E. C., Tsai, W., & Sanna, L. J. (2010). Examining the relations between rumination and adjustment: Do ethnic differences exist between Asian and European Americans? *Asian American Journal of Psychology, 1*, 46–56. http://dx.doi.org/10.1037/a0018821

Chang, E. C., Tugade, M. M., & Asakawa, K. (2006). Stress and coping among Asian Americans: Lazarus and Folkman's model and beyond. In P. P. Wong & L. J. Wong (Eds.), *Handbook of multicultural perspectives on stress and coping* (pp. 439–455). Dallas, TX: Springer. http://dx.doi.org/10.1007/0-387-26238-5_19

Cheung, F. M., Cheung, S., & Zhang, J. (2004). What is "Chinese personality"? Subgroup differences in the Chinese Personality Assessment Inventory (CPAI-2). *Acta Psychologica Sinica, 36*, 491–499.

Cheung, F. M., Leung, K., Fan, R. M., Song, W., Zhang, J., & Zhang, J. (1996). Development of the Chinese Personality Assessment Inventory. *Journal of Cross-Cultural Psychology, 27*, 181–199. http://dx.doi.org/10.1177/0022022196272003

Confucius. (2013). *The great learning* (A. C. Muller, Trans.). Retrieved from http://www.acmuller.net/con-dao/greatlearning.html

Cook, D., & Hayes, S. C. (2010). Acceptance-based coping and the psychological adjustment of Asian and Caucasian Americans. *International Journal of Behavioral Consultation and Therapy, 6*, 186–197. http://dx.doi.org/10.1037/h0100907

Crocker, J., Luhtanen, R. K., Blaine, B., & Broadnax, S. (1994). Collective self-esteem and psychological well-being among White, Black, and Asian college students. *Personality and Social Psychology Bulletin, 20*, 503–513. http://dx.doi.org/10.1177/0146167294205007

Diener, E., Emmons, R. A., Larsen, R. J., & Griffin, S. (1985). The satisfaction with life scale. *Journal of Personality Assessment, 49*, 71–75. http://dx.doi.org/10.1207/s15327752jpa4901_13

Fuligni, A. J., Tseng, V., & Lam, M. (1999). Attitudes toward family obligation among American adolescents with Asian, Latin American, and European backgrounds. *Child Development, 70*, 1030–1044. http://dx.doi.org/10.1111/1467-8624.00075

Fuligni, A. J., & Zhang, W. (2004). Attitudes toward family obligation among adolescents in contemporary urban and rural China. *Child Development, 75*, 180–192. http://dx.doi.org/10.1111/j.1467-8624.2004.00662.x

Hayes, S. C. (2002). Buddhism and acceptance and commitment therapy. *Cognitive and Behavioral Practice, 9*, 58–66. http://dx.doi.org/10.1016/S1077-7229(02)80041-4

Ho, M. Y., Cheung, F. M., & Cheung, S. F. (2008). Personality and life events as predictors of adolescents' life satisfaction: Do life events mediate the link between personality and life satisfaction? *Social Indicators Research, 89,* 457–471. http://dx.doi.org/10.1007/s11205-008-9243-6

Hui, E. P., Sun, R. F., Chow, S., & Chu, M. (2011). Explaining Chinese students' academic motivation: Filial piety and self-determination. *Educational Psychology, 31,* 377–392. http://dx.doi.org/10.1080/01443410.2011.559309

Humes, K. R., Jones, N. A., & Ramirez, R. R. (2011). *Overview of race and Hispanic origin: 2010. 2010 Census Brief* (C2010BR-02, pp. 1–24). Washington, DC: U.S. Census Bureau. Retrieved from http://www.census.gov/prod/cen2010/briefs/c2010br-02.pdf

Ip, P. (2014). Harmony as happiness? Social harmony in two Chinese societies. *Social Indicators Research, 117,* 719–741. http://dx.doi.org/10.1007/s11205-013-0395-7

Kawahara, D. M., Pal, M. S., & Chin, J. L. (2013). The leadership experiences of Asian Americans. *Asian American Journal of Psychology, 4,* 240–248. http://dx.doi.org/10.1037/a0035196

Kiang, L., Andrews, K., Stein, G. L., Supple, A. J., & Gonzalez, L. M. (2013). Socioeconomic stress and academic adjustment among Asian American adolescents: The protective role of family obligation. *Journal of Youth and Adolescence, 42,* 837–847. http://dx.doi.org/10.1007/s10964-013-9916-6

Kiang, L., Witkow, M. R., & Champagne, M. C. (2013). Normative changes in ethnic and American identities and links with adjustment among Asian American adolescents. *Developmental Psychology, 49,* 1713–1722. http://dx.doi.org/10.1037/a0030840

Kim, B. K., Atkinson, D. R., & Yang, P. H. (1999). The Asian Values Scale: Development, factor analysis, validation, and reliability. *Journal of Counseling Psychology, 46,* 342–352. http://dx.doi.org/10.1037/0022-0167.46.3.342

Kim, B. K., Li, L. C., & Ng, G. F. (2005). The Asian American Values Scale—Multidimensional: Development, reliability, and validity. *Cultural Diversity and Ethnic Minority Psychology, 11,* 187–201. http://dx.doi.org/10.1037/1099-9809.11.3.187

Kim, B. S., Yang, P. H., Atkinson, D. R., Wolfe, M. M., & Hong, S. (2001). Cultural value similarities and differences among Asian American ethnic groups. *Cultural Diversity and Ethnic Minority Psychology, 7,* 343–361. http://dx.doi.org/10.1037/1099-9809.7.4.343

Kim, E., & Lee, D. (2011). Collective self-esteem: Role of social context among Asian-American college students. *Psychological Reports, 109,* 1017–1037. http://dx.doi.org/10.2466/07.17.21.PR0.109.6.1017-1037

Kim, I. (2014). The role of critical ethnic awareness and social support in the discrimination-depression relationship among Asian Americans: Path analysis. *Cultural Diversity and Ethnic Minority Psychology, 20,* 52–60. http://dx.doi.org/10.1037/a0034529

Lee, Y., Haught, H., Chen, K., & Chan, S. (2013). Examining Daoist big-five leadership in cross-cultural and gender perspectives. *Asian American Journal of Psychology, 4*, 267–276. http://dx.doi.org/10.1037/a0035180

Lee, Y., Lin, Y., Huang, C., & Fredrickson, B. L. (2013). The construct and measurement of peace of mind. *Journal of Happiness Studies, 14*, 571–590. http://dx.doi.org/10.1007/s10902-012-9343-5

Lemola, S., Räikkönen, K., Gomez, V., & Allemand, M. (2013). Optimism and self-esteem are related to sleep. Results from a large community-based sample. *International Journal of Behavioral Medicine, 20*, 567–571. http://dx.doi.org/10.1007/s12529-012-9272-z

Liao, K. Y., & Wei, M. (2014). Academic stress and positive affect: Asian value and self-worth contingency as moderators among Chinese international students. *Cultural Diversity and Ethnic Minority Psychology, 20*, 107–115. http://dx.doi.org/10.1037/a0034071

Luhtanen, R., & Crocker, J. (1992). A collective self-esteem scale: Self-evaluation of one's social identity. *Personality and Social Psychology Bulletin, 18*, 302–318. http://dx.doi.org/10.1177/0146167292183006

Lyubomirsky, S., & Lepper, H. S. (1999). A measure of subjective happiness: Preliminary reliability and construct validity. *Social Indicators Research, 46*, 137–155. http://dx.doi.org/10.1023/A:1006824100041

Masuda, A., Wendell, J. W., Chou, Y., & Feinstein, A. B. (2010). Relationships among self-concealment, mindfulness and negative psychological outcomes in Asian American and European American college students. *International Journal for the Advancement of Counselling, 32*, 165–177. http://dx.doi.org/10.1007/s10447-010-9097-x

Moksnes, U. K., & Espnes, G. A. (2013). Self-esteem and life satisfaction in adolescents—gender and age as potential moderators. *Quality of Life Research: An International Journal of Quality of Life Aspects of Treatment, Care and Rehabilitation, 22*, 2921–2928. http://dx.doi.org/10.1007/s11136-013-0427-4

Nadal, K. L. (2011). The Racial and Ethnic Microaggressions Scale (REMS): Construction, reliability, and validity. *Journal of Counseling Psychology, 58*, 470–480. http://dx.doi.org/10.1037/a0025193

Norem, J. K., & Chang, E. C. (2002). The positive psychology of negative thinking. *Journal of Clinical Psychology, 58*, 993–1001. http://dx.doi.org/10.1002/jclp.10094

Okazaki, S., & Sue, S. (2000). Implications of test revisions for assessment with Asian Americans. *Psychological Assessment, 12*, 272–280. http://dx.doi.org/10.1037/1040-3590.12.3.272

Ong, A. D., Burrow, A. L., Fuller-Rowell, T. E., Ja, N. M., & Sue, D. W. (2013). Racial microaggressions and daily well-being among Asian Americans. *Journal of Counseling Psychology, 60*, 188–199. http://dx.doi.org/10.1037/a0031736

Orth, U., & Robins, R. W. (2013). Understanding the link between low self-esteem and depression. *Current Directions in Psychological Science, 22*, 455–460. http://dx.doi.org/10.1177/0963721413492763

O'Sullivan, G. (2011). The relationship between hope, stress, self-efficacy, and life satisfaction among undergraduates. *Social Indicators Research*, *101*, 155–172. http://dx.doi.org/10.1007/s11205-010-9662-z

Pan, J., & Chan, C. (2007). Resilience: A new research area in positive psychology. *Psychologia*, *50*, 164–176. http://dx.doi.org/10.2117/psysoc.2007.164

Perera, M. J., & Chang, E. C. (2015). Ethnic variations between Asian and European Americans in interpersonal sources of socially prescribed perfectionism: It's not just about parents! *Asian American Journal of Psychology*, *6*, 31–37. http://dx.doi.org/10.1037/a0036175

Robitschek, C. (1998). Personal growth initiative: The construct and its measure. *Measurement and Evaluation in Counseling and Development*, *30*, 183–198.

Robitschek, C., Ashton, M. W., Spering, C. C., Geiger, N., Byers, D., Schotts, G. C., & Thoen, M. A. (2012). Development and psychometric evaluation of the Personal Growth Initiative Scale-II. *Journal of Counseling Psychology*, *59*, 274–287. http://dx.doi.org/10.1037/a0027310

Rosenberg, M. (1965). *Society and the adolescent self-image*. Princeton, NJ: Princeton University Press.

Shek, Y., & McEwen, M. K. (2012). The relationships of racial identity and gender role conflict to self-esteem of Asian American undergraduate men. *Journal of College Student Development*, *53*, 703–718. http://dx.doi.org/10.1353/csd.2012.0065

Smith, H. A. (2003). *Chinese characteristics* (4th ed., rev. with illus.). New York, NY: Fleming H. Revell. (Original work published 1894)

Snyder, C. R., Harris, C., Anderson, J. R., Holleran, S. A., Irving, L. M., Sigmon, S. T., . . . Harney, P. (1991). The will and the ways: Development and validation of an individual-differences measure of hope. *Journal of Personality and Social Psychology*, *60*, 570–585. http://dx.doi.org/10.1037/0022-3514.60.4.570

Snyder, C. R., Sympsom, S. C., Michael, S. T., & Cheavens, J. (2001). Optimism and hope constructs: Variants on a positive expectancy theme. In E. C. Chang (Ed.), *Optimism and pessimism: Implications for theory, research, and practice* (pp. 101–125). Washington, DC: American Psychological Association. http://dx.doi.org/10.1037/10385-005

Sprecher, S., Brooks, J. E., & Avogo, W. (2013). Self-esteem among young adults: Differences and similarities based on gender, race, and cohort (1990–2012). *Sex Roles*, *69*, 264–275. http://dx.doi.org/10.1007/s11199-013-0295-y

Sue, D. W., Bucceri, J., Lin, A. I., Nadal, K. L., & Torino, G. C. (2009). Racial microaggressions and Asian American experience. *Asian American Journal of Psychology*, *S*, 88–101. http://dx.doi.org/10.1037/1948-1985.S.1.88

Sue, S., & Morishima, J. K. (1982). *The mental health of Asian-Americans*. San Francisco, CA: Jossey-Bass.

Suinn, R. M., Rickard-Figueroa, K., Lew, S., & Vigil, P. (1987). The Suinn-Lew Asian Self-Identity Acculturation Scale: An initial report. *Educational and Psychological Measurement*, *47*, 401–407. http://dx.doi.org/10.1177/0013164487472012

Taormina, R. J., & Gao, J. H. (2010). A research model for Guangxi behavior: Antecedents, measures, and outcomes of Chinese social networking. *Social Science Research, 39*, 1195–1212. http://dx.doi.org/10.1016/j.ssresearch.2010.07.003

Tobin, D. L., Holroyd, K. A., & Reynolds, R. V. (1984). *User's manual for the Coping Strategies Inventory*. Unpublished manuscript, Ohio University, Athens.

Tsai, J. L., Ying, Y. W., & Lee, P. A. (2001). Cultural predictors of self-esteem: A study of Chinese American female and male young adults. *Cultural Diversity and Ethnic Minority Psychology, 7*, 284–297. http://dx.doi.org/10.1037/1099-9809.7.3.284

Tsai, W., Chang, E. C., Sanna, L. J., & Herringshaw, A. J. (2011). An examination of happiness as a buffer of the rumination–adjustment link: Ethnic differences between European and Asian American students. *Asian American Journal of Psychology, 2*, 168–180. http://dx.doi.org/10.1037/a0025319

Uba, L. (1994). *Asian Americans: Personality patterns, identity, and mental health*. New York, NY: Guilford Press.

Watson, D., Clark, L. A., & Tellegen, A. (1988). Development and validation of brief measures of positive and negative affect: The PANAS scales. *Journal of Personality and Social Psychology, 54*, 1063–1070. http://dx.doi.org/10.1037/0022-3514.54.6.1063

Wei, M., Yeh, C. J., Chao, R. C., Carrera, S., & Su, J. C. (2013). Family support, self-esteem, and perceived racial discrimination among Asian American male college students. *Journal of Counseling Psychology, 60*, 453–461. http://dx.doi.org/10.1037/a0032344

Werner, S. (2012). Subjective well-being, hope, and needs of individuals with serious mental illness. *Psychiatry Research, 196*, 214–219. http://dx.doi.org/10.1016/j.psychres.2011.10.012

Wirtz, D., Chiu, C. Y., Diener, E., & Oishi, S. (2009). What constitutes a good life? Cultural differences in the role of positive and negative affect in subjective well-being. *Journal of Personality, 77*, 1167–1196. http://dx.doi.org/10.1111/j.1467-6494.2009.00578.x

Wong, A., Wong, Y. J., & Obeng, C. S. (2012). An untold story: A qualitative study of Asian American family strengths. *Asian American Journal of Psychology, 3*, 286–298. http://dx.doi.org/10.1037/a0025553

Wong, Y. J., Ho, R. M., Li, P., Shin, M., & Tsai, P. (2011). Chinese Singaporeans' lay beliefs, adherence to Asian values, and subjective well-being. *Personality and Individual Differences, 50*, 822–827. http://dx.doi.org/10.1016/j.paid.2011.01.003

Wu, M. (2013). Ren-li, reciprocity, judgment, and the question of openness to the other in the Confucian Lunyu. *Journal of Moral Education, 42*, 430–442. http://dx.doi.org/10.1080/03057240.2013.791261

Yakunina, E. S., Weigold, I. K., & Weigold, A. (2013). Personal growth initiative: Relations with acculturative stress and international student adjustment. *International Perspectives in Psychology: Research, Practice, Consultation, 1*, 62–71.

Yang, H. (2006). A primary study on attachment and detachment in goal striving. *Psychological Science, 29*, 395–397.

Yang, H., & Chang, E. C. (2014). Examining the structure, reliability, and validity of the Chinese personal growth initiative scale–II: Evidence for the importance of intentional self-change among Chinese. *Journal of Personality Assessment, 96*, 559–566. http://dx.doi.org/10.1080/00223891.2014.886256

Yang, K. S., & Ye, M. H. (1997). Zhongguoren De Jiazuzhuyi: Gainian, Fenxi Yu Shizhenghengjian [Chinese familism: Concept, analysis and empirical measurement]. *Bulletin of the Institute of Ethnology. Academia Sinica (Taiwan), 83,* 169–225.

Yee, B. W. K., DeBaryshe, B. D., Yuen, S., Kim, S. Y., & McCubbin, H. I. (2007). Asian American and Pacific Islander families: Resiliency and life-span socialization in a cultural context. In F. T. L. Leong, A. Ebreo, L. Kinoshita, A. G. Inman, L. H. Yang, & M. Fu (Eds.), *Handbook of Asian American psychology* (2d ed., pp. 69–86). Thousand Oaks, CA: Sage.

Yeh, K., & Bedford, O. (2003). A test of the dual filial piety model. *Asian Journal of Social Psychology, 6*, 215–228. http://dx.doi.org/10.1046/j.1467-839X.2003.00122.x

Zane, N. (1991). *An empirical examination of loss of face among Asian Americans.* Unpublished manuscript, Graduate School of Education, University of California, Santa Barbara.

8

POSITIVE PSYCHOLOGY ASSESSMENT AMONG LATINOS

ROSEMARY GONZALEZ AND AMADO M. PADILLA

Little of the research that has been done with the Latino community has taken an asset-based approach and identified cultural based strengths rather than deficit views. This chapter builds upon the emerging research in positive psychology and highlights the innumerable cultural strengths of Latinos that have largely gone unrecognized or understudied. We emphasize ways in which the field of positive psychology can incorporate the experience of Latinos who face economic, educational, and linguistic challenges and who also display enormous resilience as they navigate American society. We identify affective, behavioral, and cognitive-based assessment methods and strategies that have high cultural and linguistic validity and that hold promise for future research with Latinos.

We begin with a brief overview of relevant statistics and then provide a selective commentary on the importance of assessing positive strengths among Latinos. We refer to three critical dimensions of the Latino experience as it

http://dx.doi.org/10.1037/14799-008

Positive Psychology in Racial and Ethnic Groups: Theory, Research, and Practice, E. C. Chang, C. A. Downey, J. K. Hirsch, and N. J. Lin (Editors)

relates to the field of positive psychology: (a) the need to acknowledge that optimal functioning may develop under strain, (b) the need to incorporate culturally laden constructs such as familism and collectivism as core values that provide support at both the individual and family level, and (c) the need to strive for social justice reforms that are necessary to achieve optimal functioning.

VALUE OF ASSESSING POSITIVE STRENGTHS IN LATINO AMERICANS

As noted in Chapter 4 of this volume, the term *Latino* refers to an ethnic group that shares common cultural origins but whose members come from diverse Latin American countries and backgrounds with distinctive histories and socioeconomic, political, and racial experiences. Among the Latino population, differences are based on country of origin, language preference and proficiency, acculturation level, generation or length of residence in the United States, and history of assimilation within the mainstream U.S. population. Latinos are the largest and fastest-growing ethnic group; with a population of 50.5 million in 2010, they account for about 16.3% of the total U.S. population (Passel, Cohn, & Lopez, 2011). About 66% of all Latinos are of Mexican origin, and it is a youthful population: 23% of the group are 17 years of age or younger (Passel et al., 2011). In 2011 Latino households were more likely to be headed by a single female than White households (23.5% vs. 11.6%), to have a larger percentage of children under the age of 18 living in poverty (34.1% vs. 13.6%), to have lower median personal and household incomes ($20,000 and $39,000 vs. $32,000 and $54,000), and to have fewer college graduates (13.4% vs. 31.8%; Motel & Patten, 2011). Overall, Latinos are overrepresented among groups who live in poverty (Marotta & Garcia, 2003), and Latino youth fare worse than White majority youth on several indicators of well-being, especially in academic achievement and educational attainment (Eamon & Mulder, 2005). Moreover, Latinos of all ages report many incidences of overt or indirect discrimination that include negative stereotypes, microaggressions, and exclusion (e.g., Delgado-Romero, Nevels, Capielo, Galvan, & Torres, 2013). The effects of discrimination are correlated with higher rates of anxiety and depression and greater overall distress (Cervantes, Padilla, Napper, & Goldbach, 2013; Umaña-Taylor & Updegraff, 2007).

It is against this background of risk that we incorporate a positive psychology lens and examine constructs such as familism, humility, and faith. Our purpose is to identify instruments and strategies to assess cultural strengths among Latino individuals, families, and communities. The goal is to describe the inherent strengths in Latino culture and begin to identify areas where current assessments can increasingly reflect this reality. Sue and Constantine (2003) reviewed the concept of optimal human functioning among people of color in the United States and observed that in collectivistic cultures, it may entail "working for the good of the family, group, community, or society" (p. 154). In other words, well-being is not based solely on individual notions of success but is also intricately tied to relationships with others.

Since 1991 (Alva, 1991; Gandara, 1995), a growing body of literature emerged that specifically examined the environmental and individual factors that foster resilience among Latinos (e.g., Borrero, Lee, & Padilla, 2012; Gonzalez & Padilla, 1997). During the same time, the field of positive psychology also grew; however, research conducted among Latinos is scant. Whereas resilience studies examine how individuals achieve successful outcomes despite adversity (e.g., Masten, 2001), the field of positive psychology seeks to identify the processes by which individuals flourish and cultivate optimal well-being. A related concept, *integra/o*, is used in Spanish to describe an individual who embodies physical, emotional, and spiritual wholeness. We concur with Seligman (2002), who described authentic happiness as a process of both alleviating suffering and increasing well-being. Even in the face of difficult life circumstances, many Latinos flourish (i.e., they radiate a fullness of joy, express a humble openness to learning, demonstrate a deep appreciation of the small gifts in life, show a desire to contribute to the lives of others, and exhibit a vibrancy that can co-exist with a deep sense of peace and serenity rooted in compassion and respect for others). However, as M. E. Hall, Langer, and McMartin (2010) noted, suffering should not be sought for its own sake, nor tolerated passively. Nevertheless, it can promote long-term character change and strengthen the development of virtues such as courage, compassion, and faith.

Key Measures of Positive Affect

Consistent with the points raised above, research suggests that negative and positive emotions can coexist (Larsen & McGraw, 2011). As Fredrickson (2001) showed, positive emotions are correlated with many aspects of positive development (e.g., optimism). Although it may seem counterintuitive to discuss negative emotions in this chapter, certain virtues (e.g., patience, courage) become stronger through repeated challenges. The research on posttraumatic growth (e.g., Linley & Joseph, 2004) captures the idea that an individual may not merely survive traumatic events, but may actually become transformed as she or he emerges from traumatic situations. Various dimensions of posttraumatic growth include relevant positive psychology constructs: a greater appreciation of life, an insight about a personal strength that emerged, a greater sense of connection with others, and a deepened spirituality (Tedeschi

& Calhoun, 2004). In assessing positive emotions, we recommend that measures of positive affect ascertain positive emotions that coexist in the presence of negative emotional experiences. For instance, a sample item may ask, "To what extent do you feel a sense of peace when you visit your spouse in the hospital?"

Lucas, Diener, and Larsen (2003) reviewed measures of positive emotions and described self-report measures as being reliable, valid, and "the easiest and most efficient way to assess positive emotions" (p. 210). In particular, we highlight their recommendation to further explore the use of visual analog techniques. For instance, the use of faces to indicate pleasure–displeasure or a thermometer to denote the intensity of an emotional experience may be especially useful with less acculturated Latinos. The stress due to linguistic and culture differences likely affects the accuracy of responses. Lucas et al. (2003) also noted the use of cognitive tasks as useful to the study of positive emotions. We underscore the use of measures in Spanish and English and in a combination of both languages (e.g., code switching, Spanglish) because language can activate certain emotion schemas (e.g., Spanish used to express parental displeasure). In an exhaustive review of the literature with bilinguals, Pavlenko (2006) found that the language in which a bilingual experiences intense emotions, and how such experiences are represented in memory, affects how the person is bound by the linguistic and cultural context when describing or acting on the experience at a later time. According to Pavlenko, bilingual individuals compartmentalize their positive emotions based on the language in which the emotion was or is being experienced. In working with Latinos, it is important to know whether Spanish or English was the person's first language and whether they prefer one or the other of their languages in interacting with close acquaintances or strangers. Accordingly, we see this as a fruitful area of research in positive psychology since many Latinos are bilingual.

We also contend that the use of culturally relevant methods may better elicit and accurately assess the vibrancy and fullness of positive emotions. In particular, multisensory methods and methods like savoring or capitalizing (Bryant, 2003) are consistent with rich Latino cultural traditions of music and storytelling, or *cuentos*. In fact, art therapy with Latinos has shown its effectiveness in discussing of oppression, familial conflict, acculturative stress, and gentrification of Latino communities (Linesch, Aceves, Quezada, Trochez, & Zuniga, 2012; Moxley, 2013). Murals and graffiti art are two forms of artistic expression found in the Latino community. As Donahue (2011) stated, "public mural art represents the wealth of history, stories, and symbols in a community, it is a means of including voices and perspectives often excluded from curriculum" (p. 70). After-school or community-based programs that engage youth in artistic expression are particularly promising because they inspire hope (e.g., Tucker-Raymond, Rosario-Ramos, & Rosario, 2011) and a sense of empowerment among marginalized Latino youth (Delgado & Barton, 1998; Donahue, 2011). How Latinos feel about their culture and their ethnic identity is a critical aspect of optimal well-being.

Among Latino youth, both self-esteem and ethnic identity have been found to mediate the relationship between the risks associated with perceived discrimination and depressive symptoms (Umaña-Taylor & Updegraff, 2007). Specifically, Latinos with greater self-esteem and higher ethnic identity are less likely to suffer from distress as a result of perceived discrimination. Self-esteem is a widely studied area of research among Latinos in the assessment of positive affect. In Heatherton and Wyland's (2003) review of self-esteem, they suggested that William James would support the notion that "people have high self-esteem to the extent that they feel good about those things that matter to them" (p. 224). As Markus and Kitayama (1991) noted, in some cultures self-esteem can be related to experiences that detract attention from individual achievements but rather emphasize a sense of self-in-relation to others. Consistent with the notion that one's sense of self is also tied to relationships with others, measures of self-esteem are increasingly reflecting collectivistic notions of self. Based on social identity theory, Luhtanen and Crocker (1992) argued that there are two distinct aspects of self-esteem: personal identity and collective identity. Luhtanen and Crocker were among the first to develop a scale to assess individual differences in collective, rather than personal, self-esteem, with four subscales (Membership esteem, Public collective self-esteem, Private collective self-esteem, and Importance to identity). They have obtained good reliability and validity for their scales, but as of yet, little research of collective self-esteem has been conducted with Latinos.

Trying to understand the unique processes by which positive emotions affect an individual is an extremely fascinating area of research. In comparison with negative emotions, positive emotions may not necessarily have an immediate effect (e.g., readiness for action, flee from danger) on overall well-being. Fredrickson (2001) proposed that one mechanism by which positive emotions are correlated to optimal well-being is by expanding one's cognitive flexibility in a situation. Given the unique process by which positive emotions affect well-being, the assessment of positive emotions may entail different methodologies and units of analysis and languages. There is still much work to be done, but we envision many productive avenues for future research.

Key Measures of Positive Behaviors

In addition to positive emotions, positive relationships are another central component of well-being (Seligman, 2011). Although family relationships are universal, how a family is defined and how family obligations are viewed are culture specific (Villarreal, Blozis, & Widaman, 2005). Latinos, regardless of national origin or length of residence in the United States, make frequent reference to the central role that family plays in their life (Arellano & Padilla, 1996; Ceballo, 2004; Enriquez, 2011; Gandara, 1995). Familism is a cultural value that can be measured as a perception or strong identification with, and attachment to, one's nuclear and extended families. The emotional component of familism is characterized by strong feelings of loyalty and solidarity. Valenzuela and Dornbusch (1994) measured familism among Latinos along structural–demographic, behavioral, and attitudinal dimensions. On a behavioral level, familism entails mutual interdependence between extended family members to provide emotional, financial, or social support. According to Yahirun, Perreira, and Fuligni (2013), the behavioral dimension of familism includes activities that individuals engage in that fulfill family obligations such as providing economic, social support, and instrumental assistance. Behaviors such as calling family members on the telephone or visiting relatives regularly are examples of this dimension. Familistic behaviors often entail prioritizing family goals over individualistic goals and hence making sacrifices for the benefit of the family.

We encourage researchers to develop more behavioral measures of the core Latino value of familism because of the effect of familism on optimal well-being. Calderón-Tena, Knight, and Carlo (2011) showed that a strong familism orientation is associated with parental involvement and to prosocial modeling by parents. Thus, behaviors that undergird familism may be generalizable to a broader set of prosocial behaviors. It is interesting that in a recent study of familistic attitudes among day laborers (Ojeda & Piña-Watson, 2013) did not find a significant relation between familism and an aspect well-being (i.e., life satisfaction) in the face of discrimination. However, Campa (2013) hypothesized that familism often provides a safety net in the face of poverty and also provides support to cope with racism.

Given the reality that behaviors can rectify discrimination, we describe a widely used attitudinal measure of familism and identify items that can be phrased to create behavioral measures of familism. One of the earliest familism scales was an attitudinal scale developed by Sabogal, Marin, Otero-Sabogal, Marin, and Perez-Stable (1987) with Mexican, Central American, and Cuban American respondents. These researchers defined the *familismo* value system with three basic dimensions: (a) familial obligations (e.g., providing material and emotional support to family members), (b) perceived support from the family (e.g., family reliably providing help and support to solve problems), and (c) family as referents (e.g., decisions and behavior are based on conforming and consulting with family members). This study was among the first to show that familism was a central core value of Latinos: There was considerable uniformity across the three samples of Latinos and among high and low acculturated individuals. Current attitudinal measures of familism draw upon many of the items in the Sabogal et al. measure.

Germán, Gonzalez, and Dumka (2009) developed a promising new scale based on a 50-item Mexican American Cultural Values Scale (Knight et al., 2010). The original scale was derived from focus-group interviews with Mexican origin mothers, fathers, and adolescents (in English and Spanish) and subjected to confirmatory factor analysis. In their analysis, Germán et al. (2009) identified three family-related subscales comprising 16 items measuring self in relation to family, concrete family obligations, and family emotional support (Knight et al., 2010). Consistent with the literature, the scale measures familism beliefs, but several items can be rephrased to identify familistic behaviors. (Items related to respect were noted to be distinct, although related to familism.) Key items that could be rephrased to reflect familistic behaviors include older children caring for younger children, caring for elderly parents, spending holidays with nuclear and extended family, maintaining contact with extended family, assisting family members financially, seeking advice from family members when making important decisions, and expressing love and affection toward family (see Knight et al., 2010). In placing a high value on the family, group members gain social support and assistance.

Having an ever-present awareness of one's connection and sense of self in relation to others may lead to the development and value of unique characteristics. One such cultural value among traditional Latinos is that of humility. Davis et al. (2011) defined *relational humility* as "an observer's judgment that a target person (a) is interpersonally other-oriented rather than self-focused, marked by a lack of superiority; and (b) has an accurate view of self—not too inflated or too low" (p. 226). For instance, as children become the first to attend college in their families, their families remind them that they are not any better because of their formal education (Arellano & Padilla, 1996). As noted in the definition, humility is not characterized by low self-esteem or self-deprecation, nor should a humble person be expected to be unassertive, passive, and accepting of injustices (e.g., Exline & Geyer, 2004). In fact, having humility can contribute to fostering the healthy relationships that are central to positive development (Seligman, 2002). Although humility has been measured in various ways, research suggests that it is related to positive outcomes such as forgiveness (e.g., Davis, Hook, et al., 2010), helping behavior (e.g., LaBouff, Rowatt, Johnson, Tsang, & Willerton, 2012), and higher academic grades (e.g., Rowatt et al., 2006). As Davis, Hook, et al. (2010) aptly stated, humility allows for relationships to deepen, as opposed to deteriorate.

We agree with Davis et al. (2011) that self-reports of one's own humility are counterintuitive and are not likely to be valid if one is truly humble (see also Davis, Worthington, & Hook, 2010; Tangney, 2000). Thus, informant reports are likely to be more valid measures of humility. Moreover, we contend that behavioral observations of a target's humility are better suited to be valid measures of the construct. Thus far, most scales measure humility as a perception or judgment (e.g., Davis et al., 2011). We suggest that items emphasize observable behaviors given that false humility exists and that an individual may try to appear humble and make comments that would elicit praise from another individual (e.g., "No, I'm not good at . . ."). With respect to other behavioral items of humility, it is likely that a person who is authentically humble would rarely, if at all, speak of or use the phrase "I/we deserve," unless it was based on a grave injustice (e.g., a right to safe working conditions). Moreover, we would advise not using the term *humble* in measures of humility for Latinos (e.g., Davis et al., 2011; he has a humble character, she is truly a humble person). A primary reason is that in Spanish, the word *humble*, or *humilde*, is also used to refer to an individual who is poor or comes from meager beginnings. In addition, the term *humility* itself is value-laden and may be perceived as referring to an individual with low self-esteem.

Given the salience of the concept of *humildad* in the Latino community, we propose possible behavioral items to measure humility. Prior to presenting those items, we first identify key core values that are held by an individual who is humble that have not been explicitly articulated in the literature. In reviewing the literature, we were able to deduce three core values that help provide clarity to the study of humility. One core essential value is recognizing the frailty of humanity. A second core essential value is the belief that every human being has equal dignity and worth. Behaviorally, this is observed in individuals who are willing to do tasks that are considered menial to others and helping even when not asked to help. The third core value is that meaning and happiness in life are not based on possessions or seeking praise or social dominance. In other words, an authentically humble individual is detached from material possessions and praise. Exline (2012) endorsed humility as a core value and wrote, "Humble individuals do not strive for social dominance or seek to prove themselves superior to others" (p. 42). In fact, Exline (2012) found that humility is negatively associated with a sense of entitlement.

The study of humility is an exciting and ever-growing field (Davis & Hook, 2013). It is especially challenging to assess a construct that is best captured in the face of a transgression or threats to one's ego (Exline, 2008) where a prideful response is common (e.g., a conversation with someone who is abrasive). Some of the sample items in Exhibit 8.1 reflect these situations (e.g., "Expresses gratitude even during times of suffering," "Does not have to have the 'last word' during an argument"). The five types of behaviors listed in the exhibit are based on Tangney (2000).

In summary, both familism and humility are related to core values in the Latino culture. Whereas familism is a construct that has been measured

EXHIBIT 8.1
Proposed Sample Items of Behavioral Facets of Humility
Rooted in Three Core Values

Humility behavior	Sample items
Readily acknowledges one's limitations	Expresses awe in God's majesty
	Expresses gratitude even during times of suffering
	Talks about how much she or he learns from others—rarely complains
	Not defensive when receiving constructive criticism
	Receives gifts from others without strong resistance
Acknowledges one's strengths	Finds opportunities to improve on strengths
	Simply says thank you when a compliment is given
Readily takes responsibility and admits mistakes to others	Quick to ask for forgiveness
	Kind (and firm) when correcting others
Actively seeks the perspectives and ideas of others	Does not impose ideas on others
	Patient
	Actively listens more than they talk
	Does not have to have the "last word" during an argument
Readily praises others' efforts and contributions	Not judgmental or critical of others' ideas
	Compassionate toward those in need
	Compassionate to individuals who are difficult to love
	Willing to do tasks others perceive as menial

Note. The three core values refer to (a) the frailty of humanity, (b) the belief that every human being has equal dignity and worth, and (c) the belief meaning and happiness in life are not based on possessions or seeking praise or social dominance. For more information about key elements of humility, see Tangney (2000).

and validated with Latino populations, the construct of humility has not. To this end, the field of positive psychology can aid in understanding this central value in the Latino culture. Although the aforementioned constructs can be measured as perceptions, we suggest examining the concrete behavioral facets that can contribute to high-quality relationships. An individual who sacrifices for another (e.g., familism) is consistent with a self-giving love, while a person who exemplifies humility is likely to be forgiving of the human weakness we all have (e.g., Davis, Hook, et al., 2010). Such core values beautifully encompass the concepts of human flourishing and optimal well-being.

Key Measures of Positive Cognitions

In the face of challenges, our thoughts can help us grow or can disable and paralyze us. A growing body of research has shown the cognitive benefits of being bilingual/biliterate (Bialystok, Craik, Green, & Gollan, 2009). An individual who has flexible thinking is also likely to be creative and to be able to generate multiple problem-solving strategies, skills that have a lifelong impact (Bialystok et al., 2009). In situations that appear to be hopeless, a growth mind-set and a deep religious/spiritual faith can circumvent falling into despair and instead foster hope.

Dweck (2000, 2006) has distinguished between individuals who hold a fixed mind-set about their cognitive abilities and individuals who hold a growth mind-set. A *growth mind-set* is characterized by mastery-oriented beliefs or goals and beliefs that one's intelligence is malleable (Dweck, 2000). In contrast, individuals who believe they have a certain amount of intelligence, on a global or domain-specific level, and that they really cannot do much to become smarter, have a *fixed mind-set* (Dweck, 2000). Experimental research has shown that a fixed mind-set is associated with lower levels of persistence in the face of a challenge (Dweck, 2006). Cultivating a growth mind-set is especially significant to Latinos because it is connected to negative messages that minority (Latino) students frequently internalize when they hear about the achievement gap between their racial group and that of White or Asian students (Conchas, 2001). Although interventions have been effective (Blackwell, Trzesniewski, & Dweck, 2007), measures of growth mind-set interventions have yet to be identified. A composite measure of facilitating growth mind-sets among Latinos may include three core factors: beliefs of intelligence (fixed vs. malleable), attributions of failure, and self-efficacy. From a measurement perspective, the scales Dweck used to assess a person's implicit theory of intelligence are simple and entail asking a small set of questions, usually 10 or fewer on a Likert scale with response options ranging from *strongly agree* to *strongly disagree*, about their belief in whether they have a limited amount of intelligence or whether intelligence can be increased by effort. The scales have appeal because they are short and simple to administer and score, and they have face validity. We are greatly encouraged with the emerging evidence for growth mind-sets and suggest the construct can be central in aiding Latinos flourish academically. As yet, no Latino specific growth mind-set scale has appeared, so this would be a worthy research endeavor for someone with this interest.

A growth mind-set is likely to be activated in contexts where one has some level of perceived control; however, many life circumstances have multiple unknowns and we rely on probabilities (e.g., expected likelihood of survival from a certain medical treatment or surgery). In situations like this, the constructs of faith and hope become central to being able to thrive. Within the Latino culture, expressions of faith abound in everyday expressions (e.g., *Nos vemos mañana, si Dios quiere* [We'll see each other tomorrow, God willing], *Que bueno. Gracias a Dios* [How wonderful. Thanks be to God], *Que Dios te bendiga* [May God bless you], *Que Dios te ilumine* [May God enlighten you/your mind] and *Bendicion mami* [Bless me, mom]). In the context of immigrants who flee economic or political persecution, or Latinos who experience discrimination, faith may help one persist and have hope even in the absence of positive affect.

An examination of the multifaceted nature of the effect of religion and spirituality on well-being is a complex endeavor (e.g., extrinsic religious orientation, perceived sanctification of roles and relationships, perceptions of a benevolent God, spiritual experiences, negative religious coping). Thus far, two culturally relevant measures are beginning to emerge in the literature. The developers of the Latino Spiritual Perspectives Scale (LSPS; Campesino, Belyea, & Schwartz, 2009) are in the initial stages of validating a 32-item measure that began when a questionnaire was given to a convenience sample of predominantly Catholic, Latino attendees at a nursing conference (Campesino & Schwartz, 2006). Items were developed based on an understanding of Latino culture (e.g., familism, devotion to our Lady of Guadalupe, liberation theology), with the goal of assessing emotional and behavioral aspects of person's relationship with various divine entities and how a spiritual perspective manifests itself in one's daily life (Campesino et al., 2009). Latinos rated a majority of the items as significantly more important to their lives compared to non-Latinos (Campesino et al., 2009). Sample items include "My well-being is in God's/higher power's hands," "God/Higher Power is loving and kind," "Talking every day with God/Higher Power is important to me," "Feel close to Virgin Mary," "Doing something about injustice is part of my spirituality," and "I help church/community at least once" (Campesino et al., 2009, pp. 76–77).

Another measure making its appearance in the field is a subscale of the Mexican American Values Scale mentioned earlier in the description of familism. Based on focus group interviews and confirmatory factor analysis, a seven-item subscale reflects spiritual beliefs and faith in God (Knight et al., 2010). It is worth noting that the subscale had high factor loadings in both the English and Spanish versions of the measure. Survey participants were asked to rate their beliefs on a 5-point Likert scale (1 = not at all; 5 = completely). Sample items include "If everything is taken away, one still has their faith in God"; "One's belief in God gives inner strength and meaning to life"; and "It is important to thank God every day for all one has." The items constitute a single factor that reflects the centrality and strength derived from one's faith in life. Latinos are often described as having a strong faith in God, but few measures seem to tap into this type of tenacity. Thus, the two measures described above make excellent contributions to the study of Latino faith and positive psychology.

As scale development continues, concepts from current measures developed and administered with non-Latinos could be potentially helpful for Latino faith measures. T. W. Hall and Edwards (1996) developed a Judeo–Christian scale of spiritual maturity and identified a factor of realistic acceptance. It examines whether one is able to maintain contact and communication with God, even in times of spiritual doubt and frustration (e.g., "During the times when I feel frustrated by God for not responding to my prayers, I am able to talk it through with God"). In addition, Rosmarin, Krumrei, and Andersson (2009) developed a measure of Trust/Mistrust in God (e.g., "God loves me immensely"; "No matter how bad things may seem, God's kindness to me never ceases") based on beliefs of God's omnipotence, omniscience, and omnibenevolence. Moreover, a qualitative study among women, who self-identified as Seventh Day Adventists, revealed the robust finding that spirituality was a pervasive theme in the survival, healing, and restoration of survivors of interpersonal violence (Drumm et al., 2014). The interview-based study included a question about resilience (e.g., "How did your spiritual life help you cope with the difficulties?"). Consistent with the work in post-traumatic growth, the women turned to God as their sole source of support, which began a deepening of their spiritual development: "Really, truly, each day was just a matter of prayer"; "I would read my Bible and I would pray and I would get strength for the day"; "I wasn't sleeping a lot but somehow God would give me strength for the day; there have been so many miracles just in the last year and a half . . . we got an eviction notice, and it was only because of God's goodness that He found us another house, not an apartment. He [God] paid the deposit on it through somebody else." The transcripts reveal the power of a strong faith that helps one move beyond mere survival into a realm of healing and restoration. We look forward to seeing measures that capture the richness of a strong faith as an aspect of personal growth, transformation, and well-being.

DEVELOPMENT OF POSITIVE ASSESSMENT TOOLS FOR LATINO AMERICANS

It is evident that in today's increasingly complex world, people are hungering for well-being (e.g., social connection, spirituality). This is evident in our constant use of various forms of social media, growth in programs that incorporate meditation, and other forms of relaxation. However, these practices are still limited in their ability to enable people to develop emotionally intimate interpersonal relationships. If positive psychology is to capture the dynamic nature and vibrancy of individuals who radiate joy and serenity, it follows that our approach to assessment should reflect authentic assessments. We strongly believe that future assessments of positive psychology among Latinos would benefit from more authentic assessments and motivational interviewing approaches. Such approaches would view individuals as active agents and producers of knowledge.

One interesting methodological approach to assessing Latino strengths is the coresearcher methodology whereby even first-grade youth can formulate research questions and then think carefully about whom they would want to interview (e.g., Norton, 2006). In a study on concepts of spirituality among Black and Latino youth, Norton (2006) examined how the young coresearchers interviewed their family members. The researcher first interviewed the children (four separate semistructured interviews and three focus group meetings) and then, in a coresearcher training session, asked young researchers to identify a family member who supported them in their spirituality and who would agree to be interviewed. These children serving as researchers were guided to recall the questions they had been asked in the interview and to develop questions they wanted to ask their family member. One of the five coresearchers was later asked why he chose to interview his brother and he replied,

> I chose Jose because he didn't really know stuff about God so I think it would be a good experience to learn about God. I think he learned why people don't believe in God's spirit. He learned new things and bad stuff. (Norton, 2006, p. 328)

The quote shows that the child coresearcher is authentically and emotionally invested in the research enterprise and is extremely thoughtful about the questions posed. Such an approach has the potential to yield rich and meaningful information into the fullness of a person's life because it honors the inherent dignity and knowledge of the person being interviewed.

Another powerful approach that taps into the inherent and dynamic strengths of an individual is reflected in clinical assessments that use motivational interviewing techniques. Motivational interviewing is designed to strengthen personal motivation for and commitment to change by eliciting and exploring the client's own reasons for wanting change within an atmosphere of acceptance and compassion (Miller & Rollnick, 2002). Even in the face of resistance to therapy, the role of the clinician is to always interact in a manner of acceptance and compassion by asking questions that validate the client's own quest to seek change. Once a client identifies their self-defined goals, their resistance decreases, and this opens the possibility that treatment will be successful. These shifts in clinical practice are consistent with Fredrickson's approach to broadening and theory development based on positive emotions (e.g., Fredrickson, 2001).

Wright and Lopez (2002) emphasized the importance of investigating personal and environmental assets in clients during the first meeting with a client. Such assessments of Latinos may include concepts of familism (e.g., "How do your family members support you?") and faith (e.g., "In what ways do you consider yourself a spiritual person?"). Consistent with the premise of this chapter, Tomasulo and Rashid (2013) recognized that both pain and positive strengths coexist and must be acknowledged. They underscored the importance of never dismissing a client's pain, but rather drawing out the coexistence of positive experiences. For instance, if a client shares that he or she is in therapy only because of complaints from others, a therapist may respond by saying, "It sounds like there are people in your life who care about you" (Tomasulo & Rashid, 2013). In essence, such approaches of clinical assessment are rooted in love and honoring the dignity of the individual.

Throughout this chapter, we have highlighted the importance of recognizing that the study of Latinos must examine the coexistence of positive emotions with negative emotions and incorporate culturally relevant beliefs. We sought to identify a constellation of key strengths, skills, and supports central to optimal well-being and growth at the level of the individual and in relationship with others (e.g., familism, humility, faith). Although certain concepts may not necessarily be immediately viewed as central to flourishing in American society, new fields of study are beginning to uncover the benefits of collectivistic, self-giving leadership styles in the United States (van Dierendonck, 2011). Being able to give of one's self is a key aspect of love.

Fredrickson (2013) operationalized the concept of love (a positive emotion) as positivity resonance and behavioral synchrony (e.g., mutual eye contact) and described the benefits of increased oxytocin on the immune system and emotion regulation. That positive psychology can stimulate study of core values in the social sciences is inspiring. We believe that any individual who flourishes and has a deep sense of fulfillment and purpose also has a profound sense that he or she is loved. We contend that regardless of a person's strengths, optimal development (e.g., a sense of fulfillment and purpose) requires a profound belief that one is loved and that one can see the beauty in oneself and bring it out in others. This dynamic between giving and receiving love can be from a spouse (in humility), parent (rooted in familism), higher power (rooted in faith), child, friend, or even a stranger. A self-giving love entails seeking the good of the other, while also honoring ones dignity and self-respect (not rooted in hedonistic desires/pleasures).

To truly flourish also entails actively empowering individuals on a sociopolitical level (Goodman et al., 2007). We are hopeful that the recommendations made in this chapter can move the field of positive psychology assessment in ways that honor the dignity and recognize the inherent strengths of the Latino population but that also offer a critical hope rooted in solidarity and that address social injustice (Duncan-Andrade, 2009).

REFERENCES

Alva, S. A. (1991). Academic invulnerability among Mexican-American students: The importance of protective resources and appraisals. *Hispanic Journal of Behavioral Sciences, 13,* 18–34. http://dx.doi.org/10.1177/07399863910131002

Arellano, A., & Padilla, A. M. (1996). Academic invulnerability among a select group of Latino university students. *Hispanic Journal of Behavioral Sciences, 18,* 485–507. http://dx.doi.org/10.1177/07399863960184004

Bialystok, E., Craik, F. I. M., Green, D. W., & Gollan, T. H. (2009). Bilingual minds. *Psychological Science in the Public Interest, 10,* 89–129. http://dx.doi.org/10.1177/1529100610387084

Blackwell, L. S., Trzesniewski, K. H., & Dweck, C. S. (2007). Implicit theories of intelligence predict achievement across an adolescent transition: A longitudinal study and an intervention. *Child Development, 78,* 246–263. http://dx.doi.org/10.1111/j.1467-8624.2007.00995.x

Borrero, N., Lee, D., & Padilla, A. M. (2012). Developing a culture of resilience for low-income immigrant youth. *The Urban Review, 45,* 99–116. http://dx.doi.org/10.1007/s11256-012-0215-4

Bryant, F. (2003). Savoring Beliefs Inventory (SBI): A scale for measuring beliefs about savoring. *Journal of Mental Health, 12,* 175–196. http://dx.doi.org/10.1080/0963823031000103489

Calderón-Tena, C. O., Knight, G. P., & Carlo, G. (2011). The socialization of prosocial behavioral tendencies among Mexican American adolescents: The role of familism values. *Cultural Diversity and Ethnic Minority Psychology, 17*(1), 98–106. http://dx.doi.org/10.1037/a0021825

Campa, B. (2013). Pedagogies of survival: Cultural resources to foster resilience among Mexican-American community college students. *Community College Journal of Research and Practice, 37,* 433–452.

Campesino, M., Belyea, M., & Schwartz, G. (2009). Spirituality and cultural identification among Latino and non-Latino college students. *Hispanic Health Care International: The Official Journal of the National Association of Hispanic Nurses, 7*(2), 72–79.

Campesino, M., & Schwartz, G. E. (2006). Spirituality among Latinas/os: Implications of culture in conceptualization and measurement. *Advances in Nursing Science, 29*(1), 69–81. http://dx.doi.org/10.1097/00012272-200601000-00007

Ceballo, R. (2004). From the barrios to Yale: The role of parenting strategies in Latino families. *Hispanic Journal of Behavioral Sciences, 26,* 171–186. http://dx.doi.org/10.1177/0739986304264572

Cervantes, R. C., Padilla, A. M., Napper, L. E., & Goldbach, J. T. (2013). Acculturation-related stress and mental health outcomes among three generations of Hispanic adolescents. *Hispanic Journal of Behavioral Sciences, 35,* 451–468. http://dx.doi.org/10.1177/0739986313500924

Conchas, G. Q. (2001). Structuring failure and success: Understanding the variability in Latino school engagement. *Harvard Educational Review, 71*, 475–505. http://dx.doi.org/10.17763/haer.71.3.280w814v1603473k

Davis, D. E., & Hook, J. N. (2013, October). Measuring humility and its effects. *Observer: Newsletter of the Association for Psychological Science, 26*(8). Retrieved from https://www.psychologicalscience.org/index.php/publications/observer/2013/october-13/measuring-humility-and-its-positive-effects.html

Davis, D. E., Hook, J. N., Worthington, E. L., Van Tongeren, D. R., Gartner, A. L., & Jennings, D. J. (2010). Relational spirituality and forgiveness: Development of the Spiritual Humility Scale (SHS). *Journal of Psychology and Theology, 38*, 91–100.

Davis, D. E., Hook, J. N., Worthington, E. L., Jr., Van Tongeren, D. R., Gartner, A. L., Jennings, D. J., II, & Emmons, R. A. (2011). Relational humility: Conceptualizing and measuring humility as a personality judgment. *Journal of Personality Assessment, 93*, 225–234. http://dx.doi.org/10.1080/00223891.2011.558871

Davis, D. E., Worthington, E. L., Jr., & Hook, J. N. (2010). Humility: Review of measurement strategies and conceptualization as personality judgment. *The Journal of Positive Psychology, 5*, 243–252. http://dx.doi.org/10.1080/17439761003791672

Delgado, M., & Barton, K. (1998). Murals in Latino communities: Social indicators of community strengths. *Social Work, 43*, 346–356. http://dx.doi.org/10.1093/sw/43.4.346

Delgado-Romero, E. A., Nevels, B. J., Capielo, C., Galvan, N., & Torres, V. (2013). Latina/o Americans. In G. McAuliffe (Ed.), *Culturally alert counseling: A comprehensive introduction* (2d ed., pp. 293–314). Thousand Oaks, CA: Sage.

Donahue, D. M. (2011). Connecting classrooms and communities through Chicano mural art. *Multicultural Perspectives, 13*(2), 70–78. http://dx.doi.org/10.1080/15210960.2011.571548

Drumm, R., Popescu, M., Cooper, L., Trecartin, S., Seifert, M., Foster, T., & Kilcher, C. (2014). "God just brought me through it": Spiritual coping strategies for resilience among intimate partner violence survivors. *Journal of Clinical Social Work, 42*, 385–394. http://dx.doi.org/10.1007/s10615-013-0449-y

Duncan-Andrade, J. M. (2009). Note to educators: Hope required when growing roses in concrete. *Harvard Educational Review, 79*, 181–194. http://dx.doi.org/10.17763/haer.79.2.nu3436017730384w

Dweck, C. S. (2000). *Self-theories: Their role in motivation, personality, and development.* New York, NY: Psychology Press.

Dweck, C. S. (2006). *Mindset: The new psychology of success.* New York, NY: Ballantine Books.

Eamon, M. K., & Mulder, C. (2005). Predicting antisocial behavior among Latino young adolescents: An ecological systems analysis. *American Journal of Orthopsychiatry, 75*(1), 117–127.

Enriquez, L. E. (2011). "Because we feel the pressure and we feel the support": Examining the educational success of undocumented immigrant Latina/o students. *Harvard Educational Review, 81*, 476–499. http://dx.doi.org/10.17763/haer.81.3.w7k703q050143762

Exline, J. J. (2008). Taming the wild ego. In J. A. Bauer & H. A. Wayment (Eds.), *Transcending self-interest: Psychological explorations of the quiet ego* (pp. 53–62). Washington, DC: American Psychological Association. http://dx.doi.org/10.1037/11771-005

Exline, J. J. (2012). Humility and the ability to receive help from others. *Journal of Psychology and Christianity, 31*(1), 40–50.

Exline, J. J., & Geyer, A. L. (2004). Perceptions of humility: A preliminary study. *Self and Identity, 3*, 95–114. http://dx.doi.org/10.1080/13576500342000077

Fredrickson, B. L. (2001). The role of positive emotions in positive psychology. The broaden-and-build theory of positive emotions. *American Psychologist, 56*, 218–226. http://dx.doi.org/10.1037/0003-066X.56.3.218

Fredrickson, B. (2013). *Love 2.0: Finding health and happiness in moments of connection.* New York, NY: Hudson Street Press.

Gandara, P. (1995). *Over the ivy walls: The educational mobility of low-income Chicanos.* Albany: State University of New York Press.

Germán, M., Gonzales, N. A., & Dumka, L. (2009). Familism values as a protective factor for Mexican-origin adolescents exposed to deviant peers. *The Journal of Early Adolescence, 29*(1), 16–42. http://dx.doi.org/10.1177/0272431608324475

Gonzalez, R., & Padilla, A. M. (1997). The academic resilience of Mexican American high school students. *Hispanic Journal of Behavioral Sciences, 19*, 301–317. http://dx.doi.org/10.1177/07399863970193004

Goodman, L. A., Litwin, A., Bohlig, A., Weintraub, S. R., Green, A., Walker, J., . . . Ryan, N. (2007). Applying feminist theory to community practice: A multilevel empowerment intervention for low-income women with depression. In E. Aldarondo (Ed.), *Advancing social justice through clinical practice* (pp. 267–290). Mahwah, NJ: Lawrence Erlbaum.

Hall, M. E., Langer, R., & McMartin, J. (2010). The role of suffering in human flourishing: Contributions from positive psychology, theology, and philosophy. *Journal of Psychology and Theology, 38*, 111–121.

Hall, T. W., & Edwards, K. J. (1996). The initial development and factor analysis of the spiritual assessment inventory. *Journal of Psychology and Theology, 24*, 233–246.

Heatherton, T. F., & Wyland, C. L. (2003). Assessing self-esteem. In S. J. Lopez & C. R. Synder (Eds.), *Positive psychology assessment* (pp. 219–233). Washington, DC: American Psychological Association. http://dx.doi.org/10.1037/10612-014

Knight, G. P., Gonzales, N. A., Saenz, D. S., Bonds, D. D., Germán, M., Deardorff, J., . . . Updegraff, K. A. (2010). The Mexican American Cultural Values Scales for adolescents and adults. *The Journal of Early Adolescence, 30*, 444–481. http://dx.doi.org/10.1177/0272431609338178

LaBouff, J. P., Rowatt, W. C., Johnson, M. K., Tsang, J., & Willerton, G. M. (2012). Humble persons are more helpful than less humble persons: Evidence from three studies. *The Journal of Positive Psychology, 7*(1), 16–29. http://dx.doi.org/10.1080/17439760.2011.626787

Larsen, J. T., & McGraw, A. P. (2011). Further evidence for mixed emotions. *Journal of Personality and Social Psychology, 100,* 1095–1110. http://dx.doi.org/10.1037/a0021846

Linesch, D., Aceves, H. C., Quezada, P., Trochez, M., & Zuniga, E. (2012). An art therapy exploration of immigration with Latino families. *Art Therapy, 29,* 120–126. http://dx.doi.org/10.1080/07421656.2012.701603

Linley, P. A., & Joseph, S. (2004). Positive change following trauma and adversity: A review. *Journal of Traumatic Stress, 17*(1), 11–21. http://dx.doi.org/10.1023/B:JOTS.0000014671.27856.7e

Lucas, R. E., Diener, E., & Larsen, R. J. (2003). Measuring positive emotions. In S. J. Lopez & C. R. Snyder (Eds.), *Positive psychology assessment: A handbook of models and measures* (pp. 139–155). Washington, DC: American Psychological Association. http://dx.doi.org/10.1037/10612-013

Luhtanen, R., & Crocker, J. (1992). A Collective Self-esteem Scale: Self-evaluation of one's social identity. *Personality and Social Psychology Bulletin, 18,* 302–318. http://dx.doi.org/10.1177/0146167292183006

Markus, H. R., & Kitayama, S. (1991). Culture and the self: Implications for cognition, emotion, and motivation. *Psychological Review, 98,* 224–253. http://dx.doi.org/10.1037/0033-295X.98.2.224

Marotta, S. A., & Garcia, J. G. (2003). Latinos in the United States in 2000. *Hispanic Journal of Behavioral Sciences, 25,* 13–34. http://dx.doi.org/10.1177/0739986303251693

Masten, A. S. (2001). Ordinary magic. Resilience processes in development. *American Psychologist, 56,* 227–238. http://dx.doi.org/10.1037/0003-066X.56.3.227

Miller, W. R., & Rollnick, S. (2002). *Motivational interviewing: Preparing people to change* (2nd ed.). New York, NY: Guilford Press.

Motel, S., & Patten, E. (2011). *Statistical portrait of Hispanics in the U.S. 2011.* Retrieved from http://www.pewhispanic.org/2013/02/15/statistical-portrait-of-hispanics-in-the-united-states-2011/

Moxley, D. P. (2013). Incorporating art-making into the cultural practice of social work. *Journal of Ethnic and Cultural Diversity in Social Work, 22*(3-4), 235–255. http://dx.doi.org/10.1080/15313204.2013.843136

Norton, N. E. L. (2006). Talking spirituality with family members: Black and Latina/o children co-researcher methodologies. *The Urban Review, 38,* 313–334. http://dx.doi.org/10.1007/s11256-006-0036-4

Ojeda, L., & Piña-Watson, B. (2013). Day laborers' life satisfaction: The role of familismo, spirituality, work, health, and discrimination. *Cultural Diversity and Ethnic Minority Psychology, 19,* 270–278. http://dx.doi.org/10.1037/a0032961

Passel, J. S., Cohn, D., & Lopez, M. H. (2011, March 24). *Census 2010: 50 million Latinos: Hispanics account for more than half of nation's growth in past decade.* Washington, DC: Pew Research Hispanic Center.

Pavlenko, A. (Ed.). (2006). *Bilingual minds: Emotional experience, expression and representation.* Clevedon, England: Multilingual Matters.

Rosmarin, D. H., Krumrei, E. J., & Andersson, G. (2009). Religion as a predictor of psychological distress in two religious communities. *Cognitive Behaviour Therapy, 38*(1), 54–64. http://dx.doi.org/10.1080/16506070802477222

Rowatt, W. C., Powers, C., Targhetta, V., Comer, J., Kennedy, S., & Labouff, J. (2006). Development and initial validation of an implicit measure of humility relative to arrogance. *The Journal of Positive Psychology, 1*(4), 198–211. http://dx.doi.org/10.1080/17439760600885671

Sabogal, F., Marin, G., Otero-Sabogal, R., Marin, B. V., & Perez-Stable, E. J. (1987). Hispanic familism and acculturation: What changes and what doesn't? *Hispanic Journal of Behavioral Sciences, 9,* 397–412. http://dx.doi.org/10.1177/07399863870094003

Seligman, M. E. P. (2002). *Authentic happiness: Using the new positive psychology to realize your potential for lasting fulfillment.* New York, NY: Free Press.

Seligman, M. (2011). *Flourish: A visionary new understanding of happiness and well-being.* New York, NY: Free Press.

Sue, D. W., & Constantine, M. G. (2003). Optimal human functioning in people of color in the United States. In W. B. Walsh (Ed.), *Counseling psychology and optimal human functioning* (pp. 151–169). Mahwah, NJ: Erlbaum.

Tangney, J. P. (2000). Humility: Theoretical perspectives, empirical findings and directions for future research. *Journal of Social and Clinical Psychology, 19,* 70–82. http://dx.doi.org/10.1521/jscp.2000.19.1.70

Tedeschi, R. G., & Calhoun, L. G. (2004). Posttraumatic growth: Conceptual foundations and empirical evidence. *Psychological Inquiry, 15,* 1–18. http://dx.doi.org/10.1207/s15327965pli1501_01

Tomasulo, D. J., & Rashid, T. (2013, June). *Words and well-being: Health and growing through stories.* Workshop presented at the Third World Congress of Positive Psychology, Los Angeles, CA.

Tucker-Raymond, E., Rosario-Ramos, E., & Rosario, M. L. (2011). Cultural persistence, political resistance, and hope in the community and school-based art of a Puerto Rican Diaspora neighborhood. *Equity & Excellence in Education, 44,* 270–286. http://dx.doi.org/10.1080/10665684.2011.563678

Umaña-Taylor, A. J., & Updegraff, K. A. (2007). Latino adolescents' mental health: Exploring the interrelations among discrimination, ethnic identity, cultural orientation, self-esteem, and depressive symptoms. *Journal of Adolescence, 30,* 549–567. http://dx.doi.org/10.1016/j.adolescence.2006.08.002

Valenzuela, A., & Dornbusch, S. M. (1994). Familism and social capital in the academic-achievement of Mexican origin and Anglo adolescents. *Social Science Quarterly, 75*(1), 19–36.

van Dierendonck, D. (2011). Servant leadership: A review and synthesis. *Journal of Management, 37,* 1228–1261. http://dx.doi.org/10.1177/0149206310380462

Villarreal, R., Blozis, S. A., & Widaman, K. F. (2005). Factorial invariance of a pan-Hispanic familism scale. *Hispanic Journal of Behavioral Sciences, 27,* 409–425. http://dx.doi.org/10.1177/0739986305281125

Wright, B. A., & Lopez, S. J. (2002). Widening the diagnostic focus: A case for including human strengths and environmental resources. In C. R. Snyder & S. J. Lopez (Eds.), *Handbook of positive psychology* (pp. 26–44). New York, NY: Oxford University Press.

Yahirun, J. J., Perreira, K. M., & Fuligni, A. J. (2013). Family obligation across contexts: Hispanic youth in North Carolina and southern California. *Journal of Family Issues.* Advance online publication. http://dx.doi.org/10.1177/0192513X13501664

9

POSITIVE PSYCHOLOGY ASSESSMENT IN AFRICAN AMERICANS

LAURA P. KOHN-WOOD AND ALVIN THOMAS

Despite a few notable exceptions, the field of positive psychology has largely ignored the rich and prescriptive tradition of understanding how sociocultural factors influence adaptive characteristics. This omission has been most specific to positive psychology assessment. Many assessment tools for measuring strengths ignore culturally imposed variance in the levels of power that individuals can exert to change their lives; cultural differences in the valence of negative and positive emotion and emotional regulation orientations; and the experiences of discrimination, racism, racial identity development, acculturation, and immigration. All of these experiences indicate that individuals live their lives within systems and contexts and that the interactions between individuals and these systems can explain human behavior much more clearly than simply focusing on individual factors or ecological factors in isolation (Bronfenbrenner, 1979; Lazarus & Folkman, 1984). The missed opportunity to articulate sociocultural determinants in

http://dx.doi.org/10.1037/14799-009
Positive Psychology in Racial and Ethnic Groups: Theory, Research, and Practice, E. C. Chang, C. A. Downey, J. K. Hirsch, and N. J. Lin (Editors)

positive psychology and to develop assessment tools for understanding positive psychological constructs in ethnocultural groups has stunted the value of the field as applied to diverse populations.

VALUE OF ASSESSING POSITIVE STRENGTHS IN AFRICAN AMERICANS

African American populations are largely absent in the burgeoning literature on positive psychology assessment. This is unfortunate given the historical and contemporary psychological literature that examines sociocultural constructs related to race, as well as between- and within-group differences. There is relatively little to draw on to understand the assessment of characteristics that have come to be known as *positive psychology constructs* among African American populations. Independent of the positive psychology field, however, some assessment tools have been developed to understand factors such as group affiliation and racial identity, coping, religious involvement, and spirituality among African Americans. Also, the application of assessment tools for understanding the role of self-esteem, positive emotions, humor, forgiveness, gratitude, optimism, and hope among African American groups has yielded important distinctions, many similarities, and promise for the future development of culturally specific tools.

KEY MEASURES OF POSITIVE AFFECT IN AFRICAN AMERICANS

Research on cultural differences in positive emotion has largely involved comparative studies of Asian, Asian American, and White American groups (Leu, Wang, & Koo, 2011; Miyamoto, Uchida, & Ellsworth, 2010; Tsai, Knutson, & Fung, 2006), perhaps because of previous psychological evidence of differences in emotion, cognition, and behaviors between collectivist and individualist cultures (Mattis & Jagers, 2001; Utsey, Adams, & Bolden, 2000). African Americans share an individualist cultural context with White Americans with respect to international comparisons, but there is some (limited) evidence of nuanced cultural differences in emotion expression among ethnocultural groups in the United States, evidence that is primarily focused on mental health assessment. Therefore, the need to develop more culturally specific or culturally adapted tools to adequately understand emotion in diverse populations is clear.

Positive Emotions and Affect

Similar to studies of the differences between Asians and European Americans in the association of positive emotion and depression, Ayalon and Young (2003) found significant differences between African American and White American clinical patients; notably, self-dislike was a stronger factor in depression severity for White Americans, whereas in African Americans depression severity was associated with somatic symptoms of sleep, libido, and appetite. At equivalent levels of depression, African Americans reported less pessimism, self-blame, suicidal ideation, and dissatisfaction than White Americans. Another study, investigating the factor structure of the Center for Epidemiologic Studies Depression Scale (Radloff, 1977), found evidence for factorial variance between African American and White American adults; items assessing positive emotional states, including enjoyment of life, feelings of energy, and feelings of being cared for, were more often endorsed by African Americans (Kohn-Wood, Banks, Lee, & Ivey, 2013). Furthermore, robust evidence for differences in the prevalence of diagnosed depression by race exists, with African Americans showing consistently lower risk for diagnosed mood disorder than did White Americans (Breslau, Kendler, Su, Gaxiola-Aguilar, & Kessler, 2005; Williams et al., 2007). These studies demonstrate possible differences in negative affective states, but it is possible that the absence of positive emotion drives race differences (Hirsch, Visser, Chang, & Jeglic, 2012).

Decreased risk for diagnosed psychiatric disorders among minority populations is somewhat counter to the evidence that African Americans report increased depressive symptom levels on measures of symptom intensity and frequency. For example, African Americans and Latinos score higher than White Americans on mental health symptom scales (Ostrove et al., 1999; Plant & Sachs-Ericsson, 2004) and general measures of psychological distress (Vega & Rumbaut, 1991), leading some to conclude that African Americans are at greater risk for psychiatric problems. Discrepant findings are likely related to measurement issues, however, as symptom scales and general measures of distress likely include statistical noise related to individual assessments of life stress and social disadvantage unrelated to diagnostic criterion (Coyne, Fechner-Bates, & Schwenk, 1994; McGonagle & Kessler, 1990). This assertion has been supported, for instance, in studies of African American primary care patients, who are significantly more likely to report greater levels of stress, poor health-related quality of life, and physical disability in comparison with White American patients (C. Brown, Schulberg, & Madonia, 1996; Jackson-Triche et al., 2000). Nondiagnostic mental health symptom scales are likely to overestimate risk for psychiatric problems because items on these tools may confound diagnostic risk with psychosocial difficulty unrelated to psychiatric illness. An alternative explanation to these contradictory findings is that diagnoses found in various editions of the American Psychiatric Association's *Diagnostic and Statistical Manual of Mental Disorders* do not adequately capture racial differences in disorder nosology (T. N. Brown, 2003; Mabry & Kiecolt, 2005).

Similarly, with regard to emotion regulation and emotion socialization, evidence for cultural differences is sparse, but limited research suggests that differences exist between African American and White American children's regulation strategy and future externalizing behaviors (Supplee, Skuban, Shaw, & Prout, 2009). Cultural differences in emotion socialization behaviors, however, may be strongest between Asian and both African American and White groups, given retrospective reports of positive emotion expression (Morelen, Jacob, Suveg, Jones, & Thomassin, 2013); indeed, valuation of positive emotion appears to vary by culture, with Chinese individuals perceiving less value for high-arousal positive affect than Americans (Tsai et al., 2006). Finally, in a study of emotion regulation involving several methods of assessment, constructs predictive of adaptive regulation for middle-income White American children (e.g., child–parent attachment or vagal tone) do not similarly predict adaptive regulation for low-income African American children (Kidwell & Barnett, 2007); for the African American sample, however, neither construct was sufficient in isolation—both assessments were needed to provide significant prediction. These results suggest that validation of existing assessments is necessary for diverse populations, and the development of culturally specific tools for assessing emotion may be needed.

Yet, several existing assessment tools may be useful for studying affect in African Americans. For instance, the Positive and Negative Affect Schedule—Expanded predicted anxiety in African American females (Petrie, Chapman, & Vines, 2013) and, in a study examining race differences in the factor structure of two subjective well-being scales, the Life Satisfaction Index A was found to be invariant by race (Liang, Lawrence, & Bollen, 1987). The Beck Depression Inventory–Second Edition (Beck, Steer, & Brown, 1996) was tested for factorial invariance in a sample of more than 7,000 college students, and was found to be representative of the same construct (i.e., tested the same thing) across sex, race, and ethnicity (Whisman, Judd, Whiteford, & Gelhorn, 2013). Similarly, no evidence of racial bias was found for the Multidimensional Students' Life Satisfaction Scale total score in a test of factorial validity with African American and White middle school students (Huebner & Dew, 1993); however, race differences did exist for reliability indicators of the School Domain subscale (with significantly lower internal consistency for African American students' scores). On the Self Domain subscale, factor loadings for African American students on two items were substantially lower, and criterion validity scores for African American students were weaker (Huebner, 1998). Although race differences in assessment may be subtle and difficult to detect with tests of invariance using total scale scores, these examples suggest there are appropriate, adequate tools available for assessing emotion among African Americans. However, care should be used and tools that have not been validated by race should be subject to rigorous psychometric evaluation.

Self-Esteem

Self-esteem has been considered a crucial element of positive human development even before positive psychology emerged as a field of study, and it exhibits cultural variance (e.g., African Americans report higher levels of self-esteem than other ethnic groups, including White Americans, across the lifespan). Several problematic issues with self-esteem assessment have been identified, however.

In a meta-analytic review of 261 studies, self-esteem scores were consistently higher for African American children, adolescents, and young adults, in comparison with White Americans, and this race difference increased with age and for female sex, but varied based on whether the assessment tool measured general versus domain-specific self-esteem (Gray-Little & Hafdahl, 2000). The largest difference in effect sizes was for the Rosenberg (1965) Self-Esteem Scale, with approximately a quarter of a standard deviation advantage for African American subjects in comparison with White Americans. Smaller advantages were apparent for the Self-Esteem Inventory (Coopersmith, 1981), the Tennessee Self-Concept Scale (Fitts & Roid, 1964), and the Piers-Harris Children's Self-Concept Scale (Piers, 1969). Gray-Little and Hafdahl (2000) offered social identity theory as the most likely explanation of the African American advantage for self-esteem, such that racial/ethnic identity is more meaningful for African Americans than White Americans, and it is more strongly associated with individual self-esteem. However, other researchers have investigated whether differences in scores represent true differences in self-esteem or instances of factorial variance such that existing measures are not capturing the same construct across groups.

Examinations of the factorial structure and psychometric properties of self-esteem have found mixed evidence for invariance across race/ethnicity. Michaels, Barr, Roosa, and Knight (2007) used an adapted form of the Harter (1985) Self-Perception Profile for Children in a sample of more than 1,300 diverse students ages 9 to 14 years and found invariance in the factor structure of three of the Harter scales for African American students (physical appearance, behavioral conduct, and social acceptance). In a study of the psychometric properties of the Harter with a sample of African American adolescent girls, the domain-specific subscales were found to be problematic in three ways: (a) the obtained factor structure was discrepant from normative data, with not a single factor identical to those obtained in published psychometric results using White American samples; (b) the domain subscale correlations were higher than those reported previously with White American samples, indicating significantly greater overlap of self-perception items among African American girls; and (c) the correlation with the Rosenberg scale was much lower in the study, indicating poor convergent validity (Stewart, Roberts, & Kim, 2010).

Nevertheless, some evidence indicates adequate internal consistency and partial validity of the Rosenberg scale for use with African American single mothers, perhaps because self-esteem is conceptualized as a bidimensional construct unique to this population that separately considers racial esteem and rejection of negative stereotyping (Hatcher & Hall, 2009). These findings map on to earlier conceptualizations of preservation of self-esteem by African American college students in the face of negative stereotyping, through psychological disengagement, whereby African Americans maintain self-worth and agency when they discount negative information about their group or devalue such information (Crocker & Major, 2003). Other researchers have suggested that self-esteem measurement conflates self-worth with other constructs, thereby artificially increasing reported self-esteem among African Americans. Specifically, Zeigler-Hill and colleagues have indicated that the African American self-esteem advantage is due to either greater levels of impression management (Zeigler-Hill, Wallace, & Meyers, 2012) or narcissism (Zeigler-Hill & Wallace, 2011).

Overall, the literature examining self-esteem assessment among African Americans indicates that existing measures should be used with caution because of possible variance in the construct. In addition, most studies can be critiqued on the basis that all comparisons are between an ethnic group and the White American group, as if White Americans represent the normative criterion group against which all others are measured. This type of approach has limited our understanding of ethnic and cultural variation in psychological phenomena in the field in general, plaguing our understanding of African Americans' self-worth ever since the misinterpreted doll studies that supported school desegregation (Clark & Clark, 1939). A modern conceptualization of self-esteem is needed, which applies a conceptual framework that uses positive constructs such as resilience, character strengths, and social identity theory rather than processes involving pathology or deception. In this way, the specific cultural strengths of African American self-concept development could contribute more broadly to the comprehension of human thriving.

KEY MEASURES OF POSITIVE BEHAVIORS
IN AFRICAN AMERICANS

Based on national survey data, the prevalence rates of many psychiatric disorders are either equivalent or lower for ethnic minorities in comparison with White Americans, despite persistent disparities in physical health problems by race. African Americans experience similar or, in some age groups lower, rates of major depressive disorder than White Americans, and rates of some anxiety disorders and substance dependence are equivalent or lower among African Americans in comparison with other groups (Breslau et al., 2005; Seng, Kohn-Wood, & Odera, 2005; Williams et al., 2007). Furthermore, rates of death by suicide, a marker of severe internalized despair, are lowest among African American women compared to African American men and White American women (Perry, Pullen, & Oser, 2012). Therefore, despite major racial disparities in education, socioeconomic conditions, and physical health (perhaps caused by the effects of discrimination and racism), rates of mental disorder prevalence more often show an advantage for African Americans, yet little is known about factors that contribute to these decreased rates.

It is possible that many African Americans have developed specific positive, protective behaviors as a response to difficult life conditions that mitigate, to some extent, the emotional cost of discrimination and minority or low socioeconomic status. Developing specific tools for assessing potentially protective behaviors is therefore a critical role for positive psychology and, with regard to African Americans, may focus on topics such as forgiveness, religious or spiritual involvement and behaviors, and culturally unique coping strategies.

Forgiveness

Forgiveness has become a focus of inquiry for positive psychologists because it has a beneficial effect on deleterious mental and physical health problems that result from perceived offenses and difficult life events. As such, the assessment of forgiveness has advanced, with the construct being defined in many ways (McCullough, 2008), including as an aspect of, but not limited to, religious or spiritual practice (Worthington, Witvliet, Pietrini, & Miller 2007), consisting of cognitive, emotional, and behavioral elements that may be related to mental health (Harris et al., 2006) and involving several targets, self, others, or God (Hirsch, Webb, & Jeglic, 2012). As an example of how forgiveness may be important for mental health, Hirsch, Webb, and Jeglic (2012) assessed forgiveness of self and others and being forgiven by

God as moderators of the relation between anger and suicidal behavior, in a racially and ethnically diverse sample of college students. They found that self-forgiveness significantly moderated both inward and outward anger and suicidal thoughts and behavior, after covarying ethnicity. Thus, in this study, differences in forgiveness were not noted across racial and ethnic groups.

Other studies, however, have found robust evidence for differences in the amount and function of forgiveness between African American and White American adults. For example, older African Americans are more likely to forgive themselves and others and to feel that they have God's forgiveness than are older White Americans, and they are more likely to have expectations of acts of contrition and initiate processes of reconciliation (Krause, 2012). In another study, using a large national data set, forgiveness acted as a protective factor for increased self-reported health, decreased alcohol use, and chronic health conditions for African Americans but not for White Americans (McFarland, Smith, Toussaint, & Thomas, 2012). Finally, forgiveness was a significantly more powerful buffer for reducing views of discrimination, reducing negative affect, and increasing cognitive performance in ethnic minorities compared with White Americans, although it had a salubrious overall effect for the total sample (Burrow & Hill, 2012). Given such inconsistencies and significant differences in religious/spiritual behavior associated with psychopathology for African Americans compared with White Americans (Kohn-Wood, Hammond, Haynes, Ferguson, & Jackson, 2012), this area of inquiry is an important focus of assessment.

Religious Involvement, Behavior, and Coping

The field of assessment of religion, religious involvement, and religious behavior among African Americans had been firmly established prior to and separate from the field of positive psychology. Religious beliefs are integral to the lives of African Americans, with eight out of 10 respondents from seven national surveys reporting that religious beliefs were very important (Chatters, Taylor, & Lincoln, 1999). African Americans have demonstrated higher levels of both public and private religious behaviors, including religious participation (i.e., church attendance), spiritual readings, and prayer than White Americans (R. J. Taylor, Chatters, & Levin, 2004), suggesting that organized religion and engagement with religious and spiritual practices are ubiquitous aspects of life among African Americans (Boyd-Franklin, 2010; Mattis & Jagers, 2001). Moreover, African American college students report significant and varied use of religious participation and religious problem solving (Constantine, Wilton, Gainor, & Lewis, 2002), and religious coping is significantly higher among African Americans and Black Caribbean individuals than White Americans (Chatters, Taylor, Jackson, & Lincoln, 2008).

Previous research has also assessed the protective role of *religious coping*, defined as the use of religious-based beliefs as problem solving or coping mechanisms (Pargament et al., 1994) and as "the extent to which persons use their religious beliefs and practices to help adapt to difficult life situations and stressful life events" (Koenig, McCullough, & Larson, 2001, p. 502). Dimensions of religious coping include *collaborative religious coping*, defined as working together with God to solve problems; *deferred religious coping*, or relying more heavily on God to solve the problem; and *self-directed religious coping*, which emphasizes that people have (God-given) freedom to direct the course of their lives (Pargament et al., 1988). In addition, the 14-item Brief RCOPE that measures positive (e.g., sense of spiritual connectedness) and negative (e.g., signs of spiritual tension or negative reappraisals of God) religious coping strategies demonstrates robust psychometric properties (Pargament, Feuille, & Burdzy, 2011).

In previous research, African Americans reported the use of religious resources and engagement as coping techniques for negative life circumstances, including daily and chronic stress and distress (Pargament, Koenig, & Perez, 2000). Religious coping, therefore, may be an important positive psychological factor that offsets difficulties of everyday life but perhaps impedes use of formal mental health resources.

Others have suggested that religion may serve as an important coping method for individuals with mental illness, including African Americans. Religious participation by African Americans may be a protective factor that could explain lower lifetime prevalence rates of psychiatric disorders (Lee & Newberg, 2005). In a meta-analytic study examining religiosity and depression, a significant though small effect size exists for the negative association between religious coping and depression, although most individual studies do not examine the effects of race or ethnicity across the different types of religious coping (Smith, McCullough, & Poll, 2003). Thus, the assessment of specific components of African American coping, of which religious coping is just one form, is needed.

Coping

Some researchers have speculated that African Americans may engage in culturally specific coping strategies or exhibit other forms of resilience, such as preservation of esteem and avoidance of psychological insult, that buffer negative life experiences and prevent the onset of psychopathology (Breslau et al., 2005; Williams, Spencer, & Jackson, 1999) in the face of social disadvantage. Self-esteem formation theory (Crocker & Major, 1989; Gecas & Schwalbe, 1983) posits that individuals prevent threats to self-esteem through appraisal and coping strategies that deflect negative, threatening information or events. Some researchers have suggested that individuals who consider a given group membership (e.g., African American) to be an important source of identity have a stronger motivation to engage in behavioral and psychological strategies that protect and maintain that social identity (Schmader, 2002). Major and Schmader (1998) assessed a particular form of coping called *psychological disengagement*, defined as attempts to discount or devalue negative information or experiences in order to offset deleterious effects, that is used by members of stigmatized minority groups to protect self-esteem, often in response to discrimination (Crocker & Major, 1994). Racial identity may be related to variance in the degree to which African Americans engage in strategies to cope with stereotypes (Major & Schmader, 1998).

Unfortunately, research on psychological disengagement and other racially unique cognitive coping strategies has been limited to studies of academic achievement and, thus, it is not clear whether strategies developed by ethnic minorities as a response to negative stereotyping or social inferiorization can generalize as coping strategies for other kinds of emotionally distressing, negative events. It is possible that these coping strategies are limited to racially loaded situations where negative expectations of minorities' performances are common (e.g., situations such as academic examination that may be characterized by stereotype threat; Steele & Aronson, 1995). Additional evidence is needed to link psychological disengagement strategies to mental health.

The development of coping models and assessment tools specific to African Americans has been restricted largely to research examining coping with stress from race-related oppression, discrimination, and minority status. Researchers have suggested that historically based spiritual beliefs and rituals, with roots in West African cultural values, have shaped coping among African Americans (Plummer & Slane, 1996; Utsey et al., 2000). Others have emphasized collectivity and interconnectedness among African Americans, which results in a naturalistic support system, such as the support of family, friends, and colleagues (Post & Weddington, 1997). Several examples of conceptual models have been proposed for explaining African Americans' responses to race-related stress. Harrell (1979) identified several coping styles among African Americans responding to racism ranging from continued apathy to cognitive flexibility. The Africultural Coping Systems Inventory (Utsey et al., 2000) was developed to measure culture-specific coping strategies used by African Americans when faced with stressful situations. Similarly, the TRIOS model (a model that is based on the cultural elements time, rhythm, improvisation, orality, and spirituality) conceptualizes a reactive worldview and coping method, developed and adapted over time by African Americans to cope with a context of racism (Jones, 2003). The model comprises ego-resilient, self-protective mechanisms and self-enhancing motivations used by African

Americans in the context of threat, such as persistent racism. With regard to gender and race, the Multi-Axial Model of Coping suggests that low-income, inner city African women engage in coping strategies that fall along three axes: prosocial–antisocial, active–passive, and direct–indirect (Riley-Eddins, Hobfall, & Jackson, 2000). The term *armoring* has been used to describe a strategy used by African American women as a mechanism of adaptation for coping with racial oppression (Edmonson Bell & Nkomo, 1998), consisting of recognizing and labeling racism, identifying positive role models, and understanding the racist experience as containing feelings of rejection, confusion, and difference (Greene, 1994).

Theoretical models represent unique conceptualizations of coping strategies among African Americans, but empirical support and specific assessment tools are scant. One of the few empirical studies of coping responses among African Americans used Lazarus and Folkman's (1984) Ways of Coping measure to examine coping patterns by race and found that African Americans used more problem-focused coping than White Americans, including confrontive coping and planful problem solving, and were more likely to seek social support (Plummer & Slane, 1996). African Americans were also more likely to engage in distancing, escape avoidance, positive reappraisal, and self-controlling strategies. However, in the context of racial stress, African Americans used less distancing, less support seeking, and less planful problem solving than White Americans. In another study, the relationship between poor problem solving and suicidal behavior was exacerbated by loneliness across ethnic groups in a sample of African American, White American, and Asian college students (Hirsch, Chang, & Jeglic, 2012). This and other studies suggest that race differences exist in coping, yet little is known regarding the assessment and role of this variation.

KEY MEASURES OF POSITIVE COGNITIONS IN AFRICAN AMERICANS

Assessment of positive cognitions, such as optimism, hope, creativity, and courage, is arguably the area to which the field of positive psychology has contributed most in terms of opening new fields of inquiry. However, scholarship specific to African American populations has been limited.

Optimism

The popularity of optimism in positive psychology is, in part, based on the utility of this construct for promoting resilience, combating psychopathology, and offering improved quality of life and longevity. Researchers who have assessed optimism cross-culturally, however, have found that it does not offer uniform benefits across ethnic groups, including Japanese Americans (Chang & Asakawa, 2003) and African Americans (Cardemil, Reivich, Beevers, Seligman, & James, 2007).

Despite this, there have been some investigations of the assessment and function of optimism among African American youth. Researchers conducting the Penn Resiliency Program reported results from a preventive intervention program for low-income minority children designed to reduce or prevent depressive symptoms, decrease negative thoughts and hopelessness, and increase perceived competence (Cardemil et al., 2007). Measures included the Hopelessness Scale (Kazdin, Rodgers, & Colbus, 1986), which assesses the degree to which children feel hopeless about the future. Postintervention and 2-year follow-up analyses showed no effects for African American children, despite some benefit among Latino children, perhaps because of a natural symptom reduction over time. It is possible that the study is limited by the lack of validation of self-report measures with low-income minority populations (Cardemil et al., 2007), an issue that severely hampers scholarship.

Other researchers have evaluated the Youth Life Orientation Test (Ey et al., 2005), a 16-item self-report measure of optimism (e.g., "I usually expect to have a good day") and pessimism (e.g., "Things usually go wrong for me"), in a sample of African American girls in third through sixth grade, participating in a study of diet and activity (W. C. Taylor et al., 2004); they found the test to have acceptable psychometric properties (Cronbach's alpha for subscales greater than .70) and low to moderate, yet significant, test–retest correlations. In addition, pessimism was more related to health behaviors than optimism. In additional psychometric evaluation of the Youth Life Orientation Test, Ey et al. (2005) found acceptable reliability and validity of the scale, and African American children endorsed significantly higher levels of optimism and marginally significant lower levels of pessimism than their White American peers, despite no race differences in depression. It may be that African American children are less vulnerable to developing pessimistic expectations either because of lack of knowledge or experience or, alternatively, because they are "preoccupied with more pressing threats to their well-being such as poverty, violence and racism" (Ey et al., 2000, p. 431). African American youth may also perceive themselves as particularly competent because, rather than compare themselves with a perceived universal peer group, they instead think of themselves in relation to their own (racial) group (Ey et al., 2005). They may also hold differing appraisals of their lives influenced by religiosity, such as perceiving themselves to be blessed as opposed to lucky. Such complexity suggests that more research is needed to carefully evaluate potential race differences in manifestation of future expectations.

Established measures of optimism should be used with caution with adult African American samples. The Life Orientation Test–Revised (LOT-R; Scheier, Carver, & Bridges, 1994) is a commonly used measure, modified from the original LOT (Scheier & Carver, 1985), to examine optimism and pessimism among adults, and it is the scale from which Youth Life Orientation Test items were derived. The LOT-R has not been psychometrically validated specifically for African American populations, and the original psychometric article insufficiently describes the race/ethnicity demographic composition of the validation sample. The instrument, however, has been used with African American samples and has been validated in the United States, Brazil, Germany, Norway, and China (Moyer et al., 2008). For instance, use of the four positively worded LOT-R optimism items in a study of religiosity, racism, and optimism in African American adults yielded adequate internal consistency (0.73; Mattis, Fontenot, & Hatcher-Kay, 2003), and the LOT-R has been used in studies with diverse samples focused on optimism–pessimism, quality of life, and knowledge and attitudes toward HIV screening among pregnant African women in Ghana (Moyer et al., 2008) and on spiritual well-being and depressive symptoms among African American female suicide attempters (Hirsch, Nsamenang, Chang, & Kaslow, 2014), with resulting scores comparable with those of non-African American samples and with outcomes as expected according to theory and previous research.

In general, however, the assessment of optimism among African Americans needs further development. Specifically, cognitive positive psychology constructs should be investigated to determine the degree to which they are determinants of a general worldview that may be influenced by cultural norms and beliefs (Ey et al., 2005). There is some evidence for overlap between positive psychology constructs across the affective, behavioral, and cognitive domains outlined in this chapter, such that they may not be discrete processes. For example, among African Americans, the perception of having a good relationship with God was positively associated with optimism, and the perception of a negative relationship with God was associated with pessimism (Mattis, Fontenot, Hatcher-Kay, Grayman, & Beale, 2004). This overlap could explain the race differences observed in comparative studies of optimism and could, therefore, engender the development of new assessment tools that consider the culturally relevant intersections of positive psychology constructs such as optimism and religious beliefs.

Hope

Hope has been assessed among African Americans across the lifespan, and evidence suggests that it is a valid and reliable construct for this group.

Even qualitative assessment of hope has been conducted with diverse groups of African Americans. For example, among African American adolescent gang members, hope emerged as a "caring" construct that varied by age, with youth expressing hope about their future prior to age 12 but feelings of hopelessness and despair after their 13th birthday (Morris & Fry-McComish, 2012). Among adult African American women coping with the aftermath of Hurricane Katrina, hope and spirituality emerged as themes related to resilience (Hamilton-Mason et al., 2012). Finally, in an examination of why highly religious African Americans (e.g., attend worship services more than once/week) live significantly longer than those who never attend worship services, the absence of hope emerged as key predictor of decreased longevity (Marks, Nesteruk, Swanson, Garrison, & Davis, 2005). These studies suggest that hope is an important and explicitly recognized construct associated with positive outcomes among African Americans.

Quantitative assessment of hope has been related to a variety of outcomes in African American samples. For example, in a study of quality of life among aging African Americans, interviews were conducted 12 years apart, and feelings of hope (as measured by a single item assessing "feeling life would work out or not") were related to greater life satisfaction across three age cohorts (Adams & Jackson, 2000). In contrast, hope as measured by the dispositional version of Snyder et al.'s (1997) Hope Scale did not appear to be directly related to life satisfaction among approximately 100 African American college students, although hope was significantly related to coping efficacy and moderated the relationship between coping and life satisfaction (Danoff-Burg, Prelow, & Swenson, 2004). This version of the Hope Scale contained four items assessing agency, or the personal efficacy to meet goals (e.g., "I meet the goals I set for myself"), and four items assessing pathways, or the ability to successfully plan for or acquire resources for goal attainment (e.g., "There are lots of ways around any problems"). Reliability coefficients for the sample were 0.84, 0.80, and 0.73 for the full scale, agency, and pathways, respectively.

The assessment of hope among African American children and youth has been facilitated by the development of the Children's Hope Scale (Snyder et al., 1997), a self-report measure with six items, three each for an agency subscale (e.g., "I think the things I have done in the past will help me in the future") and a pathways subscale (e.g., "When I have a problem, I can come up with lots of ways to solve it"). In a sample of more than 100 low-income African American fifth graders, hope levels were consistent with that of the school-age sample of children used to norm the scale (Cedeno, Elias, Kelly, & Chu, 2010), were directly related to externalizing behavior, and moderated the relation between victimization and witnessing violence and self-concept. In general, however, researchers have concluded that hope is not sufficient to protect youth from the negative effects of violence in their environments (Cedeno et al., 2010). Like optimism, hope may be one of several factors in a confluence of overlapping constructs that confer protection from social disadvantage. For example, Chang et al. (2013) found that both agency and pathway forms of hope mediate the relation between religiosity, spirituality, and the experience of depressive symptoms among diverse adult primary care patients (albeit mostly White, rural, and low-income). This study, in particular, is important because it samples individuals other than college students, who often represent a convenient but not representative population.

Other studies have used revised scales of hopefulness. Shorey and Snyder's (2004) Revised Trait Hope Scale, a self-report, Likert response 18-item scale with three subscales (goals, pathways, agency) of six items each was used in a study of 115 African American college students to examine the association of hope and suicidal risk (Davidson, Wingate, Slish, & Rasmussen, 2010). The scale demonstrated good reliability for the overall hope score in the study sample (0.84), was significantly associated with suicidal ideation, and both overall hope and the pathways subscale buffered suicide risk (Davidson et al., 2010). Assessing hope as a buffer for mental health among diverse samples has yielded important information about cultural variation in the function of hope as a moderator of risk. For example, Hirsch, Visser, et al. (2012) used Snyder and colleagues' (1997) Trait Hope Scale with a sample of African American, White, Latino, and Asian college students, and they found that although low hopelessness served as a buffer for the entire sample, trait hope did not serve as a buffer for African American students, suggesting that different processes may exist for this group. Rather than hopelessness being associated with "more severe cognitive and emotional impairment" (Hirsch, Visser, et al., 2012, p. 121) or "the adoption of maladaptive coping strategies" (p. 122), the authors suggested that social factors including discrimination may make feelings of hope less accessible and feelings of hopelessness more accessible to African Americans (Hirsch, Visser, et al., 2012). In a later study, using the same Trait Hope Scale with (predominantly) Latino, African American, White, Asian, and Native American (less than 1%) college students, there were no ethnic differences in the moderating effect of hope on the relation between negative life events and depressive symptoms (Visser, Loess, Jeglic, & Hirsch, 2013); regardless of ethnicity, those reporting greater hope were less likely to experience depressive symptoms associated with negative life events. One explanation of race/ethnic differences in hope may be related to the finding that African American college students report greater pathways thinking than do their White American peers, and a different pattern of relations between agentic thinking and problem solving, affect, and life satisfaction—despite overall similar levels of hope (Chang & Banks, 2007). These nuanced yet significant differences are likely the nature of cultural variation and deserve more careful attention.

DEVELOPING POSITIVE ASSESSMENT TOOLS FOR AFRICAN AMERICANS

Prior to the growth of positive psychology, several empirical traditions within the field of psychology emphasized the importance of contextual or ecological perspectives to explain human behavior. To understand the constructs of importance to positive psychologists, it is critical that the field advance in the development of assessment tools that take into account potential race differences in the underlying mechanisms of constructs like positive emotion, optimism, religion and spirituality, coping, and hope. Caldwell-Colbert, Parks, and Eshun (2009) reviewed positive psychology in connection with African Americans and called for an understanding of positive personal characteristics and forms of optimal functioning that have evolved among African Americans within a context of socioeconomic inequities. They also suggested that positive psychologists pay greater attention to multicultural and strengths-based research that has previously examined protective factors such as resilience, hope, and faith in African American populations.

In this chapter, we reviewed the evidence for the importance of assessment of positive psychology constructs among African Americans, including both between- and within-group investigations. In general, the studies we reviewed indicate that positive psychology constructs are important factors in directly and indirectly influencing a variety of outcomes, with some nuanced differences for African Americans that may represent cultural variation in how positive psychology constructs are perceived and processed. We join Flores and Obasi (2003) in calling for increased scholarship focused specifically on assessment tools for understanding positive psychological constructs in African American groups, particularly community-based samples.

REFERENCES

Adams, V. H., III, & Jackson, J. S. (2000). The contribution of hope to the quality of life among aging African Americans: 1980–1992. *International Journal of Aging and Human Development, 51*, 279–296. http://dx.doi.org/10.2190/AWB4-7CLU-A2EP-BQLF

Ayalon, L., & Young, M. A. (2003). A comparison of depressive symptoms in African Americans and Caucasian Americans. *Journal of Cross-Cultural Psychology, 34*(1), 111–124. http://dx.doi.org/10.1177/0022022102239158

Beck, A. T., Steer, R. A., & Brown, G. K. (1996). *Beck Depression Inventory—Second edition manual*. San Antonio, TX: The Psychological Corporation.

Boyd-Franklin, N. (2010). Incorporating spirituality and religion into the treatment of African American clients. *The Counseling Psychologist, 38,* 976–1000. http://dx.doi.org/10.1177/0011000010374881

Breslau, J., Kendler, K. S., Su, M., Gaxiola-Aguilar, S., & Kessler, R. C. (2005). Lifetime risk and persistence of psychiatric disorders across ethnic groups in the United States. *Psychological Medicine, 35,* 317–327. http://dx.doi.org/10.1017/S0033291704003514

Bronfenbrenner, U. (1979). Contexts of child rearing: Problems and prospects. *American Psychologist, 34,* 844–850. http://dx.doi.org/10.1037/0003-066X.34.10.844

Brown, C., Schulberg, H. C., & Madonia, M. J. (1996). Clinical presentations of major depression by African Americans and whites in primary medical care practice. *Journal of Affective Disorders, 41,* 181–191.

Brown, T. N. (2003). Critical race theory speaks to the sociology of mental health: Mental health problems produced by racial stratification. *Journal of Health and Social Behavior, 44,* 292–301.

Burrow, A. L., & Hill, P. L. (2012). Flying the unfriendly skies? The role of forgiveness and race in the experience of racial microaggressions. *The Journal of Social Psychology, 152,* 639–653. http://dx.doi.org/10.1080/00224545.2012.686461

Caldwell-Colbert, A., Parks, F. M., & Eshun, S. (2009). Positive psychology: African American strengths, resilience, and protective factors. In H. A. Neville, B. M. Tynes, & S. O. Utsey (Eds.), *Handbook of African American psychology* (pp. 375–384). Thousand Oaks, CA: Sage.

Cardemil, E. V., Reivich, K. J., Beevers, C. G., Seligman, M. E., & James, J. (2007). The prevention of depressive symptoms in low-income, minority children: Two-year follow-up. *Behaviour Research and Therapy, 45,* 313–327. http://dx.doi.org/10.1016/j.brat.2006.03.010

Cedeno, L. A., Elias, M. J., Kelly, S., & Chu, B. C. (2010). School violence, adjustment, and the influence of hope on low-income, African American youth. *American Journal of Orthopsychiatry, 80,* 213–226. http://dx.doi.org/10.1111/j.1939-0025.2010.01025.x

Chang, E. C., & Asakawa, K. (2003). Cultural variations on optimistic and pessimistic bias for self versus a sibling: Is there evidence for self-enhancement in the west and for self-criticism in the east when the referent group is specified? *Journal of Personality and Social Psychology, 84,* 569–581. http://dx.doi.org/10.1037/0022-3514.84.3.569

Chang, E. C., & Banks, K. H. (2007). The color and texture of hope: Some preliminary findings and implications for hope theory and counseling among diverse racial/ethnic groups. *Cultural Diversity and Ethnic Minority Psychology, 13*(2), 94–103. http://dx.doi.org/10.1037/1099-9809.13.2.94

Chang, E. C., Kahle, E. R., Yu, E. A., Lee, J. Y., Kupfermann, Y., & Hirsch, J. K. (2013). Relations of religiosity and spirituality with depressive symptoms in primary care adults: Evidence for hope agency and pathway as mediators. *The Journal of Positive Psychology, 8,* 314–321.

Chatters, L. M., Taylor, R. J., Jackson, J. S., & Lincoln, K. D. (2008). Religious coping among African Americans, Caribbean Blacks and Non-Hispanic Whites. *Journal of Community Psychology, 36,* 371–386. http://dx.doi.org/10.1002/jcop.20202

Chatters, L. M., Taylor, R. J., & Lincoln, K. D. (1999). African American religious participation: A multi-sample comparison. *Journal for the Scientific Study of Religion, 38*(1), 132–145. http://dx.doi.org/10.2307/1387589

Clark, K. B., & Clark, M. P. (1939). The development of consciousness of self and the emergence of racial identification in Negro preschool children. *The Journal of Social Psychology, 10,* 591–599. http://dx.doi.org/10.1080/00224545.1939.9713394

Constantine, M. G., Wilton, L., Gainor, K. A., & Lewis, E. L. (2002). Religious participation, spirituality, and coping among African American college students. *Journal of College Student Development, 43,* 605–613.

Coopersmith, S. (1981). *Self-Esteem Inventory.* Palo Alto, CA: Counseling Psychologists.

Coyne, J. C., Fechner-Bates, S., & Schwenk, T. L. (1994). Prevalence, nature, and comorbidity of depressive disorders in primary care. *General Hospital Psychiatry, 16,* 267–276.

Crocker, J., & Major, B. (1989). Social stigma and self-esteem: The self-protective properties of stigma. *Psychological Review, 96,* 608–630. http://dx.doi.org/10.1037/0033-295X.96.4.608

Crocker, J., & Major, B. (1994). Reactions to stigma: The moderating role of justifications. In M. P. Zanna & J. M. Olson (Eds.), *The psychology of prejudice: The Ontario Symposium* (Vol. 7, pp. 289–314). Hillsdale, NJ: Erlbaum.

Crocker, J., & Major, B. (2003). The self-protective properties of stigma: Evolution of a modern classic. *Psychological Inquiry, 14*(3-4), 232–237. http://dx.doi.org/10.1080/1047840X.2003.9682885

Danoff-Burg, S., Prelow, H. M., & Swenson, R. R. (2004). Hope and life satisfaction in Black college students coping with race-related stress. *Journal of Black Psychology, 30,* 208–228. http://dx.doi.org/10.1177/0095798403260725

Davidson, C. L., Wingate, L. R., Slish, M. L., & Rasmussen, K. A. (2010). The great Black hope: Hope and its relation to suicide risk among African Americans. *Suicide and Life-Threatening Behavior, 40*(2), 170–180. http://dx.doi.org/10.1521/suli.2010.40.2.170

Edmonson Bell, E. L. J., & Nkomo, S. M. (1998). Armoring: Learning to withstand racial oppression. *Journal of Comparative Family Studies, 29,* 285–295.

Ey, S., Hadley, W., Allen, D. N., Palmer, S., Klosky, J., Deptula, D., . . . Cohen, R. (2005). A new measure of children's optimism and pessimism: The youth life orientation test. *Journal of Child Psychology and Psychiatry, 46,* 548–558. http://dx.doi.org/10.1111/j.1469-7610.2004.00372.x

Ey, S., Klesges, L. M., Patterson, S. M., Hadley, W., Barnard, M., & Alpert, B. S. (2000). Racial differences in adolescents' perceived vulnerability to disease and

injury. *Journal of Behavioral Medicine, 23*, 421–435. http://dx.doi.org/10.1023/
A:1005568930849

Fitts, W. H., & Roid, G. H. (1964). *Tennessee Self Concept Scale.* Nashville, TN:
Counselor Recordings and Tests.

Flores, L. Y., & Obasi, E. M. (2003). Positive psychological assessment in an increasingly diverse world. In S. J. Lopez & C. R. Snyder (Eds.), *Positive psychological
assessment: A handbook of models and measures* (pp. 41–54). Washington, DC:
American Psychological Association. http://dx.doi.org/10.1037/10612-003

Gecas, V., & Schwalbe, M. L. (1983). Beyond the looking-glass self: Social structure
and efficacy-based self-esteem. *Social Psychology Quarterly, 46*, 77–88. http://
dx.doi.org/10.2307/3033844

Gray-Little, B., & Hafdahl, A. R. (2000). Factors influencing racial comparisons of
self-esteem: A quantitative review. *Psychological Bulletin, 126*, 26–54.

Greene, B. (1994). African American women. In L. Comas-Díaz & B. Greene (Eds.),
Women of color: Integrating ethnic and gender identities in psychotherapy (pp. 10–29).
New York, NY: Guilford Press.

Hamilton-Mason, J., Everett, J., Hall, J. C., Harden, S., Lecloux, M., Mancini, S., &
Warrington, R. (2012). Hope floats: African American women's survival experiences after Katrina. *Journal of Human Behavior in the Social Environment, 22*,
479–499. http://dx.doi.org/10.1080/10911359.2012.664982

Harrell, J. P. (1979). Analyzing Black coping styles: A supplemental diagnostic system. *Journal of Black Psychology, 5*, 99–108. http://dx.doi.org/10.1177/
009579847900500204

Harris, A. H., Luskin, F., Norman, S. B., Standard, S., Bruning, J., Evans, S., &
Thoresen, C. E. (2006). Effects of a group forgiveness intervention on forgiveness, perceived stress, and trait-anger. *Journal of Clinical Psychology, 62*, 715–733.
http://dx.doi.org/10.1002/jclp.20264

Harter, S. (1985). *Manual for the self-perception profile for children.* University of
Denver, CO.

Hatcher, J., & Hall, L. A. (2009). Psychometric properties of the Rosenberg Self-
esteem Scale in African American single mothers. *Issues in Mental Health
Nursing, 30*(2), 70–77. http://dx.doi.org/10.1080/01612840802595113

Hirsch, J. K., Chang, E. C., & Jeglic, E. L. (2012). Social problem solving and suicidal behavior: Ethnic differences in the moderating effects of loneliness and
life stress. *Archives of Suicide Research, 16*, 303–315. http://dx.doi.org/10.1080/
13811118.2013.722054

Hirsch, J. K., Nsamenang, S. A., Chang, E. C., & Kaslow, N. J. (2014). Spiritual well-
being and depressive symptoms in female African American suicide attempters:
Mediating effects of optimism and pessimism. *Psychology of Religion and Spirituality,
6*, 276–283. http://dx.doi.org/10.1037/a0036723

Hirsch, J. K., Visser, P. L., Chang, E. C., & Jeglic, E. L. (2012). Race and ethnic differences in hope and hopelessness as moderators of the association between

depressive symptoms and suicidal behavior. *Journal of American College Health*, 60, 115–125. http://dx.doi.org/10.1080/07448481.2011.567402

Hirsch, J. K., Webb, J. R., & Jeglic, E. L. (2012). Forgiveness as a moderator of the association between anger expression and suicidal behaviour. *Mental Health, Religion & Culture*, 15, 279–300. http://dx.doi.org/10.1080/13674676.2011. 571666

Huebner, E. S. (1998). Cross-racial application of a children's multidimensional life satisfaction scale. *School Psychology International*, 19, 179–188. http://dx.doi.org/ 10.1177/0143034398192006

Huebner, E. S., & Dew, T. (1993). An evaluation of racial bias in a life satisfaction scale. *Psychology in the Schools*, 30, 305–309. http://dx.doi.org/10.1002/1520-6807(199310)30:4<305::AID-PITS2310300404>3.0.CO;2-F

Jackson-Triche, M. E., Sullivan, J. G., Wells, K. B., Rogers, W., Camp, P., & Mazel, R. (2000). Depression and health-related quality of life in ethnic minorities seeking care in general medical settings. *Journal of Affective Disorders*, 58, 89–97.

Jones, J. M. (2003). TRIOS: A psychological theory of the African legacy in American culture. *Journal of Social Issues*, 59, 217–242.

Kazdin, A. E., Rodgers, A., & Colbus, D. (1986). The hopelessness scale for children: Psychometric characteristics and concurrent validity. *Journal of Consulting and Clinical Psychology*, 54, 241–245. http://dx.doi.org/10.1037/0022-006X.54.2.241

Kidwell, S. L., & Barnett, D. (2007). Adaptive emotion regulation among low-income African American children. *Merrill-Palmer Quarterly*, 53, 155–183. http://dx.doi. org/10.1353/mpq.2007.0011

Koenig, H. G., McCullough, M. E., & Larson, D. B. (2001). *Handbook of religion and health*. New York, NY: Oxford University Press.

Kohn-Wood, L. P., Banks, K. H., Lee, D., & Ivey, A. (2013). *Examining factor variability of depressive symptom intensity in Black and White Americans*. Unpublished manuscript.

Kohn-Wood, L. P., Hammond, W. P., Haynes, T. F., Ferguson, K. K., & Jackson, B. A. (2012). Coping styles, depressive symptoms and race during the transition to adulthood. *Mental Health, Religion & Culture*, 15, 363–372. http://dx.doi.org/ 10.1080/13674676.2011.577059

Krause, N. (2012). Studying forgiveness among older Whites, older Blacks, and older Mexican Americans. *Journal of Religion, Spirituality & Aging*, 24, 325–344. http://dx.doi.org/10.1080/15528030.2012.706738

Lazarus, R. S., & Folkman, S. (1984). *Stress, appraisal, and coping*. New York, NY: Springer.

Lee, B. Y., & Newberg, A. B. (2005). Religion and health: A review and critical analysis. *Zygon*, 40, 443–468. http://dx.doi.org/10.1111/j.1467-9744.2005.00674.x

Leu, J., Wang, J., & Koo, K. (2011). Are positive emotions just as "positive" across cultures? *Emotion*, 11, 994–999. http://dx.doi.org/10.1037/a0021332

Liang, J., Lawrence, R. H., & Bollen, K. A. (1987). Race differences in factorial structures of two measures of subjective well-being. *Journal of Gerontology, 42,* 426–428. http://dx.doi.org/10.1093/geronj/42.4.426

Mabry, J. B., & Kiecolt, K. J. (2005). Anger in black and white: Race, alienation, and anger. *Journal of Health and Social Behavior, 46,* 85–101.

Major, B., & Schmader, T. (1998). Coping with stigma through psychological disengagement. In J. Swim & C. Stangor (Eds.), *Prejudice: The target's perspective* (pp. 219–241). San Diego, CA: Academic Press. http://dx.doi.org/10.1016/B978-012679130-3/50045-4

Marks, L., Nesteruk, O., Swanson, M., Garrison, B., & Davis, T. (2005). Religion and health among African Americans: A qualitative examination. *Research on Aging, 27,* 447–474. http://dx.doi.org/10.1177/0164027505276252

Mattis, J. S., Fontenot, D. L., & Hatcher-Kay, C. A. (2003). Religiosity, racism, and dispositional optimism among African Americans. *Personality and Individual Differences, 34,* 1025–1038. http://dx.doi.org/10.1016/S0191-8869(02)00087-9

Mattis, J. S., Fontenot, D. L., Hatcher-Kay, C. A., Grayman, N. A., & Beale, R. L. (2004). Religiosity, optimism, and pessimism among African Americans. *Journal of Black Psychology, 30,* 187–207. http://dx.doi.org/10.1177/0095798403260730

Mattis, J. S., & Jagers, R. (2001). A relational framework for the study of religiosity and spirituality in the lives of African Americans. *Journal of Community Psychology, 29,* 519–539. http://dx.doi.org/10.1002/jcop.1034

McCullough, M. E. (2008). *Beyond revenge: The evolution of the forgiveness instinct.* San Francisco, CA: Jossey-Bass.

McFarland, M. J., Smith, C. A., Toussaint, L., & Thomas, P. A. (2012). Forgiveness of others and health: Do race and neighborhood matter? *The Journals of Gerontology: Series B: Psychological Sciences and Social Sciences, 67*(1), 66–75. http://dx.doi.org/10.1093/geronb/gbr121

McGonagle, K. A., & Kessler, R. C. (1990). Chronic stress, acute stress, and depressive symptoms. *American Journal of Community Psychology, 18,* 681–706.

Michaels, M. L., Barr, A., Roosa, M. W., & Knight, G. P. (2007). Self-esteem assessing measurement equivalence in a multiethnic sample of youth. *The Journal of Early Adolescence, 27,* 269–295. http://dx.doi.org/10.1177/0272431607302009

Miyamoto, Y., Uchida, Y., & Ellsworth, P. C. (2010). Culture and mixed emotions: Co-occurrence of positive and negative emotions in Japan and the United States. *Emotion, 10,* 404–415. http://dx.doi.org/10.1037/a0018430

Morelen, D., Jacob, M. L., Suveg, C., Jones, A., & Thomassin, K. (2013). Family emotion expressivity, emotion regulation, and the link to psychopathology: Examination across race. *British Journal of Psychology, 104,* 149–166.

Morris, E. J., & Fry-McComish, J. (2012). Hope and despair: Diverse voices of hope from urban African American adolescent gang members. *International Journal for Human Caring, 16*(4), 50–57.

Moyer, C. A., Ekpo, G., Calhoun, C. L., Greene, J., Naik, S., Sippola, E., . . . Anderson, F. J. (2008). Quality of life, optimism/pessimism, and knowledge and attitudes toward HIV Screening among pregnant women in Ghana. *Women's Health Issues*, *18*, 301–309. http://dx.doi.org/10.1016/j.whi.2008.02.001

Ostrove, J. M., Feldman, P., & Adler, N. E. (1999). Relations among socioeconomic status indicators and health for African-Americans and whites. *Journal of Health Psychology*, *4*, 451–463.

Pargament, K., Feuille, M., & Burdzy, D. (2011). The Brief RCOPE: Current psychometric status of a short measure of religious coping. *Religions*, *2*(1), 51–76. http://dx.doi.org/10.3390/rel2010051

Pargament, K. I., Ishler, K., Dubow, E. F., Stanik, P., Rouiller, R., Crowe, P., . . . Royster, P. J. (1994). Methods of religious coping with the Gulf War: Cross-sectional and longitudinal analyses. *Journal for the Scientific Study of Religion*, *33*, 347–361. http://dx.doi.org/10.2307/1386494

Pargament, K. I., Kennell, J., Hathaway, W., Grevengoed, N., Newman, J., & Jones, W. (1988). Religion and the problem-solving process: Three styles of coping. *Journal for the Scientific Study of Religion*, *27*, 90–104. http://dx.doi.org/10.2307/1387404

Pargament, K. I., Koenig, H. G., & Perez, L. M. (2000). The many methods of religious coping: Development and initial validation of the RCOPE. *Journal of Clinical Psychology*, *56*, 519–543. http://dx.doi.org/10.1002/(SICI)1097-4679(200004)56:4<519::AID-JCLP6>3.0.CO;2-1

Perry, B. L., Pullen, E. L., & Oser, C. B. (2012). Too much of a good thing? Psychosocial resources, gendered racism, and suicidal ideation among low socioeconomic status African American women. *Social Psychology Quarterly*, *75*, 334–359.

Petrie, J. M., Chapman, L. K., & Vines, L. M. (2013). Utility of the PANAS-X in predicting social phobia in African American females. *Journal of Black Psychology*, *39*, 131–155. http://dx.doi.org/10.1177/0095798412454677

Piers, E. V. (1969). *Manual for the Piers-Harris Children's Self-Concept Scale*. Nashville, TN: Counselor Recording & Tests.

Plant, E. A., & Sachs-Ericsson, N. (2004). Racial and ethnic differences in depression: The roles of social support and meeting basic needs. *Journal of Consulting and Clinical Psychology*, *72*, 41–52.

Plummer, D. L., & Slane, S. (1996). Patterns of coping in racially stressful situations. *Journal of Black Psychology*, *22*, 302–315. http://dx.doi.org/10.1177/00957984960223002

Post, D. M., & Weddington, W. (1997). The impact of culture on physician stress and coping. *Journal of the National Medical Association*, *89*, 585–590.

Radloff, L. S. (1977). The CES-D Scale: A self report depression scale for research in the general population. *Applied Psychological Measurement*, *1*, 385–401. http://dx.doi.org/10.1177/014662167700100306

Riley-Eddins, E. A., Hobfall, S. E., & Jackson, A. P. (2000, Winter). Ways of coping among low-income inner-city women: The multi-axial model of coping. *African American Research Perspectives*, 30–40.

Rosenberg, M. (1965). *Society and the adolescent self-image*. Princeton, NJ: Princeton University Press.

Scheier, M. F., & Carver, C. S. (1985). Optimism, coping, and health: Assessment and implications of generalized outcome expectancies. *Health Psychology, 4*(3), 219–247. http://dx.doi.org/10.1037/0278-6133.4.3.219

Scheier, M. F., Carver, C. S., & Bridges, M. W. (1994). Distinguishing optimism from neuroticism (and trait anxiety, self-mastery, and self-esteem): A reevaluation of the Life Orientation Test. *Journal of Personality and Social Psychology, 67*, 1063–1078. http://dx.doi.org/10.1037/0022-3514.67.6.1063

Schmader, T. (2002). Gender identification moderates stereotype threat effects on women's math performance. *Journal of Experimental Social Psychology, 38*, 194–201. http://dx.doi.org/10.1006/jesp.2001.1500

Seng, J. S., Kohn-Wood, L. P., & Odera, L. A. (2005). Exploring racial disparity in posttraumatic stress disorder diagnosis: Implications for care of African American women. *Journal of Obstetric, Gynecologic, and Neonatal Nursing, 34*, 521–530. http://dx.doi.org/10.1177/0884217505278296

Shorey, H. S., & Snyder, C. R. (2004). *The revised domain specific hope scale*. Unpublished manuscript, Department of Psychology, University of Kansas, Lawrence.

Smith, T. B., McCullough, M. E., & Poll, J. (2003). Religiousness and depression: Evidence for a main effect and the moderating influence of stressful life events. *Psychological Bulletin, 129*, 614–636. http://dx.doi.org/10.1037/0033-2909.129.4.614

Snyder, C. R., Hoza, B., Pelham, W. E., Rapoff, M., Ware, L., Danovsky, M., . . . Stahl, K. J. (1997). The development and validation of the Children's Hope Scale. *Journal of Pediatric Psychology, 22*, 399–421. http://dx.doi.org/10.1093/jpepsy/22.3.399

Steele, C. M., & Aronson, J. (1995). Stereotype threat and the intellectual test performance of African Americans. *Journal of Personality and Social Psychology, 69*, 797–811. http://dx.doi.org/10.1037/0022-3514.69.5.797

Stewart, P. K., Roberts, M. C., & Kim, K. L. (2010). The psychometric properties of the Harter Self-perception Profile for Children with at-risk African American females. *Journal of Child and Family Studies, 19*, 326–333. http://dx.doi.org/10.1007/s10826-009-9302-x

Supplee, L. H., Skuban, E. M., Shaw, D. S., & Prout, J. (2009). Emotion regulation strategies and later externalizing behavior among European American and African American children. *Development and Psychopathology, 21*, 393–415. http://dx.doi.org/10.1017/S0954579409000224

Taylor, R. J., Chatters, L. M., & Levin, J. (2004). *Religion in the lives of African Americans: Social, psychological, and health perspectives*. Thousand Oaks, CA: Sage.

Taylor, W. C., Baranowski, T., Klesges, L. M., Ey, S., Pratt, C., Rochon, J., & Zhou, A. (2004). Psychometric properties of optimism and pessimism: Results from the Girls' Health Enrichment Multisite Studies. *Preventive Medicine, 38*(Suppl.), S69–S77. http://dx.doi.org/10.1016/j.ypmed.2003.10.015

Tsai, J. L., Knutson, B., & Fung, H. H. (2006). Cultural variation in affect valuation. *Journal of Personality and Social Psychology, 90,* 288–307. http://dx.doi.org/10.1037/0022-3514.90.2.288

Utsey, S. O., Adams, E. P., & Bolden, M. (2000). Development and initial validation of the Africultural Coping Systems Inventory. *Journal of Black Psychology, 26,* 194–215. http://dx.doi.org/10.1177/0095798400026002005

Vega, W. A., & Rumbaut, R. G. (1991). Ethnic minorities and mental health. *Annual Review of Sociology, 17,* 351–383.

Visser, P. L., Loess, P., Jeglic, E. L., & Hirsch, J. K. (2013). Hope as a moderator of negative life events and depressive symptoms in a diverse sample. *Stress and Health, 29*(1), 82–88. http://dx.doi.org/10.1002/smi.2433

Whisman, M. A., Judd, C. M., Whiteford, N. T., & Gelhorn, H. L. (2013). Measurement invariance of the Beck Depression Inventory—Second Edition (BDI-II) across gender, race, and ethnicity in college students. *Assessment, 20,* 419–428.

Williams, D. R., González, H. M., Neighbors, H., Nesse, R., Abelson, J. M., Sweetman, J., & Jackson, J. S. (2007). Prevalence and distribution of major depressive disorder in African Americans, Caribbean blacks, and non-Hispanic whites: Results from the National Survey of American Life. *Archives of General Psychiatry, 64,* 305–315. http://dx.doi.org/10.1001/archpsyc.64.3.305

Williams, D. R., Spencer, M. S., & Jackson, J. S. (1999). Race, stress, and physical health: The role of group identity. In R. J. Contrada & R. D. Ashmore (Eds.), *Self, social identity, and physical health: Interdisciplinary explorations* (pp. 71–100). New York, NY: Oxford University Press.

Worthington, E. L., Jr., Witvliet, C. V. O., Pietrini, P., & Miller, A. J. (2007). Forgiveness, health, and well-being: A review of evidence for emotional versus decisional forgiveness, dispositional forgivingness, and reduced unforgiveness. *Journal of Behavioral Medicine, 30,* 291–302. http://dx.doi.org/10.1007/s10865-007-9105-8

Zeigler-Hill, V., & Wallace, M. T. (2011). Racial differences in narcissistic tendencies. *Journal of Research in Personality, 45,* 456–467. http://dx.doi.org/10.1016/j.jrp.2011.06.001

Zeigler-Hill, V., Wallace, M. T., & Myers, E. M. (2012). Racial differences in self-esteem revisited: The role of impression management in the Black self-esteem advantage. *Personality and Individual Differences, 53,* 785–789. http://dx.doi.org/10.1016/j.paid.2012.06.007

10

POSITIVE PSYCHOLOGY ASSESSMENT IN AMERICAN INDIANS

JEFF KING

> Our ancestors lived in a spiritual universe. We are still conscious of it but many immigrants from Europe do not experience it because they do not see that all things are imbued with spirit.
>
> —Phillip Duran (Tigua Pueblo)

Positive psychology focuses on people's strengths, virtues, and well-being. This relatively young discipline has been substantially grounded in the Western tradition, with its individualistic features shared by only a few cultures. For example, one of the key features of positive psychology is a focus on well-being. However, the definition and evaluation of *well-being* across cultures do not necessarily coincide with Western ones. This is true for American Indian[1] conceptions of well-being. In this chapter, I provide

---

[1]*American Indian, Native people, Native American, North American Indigenous tribes*, and *American Indian/ Alaska Native* are used interchangeably in this chapter.

http://dx.doi.org/10.1037/14799-010
Positive Psychology in Racial and Ethnic Groups: Theory, Research, and Practice, E. C. Chang, C. A. Downey, J. K. Hirsch, and N. J. Lin (Editors)

(a) a brief critique of the historical context for assessment within American Indian/Alaska Native communities, (b) examples of traditional means of assessment across tribes, (c) recommendations for a gold standard or ideal approach to assessment, and (d) examples of current practical types of positive psychological assessment within Indian Country.[2]

VALUE OF ASSESSING POSITIVE STRENGTHS IN AMERICAN INDIANS

It is necessary to provide the appropriate context for a phrase such as "assessing positive strengths in American Indians" because the phrase takes on different meanings in Native cultures. A personal anecdote might help to illustrate this. I was in discussion with a medicine man from my own tribe, the Muscogee Nation, regarding how our medicine people were able to assess the well-being or ill-health of our people. He began our conversation by stating, "The *este hvtke* (White man) and the *este cate* (Red man) live in two totally different existences" (Sam Proctor, personal communication, March 26, 2011). The implication here is that there is a deep-felt sense by traditional Native people that the Western European (White) view of the world is significantly different from tribal worldviews, a belief that is fundamental to the issues to be covered herein.

This statement is echoed by numerous researchers and scholars who have worked with American Indian culture. In his book, *The Spiritual Life of Children*, Harvard psychiatrist Robert Coles told of meeting a young American Indian (Hopi) girl who explained to him why he wasn't getting much response from the tribe to his inquiries: "My grandmother says they [you] live to conquer the sky, and we live to pray to it, and you can't explain yourself to people who conquer—just pray for them, too" (Coles, 1990, p. 29). Robert Bergman (1973), a psychiatrist who worked for many years among the Diné (Navajo), wrote, "Some familiarity with Navajo tradition has helped me to focus my dissatisfaction with the way we [psychiatrists] organize our work and to see alternatives to our methods that I wouldn't have seen otherwise" (p. 8). In other words, if we do not open ourselves to "see alternatives to our methods," we cannot perceive the world in which Native people move and exist. Fixico (2003) stated:

> Can non-Indians "see" in an Indian way like a traditionalist? This perplexing question for the 1980s and 1990s has continued into the twenty-first century as indigenous knowledge and the academic writings of indigenous

---

[2]*Indian Country* is a term used for North American Indigenous people and wherever they reside.

scholars have received increasing respect from the mainstream academy. The answer is affirmative, if the non-Indian learns the traditional ways of an Indian community and accepts the values and beliefs of the indigenous culture. Seeing and learning is accepting that you will be enlightened by listening and witnessing the signs. Non-Indians can "see" in this manner, if they believe in the same ethos of the native community or tribe. (pp. 7–8)

The reader is asked to do the same with this chapter in order to grasp the worldview of traditional North American Indigenous peoples and the associated systems of assessment, strengths, and well-being. Historically, for many tribes, the person making assessments of well-being and ill-being was the traditional healer, but all community members had common understandings of what was healthy and unhealthy (Jacob, 2008).

The primary focus of this book is to highlight the importance of race and ethnicity in developing theory, conducting research, making assessments, and implementing treatments, within the context of positive psychology, in ways that will be meaningful and effective for understanding and working with diverse populations. It is within this purview that the first question to be asked in this chapter is, How did Native people make assessments of well-being and illness? Although a number of studies have addressed or included cultural factors that are relevant to American Indians, the focus and instrumentation have inevitably been with measures developed within a Western scientific framework and have, by default, overlooked this primary question (Gone, 2010; Goodkind, LaNoue, & Milford, 2010; Kenyon & Carter, 2011; Yu & Stiffarm, 2010). In fact, the importance of traditional value systems in well-being, assessment, and treatment for Native people has been noted by many researchers, yet those with traditional knowledge have not been consulted for their understanding in these areas (Duran, 2006; Gone, 2010; LaFromboise et al., 1990; Wolsko, Lardon, Hopkins, & Ruppert, 2006). Thus, it is all the more notable that we do not know the answer to how well-being and illness were traditionally assessed, and it is equally notable that we have not asked the question. Some scholars link this lack of inquisitiveness to an underlying assumption of the superiority of scientific thinking over all other ways of knowing (Scheurich & Young, 2002; L. T. Smith, 2012). The notion that only Western science is qualified to make assessments of well-being and ill-health is by and large taken for granted within the scientific community (Scheurich & Young, 2002; L. T. Smith, 2012). This is to our detriment, because without careful scrutiny, attention, and respect for other cultural epistemologies and how they apply to assessment strategies, we may overlook important aspects of cultural knowledge that could benefit everyone. Lopez and Snyder (2003) asserted that "the uncovering of hidden resources can make a difference in the lives of people" (p. 461). One cannot fully grasp the realm of assessment in Indian Country without visiting historical, traditional approaches.

As many have noted, the current field of scientific pursuit is grounded in Western European epistemology that essentially dismisses indigenous knowledge as outdated, primitive, and irrational (Bodeker, 2009; Cajete, 2000; Deloria, 1997; L. T. Smith, 2012; Whitt, 2009). These statements are typically made without serious investigation (Gone, 2010). Furthermore, Eurocentric science has shaped the focus of inquiry to primarily White populations and, when investigating non-White cultures, has used the tools of Western European (White) populations. Psychological science, including positive psychology, has followed in this pattern (Richards, 2012). The result has been a history of assessment tools based on the deficit model (Gould, 1996; Hilliard, 1995), inappropriate item content, insensitivity, misinterpretation, inappropriate placement, and many other forms of test bias and outcomes (Allen, 2002; Hill, Pace, & Robbins, 2010; King & Fletcher-Janzen, 2000; Reynolds & Suzuki, 2013). Assessment bias has been prominent; so too has been the lack of demonstrable efficacy of psychological measures among American Indians and Alaska Natives (Allen, 1998; Hagie, Gallipo, & Svien, 2003; Jervis, Beals, Fickenscher, & Arciniegas, 2007; Jervis, Cullum & Manson, 2006; Stone, 2002). The most recent literature reviews called for greater attention to emic perspectives and emically derived assessments; such a perspective is culturally congruent and, to the extent such congruence can be maintained, this may serve as a strength for individuals and communities (Garrett & Garrett, 1994; T. B. Smith & Silva, 2011), and the inclusion of culture as a component of behavioral health treatment is strongly related to better treatment outcomes (Trimble, King, LaFromboise, Bigfoot, & Norman, 2014; Wexler, 2014). Yet, to date this has not been adequately addressed (Dauphinais & King, 1992; King & Fletcher-Janzen, 2000). A recent literature search using the terms *positive psychology, assessment, American Indian*, and *Native American* yielded no results regarding the use of positive psychology in assessment. However, positive psychology's commitment to strengths-driven research and assessment (Buckingham & Clifton, 2001) has the potential to reverse the past trends of focusing on negatives and thus holds the potential to gain greater knowledge regarding the deep strengths that have sustained Native people through the generations. More specifically, positive psychology can play a major role in using a strengths-based approach, as well as its own principles, to understand, accept, and support indigenous knowledge as pertaining to health and well-being among Native people. In particular, positive psychology can ask and seek out the answer to this basic question of assessment, diagnosis, and treatment from tribal perspectives.

APPROACHES AND ISSUES WITH ASSESSMENT OF AMERICAN INDIAN WELL-BEING

A discussion of Native American Indian notions of well-being and self is necessary to provide an appropriate context for addressing positive psychology assessment factors, because they emerge from a different worldview than Western European culture. These concepts inform the reader as to how the various strengths and resiliencies, seemingly similar to Western culture concepts, take on culturally unique meanings and contexts and thus are significantly different in substance and form than their Western counterparts. Several positive psychology dimensions are addressed in this chapter as a means to demonstrate these differences.

Although Native peoples' beliefs, customs, and lifeways (i.e., way of life or manner of living) differ in many ways from one tribe to another, the core perceptions or ideas of health or well-being across tribes are remarkably similar. North American Indigenous people view well-being as keeping oneself and the community in balance and harmony. This balance is maintained within physical, mental, emotional, and relational well-being dimensions and may often include balance with the land and all that is part of it. The key to understanding this is that Native people saw themselves in a mutual, reciprocal *relationship* to all things. It is through relationship that balance and harmony are maintained (Vine Deloria, quoted in Jensen, 2000). Many of the tribal ceremonies reflect the mutual respect for the animals, plants, and land that permits the tribe to live sustainable and healthy lives (Cajete, 2000; Martin, 2001; Ruby, Brown, & Collins, 2010). Many tribes believe that if you do not treat a plant or animal with respect, the plant or animal will not share its power with you and will cease to be as plentiful in the years to come. In conducting business or making requests, typically the parties involved will initially discuss their families and what is happening in the community. This is akin to what others might call "visiting." However, within tribal communities there is an underlying meaning of the importance of relationship over business or other types of dealings. To ignore the relationship and "get down to business" would cheapen the meaning of the transaction and be considered disrespectful (G. Coser, personal communication, June 14, 2014).

Thus, the healthy "individual" among many tribes is viewed always as in relationship—not viewed in isolation from family, community, or even the land. In my tribe (Muscogee), for example, the words for a healthy individual are *heyv este hermemahet omet, cemvnice tayet omes*, meaning "This person is there, a person of good repute, around and available to help" (A. King, personal communication, July 3, 2009). Lakota terminology for healthiness is *tiwahe eyecinka egloiyapi nahan oyate op unpi kte*, meaning "the family moving forward interdependently while embracing the values of generosity and interdependence" (Moves Camp, 2014). The Navajo concept of *hózhó* is similar. Implying a state of well-being, it is a much deeper, transcendent word, not easily translatable in English. It implies a unity or balance at all levels of life, including people, community, animals, the spiritual, and the land (Drake, 2004). In Tewa (Pueblo), the phrase *ta e go mah ana thla mah* is translated as, "This person is of good demeanor, kind and empathetic to the people and generous to those in need, including the animals" (A. Martinez, personal communication, August 28, 2006). In all these tribal terms, the concept of well-being is not located solely in the individual; it is inseparable from family, community, and environment.

In addition to the concept of well-being for many traditional Native people, the concept of self is not the autonomous self that is understood through Western ideology. In fact, some tribes do not have a word for *self*. Leroy Little Bear, a *Siksika* (Blackfoot) elder from Canada, once addressed a group of American Indian psychologists with this statement: "You psychologists talk about identity crises. I'll tell you what an identity crisis is: it is when you do not know the land and the land does not know you" (Blood, HeavyHead, & Little Bear, 2007). Not separate from their construction of "self," the Blackfoot have core values of *kimmapiiyipitssini*, meaning "unconditional positive regard for all other social members," and *ainna'kootsiiyo'p*, meaning "cooperative co-existence; a form of mutual respect that includes, at its base, a conservation ethic [respect for all that is in the environment]" (R. HeavyHead, personal communication, October 13, 2011). Abraham Maslow glimpsed this manner of self and well-being among the Blackfeet and made this observation while conducting research at *Siksika* and linked it to self-esteem: "With respect to self-esteem, it was found that a completely different quality of self-esteem was found in about 80–90% of the Blackfoot tribe, a quality that is found in only about 5–10% of our population" (Maslow, 1939).

Similarly, the Lakota have a saying, *mitakuye oyas'in* ("all my relatives"), which conveys a very deep meaning through time and space, that all things are relatives and must be respected, acknowledged, and listened to as a vital aspect of living well. One finds the equivalent among the Pacific Northwest Indian Coastal Salish people, among whom wellness was achieved through balance and harmony with others and the environment. Illness was related to loss of this balance and a disturbance in or confusion of identity. Specific ceremonies were used to restore this balance (Strickland, 2001). In all this, the self is not autonomous; the self is part of "all my relatives." Thus, one of the oft-cited components of positive psychology, autonomy, or the autonomous self, seen as universal, does not fit within many Native cultures (Wong, 2013).

Self-in-relationship manifests itself throughout tribal lifeways. Within this way of viewing the world, all things are seen as sacred and life events are treated similarly. For example, traditional Lakota people believe we are all gifted from the time we were created and we have a choice to share those gifts with others and make a difference. For the Lakota, there is no impairment in intellectual functioning, because the full range of intelligence is considered to be normal. Lakota recognize that some people are intellectually quicker or slower than others, but they consider this to be simply part of the normal range of human possibilities. Differences in intellectual functioning are neither disabling nor handicapping, although they may account for how the person contributes to the group. Furthermore, Lakota individuals born with what we call "birth defects" are considered to be sacred and carry special abilities that benefit the tribe. Every individual "belongs" to the tribe, and his or her characteristics are seen within this context. There is an abiding, collective sense of belonging from prebirth through old age (Nichols & Keltner, 2005; Patterson, 1997). Children are given viable social roles and respect among tribal members. Children who have conditions such as fetal alcohol syndrome or mental retardation are accepted and are valued to the same degree as other children (DuBray & Sanders, 1999).

"Today is a good day to die!" These words have been attributed to Lakota holy man Crazy Horse and reflect many indigenous tribal beliefs about living well. The goal in life is not happiness, a construct often cited in the positive psychology literature and seen as a universal (see Wong, 2013), but rather to live life well, through good times and bad times. Similarly, Pacific Northwest Coast tribal peoples view pain as something to be endured and/or overcome through spiritual strength (Strickland, 2001). Many of the current assessments for happiness are worded for the individual (Forgeard, Jayawickreme, Kern, & Seligman, 2011), and individuality is not a relevant construct for many tribal peoples.

Similar to happiness, positive emotion is highlighted within the positive psychology literature as a component of well-being (Forgeard et al., 2011) and yet may be misleading within traditional Native values. Living life well does not necessarily include positive emotion for Native people. A brief case study can highlight this dynamic. Social Services was called in by school administrators because a woman who was raising 11 grandchildren (including students at that school) was thought to be "depressed," and thus, her ability to care for the children was called into question. Fortunately, a Native family organization was consulted, and it arranged for a culturally sensitive evaluation by a Native American psychologist. Because there are no culturally congruent psychological measures, the psychologist used a number of standardized tests as well as an extended interview with the grandmother. The test scores indicated depression, chronic stress, and poor coping skills, but the psychologist reframed the score outcomes as indicative of being overwhelmed with responsibility and struggling and of appearing to be depressed;

yet at her core, she was maintaining a deep fortitude learned through life that despite significant difficulties, one can still persevere. Recognizing the impact of tribal values lived out over a lifetime allowed for a reinterpretation of test data that could have easily been misunderstood. Such a misunderstanding could have vastly different outcomes for this grandmother and her grandchildren. Although positive psychology acknowledges the value of addressing difficulty and trauma in life by embracing positive attitudes of fortitude, perseverance, and growth after adversity (Hall, Lewis, Langer, & McMartin, 2010), the positive psychology literature also tends to view suffering more as an anomaly than an integral part of life (Miller, 2008) and has yet to address critical issues such as dealing with historical trauma among American Indians (Gone & Alcántara, 2007; Whitbeck, Adams, Hoyt, & Chen, 2004).

CURRENT TRENDS IN ADDRESSING CULTURAL DIFFERENCES IN RESEARCH AND ASSESSMENT

Social constructions of positive psychology dimensions differ between Western and Native cultures, but there are some promising approaches that address these differences. Researchers and practitioners are moving toward "practice-based evidence" or "community-defined evidence," in contrast to "evidence-based practice" (Isaacs et al., 2008; Martínez, Callejas, & Hernandez, 2010). The former two recognize the strengths in emic-based approaches and hold promise for yielding more accurate information and affording proper respect to the particular culture or individual. Contrastingly, the concept of evidence from a Western worldview is typically based on Western assessment tools and use of behavioral indices derived from quantitative measures of outcomes. The concept of evidence from an Indigenous perspective is more likely based on the community view of wellness, health, or improvement indices that are based on local environmental and cultural factors and a qualitative description of improvement.

More specifically, *evidence-based practices* are defined as "the integration of the best available research with clinical expertise in the context of patient characteristics, culture and preferences" (American Psychological Association, 2005, p. 5); *practice-based evidence* is

> a range of treatment approaches and supports that are derived from, and supportive of, the positive cultural attributes of the local society and traditions . . . they are accepted as effective by the local community, through community consensus, and address the therapeutic and healing needs of individuals and families from a culturally–specific framework. (Martínez et al., 2010, p. 12)

Community-defined evidence is similar to practice-based evidence: "a set of practices that communities have used and determined to yield positive results as determined by community consensus over time and which may or may not have been measured empirically but have reached a level of acceptance by the community" (Martínez et al., 2010, p. 12).

Practice-based evidence has also been defined as "a culturally specific healing/wellness practice that works and has the community's sanction" (Technical Assistance Partnership for Child and Mental Health, n.d., para. 4). Critical and most challenging to the scientific community is that practice-based evidence is typically not scientifically studied, nor is it necessarily documented. For many Native communities, these practices are intricately tied to their spiritual practices and are not to be broadcast to the broader population. For example, I requested several tribally based assessments from different tribal organizations, but they did not feel comfortable releasing this information to the outside community.

This is not to say that some practice-based evidence cannot be subjected to scientific examination. However, in the context of culture and the positive psychology paradigm, practice-based evidence should not necessarily be compelled to follow scientific guidelines; to do so might undermine the trust of the tribe or community. As mentioned previously, many of these practices are either religiously or culturally protected practices that do not belong in the public domain, and they should not or cannot be replicated.

In summary, recognition of the culturally congruent approach embraced by practice-based-evidence approaches provides context for understanding the importance of assessment strategies and instrumentation among Native peoples. We can see the facility of practice-based evidence over evidence-based practice in terms of the accuracy of the data obtained, *how* the data are obtained, and the source for measurement. Emic (within-group) assessments, by far, hold the greatest promise for cultural sensitivity and the use of appropriate strategies.

These strategies must also be understood within the framework of acculturative status (Lucero, 2010). This chapter focuses primarily on Native people who are more traditional in their lifeways and beliefs. However, Native people range from very traditional to very assimilated to White culture. Those whose acculturative status is closer to White culture tend to be better served by assessments, practices, and services that are more situated for that culture (Thomason, 2011), whereas those who continue to hold to their traditional beliefs respond better to services that include, at minimum, elements of their culture. Community-defined evidence and practice-based evidence are designed for use with individuals who retain their cultural values and lifeways (Isaacs et al., 2008; Martínez, Callejas, & Hernandez, 2010).

AMERICAN INDIAN/ALASKA NATIVE EMIC
METHODS OF ASSESSMENT

We must acknowledge and respect the traditional approaches to assessment. Many tribes have multiple means for diagnosing and assessing. The Navajo have sand paintings, hand-tremblers, and ceremonial songs that perform both diagnosis and assessment. A more specific example for the Navajo sand painting is that it is a symbolic design created in the soil by the tribe's spiritual healers. This intricate work represents both the spiritual and physical landscapes in which the clients and their sicknesses exist. At the same time, the sand painting is understood to portray the cause of the disease and the meaning and function of the treatment that has been chosen by the healer for its cure. Non-Navajo mental health professionals have remarked about the efficacy of these practices, to the extent that they observed cures that Western medicine could not perform (Bergman, 1973; G. Mohatt & Eagle Elk, 2000). Some of these cures were for schizophrenia (Bergman, 1973), broken bones (G. Mohatt & Eagle Elk, 2000), cancer (D. Lewis, personal communication, July 6, 2009; G. Mohatt & Eagle Elk, 2000), and depression (D. Goodteacher, personal communication, September 15, 1998). The Muscogee have various types of healers, who are consulted according to type of concern. They may use a *keera* ("one who knows") for "seeing" what the problem or issue might involve and the type of treatment necessary. Other healers who specialize in herbal treatments also have the ability to identify problems of "imbalance" in the individual (Chaudhuri & Chaudhuri, 2001; Lewis & Jordan, 2002). Lakota healers may often consult with the *wanage* (spirits) to determine the nature of the problem and how to resolve it (G. Mohatt & Eagle Elk, 2000). Furthermore, healers may use a discussion of one's symptoms, family and personal history, and observations of nonverbal cues such as posture, facial expression, voice tone, or gait (G. Coser, personal communication, June 6, 2014). Many Native stories include animals, plants, or elements such as wind, fire, or thunder that provided the tribe with information or gifts that helped them survive or solve a problem. Sometimes remedies and cures came through a dream or vision. With most tribes, the responsibility for assessing the health status of an individual or community was typically relegated to the traditional healers or elders.

Although a Western-scientific-minded person may think these approaches far-fetched, they are not too dissimilar from the fact that some very significant scientific discoveries were made as a result of dreams: for example, Frederick Banting's making the connection between insulin and diabetes; Niels Bohr's discovering the atomic structure; Friedrick Kekule and the Benzene ring; Otto Loewi and how nerve transmissions work; and Albert Einstein, who credited a dream for his theory of relativity (Taylor, 1992).

Tribal members with these particular roles were evaluated by the larger tribe on the basis of their success, both in diagnosis and outcome. Historically, tribal communities were small, and personal knowledge and word of mouth were the methods of evaluation. However, some diagnosticians and healers gained such reputations for their skills that people would travel great distances to seek their help (Lévi-Strauss, 1976). Often, these help seekers were from a different tribe. These evaluations and behaviors still hold true today.

GOLD STANDARD OR IDEAL ASSESSMENT IN INDIAN COUNTRY

In the preceding sections, I provided historical and traditional assessment methods and their meanings; here I review newer emic-derived assessment strategies that some tribes have developed. I believe that these represent the gold standard for assessment among North American indigenous peoples. The *Lakota Oyate Wakanyeja Owicakiyapi* (LOWO–Oglala Lakota Integrated Tribal Child and Family Services Agency) child protection and foster care program has built a system based on seven tribal values (and we can see positive psychology dimensions within them): *Wocekiye* (prayer); *Wowaunshila* (generosity); *Woksape* (wisdom); *Wowacintunka* (fortitude); *Wonagi Ksapi* (healthy mind, spirit); *Wacanteoganke* (keep people in heart); and *Wauonihan* (respect and honor). In a tribal context, families who have become part of the foster care system or child welfare system are offered the opportunity to receive services from a more Western-based approach or a traditional approach. Within the traditional approach, there are three levels of assessment: (a) cultural assessment to determine degree of identification with the tribe; (b) spiritual assessment made by a medicine person; and (c) a tribal mental health assessment, which is more of a hybrid assessment using both Western and traditional means for assessing the individual's mental health. *Sung Nagi Okolakiciye* is the Lakota wording for "Horse Spirit Society" and is an organization on the Pine Ridge Indian Reservation that supports traditional Lakota culture and values by offering horse camps (equine therapy from a Lakota perspective) to youth and visitors to Pine Ridge. They use traditional assessments but have declined to share them because of their sacred nature. Not all (and in fact, perhaps very few) mental health agencies can be afforded emically derived instrumentation, and I believe this is a standard that should guide assessment practices in Indian Country. Such instruments capture the core strengths of the community, acknowledge and respect the culture, and offer the best strategies for fully capturing the positive features of the community, family, and individual. Community experts should be consulted for the following: (a) historical, traditional means for assessing;

(b) how well-being and other strengths are construed within the community; (c) what traditional values underlie community functioning; (d) who would be the best person or persons to administer these assessments; and (e) who should own the data.

Using community-derived assessments should be a gold standard, and, recognizing that our current approaches fall well short, it is worth every effort to pursue this goal. This will require much time and quite possibly a major shift in scientific paradigm. Many will wonder at the basis for this approach and the conundrums it poses. How do we know for certain that these assessments are effective if we are not able to access them? This speaks to the socio-historical context that has created the reluctance to share indigenous knowledge with systems that have been historically hostile to tribes. The practice-based or community-defined efforts speak to this very dynamic (Isaacs et al., 2008; Martínez, Callejas, & Hernandez, 2010). To bridge this gap, there has to be a recognition, respect, and support for these efforts and suspension of judgment as well. From a Western scientific worldview this is risky, but without this the gap between our science and indigenous ways will not be narrowed. To not do this is to limit our knowledge and limit our ability to accurately and adequately address both the strengths and needs in Indian Country. It is, indeed, a public health issue. However, the question remains: What do we do in the meantime? While research is incredibly sparse in the area of positive psychology and Native American assessment, there are some transitional models of assessment that bridge culture and Western psychology.

TRANSITIONAL ASSESSMENT MODELS AMONG AMERICAN INDIANS

Dana (2005) suggested an overall multicultural assessment-intervention process. Emphasizing that both therapist and assessor must use frequent and careful selections from among traditional and appropriate psychometric devices, he recommended the following procedures: (a) assess the client's cultural identity; (b) assess the client's acculturative status; (c) provide a culture-specific style of delivering services using local nomenclature and etiquette; (d) use the client's preferred language, if possible; (e) select assessment tools that are culturally appropriate to the client; and (f) use culture-specific strategies to inform the client about the assessment results. These are presented as guidelines for multicultural assessment in general, but they are useful strategies for conducting assessment in Indian Country.

Hodge and Limb (2011) noted that assessments conducted among Native people are a difficult endeavor. Their efforts at developing a measure of spirituality found that verbally based spiritual histories were the most informative; the more structured aspects of the assessment yielded less informative results. Furthermore, they found that the practitioner's level of spiritual competence played a crucial role in ensuring the instruments validity in a culturally congruent manner. Pace et al. (2006) strongly recommended qualitative validation research in which Native Americans familiar with the particular tribe or community are used for feedback on items from more standardized tests. These findings further support practice-based-evidence approaches.

Naturally emerging as a positive psychology practice, the Awareness of Connectedness Scale (N. V. Mohatt, Fok, Burket, Henry, & Allen, 2011) is congruent with well-being constructs for Alaska Native Yup'ik communities. This scale identifies strengths from a Yup'ik worldview including constructs related to (a) relatedness to nature, (b) community importance, (c) family importance, and (d) generosity. This scale was found to be useful, and the factors were positively related to well-being and perform a protective-factor role for the dangers of suicide and substance abuse.

Another model for assessing American Indians that is more grounded in scientific psychometric evaluation, but included input and participation from tribal members, is the American Indian Service Utilization, Psychiatric Epidemiology, Risk and Protective Factors Project (AI-SUPERPFP). It uses scientific assessments with the goal of being "good science" and "locally meaningful" (Beals, Manson, Mitchell, Spicer, & the AI-SUPERPFP Team, 2003). The team spent 2 years developing and framing research questions and activities that met the needs of the communities; balanced the needs for comparability and cultural specificity; and upheld scientific standards but remained realistic given the cultural context. Although it does not emphasize a strengths-based approach, it is clearly a model for sensitivity and community input seeking, and it can provide a template for the necessary steps toward developing positive psychology assessments within Native communities.

CURRENT APPROACHES GIVEN SOCIOCULTURAL REALITY

The reality is that very few culturally congruent measures in Indian Country fall within the positive psychology framework. Furthermore, our current psychological assessments are rooted in Western-based assessment. Professionals who use various assessments have had to be innovative, creative, and adaptive in their use of Western-based instruments when assessing Native people.

Thomason (2011) interviewed counselors and psychologists and other professionals who had worked substantially with Native American populations and asked how they approached psychological assessment. Responses were mixed across providers, but there were some overarching themes. Most believed that degree of acculturation should be assessed, but many also stated there were no tribal-specific acculturation scales, and the existing scales tended not to have well-established validity and reliability. Most of the respondents used standard psychological tests with their Native clients. However, many of their comments emphasized the need to recognize the cultural nuances that show up in the testing, which can be easily misinterpreted (Hodge & Limb, 2011). Further complicating this matter is that courts, mental health organizations, insurance companies, educational institutions, and social service organizations often require the most commonly used standardized, validated assessments in order to make determinations for these clients. Certainly, a tribally based assessment presented as a key factor for an individual would not be given credence in a court of law. Thus, mental health professionals and educators working in Indian Country are constrained by the dominant cultural milieu.

The current sociopolitical reality is that only standardized tests are recognized and given credibility within educational, governmental, judicial, health, and mental health institutions, even though research demonstrates that culturally valid assessment approaches must be used with Native people. Hodge and Limb (2011) noted that to avoid imposing a culturally foreign value system on Native people, assessment tools must be modified. They further stated that "the suppositions that inform mainstream discourse in the mental health professions often differ substantially from those held by Native tribes" (p. 214). It is incumbent on the assessor to become familiar with the culture or to utilize "cultural experts" (Pace et al., 2006) for feedback on the extent to which items on standardized measures are culturally appropriate. Again, positive psychology has the opportunity to bridge this gap by informing practitioners, researchers, and policy makers of the central idea that for Native Americans "culture is strength." With this concept as central, positive and culturally sensitive efforts can launch cultural competency in assessment to new levels of effectiveness. This notion can inform those who serve Native communities of the importance of seeing past the mainstream interpretations of standardized tests and recognizing the cultural nuances that manifest themselves in the test results. Or they may recognize that certain assessments simply are not feasible within that particular tribe.

SUMMARY

This chapter provided a broad cultural context for the issues of assessment in Indian Country. Without this context, it is difficult to understand the issues that Native communities face. Positive psychology has the opportunity

to expand on its conceptual framework by integrating non-Western epistemologies into its approaches to psychological assessment. Much can be gained
through this endeavor, and the welfare of psychology, as well as that of North
American Indigenous peoples, is directly linked to this. Strengths must be
evaluated from the standpoint of those being assessed. Several examples of
emic-based assessments were given, as well as models that functioned more in
the "transitional" mode—integrating Western scientific approaches with traditional tribal values. The chapter offered professional guidelines that highlight
the necessary precautions when using standard psychological evaluations in
Indian Country.

REFERENCES

Allen, J. (1998). Personality assessment with American Indians and Alaska Natives:
Instrument considerations and service delivery style. *Journal of Personality Assessment, 70*, 17–42. http://dx.doi.org/10.1207/s15327752jpa7001_2

Allen, J. (2002). Assessment training for practice in American Indian and Alaska
Native settings. *Journal of Personality Assessment, 79*, 216–225. http://dx.doi.org/
10.1207/S15327752JPA7902_05

American Psychological Association. (2005). *Report of the 2005 Presidential Task Force
on evidence-based practice.* Retrieved from http://www.apapracticecentral.org/
ce/courses/ebpstatement.pdf

Beals, J., Manson, S. M., Mitchell, C. M., Spicer, P., & the AI-SUPERPFP Team.
(2003). Cultural specificity and comparison in psychiatric epidemiology: Walking the tightrope in American Indian research. *Culture, Medicine and Psychiatry,
27*, 259–289. http://dx.doi.org/10.1023/A:1025347130953

Bergman, R. L. (1973, July). Navajo medicine and psychoanalysis. *Human Behavior,*
8–15.

Blood, N., HeavyHead, R., & Little Bear, L. (2007, June). *Blackfoot influence on
Abraham Maslow.* Symposium conducted at the meeting of the Society of Indian
Psychologists, Logan, UT.

Bodeker, G. (2009). Traditional medical knowledge and twenty-first century healthcare: The interface between indigenous and modern science. In P. Sillitoe (Ed.),
*Local science versus global science: Approaches to indigenous knowledge in interna-
tional development* (pp. 23–39). New York, NY: Bergham Books.

Buckingham, M., & Clifton, D. O. (2001). *Now, discover your strengths.* New York,
NY: The Free Press.

Cajete, G. (2000). *Native science: Natural laws of interdependence.* Santa Fe, NM:
Clear Light.

Chaudhuri, J., & Chaudhuri, J. (2001). *A sacred path: The way of the Muscogee Creeks.*
Los Angeles: University of California at Los Angeles, American Indian Studies
Center.

Coles, R. (1990). *The spiritual life of children*. Boston, MA: Houghton-Mifflin.

Dana, R. H. (2005). *Multicultural assessment: Principles, applications, and examples*. Mahwah, NJ: Erlbaum.

Dauphinais, P., & King, J. (1992). Psychological assessment with American Indian children. *Applied and Preventive Psychology, 1*, 97–110. http://dx.doi.org/10.1016/S0962-1849(05)80150-7

Deloria, V. (1997). *Red earth, white lies: Native Americans and the myth of scientific fact*. Golden, CO: Fulcrum.

Drake, R. S. (2004). *Hozho: Dine concept of balance and beauty*. Unpublished manuscript, Arizona State University.

DuBray, W., & Sanders, A. (1999). Interactions between American Indian ethnicity and health care. *Journal of Health & Social Policy, 10*(4), 67–84. http://dx.doi.org/10.1300/J045v10n04_05

Duran, E. (2006). *Healing the soul wound: Counseling with American Indians and other Native peoples*. New York, NY: Teachers College Press.

Fixico, D. L. (2003). *The American Indian mind in a linear world: American Indian studies and traditional knowledge*. New York, NY: Routledge.

Forgeard, M. J. C., Jayawickreme, E., Kern, M., & Seligman, M. E. P. (2011). Doing the right thing: Measuring wellbeing for public policy. *International Journal of Wellbeing, 1*(1), 79–106.

Garrett, J. T., & Garrett, M. W. (1994). The path of good medicine: Understanding and counseling Native American Indians. *Journal of Multicultural Counseling and Development, 22*, 134–144. http://dx.doi.org/10.1002/j.2161-1912.1994.tb00459.x

Gone, J. P. (2010). Psychotherapy and traditional healing for American Indians: Exploring the prospects for therapeutic integration. *The Counseling Psychologist, 38*, 166–235. http://dx.doi.org/10.1177/0011000008330831

Gone, J. P., & Alcántara, C. (2007). Identifying effective mental health interventions for American Indians and Alaska Natives: A review of the literature. *Cultural Diversity and Ethnic Minority Psychology, 13*, 356–363. http://dx.doi.org/10.1037/1099-9809.13.4.356

Goodkind, J., Lanoue, M. D., & Milford, J. (2010). Adaptation and implementation of cognitive behavioral intervention for trauma in schools with American Indian youth. *Journal of Clinical Child and Adolescent Psychology, 39*, 858–872.

Gould, S. J. (1996). *The mismeasure of man* (Rev. ed.). New York, NY: Norton.

Hagie, M. U., Gallipo, P. L., & Svien, L. (2003). Traditional culture versus traditional assessment for American Indian students: An investigation of potential test item bias. *Assessment for Effective Intervention, 29*(1), 15–25. http://dx.doi.org/10.1177/073724770302900103

Hall, M., Lewis, E., Langer, R., & McMartin, J. (2010). The role of suffering in human flourishing: Contributions from positive psychology. *Journal of Psychology and Theology, 38*, 111–121.

Hill, J. S., Pace, T. M., & Robbins, R. R. (2010). Decolonizing personality assessment and honoring indigenous voices: A critical examination of the MMPI-2. *Cultural Diversity and Ethnic Minority Psychology, 16*(1), 16–25. http://dx.doi.org/10.1037/a0016110

Hilliard, A. G. (1995). *The maroon within us: Selected essays on African American community socialization*. Baltimore, MD: Black Classic Press.

Hodge, D. R., & Limb, G. E. (2011). Spiritual assessment and Native Americans: Establishing the social validity of a complementary set of assessment tools. *Social Work, 56*, 213–223. http://dx.doi.org/10.1093/sw/56.3.213

Isaacs, M. R., Huang, L. M., Hernandez, M., Echo-Hawk, H., Acededo-Polakovich, I. D., & Martínez, K. (2008). Service for youth and their families in culturally diverse communities. In B. A. Stroul & G. M. Blau (Eds.), *The system of care handbook: Transforming mental health services for children, youth, and families* (pp. 619–642). Baltimore, MD: Paul H. Brookes.

Jacob, M. M. (2008). "This path will heal our people": Healing the soul wound of diabetes. In S. J. C. O'Brien (Ed.), *Religion and healing in Native America: Pathways for renewal* (pp. 115–134). Westport, CT: Praeger.

Jensen, D. (2000, July). Where the buffalo go: How science ignores the living world—an interview with Vine Deloria. *The Sun Magazine, 295*, 5–8.

Jervis, L. L., Beals, J., Fickenscher, A., & Arciniegas, D. B. (2007). Performance on the Mini-Mental State Examination and Mattis Dementia Rating Scale among older American Indians. *The Journal of Neuropsychiatry and Clinical Neurosciences, 19*(2), 173–178. http://dx.doi.org/10.1176/jnp.2007.19.2.173

Jervis, L. L., Cullum, C. M., & Manson, S. (2006). American Indians, cognitive assessment, & dementia. In G. Yeo & D. Gallagher-Thompson (Eds.), *Ethnicity & the dementias* (2nd ed., pp. 87–102). Boston, MA: Routledge/Taylor & Francis.

Kenyon, D. B., & Carter, J. S. (2011). Ethnic identity, sense of community, and psychological well-being among northern plains American Indian youth. *Journal of Community Psychology, 39*(1), 1–9.

King, J., & Fletcher-Janzen, E. (2000). Neuropsychological assessment and intervention with Native Americans. In E. Fletcher-Janzen, T. L. Strickland, & C. R. Reynolds (Eds.), *The handbook of cross-cultural neuropsychology* (pp. 105–122). New York, NY: Plenum. http://dx.doi.org/10.1007/978-1-4615-4219-3_8

LaFromboise, T., Trimble, J., & Mohatt, G. (1990). Counseling intervention and American Indian tradition: An integrative approach. *The Counseling Psychologist, 18*, 628–654.

Lévi-Strauss, C. (1976). *Structural anthropology*. New York, NY: Basic Books.

Lewis, D., & Jordan, A. T. (2002). *Creek Indian medicine ways: The enduring power of Muskoke religión*. Albuquerque: University of New Mexico Press.

Lopez, S. J., & Snyder, C. R. (2003). The future of positive psychological assessment: Making a difference. In S. J. Lopez & C. R. Snyder (Eds.), *Positive psychological assessment: A handbook of models and measures* (pp. 461–468). Washington, DC: American Psychological Association. http://dx.doi.org/10.1037/10612-029

Lucero, N. M. (2010). Making meaning of urban American Indian identity: A multi-stage integrative process. *Social Work, 55,* 327–336. http://dx.doi.org/10.1093/sw/55.4.327

Martin, J. (2001). *The land looks after us: A history of Native American religion.* New York, NY: Oxford University Press.

Martínez, K. J., Callejas, L., & Hernandez, M. (2010). Community-defined evidence: A bottom–up behavioral health approach to measure what works in communities of color. *Report on Emotional & Behavioral Disorders in Youth, 10*(1), 11–16.

Maslow, A. (1939). *Psychology of the Blackfoot Indians.* Unpublished manuscript.

Miller, A. (2008). A critique of positive psychology—or "The New Science of Happiness." *Journal of Philosophy of Education, 42,* 591–608.

Mohatt, G., & Eagle Elk, J. (2000). *The price of a gift: A Lakota healer's story.* Lincoln: University of Nebraska Press.

Mohatt, N. V., Fok, C. C. T., Burket, R., Henry, D., & Allen, J. (2011). Assessment of awareness of connectedness as a culturally-based protective factor for Alaska native youth. *Cultural Diversity and Ethnic Minority Psychology, 17,* 444–455. http://dx.doi.org/10.1037/a0025456

Moves Camp, R. (2014). *The traditional Lakota practice model: Overview of the model.* Retrieved from http://www.shrdocs.com/presentations/7726/index.html

Nichols, L. A., & Keltner, B. (2005). Indian family adjustment to children with disabilities. *American Indian and Alaska Native Mental Health Research, 12*(1), 22–48. http://dx.doi.org/10.5820/aian.1201.2005.22

Pace, T. M., Robbins, R. R., Choney, S. K., Hill, J. S., Lacey, K., & Blair, G. (2006). A cultural-contextual perspective on the validity of the MMPI-2 with American Indians. *Cultural Diversity and Ethnic Minority Psychology, 12,* 320–333. http://dx.doi.org/10.1037/1099-9809.12.2.320

Patterson, J. M. (1997). Meeting the needs of Native American families and their children with chronic health conditions. *Families, Systems, & Health, 15,* 237–241. http://dx.doi.org/10.1037/h0090143

Reynolds, C. R., & Suzuki, L. (2013). Bias in psychological assessment: An empirical review and recommendations. In I. B. Weiner (Ed.), *Handbook of psychology* (2nd ed., pp. 82–113). Hoboken, NJ: John Wiley & Sons.

Richards, G. (2012). *"Race," racism and psychology: Towards a reflexive history.* New York, NY: Routledge.

Ruby, R. H., Brown, J. A., & Collins, C. C. (2010). *A guide to the Indian tribes of the Pacific Northwest* (3rd ed.). Norman: University of Oklahoma Press.

Scheurich, J. J., & Young, M. D. (2002). Coloring epistemology: Are our research epistemologies racially biased? In J. J. Scheurich (Ed.), *Anti-racist scholarship: An advocacy* (pp. 51–73). New York: State University of New York Press.

Smith, L. T. (2012). *Decolonizing methodologies: Research and indigenous peoples* (2d ed.). New York, NY: Ed Books.

Smith, T. B., & Silva, L. (2011). Ethnic identity and personal well-being of people of color: A meta-analysis. *Journal of Counseling Psychology, 58*, 42–60. http://dx.doi.org/10.1037/a0021528

Stone, J. B. (2002). Focus on cultural issues in research: Developing and implementing Native American postcolonial participatory action research. In J. D. Davis, J. S. Erickson, S. R. Johnson, C. A. Marshall, P. Running Wolf, & R. L. Santiago (Eds.), *Work Group on American Indian Research and Program Evaluation Methodology (AIRPEM), Symposium on Research and Evaluation Methodology: Lifespan issues related to American Indians/Alaska Natives with disabilities* (pp. 98–121). Flagstaff: Northern Arizona University.

Strickland, J. (2001). Pain management and health policy in a Western Washington Indian tribe. *Wicazo Sa Review: A Journal of Native American Studies, 16*, 17–30.

Taylor, J. (1992). *Where people fly and water runs uphill: Using dreams to tap into the wisdom of the unconscious.* New York, NY: Warner Books.

Technical Assistance Partnership for Child and Mental Health. (n.d.). *Mental health frequently asked questions: Evidence-based practice and practice-based evidence.* Retrieved from http://www.tapartnership.org/content/mentalHealth/faq/01evidenceBased.php

Thomason, T. (2011). Best practices in counseling Native Americans. *Journal of Indigenous Research, 1*(1), Article 3. Retrieved from http://digitalcommons.usu.edu/kicjir/vol1/iss1/3

Trimble, J. E., King, J., LaFromboise, T., Bigfoot, D. S., & Norman, D. (2014). American Indian and Alaska Native Mental Health Perspectives. In R. Parekh & D. Dominguez (Eds.), *The Massachusetts General Hospital textbook on cultural sensitivity and diversity in mental health* (pp. 119–138). New York, NY: Springer. http://dx.doi.org/10.1007/978-1-4614-8918-4_5

Wexler, L. (2014). Looking across three generations of Alaska Natives to explore how culture fosters indigenous resilience. *Transcultural Psychiatry, 51*(1), 73–92. http://dx.doi.org/10.1177/1363461513497417

Whitbeck, L. B., Adams, G. W., Hoyt, D. R., & Chen, X. (2004). Conceptualizing and measuring historical trauma among American Indian people. *American Journal of Community Psychology, 33*(3-4), 119–130. http://dx.doi.org/10.1023/B:AJCP.0000027000.77357.31

Whitt, L. (2009). *Science, colonialism, and indigenous peoples: The cultural politics of law and knowledge.* New York, NY: Cambridge University Press.

Wolsko, C., Lardon, C., Hopkins, S., & Ruppert, E. (2006). Conceptions of wellness among the Yup'ik of the Yukon-Kuskokwim Delta: The vitality of social and natural connection. *Ethnicity and Health, 11*, 345–363.

Wong, P. T. P. (2013). Cross-cultural positive psychology. In K. Keith (Ed.), *Encyclopedia of cross-cultural psychology.* Oxford, England: Wiley Blackwell. http://dx.doi.org/10.1002/9781118339893.wbeccp426

Yu, M., & Stiffman, A. R. (2010). Positive family relationships and religious affiliation as mediators between negative environment and illicit drug symptoms in American Indian adolescents. *Addictive Behaviors, 35*, 694–699.

IV

PRACTICE

11

SOCIAL CONNECTEDNESS CAN LEAD TO HAPPINESS: POSITIVE PSYCHOLOGY AND ASIAN AMERICANS

MICHI FU AND SHANNEN VONG

What is positive psychology? How does it apply to Asian Americans? Although there is a growing body of research in the field of positive psychology, few studies have examined culture, including race and ethnicity, as influential factors in the development and maintenance of well-being. In this chapter, we describe mainstream positive psychology and Asian American positive psychology and explain how such values are based on Western ideals and may not apply to some East Asian cultures. We also describe positive psychology as experienced by the Asian American population, for which we provide an overview. Finally, we offer recommendations for future research and treatment approaches that integrate positive psychological and Asian cultural elements to promote well-being in Asian Americans.

http://dx.doi.org/10.1037/14799-011
Positive Psychology in Racial and Ethnic Groups: Theory, Research, and Practice, E. C. Chang, C. A. Downey, J. K. Hirsch, and N. J. Lin (Editors)

DEMOGRAPHIC OVERVIEW

An estimated 17.3 million people of Asian descent live in the United States; they make up 5.6% of the total population (Humes, Jones, & Ramirez, 2011). In California alone, there are about 6 million Asians, one of the highest concentrations of any state in the nation (Hoeffel, Rastogi, Kim, & Shahid, 2012). The Asian American population grew faster than any other racial group in the United States between 2000 and 2010 (Hixson, Hepler, & Kim, 2012; Hoeffel et al., 2012), with an increase of approximately 43% in recent years (Hoeffel et al., 2012). Asian Americans are also a diverse group, although this is often overlooked. For instance, Asian countries represented in California include Filipinos as the largest Asian group (43.2%), followed by Vietnamese (37.3%), Japanese (32.8%), Korean (29.6%), and Asian Indian (18.5%). Yet, many people perceive this population as one homogenous group (Hong & Ham, 2001). It is important to understand the cultural diversity within and between cultural groups to avoid overgeneralization and stereotyping. For example, at least 32 different primary Asian languages are spoken in the United States, and each language has various dialects (E. Lee, 1997). Moreover, Asian Americans differ in terms of population, immigration history, language, foreign-born populations, education level, income, family, and religion (Hong & Ham, 2001).

THE MODEL MINORITY STEREOTYPE

In the field of mental health, Asian American consumers continue to be underrepresented; therefore, it is sometimes assumed that Asian Americans do not have mental health issues (Leong & Lau, 2001). Often, Asian Americans are perceived to be uniformly successful (i.e., the model minority myth), yet this group also experiences poor mental health. Specifically, the model minority myth is probably the most prevalent stereotype for Asian Americans today (Kawai, 2005); they have been narrowly described in this manner for many years (L. C. Lee & Zane, 1998). This myth assumes that all Asians are exempt from poverty, educational underachievement, poor mental health, and racial discrimination, and thus, it puts undue pressure on Asian Americans to live up to such standards, even in the face of academic, social, and financial stressors. Although this stereotype may outwardly seem to be of a positive nature, it has negative implications; some Asian Americans may buy into the positive aspects of the myth and, thus, strive to achieve those ideals. Furthermore, some Asian Americans may perceive the model minority stereotype positively because it provides positive affirmation by outsiders (Oyserman & Sakamoto, 1997). However, failure to attain such idealistic goals may result in reduced self-esteem and increased shame. Moreover, it depicts Asians as a successful group who fulfill requirements of a minority compared with other racial and ethnic groups who did not (Zinzius, 2005), which may contribute to interracial tension.

In addition to the perceived need to live up to the model minority stereotype, this community might have a tendency to keep things private, perhaps contributing to this group's low rates of treatment seeking for mental health services. Asian cultural values, such as self-reliance and fear of bringing shame upon the family, may prevent many Asian Americans from seeking psychological help (Leong & Lau, 2001). In addition, discussing problems with outsiders is considered taboo and could be reflected as a failure of the family (Herrick & Brown, 1998). In many Asian cultures, preventing *loss of face* involves maintaining a positive self-image within the family and community, to reduce the risk of being perceived as weak (Herrick & Brown, 1998). Traditionally, Asians are taught to deal with problems independently; if they cannot, they tend to seek help from family members. Confronting mental health problems may be a final option for many Asian Americans, who, as a group, tend to seek mental health services when they are in more advanced stages of mental illness (Herrick & Brown, 1998). Preventative services are needed to help address this issue, and a focus on positive psychological, potentially protective characteristics that adhere to traditional Asian values may be especially useful.

POSITIVE PSYCHOLOGY

Traditionally, the focus of the field of psychology has been on pathology, with little emphasis on positive qualities and functioning (Fernandez-Rios & Cornes, 2009), such as hope, wisdom, courage, and spirituality (Seligman & Csikszentmihalyi, 2000). Moving away from the disease model toward a more holistic view of well-being and health, positive psychology encompasses the study and application of a broad range of positive emotions, positive character traits, and enabling institutions (Seligman, Steen, Park, & Peterson, 2005). Furthermore, a positive psychological approach can be conceptualized to operate at three levels: the subjective level (individual has been content and satisfied and has hope and optimism for the future); the individual level (person has capacity to love, forgive, and persevere in life); and the group level, which includes aspects of responsibility, nurturance, altruism, moderation, and work ethic (Seligman & Csikszentmihalyi, 2000). Focusing on such factors as a supplement to traditional deficit-model mental health approaches could allow both individuals and communities to flourish.

Little is known about positive psychology among Asians and Asian American populations, and very little information exists about whether positive psychology is applicable to this sociocultural group. Therefore, it is important to establish a clear understanding of positive psychology and its values among Asians and Asian Americans in order to develop an integrative model for working with this population, which in turn could be used to develop effective therapeutic strategies and interventions.

VALUE OF POSITIVE PSYCHOLOGY PRACTICE WITH ASIAN AMERICANS

What does an Asian American culture's style of happiness look like? Many Asian American cultures emphasize moderation of emotional expression and cultivate group pride (Huang, 1997); thus, culture plays an important role in happiness (Lu, Gilmour, & Kao, 2001). Leu, Wang, and Koo (2011) found that in many Asian cultures, *happiness* may not necessarily mean what it means in the traditional Western sense. For instance, feeling happy may have certain social consequences in Asian cultures (e.g., too much of this positive emotion may disrupt familial relationships). Moreover, Asians may value social relationships more than individual success compared with Western culture (Leu et al., 2011), which might make moderation of positive emotions (e.g., happiness) an important cultural value for many Asian Americans. Given the cultural differences in such positive emotions, it is important to understand how positive psychology may operate within Asian American culture.

Facilitating Positive Affect Among Asian Americans

Facilitation of positive affect might not be the most worthwhile approach to addressing mental health problems in Asian American clients. For example, the concept of somatization can help researchers and clinicians understand the connection or disconnection of Asian American mental health from affective experience. Leu et al. (2011) found that Asians and Asian Americans might not attribute positive emotions the same way as European Americans and that positive emotions played a different role in Asians' and Asian Americans' mental health when compared with European American counterparts. For example, positive emotions such as happiness were less likely to relieve depression symptoms among the immigrant Asian participants than the European American participants. Mental health practitioners, whose work focuses on positive emotions to minimize distress, may not be using an effective treatment strategy (Leu et al., 2011). For Asian American clients, a purposeful balancing of emotions, both positive and negative, may be an important cultural value to incorporate, rather than promoting an abundance of positive emotions (Leu et al., 2011).

Miyamoto, Uchida, and Ellsworth (2010) examined cultural similarities and differences in co-occurring or mixed emotions among Japanese and Americans. Specifically, the authors hypothesized that both the Japanese and the American participants experienced mixed emotions, but *how* they were experienced depended upon cultural contexts. Three studies were conducted. In the pilot study, 33 non-Asian American undergraduates and 32 Japanese undergraduate students identified situations in which they experienced both positive and negative emotions, with findings indicating that although the situations that were commonly identified as eliciting mixed emotions tended to be similar across groups, the groups differed in the frequency with which they mentioned these situations. In one stark example, 24% of American participants reported feeling mixed emotions when they had lost someone close (e.g., loss of a loved one), whereas none of the Asian participants mentioned this. In the two main studies, the authors found evidence that Japanese participants felt more mixed emotions (a balance of both positive and negative emotions), including more negative consequences, than their European American counterparts in self-success situations (where they outperform others); the groups did not differ in mixed emotion during self-failure situations (Miyamoto et al., 2010). Japanese participants also reported more responsibility for their own feelings, whereas American participants more often attributed the source of their feelings to others (Miyamoto et al., 2010). In summary, these findings suggest that the manner in which Asians and Americans experience emotions may differ based on cultural contexts (Miyamoto et al., 2010) and that some situations or emotions deemed positive by Western standards may not be viewed similarly by Asians.

Asian Americans and other groups may express positive emotion in different ways. For example, Boehm, Lyubomirsky, and Sheldon (2011) conducted a longitudinal study comparing the effectiveness of a happiness-enhancing intervention (because happiness is generally accepted as an important value in North American culture) among a sample of 220 Anglo Americans and Asian American participants, to assess how subjective well-being (life satisfaction and positive emotions) is associated with successful interpersonal relationships. Results indicated that Anglo Americans benefited more (in the form of enhanced life satisfaction) from expressing optimism than the Asian American participants (Boehm et al., 2011).

Similarly, Tsai, Chang, Sanna, and Herringshaw (2011) found, in a sample of 422 European Americans and Asian Americans, that happy European Americans reported lower levels of rumination (e.g., self-reflection and the repetitive and passive focus on one's own negative emotions) and depressive symptoms than happy Asian Americans. Whereas happiness may serve as a buffer for European Americans, Asian Americans who describe themselves as "happy" might still be at increased risk for depression. Why might happy

Asian Americans ruminate more? The authors suggested that Western cultures tend to embrace and foster a sense of independence, believing that happiness most often results from personal achievements or gains, which can be enjoyed without guilt or concern for others; however, this may not be an acceptable display of emotion in many Eastern cultures (Tsai et al., 2011). Specifically, many individuals from Eastern cultures are collectivistic and tend to take into account family and relationships; therefore, individual happiness may have a complicated meaning for Asian Americans, which contributes to increased rumination.

At the same time, positive emotion can fulfill important needs for Asian Americans. For example, Kim, Suh, Kim, and Gopalan (2012) explored how Korean immigrants perceived acculturative stress by conducting a qualitative study that employed in-depth interviews. Based on responses from participants, the authors identified a positive emotion theme, where positive emotion acted as a buffer against acculturative stress. Although the Korean participants experienced negative emotions, the ability to have positive emotions, and focusing on such positive traits and emotions, provided them with the strength to deal with life stressors. For example, in some of the responses, participants mentioned that volunteering to teach helped them to realize that they had the strength and capacity to overcome adversity.

According to Kubokawa and Ottaway (2009), positive psychology consists of four components: subjective well-being, happiness, optimism, and self-determination. It also focuses on an individual's place in society (e.g., work ethic, nurturance, responsibility), which may also differ by culture and which might affect the applicability of positive psychological constructs to some Asian Americans because they were mainly founded on Western values. For instance, Kubokawa and Ottaway noted that the idea that a person must adhere to mainstream ideals and values in order to be happy is a narrow perception of the meaning of happiness, because emotions may differ across and within cultures (see also Leu et al., 2011). As an example, self-criticism may be perceived as negative (in Western culture) but may be positive in some Eastern cultures. Similarly, happiness may have a different meaning in some Asian cultures, perhaps being focused on sense of connection with family members, rather than on possessing material things and success (Kubokawa & Ottaway, 2009). Such findings support the argument that positive psychology practitioners should be cognizant of cultural differences and include more nonmainstream positive psychology into its field to work effectively with Asian Americans.

Facilitating Positive Behaviors in Asian Americans

Kim et al. (2012) conducted a qualitative study on how Korean immigrants perceived and coped with acculturative stress. Three themes were identified: engagement in meaningful activities, social support, and positive emotion. Engagement in meaningful activities (e.g., club activities) helped to increase participants' sense of well-being and social connections with members of their own ethnic groups (Kim et al., 2012). Helping participants engage in personally and culturally meaningful activities can help them more effectively cope with acculturative stress. Moreover, participants noted that social support from family and friends acted as a buffer against acculturative stress (Kim et al., 2012).

Helping Asian Americans participate in positive activities (e.g., family gatherings that are culturally significant to them) may help increase their sense of happiness and well-being. Assisting Asian Americans in recognizing their cultural strengths (e.g., strong social ties, resiliency) and helping them to use those strengths may boost well-being. This highlights the need for greater consideration of cultural contexts for Asian Americans; psychologists and mental health professionals who seek to work with Asian Americans should be aware of the unique cultural strengths that exist within these cultures.

Facilitating Positive Cognitions in Asian Americans

Practicing psychologists and researchers can facilitate positive cognitions in Asian Americans culture by promoting resilience. *Resilience* is defined as the ability and capacity to overcome stressors and adversities, and it often differs from one individual to another (Pan & Chan, 2007). In many Asian societies, and particularly in Chinese society, resilience is associated with pain and suffering. For Asian Americans, the experience of pain is associated with life, which is unpredictable (Chan & Chan, 2001). Family resilience is an important concept in Asian American cultures: When working with Asian American clients, it is important to keep in mind the significant role family plays against adversity (Pan & Chan, 2007) and that there are other cultural factors (e.g., spirituality/cosmic forces) that play a role in resilience.

In addition to facilitating positive cognitions in Asian Americans, it is also critical to focus on acculturation and psychological well-being. Baker, Soto, Perez, and Lee (2012) examined the relationship between acculturative status and positive psychological functioning (i.e., psychological well-being) in a sample of 96 Asian Americans (Asian identified, $n = 56$; Western identified, $n = 20$; and bicultural identified, $n = 20$). The Suinn-Lew Self Identity Acculturation Scale (Suinn, Ahuna, & Khoo, 1992), Ryff's (1989) Scales of Psychological Well-Being, and a depression scale were used. The authors found that Asian Americans who identified as bicultural reported significantly higher levels of personal growth, interpersonal relations, and overall purpose in life, as well as fewer depressive symptoms, than participants who identified as Asians and those who identified as White (Baker et al., 2012). Although having a bicultural identity may be helpful against stress and depression, some studies (e.g., Takeuchi et al., 2007) found that factors such as acculturation levels may affect Asian immigrants. The results of Baker et al.'s (2012) study indicate that bicultural Asian Americans are doing well psychologically, perhaps because of their ability to cope with both Asian and mainstream American ideals and values.

DEVELOPMENT OF AN INTEGRATIVE MODEL OF POSITIVE PRACTICE IN WORKING WITH ASIAN AMERICANS

Seligman and Csikszentmihalyi (2000) outlined a model of positive psychology that included concepts such as optimal and subjective well-being, happiness and self-determination, and how fostering those characteristics might also promote personal fulfillment and growth, as well as better mental and physical health outcomes. They also described interventions that have been shown to provide some level of benefit for some clients (mood improvement ranging from less than 1 month to 3–6 months). In this section, we look at the adaptation of some strategies of positive psychology practice that may be helpful in working with Asian Americans.

Expressing Gratitude

Expressing gratitude has been shown to provide immediate boosts of happiness of short duration (Seligman et al., 2005). Therapists can encourage their Asian American clients to engage in acts of gratitude, perhaps by having the Asian American client visit or write a letter to someone whom they think had been nice to them but never had the chance to thank them properly. The therapist can also encourage the Asian American client to give something culturally symbolic to demonstrate appreciation to the other person, such as an offering of food or red envelopes (that could include candies or some treats).

Three Good Things

The Three Good Things exercise requires clients to list three good things that happen each day and the causes of each event; the exercise provides clients with practice at redirecting negative thoughts to positive thoughts. For example, each night before going to bed, have the Asian American client list three good things that happened that day (e.g., spending time with one's own family and/or extended families, telling stories, or learning about one's own culture) and ask the client to reflect on why those experiences occurred. The "Why" component is very important because it helps the client understand the origins and purpose of the event. For instance, spending time with one's own family may indicate the closeness of the person to his or her family, or telling stories to their friends or family may indicate a willingness to learn more about one's own culture and its history. The Three Good Things exercise could be an appropriate intervention because some Asian cultures may prefer to discuss issues through stories or poems rather than directly addressing them (B.L., personal communication, July 23, 2013).

You at Your Best

In the You at Your Best exercise, clients are asked to write and reflect about a time when they were at their best. Participants were also asked to reflect on their strengths during that time. The exercise provides an increase in happiness very quickly, but the good feeling is not sustained over the long term. This intervention may be useful when used in conjunction with other exercises. For example, an Asian American client can write a positive personal story or poem (e.g., I exercised, ate well, and spent time with my family/ friends) and then list five different strengths with which she or he identifies. Part of the exercise is to have the person become aware of his or her strengths and to use those strengths daily to increase happiness. The combination of having the person list out strengths and using those strengths may be more effective. In another exercise, the Asian American client can be asked to create a story or a poem about a character with whom he or she resonates; the character should be associated with something that actually happened or reflects an actual experience that the client had.

Identifying Signature Strengths

The Identifying Signature Strengths exercise asks clients to simply identify their strengths without using them in new and different ways. Identifying these strengths can increase happiness briefly; nevertheless, the exercise is useful because it helps clients to see themselves in positive ways. Most Asian cultures discourage the disclosure of personal information about themselves (because doing so can be considered a sign of individualism and selfishness), and so clients might ask friends or family members to make a list of positive things they think or say about them, or they might be asked to imagine positive things their family and friends might say about them.

Using Signature Strengths

The Using Signature Strengths exercise allows clients to use strengths they identified (in another exercise) in new and different way; it promotes long-term improvements through the use of fun, self-reinforcing exercises. For this exercise, the Asian American client can list his or her top five "signature" strengths and how they can use these five strengths in a new and different way every day for 1 week. Examples follow. *Love of learning* can be expressed as follows: visiting a new museum, learning five new words, earning how to read/write words in a new language; *open-mindedness* can be expressed through attending a multicultural event and critically evaluating it; *group harmony* can be expressed through planning an event with one's immediate and extended family members; *kindness* can be expressed through greeting others with a smile with food (if they are family members); *hope* can be expressed by spending 15 minutes every day for a week generating optimistic ideas or visiting a temple; *humor* can be expressed through watching a funny movie, dressing up for a cultural event, telling three jokes to a friend or family member.

It is important that Asian American clients practice these short-term interventions every day for a week. However, these short-term interventions may not be helpful in the long run. According to previous research, it may be important for therapists to emphasize the importance of family and friends, prevention of loss of face or shame, and recognition of cultural and individual strengths, all of which may promote long-term well-being.

GUIDELINES AND SUGGESTIONS FOR PRACTICING PSYCHOLOGISTS

Practicing psychologists who are interested in using a positive psychology approach with Asian American clients can use the following guidelines and suggestions:

- Consider implementing gratitude exercises in their work with Asian American clients. Feelings of gratitude have been demonstrated to be strongly correlated with boosting happiness and well-being (Watkins, Van Gelder, & Frias, 2009). Because many Asian Americans engage in indirect communication, it may be necessary to see if writing "thank you" letters directly may be culturally incongruent. If so, an alternative may be to have clients write a story using fictional or nonfictional characters to help them describe the situation they are experiencing. Because many Asian cultures emphasize nonverbal behaviors, having clients use symbols may help them reframe the situation that they are experiencing. Many Asian cultures are also collectivistic, and so it may be helpful to assess whether they could share their gratitude letters or visits with their family and friends.

- Some Asian Americans may perceive positive emotions differently. As mentioned earlier, positive emotions may have both positive and negative interpretations in some Asian cultures. Therefore, psychologists should consider their clients' level of racial/ethnic identity to determine whether it has an effect on their happiness and well-being. Clients who identify more closely with Western culture are more likely to interpret positive emotions similar to mainstream culture, whereas someone who identifies as Asian may have mixed feelings about positive emotions.

- Mindfulness therapy is the process of helping clients become aware of their environment, their surroundings, and both the positive and negative events in their lives (Nagayama Hall, Hong, Zane, & Meyer, 2011). For example, mindfulness therapy may help clients appreciate the present moment and develop appropriate coping strategies. When clients become aware of events in their lives, it is important to help them interpret and reappraise the situation. Mindfulness therapy can help psychologists provide culturally competent services to their Asian American clients (Nagayama Hall et al., 2011). For example, helping Asian American clients accept the situation (both positive and negative) and gain an awareness of what is happening without disrupting relationships may be culturally appropriate. This treatment approach might work better for Asian American clients because it emphasizes both positive and negative emotions (e.g., Hayes, Strosahl, & Wilson, 1999).

- Consider how acculturation might affect therapy with Asian American clients. Leu et al. (2011) found evidence that acculturation plays a role in positive emotions and depression in Asian Americans. Leu et al.'s study demonstrated that it is crucial to take into account the concept of culture when implementing a positive psychology approach in therapy with Asian American clients. Because positive psychology interventions are discussed from the perspective of mainstream culture, it is important to apply them with caution; they might not be culturally appropriate. Discussing the exercises with clients to assess their comprehension and comfort levels may be helpful.

- Explore the cultural strengths of Asian American clients. The following questions might be helpful: What has worked or has not worked for this culture? Which coping strategies have been successfully used by members of this culture? It may be helpful to request examples of success from clients' family background or historical figures.

■ Some studies have demonstrated that happiness may mean something different in certain Asian cultures (e.g., Leu et al., 2011). If certain Asian Americans are not as happy as members of other cultures, assess how clients traditionally cope without being too happy.

■ It is imperative to build on the culture's strengths and resources that may help boost Asian Americans' psychological well-being, thereby helping them develop culturally appropriate coping strategies.

CASE STUDIES

This section describes clients seen by the first author; the case studies are included here to illustrate possible approaches to positive psychology interventions with Asian American clients that may be useful in understanding the strategies of Seligman and Csikszentmihalyi (2000). (Pseudonyms have been used and identifying details have been changed to protect client confidentiality.)

Case Study 1

Cara was a part-Chinese, part-Native Hawaiian woman, in her early 40s, referred for counseling because she had experienced intimate partner violence during her former marriage. Her children were removed by Child Protective Services because she was unable to protect them from abuse. She was diagnosed with depression. During the course of treatment, it became clear that she felt hopeless and ruminated over negative thoughts.

Her therapist (using Seligman and Csikszentmihalyi's positive psychology strategies) encouraged Cara to illustrate a story (e.g., You at Your Best exercise) with her as the heroine, highlighting strengths that she possessed as a mother and as a survivor of childhood sexual abuse. Over time, she learned to identify with the protagonist of her illustrations, and she felt empowered enough to eventually demonstrate that she could be reunited with her children. She was also instructed to engage in the exercise of expressing gratitude, which helped her relationship with her current partner. Finally, she was encouraged to use the Three Good Things exercise to focus on her strengths and positive events in her life, which seemed to help her overall mood over time.

Although the exercise used (You at Your Best) did not help with Cara's long-term happiness, it did help with temporarily decreasing her hopelessness and negative thoughts. The strategy helped increased Cara's happiness quickly so that she could focus on working on her strengths with the therapist. The intention was to focus on her strengths so that she could feel empowered to work on other issues. Expressing gratitude helped her to express her appreciation for her partner more, thus bolstering her social support. Three Good Things helped her to reframe events in her life so that she could focus on events that were going well, which she could then relay to the child welfare worker, who could then advocate on her behalf for the return of her children.

Case Study 2

Walter was a Japanese American in his middle 30s who self-referred because he experienced difficulties concentrating and feelings of social anxiety. Treatment focused on redirecting his negative thoughts; he was asked to identify positive aspects of his social interactions with others and things that he felt good about during the day. Although this exercise was initially difficult for him, he was able to depict his thoughts through characters that he created during sand-tray sessions. (A *sand tray session* is a type of play therapy that involves using sand and miniature figures for self-expression; Magnuson & Sangganjanavanich, 2011). After months of examining more positive thoughts, he was able to use first person language to own his more adaptive thoughts, which then influenced his ability to develop confidence around social interactions. He was eventually able to join a civic organization and initiate conversations with others.

The therapist used three Seligman exercises (Identify Signature Strengths, Using Signature Strengths, and Three Good Things) in therapy. Walter was asked to list his signature strengths using nonverbal strategies (e.g., using characters to illustrate his thoughts), which was culturally fun and self-reinforcing. The therapist also asked Walter to use those strengths in a different and meaningful way for every day of the week. Notice that the therapist did not immediately focus on building Walter's verbal abilities but instead first focused on his strengths. By discovering his self-confidence, Walter was able to interact socially with family and friends, which helped ease some of his social anxiety; this gave him the confidence he needed to try to practice speaking with others. Focusing on the Three Good Things exercise was initially difficult for him because of his natural tendency to worry about the negative events in his life. However, he was able to engage in this exercise over time when encouraged to identify even basic successes (e.g., able to wake up and go to school, got a seat on the bus even though it was crowded). Using a combination of exercises (Three Good Things with

Identifying Signature Strengths and Using Signature Strengths) seemed to be more effective at eventually helping him to gain the self-confidence he needed to engage in social interactions.

GUIDELINES AND SUGGESTIONS FOR RESEARCH AND EDUCATION

We propose the following guidelines and suggestions for future research and education:

- Incorporate the role of culture in psychological research and the function that culture plays in Asian American positive psychology. Although some research has demonstrated that culture plays an important role in positive emotions (e.g., Leu et al., 2011), more research is needed in this area.
- Balance research regarding positive and negative emotions. Although some positive psychology research and practice is available, further research is needed. It is recommended that future research on Asian American positive psychology examines the effect of positive and negative emotions on optimal well-being.
- More research is needed that focuses on diverse emotions experienced by different cultural groups. Therefore, research should focus on examining differences among some of the Asian subgroups to see whether qualitative or quantitative differences exist between, for example, ethnic groups or members of different acculturative generations.
- Positive psychology research emphasizes increasing optimism and positive emotions and thinking, but it might not be useful to focus solely on examining optimism in Asian American culture. It is important for researchers to include suffering as part of the road to happiness because for Asian Americans, happiness may encompass the balance of both suffering and happiness.

GENERAL CONCLUSIONS

Positive psychology can play a significant role in mental health. Although it is important to focus on optimism and resiliency when working with most clients from the mainstream culture, these strategies may not be as effective for Asian American clients. Many Asian cultures focus on having a balance (i.e., yin–yang) and incorporating both positive and negative emotions, which may be a more culturally appropriate approach. Positive emotions may help to increase coping skills and provide a buffer against stress. However, the expression of positive emotions is not similar across cultures (Leu et al., 2011). Therefore, it is important that mental health professionals recognize cultural differences in the expression of positive emotions (Leu et al., 2011). Specifically, happiness may have a different meaning when it comes to culture, so it is crucial that mental health professionals who work with Asian Americans are aware of the cultural implications of happiness. Leu et al. (2011) suggested that focusing on positive emotional experiences during therapy with recently immigrated Asians to decrease depression may not be an effective treatment approach. Instead, balancing both positive and negative emotions may be a more appropriate treatment strategy. Therefore, the field of psychology is encouraged to apply strategies from the growing study of positive psychology that are culturally appropriate for Asian Americans, after assessing for acculturation and other such culturally related factors.

REFERENCES

Baker, A. M., Soto, J. A., Perez, C. R., & Lee, E. A. (2012). Acculturative status and psychological well-being in an Asian American sample. *Asian American Journal of Psychology, 3*, 275–285. http://dx.doi.org/10.1037/a0026842

Boehm, J. K., Lyubomirsky, S., & Sheldon, K. M. (2011). A longitudinal experimental study comparing the effectiveness of happiness-enhancing strategies in Anglo Americans and Asian Americans. *Cognition and Emotion, 25*(7), 1263–1272. http://dx.doi.org/10.1080/02699931.2010.541227

Chan, C. L., & Chan, E. K. (2001). Enhancing resilience and family health in the Asian context. *Asia Pacific Journal of Social Work and Development, 11*(Suppl. 1), 5–17. http://dx.doi.org/10.1080/21650993.2001.9755870

Fernandez-Rios, L., & Cornes, J. M. (2009). A critical review of the history and current status of positive psychology. *Annuary of Clinical and Health Psychology, 5*, 7–19.

Hayes, S. C., Strosahl, K. D., & Wilson, K. G. (1999). *Acceptance and commitment therapy: An experiential approach to behavior change*. New York, NY: Guilford Press.

Herrick, C. A., & Brown, H. N. (1998). Underutilization of mental health services by Asian-Americans residing in the United States. *Issues in Mental Health Nursing, 19*, 225–240. http://dx.doi.org/10.1080/016128498249042

Hixson, L., Hepler, B. B., & Kim, M. O. (2012). *The Native Hawaiian and other Pacific Islander population: 2010*. Washington, DC: U.S. Department of Commerce, Economics and Statistics Administration, U.S. Census Bureau.

Hoeffel, E. M., Rastogi, S., Kim, M. O., & Shahid, H. (2012). *The Asian population: 2010*. Washington, DC: U.S. Department of Commerce, Economics and Statistics Administration, U.S. Census Bureau.

Hong, G. K., & Ham, M. D. C. (2001). *Psychotherapy and counseling with Asian American clients*. Thousand Oaks, CA: Sage.

Huang, L. N. (1997). Asian American adolescents. In E. Lee (Ed.), *Working with Asian Americans: A guide for clinicians* (pp. 175–195). New York, NY: Guildford Press.

Humes, K., Jones, N. A., & Ramirez, R. R. (2011). *Overview of race and Hispanic origin, 2010*. Washington, DC: U.S. Department of Commerce, Economics and Statistics Administration, U.S. Census Bureau.

Kawai, Y. (2005). Stereotyping Asian Americans: The dialectic of the model minority and the yellow peril. *Howard Journal of Communications, 16*, 109–130. http://dx.doi.org/10.1080/10646170590948974

Kim, J., Suh, W., Kim, S., & Gopalan, H. (2012). Coping strategies to manage acculturative stress: Meaningful activity participation, social support, and positive emotion among Korean immigrant adolescents in the USA. *International Journal of Qualitative Studies on Health and Well-being, 7*, 1–10. http://dx.doi.org/10.3402/qhw.v7i0.18870

Kubokawa, A., & Ottaway, A. (2009). Positive psychology and cultural sensitivity: A review of the literature. *Graduate Journal of Counseling Psychology, 1*(2), 129–138.

Lee, E. (Ed.). (1997). *Working with Asian Americans: A guide for clinicians*. New York, NY: Guilford Press.

Lee, L. C., & Zane, N. (Eds.). (1998). *Handbook of Asian American psychology*. Thousand Oaks, CA: Sage.

Leong, F. T., & Lau, A. S. (2001). Barriers to providing effective mental health services to Asian Americans. *Mental Health Services Research, 3*, 201–214. http://dx.doi.org/10.1023/A:1013177014788

Leu, J., Wang, J., & Koo, K. (2011). Are positive emotions just as "positive" across cultures? *Emotion, 11*, 994–999. http://dx.doi.org/10.1037/a0021332

Lu, L., Gilmour, R., & Kao, S. F. (2001). Cultural values and happiness: An East–West dialogue. *The Journal of Social Psychology, 141*, 477–493. http://dx.doi.org/10.1080/00224540109600566

Magnuson, S., & Sangganjanavanich, V. F. (2011). Effective techniques: Using sand trays and miniature figures to facilitate career decision making. *The Career Development Quarterly, 59*, 264–273.

Miyamoto, Y., Uchida, Y., & Ellsworth, P. C. (2010). Culture and mixed emotions: Co-occurrence of positive and negative emotions in Japan and the United States. *Emotion, 10*, 404–415. http://dx.doi.org/10.1037/a0018430

Nagayama Hall, G. C., Hong, J. J., Zane, N. W., & Meyer, O. L. (2011). Culturally-competent treatments for Asian Americans: The relevance of mindfulness and acceptance-based psychotherapies. *Clinical Psychology: Science and Practice, 18,* 215–231. http://dx.doi.org/10.1111/j.1468-2850.2011.01253.x

Oyserman, D., & Sakamoto, I. (1997). Being Asian American: Identity cultural constructs, and stereotype perception. *Journal of Applied Behavioral Science, 33,* 435–453. http://dx.doi.org/10.1177/0021886397334002

Pan, J. Y., & Chan, C. L. W. (2007). Resilience: A new research area in positive psychology. *Psychologia, 50,* 164–176. http://dx.doi.org/10.2117/psysoc.2007.164

Ryff, C. (1989). Happiness is everything, or is it? Explorations on the meaning of psychological well-being. *Journal of Personality and Social Psychology, 57,* 1069–1081.

Seligman, M. E., & Csikszentmihalyi, M. (2000). Positive psychology. An introduction. *American Psychologist, 55,* 5–14. http://dx.doi.org/10.1037/0003-066X.55.1.5

Seligman, M. E. P., Steen, T. A., Park, N., & Peterson, C. (2005). Positive psychology progress: Empirical validation of interventions. *American Psychologist, 60,* 410–421. http://dx.doi.org/10.1037/0003-066X.60.5.410

Suinn, R. M., Ahuna, C., & Khoo, G. (1992). The Suinn–Lew Asian Self-Identity Acculturation Scale: Concurrent and factorial validation. *Educational & Psychological Measurement, 52,* 1041–1046.

Takeuchi, D. T., Zane, N., Hong, S., Chae, D. H., Gong, F., Gee, G. C., ... Alegría, M. (2007). Immigration-related factors and mental disorders among Asian Americans. *American Journal of Public Health, 97,* 84–90. http://dx.doi.org/10.2105/AJPH.2006.088401

Tsai, W., Chang, E. C., Sanna, L. J., & Herringshaw, A. J. (2011). An examination of happiness as a buffer of the rumination-adjustment link: Ethnic differences between European and Asian American students. *Asian American Journal of Psychology, 2,* 168–180. http://dx.doi.org/10.1037/a0025319

Watkins, P. C., Van Gelder, M., & Frias, A. (2009). Furthering the science of gratitude. In R. Snyder & S. Lopez (Eds.), *Oxford handbook of positive psychology* (2nd ed., pp. 437–445). New York, NY: Oxford University Press.

Zinzius, B. (2005). *Chinese America: Stereotype and reality: History, present, and future of the Chinese Americans.* New York, NY: Peter Lang.

12

POSITIVE PSYCHOLOGY PRACTICE WITH LATIN AMERICANS

MARISA J. PERERA, ELIZABETH A. YU, SHAO WEI CHIA,
TINA YU, AND CHRISTINA A. DOWNEY

No medicine cures what happiness cannot.

—Gabriel García Márquez

Many cultural values and norms are aligned with leading positive lives among Latin American populations and within Latin American culture. However, there is a considerable lack of understanding of the role of positive psychology principles with Latin American clients (Garcia & Zea, 1997; Rosenthal, 2000). Attention has been drawn to particular Latino values (e.g., *familismo, respeto, destino, esperanza*) and their potential for use in improving mental health among Latin American clients. As psychology increases its focus on character strengths and virtues (Seligman, 2002), it becomes imperative to understand Latino values and their place in positive psychology practice with Latinos.

http://dx.doi.org/10.1037/14799-012
Positive Psychology in Racial and Ethnic Groups: Theory, Research, and Practice, E. C. Chang, C. A. Downey, J. K. Hirsch, and N. J. Lin (Editors)

MENTAL HEALTH CHALLENGES OF LATIN AMERICANS

There are a number of challenges to improving the mental health of Latin Americans (Ai, Pappas, & Simonsen, 2015; Paniagua & Yamada, 2013; Vega & Alegría, 2001; Vega, Kolody, Aguilar-Gaxiola, & Catalano, 1999). Although considerable gains have been made regarding some of these, others remain. We discuss underutilization of mental health services, cultural stigma of mental illness, language barriers, and health care policy as past challenges. Additional, more recent challenges include reforms of health care policy, increased immigration of many Latino subgroups, and sociodemographic status. Future challenges include a need to disaggregate our study of Latin Americans as well as an increased need for culturally competent communication with and care from mental health providers. We discuss each of these in turn.

Past and Present Challenges

One of the most critical challenges to improving mental health among Latin Americans has been their underuse of mental health services compared with the average American (Alegría et al., 2002). Studies conducted in the 1990s reported that fewer than one in five Latinos obtained general mental health services (U.S. Department of Health and Human Services, 2001), and rates are even lower for Latino immigrants (Vega et al., 1999). Although underutilization of mental health services does remain a challenge for clinicians, initial gains have been made in this area. For instance, results from the National Latino and Asian American Study found rates of mental health service use among Latinos to be higher than rates reported in the 1990s, with cultural factors related to nativity, language, age at migration, years of residence in the United States, and generational status to be linked to use of mental health services (Alegría et al., 2007). Going forward, it is thus important for clinicians to be attuned to such cultural factors among Latin Americans seeking mental health services. Additionally, foreign-born Latin Americans and those primarily speaking Spanish (vs. English) are much less likely to seek out and make use of mental health services (Weech-Maldonado et al., 2003). Their underutilization of services may be due to cultural stigma, language barriers, issues related to health policies such as insurance coverage, and other factors.

Cultural stigma regarding mental illness within Latino communities is a prominent challenge to improving mental health among Latin Americans. For instance, beliefs that the family shares responsibility for an individual's problems and that mental illness is best treated within the family (Edgerton & Karno, 1971; Sabogal, Marin, Otero-Sabogal, Marin, & Perez-Stable,

1987) can contrast with a desire to seek mental health services from a clinician or a nonfamily member. For example, looking at a large-scale study of low-income women, stigma reduced the desire for mental health treatment among immigrant Latina women with depression (Nadeem et al., 2007). In another example, Latinos had more negative views of mental illness than did Caucasian Americans and were more likely to believe that mentally ill individuals were morally inferior and should be isolated from others (Alvidrez, 1999). Indeed, Latino beliefs about the etiology of mental illness can include lack of willpower, weakness of character, result of sin, and moral transgressions (Padilla & De Snyder, 1988). Such beliefs may help explain why Latinos appear to express much psychological distress as somatic symptoms (Hernandez & Sachs-Ericsson, 2006; Husain et al., 2007). For instance, symptoms of depression or anxiety that develop as a result of immigration and culture shock are likely to be expressed as physical pains and somatic complaints by Latinos, increasing the difficulty in diagnosing and thus treating mental issues (Comas-Díaz & Griffith, 1988).

Limited English proficiency in Latin Americans is an additional known barrier to mental health service use (Prieto, McNeill, Walls, & Gómez, 2001; Vega & Alegría, 2001). Although rates of English proficiency vary across Latino subgroups, a large percentage of the Latin population in the United States speaks Spanish as their primary language. Consequently, not only is it important to increase the availability of bilingual mental health service providers and Spanish interpretation services, but it may also be important to increase awareness of such options for Latinos with limited English proficiency (Kim et al., 2011). Furthermore, because access to bilingual clinicians in the United States is limited, issues of accurate diagnosis and discrepancies in treatment are likely to result even when Latinos with limited English proficiency do choose to seek out services. Notably, some mental health programs in certain areas of the United States have developed Latino-focused programs with bilingual mental health professional staff. Such programs offer treatment based on an understanding of Latino culture and the Latino community in the United States (Martinez, Roth, Kelle, Downs, & Rhodes, 2014). They also seek to identify resources and build connections among providers serving the Latin American community to improve the mental health of Latin American clients.

Although there is a general need for bilingual clinicians in the United States, a few geographical exceptions to the lack of bilingual clinicians are worth noting (e.g., areas in California and Miami, Florida). For instance, as a result of the strong influence of Cuban culture, the Miami area boasts a number of Cuban health and mental health professionals. However, the Latino community is dispersing throughout the United States, especially as immigration rates continue to increase (U.S. Census Bureau, 2010). Subsequently, low English proficiency and lack of access to bilingual clinicians may be particularly salient barriers in rural areas, where there is a lack of mental health clinicians generally (not to mention bilingual mental health clinicians; Lambert, Agger, & Hartley, 1999; Sullivan, Jackson, & Spritzer, 1996). Some epidemiological studies have looked at Latin American mental health (Alegría et al., 2004; National Center for Health Statistics, 1985), but it is imperative to note that traditional epidemiologic studies typically conduct interviews in English. Thus, communication with and access to Latinos with lower English are likely to be understudied.

It is likely that language barriers also heighten the difficulty of completing insurance applications. Hence, an additional challenge to Latin American mental health concerns public policy restrictions regarding insurance coverage. Broadly speaking, the rate of uninsured Latin Americans is double that of European Americans; Mexican Americans report the lowest, and Puerto Ricans report the highest, rates of insurance coverage of all Latino subgroups (Alegría et al., 2006). Disproportionate insurance coverage rates among Latin Americans are, at least in part, a result of health care reforms. For instance, the Personal Responsibility and Work Opportunity Reconciliation Act of 1996 limits Latino immigrants' ability to access outpatient mental health services. Similarly, based on recent changes in Medicaid laws, immigrants are required to be residents of the United States for a minimum of 5 years before reaching eligibility for health care benefits. This requirement not only barred new immigrants from enrolling but also led to misunderstandings about requirements and fears of deportation among Latinos who had been residing in the United States for many years, creating further drops in coverage rates (Kandula, Kersey, & Lurie, 2004). In addition, Latinos receiving mental health services may experience discrimination stemming from racial and cultural bias. For example, Mexicans have been the focus of English-only laws and propositions to limit their access to health services in the state of California. With regard to newer health care reforms, the Patient Protection and Affordable Care Act (2010) signed by President Obama aligns with a transformation of the mental and behavioral health system, as well as opportunities for workforce expansion (Mechanic, 2012). Thus, insurance coverage for Latin Americans may be expanding.

With Latinos immigrating to the United States in increasing numbers, sociodemographic risk factors are of particular concern as potential barriers to mental health. In migrating to the United States, Latin Americans often experience economic challenges (Catanzarite, 2002). Indeed, low socioeconomic rates have consistently been linked to poorer mental health outcomes, such as increased risk of depression (Cuéllar & Roberts, 1997; Everson, Maty, Lynch, & Kaplan, 2002). Furthermore, treatment centers have previously been shown to be selective in accepting individuals, with an inclination for individuals from higher sociodemographic backgrounds (Garfield, 1994). Thus, Latinos from lower sociodemographic backgrounds may experience greater difficulties accessing and receiving mental health services, such as paying for costly treatments and medicines. It is also worthwhile to consider more recent mass deportations of undocumented immigrants in the United States. In the aftermath of September 11, 2001, and the global economic crisis, U.S. deportation rates surged between 1997 and 2012, and Latino working class men were targeted (Golash-Boza & Hondagneu-Sotelo, 2013). Given the lasting consequences of such deportation, there exist mental health concerns for individuals and families who are either themselves undocumented or who have undocumented family members.

Future Challenges

A growing challenge to improving mental health among Latin Americans is the recent increase in immigration to the United States of previously less-common subgroups, namely, Dominicans and South Americans (Portes & Sensenbrenner, 1993; Torres, 2004). Given preliminary findings of sizeable differences in mental and physical health among Latin American subgroups (Daviglus et al., 2012), it is especially necessary to consider subgroup differences and to disaggregate the term *Latin American* to consider subgroups such as Cuban, Dominican, Mexican, Puerto Rican, and Central and South Americans. Relatedly, there has also been an increase in migration to parts of the United States other than those that have been traditionally Latino based (i.e., California, Miami, and Texas). Thus, with migration to areas with weaker Latino communities, there is a conceivable lack of culturally competent care that will be a challenge to Latin American mental health. For instance, there are foreseeable gaps in communication with clinicians and other mental health care providers, given language barriers and differences in cultural behaviors.

VALUE OF POSITIVE PSYCHOLOGY PRACTICE WITH LATIN AMERICANS

It is increasingly important for mental health workers to understand and attend to cultural strengths that may be tapped for optimal intervention with Latin Americans. The immigrant paradox, or the idea that foreign nativity among individuals residing in the United States is protective against poor mental health outcomes as compared with non-Hispanic Whites, functions as an exemplar of resilience among Latinos in the United States (Burnam, Telles, Karno, Hough, & Escobar, 1987; Lau et al., 2013). Similarly, and despite national statistics revealing that Latino youth face significant challenges and engage in risky behaviors that often hinder positive development and well-being, many Latino youth have also been found to be socially and emotionally resilient despite exposure to considerable adversity (Reyes & Elias, 2011; see also Chapters 4 and 8, this volume). Therefore, clinicians should strive to emphasize protective factors and foster resilience stemming from Latino culture when working with Latin American clients.

Latin Americans often display characteristics of resilience at the individual, family, and community levels that can be taken into consideration during the therapeutic process (see Figure 12.1). As the figure shows, it is informative to consider the individual client, the individual in the context of his or her family, and the individual and family in the context of the community in practice with Latino American clients. At the individual level, fostering skills such as self-esteem, a sense of mastery, and a personal sense of agency is meaningful to improving long-term mental health outcomes. For example, among Latin Americans, these skills have been linked to a stronger desire for employment, education, and autonomy (Campbell, 2008). Furthermore, it may be important for clinicians to foster self-esteem among Latino American youth, as research on national samples of youth has found Latino youth to have lower self-esteem than African American and Caucasian American youth (Bachman, O'Malley, Freedman-Doan, Trzesniewski, & Donnelan, 2011; Erol & Orth, 2011).

Having a positive ethnic identity seems particularly vital to individual resilience among Latin Americans. Given that positive ethnic identity functions in a protective way in the face of discrimination, marginalization, and experiences of oppression, clients would benefit from working to maintain and increase a positive sense of their ethnic identity. Clinicians should be particularly aware of the benefits this holds for new immigrants, because they may experience (for the first time in their lives) a shift in how others treat them as a result of their ethnicity and skin color. A potentially useful model for clinicians working with Latino clients with poor or negative ethnic identity is provided by French and Chavez (2010), who focused on four dimensions of ethnic identity: centrality, public regard, private regard, and other group orientation. All four dimensions are protective of well-being and may prove helpful in working with Latino clients, especially in those clients with a high fear of confirming stereotypes and adolescents with a developing sense of ethnic identity. Thus, clinicians would also benefit from working with Latino children and adolescents to foster positive ethnic identity because they are in stages of life where they are likely to experience role conflicts and identity formation, and cultural conflicts may result (Holleran & Jung, 2005).

Broadly speaking, Latin American clients are often deeply tied to their familial and community networks, which can be beneficial or detrimental to

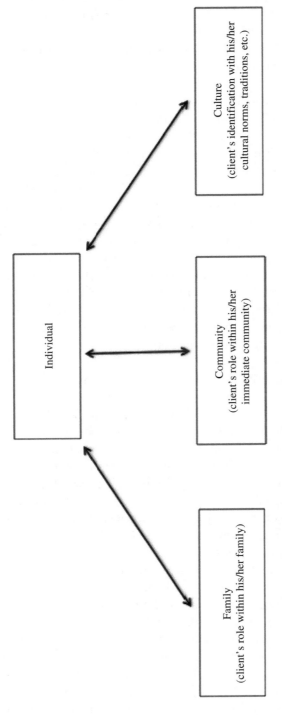

Figure 12.1. Considerations for positive practice with the Latino American client.

client engagement in mental health treatment. *Familismo* (or familism) functions as one of the most salient factors of resilience among Latinos, which strives to have cohesive families and stresses the values of family loyalty, collectivism, and cooperation with others over competition. Familismo is typical of Latinos residing in the United States and leads to expectations that one's life revolves around his or her immediate family and extended family. Keeping this value in mind, clinicians can work to reduce negative interactions among family and community members for the purpose of promoting family resilience as a protective factor. It is also worthwhile for clinicians to consider familismo in working with Latino clients, especially recent immigrants, because recently immigrated Latinos often have fractured family systems as a result of migrating. Moreover, those family members who are in the United States and are commonly working long hours with limited financial resources may have considerably less family support. Indeed, having larger support networks, including church and other religious involvement, school systems, grandparents, and romantic partners, has been linked to seeking informal care and help in dealing with mental health issues among Puerto Ricans in Puerto Rico (Pescosolido, Wright, Alegría, & Vera, 1998). Based on this discussion of Latino cultural strengths, it would seem that clinicians might benefit greatly from consideration of cultural values and strengths in working with Latin American clients.

Facilitating Positive Affect in Latin Americans

A culturally informed approach to practice with Latin Americans must attend to cultural factors that support their emotional well-being. For example, much research has emphasized the process of engaging in *personalismo* with others, or the placing of great importance on people to create strong relationships (Acevedo, 2008). This being the case, clinicians are more likely to deliver optimal treatment to their Latino clients if they deliver treatment in a manner consistent with specific aspects of this interpersonal approach. For instance, *cariño*, or warm and genuine affection and care for others, and *simpatía*, or harmonious interactions with others, are expected of relationships and are seen in everyday relationships among Latinos. Indeed, it is known that warmth and concern within Latino American families helps to buffer children against psychological dysfunction (Duarté-Vélez & Bernal, 2008; Samaan, 2000), as well as protect adult members with persistent mental health problems against relapse (Vega, Gil, & Kolody, 2002).

In keeping with cariño and simpatía, clinicians may also benefit from creating a relatively flexible environment with Latino clients. For instance, clinicians conducting individual psychosocial interventions may express warmth to their Latino American clients by being open to spontaneous peerlike disclosure with such clients (viz., *platicando*, the informal and leisurely chatting that contributes to the warm atmosphere, or *ambiente*, that humanizes the situation; Gomez & Cook, 1978). It is important for clinicians to tolerate a rather deep level of intimacy with Latino clients without exploiting the closeness. Similarly, clients may benefit when clinicians seek out additional resources for clients, as opposed to simply suggesting them to clients. This is likely to lead to more positive and productive relationships with clients than if typical Western boundaries are maintained (Añez, Paris, Bedregal, Davidson, & Grilo, 2005; Van Voorhees, Walters, Prochaska, & Quinn, 2007).

Cultural and linguistic factors influence the diagnosis process for Latin Americans. In particular, Latinos have been said to be an emotionally expressive ethnic group (Galanti, 2003). However, this heightened sense of emotional expressiveness can affect a clinician's interpretations of interviews with clients because a number of interview behaviors may change as a result of language and ethnicity. For instance, regarding nonverbal expressions, Spanish-dominant Latino clients may be more frequently diagnosed with affective disorders because of their increased intensity of emotional body gestures (e.g., touching, soothing, and stroking that are reflective of emotional states). In English interviews, however, Latinos are more likely to be diagnosed as having thought disorders (e.g., schizophrenia) because of misinterpretation of signs of the cognitive load from speaking in a nondominant language (e.g., making more speech-related hand movements reflecting active cognitive encoding; Malgady & Zayas, 2001). Regarding verbal behavior, Spanish-dominant clients may reveal more symptomatic information and be more emotionally expressive during Spanish language interviews than during English language interviews (Malgady & Zayas, 2001). Speaking in one's nondominant language produces a sense of cautiousness over expressing emotions, increasing the difficulty for English-only clinicians to make accurate diagnoses of Spanish-native clients. At the same time, bilingual clinicians should not overestimate pathology when treatment is in Spanish, given a higher incidence of emotional expressiveness in Latinos as compared with the typical "American." For instance, bilingual individuals express more anxious and depressive symptoms when speaking Spanish, regardless of their first language (Guttfreund, 1990).

Self-disclosure is another issue for clinicians working with Latin American clients to note. Recent research suggests that Latino clients disclose more personal information to friends and family than to acquaintances and more to Latino than to Caucasian American individuals (Schwartz, Galliher, & Domenech Rodríguez, 2011). This likely stems from collectivistic tendencies and is in alignment with a differential impact of self-disclosure depending on intracultural versus intercultural exchanges. Furthermore, non-U.S.-born Latinos were likely to disclose with equal frequency to friends and acquaintances, whereas U.S.-born Latinos were more likely to disclose to friends, calling attention to potential differences in acculturation. Considering these findings, clinicians should work to cultivate a nurturing and comfortable environment for Latino clients to disclose information, spending time establishing trust and some sort of meaningful relationship between clinician and client before attempting to deal directly with mental health issues.

Facilitating Positive Behaviors in Latin Americans

Clinicians should try to be aware of cultural values that may facilitate behavioral change and increase motivation among Latin American clients. For instance, *fatalismo* or *destino* is the tendency for Latinos to believe that their problems are a part of fate and God's will and cannot be changed (Flores, 2000), which is in contrast with behavioral techniques to influence one's mood and environment. Thus, when fatalismo is involved, clinicians can illustrate controllability by highlighting examples where clients' behaviors have improved their mood, events, or outcomes. With clients who are particularly devout, clinicians can focus on God's will as being actualized through actions and behaviors, using phrases such as *A quien madruga, Dios ayuda* (God helps the early riser). In addition, Latin American clients value being able to *poner de su parte* (do their part; Martínez Pincay & Guarnaccia, 2006). A self-reliant attitude among Puerto Ricans has been noted as a challenge to improving mental health (Ortega & Alegría, 2002). In other words, Puerto Ricans who feel that they should be able to cope with mental health problems on their own are less likely to seek care and utilize services. Notably, poner de su parte has also been postulated to be involved with issues of treatment adherence. Hence, it may prove worthwhile for clinicians to explore these issues with Latino clients exhibiting issues of adhering to treatment and medications. In addition, the value of contributing one's part can be stimulated when clinicians frame behavioral strategies. Specifically, using poner de su parte as a tool, clinicians can present behavioral assignments as opportunities for patients to personally contribute to improving mood and well-being (Interian & Díaz-Martinez, 2007).

Based on the salient Latino values of familismo and *respeto*, clinicians may also benefit from discourses of understanding the client's role in their family. For instance, assisting one's family on a daily basis was associated with higher levels of happiness because it provided role fulfillment in Latin American adolescents, whereas it was associated with more stress in European American adolescents (Telzer & Fuligni, 2009). It may also be worthwhile for clinicians to help clients by framing issues and potential solutions with regard to these values. For instance, a traditional gender role such as *marianismo*, or the expectation that females are to be self-sacrificing for their families and to endure the suffering of this process (Stevens, 1973), may lead to poor well-being and risk of mental illness among Latin American wives, mothers, daughters, and sisters who are expected to emphasize family needs (familismo) and respect older adults, parents, and husbands (respeto) over themselves. Using culturally adapted behavioral approach based on these Latino values, clinicians could work with clients to address personal needs to the family in framing statements within familismo and respeto ("it is important for me to express my feelings and opinions. This will make me less nervous and less sad and thus better able to raise and help my children. If I am nervous or sad, I will not be useful to my family") or to authority figures with whom issues of displaying may come before personal needs ("With all of the respect that you deserve, I feel . . ."; Comas-Díaz & Duncan, 1985; Organista, 2000).

Facilitating Positive Cognitions in Latin Americans

Unlike other ethnic and racial groups, well-being does not appear to be indexed by wealth for Latin Americans. For instance, research looking at happiness across nations found that Brazil, Chile, and Argentina had levels of subjective well-being that were higher than what was predicted by the wealth of these countries (Diener, 2000). Rather, well-being appears to be indexed by values of connection to family, community, and religiosity/spirituality (Comas-Díaz, 2006), perhaps helping to contextualize consistent findings of family therapy being successful among Latinos. Clinicians interested in facilitating positive cognitions among Latinos might consider asking clients about racial dynamics in their families; messages learned from their culture of origin regarding gender, racial identity, and ethnic identity; and how they make sense of their conflicts related to family life, migration to the United States, and the similarity of their experiences to that of other Latinos (Hernandez & Curiel, 2012). In addition, religiosity, spirituality, and related positive cognitions, such as hope and optimism, are involved with a lower risk of poor mental health among Latinos, whereas this is not the case for some other ethnic groups (Chang, Yu, Kahle, Jeglic, & Hirsch, 2013). Indeed, research has suggested the impact of facilitating positive future cognitions in reducing poor mental health in Latino adults, with particular attention to Latinos with low to modest expectations (as opposed to great expectations; Chang, Yu, & Hirsch, 2013). Clinicians may thus benefit from offering hope-based interventions when working with Latino clients at risk of depression. It may also be worthwhile to consider incorporating components of social problem-solving therapy with hope-based interventions (Cheavens, Feldman, Gum, Michael, & Snyder, 2006; D'Zurilla & Nezu, 2010). For instance, it may prove useful to teach Latin American clients how to critically and positively reappraise some of the major problems they encounter as challenges and opportunities, rather than as stressors or obstacles (Nezu, Nezu, & Lombardo, 2004), while applying hope-based strategies to increase a general sense of setting goals and being capable of reaching them.

Based on the value of fatalismo, Latin Americans may be inclined to engage in acceptance as a way of coping with the existence of mental issues. Acceptance coping may be a barrier for certain treatments, such as cognitive therapy, because their intention is to help patients to change their cognitions. Thus, clinicians should work to develop a strong treatment alliance in which rationales for cognitive tasks are understood as essential by the client. For example, clinicians can simplify the process of teaching cognitive disputation as necessary with use of the *si . . . , pero . . .* (yes . . ., but . . .) technique that seeks to counteract a negative cognitive filter associated with poor mental health (Interian & Díaz-Martinez, 2007). Clients are prompted to consider less negative interpretations of events, making this especially useful among clients who have difficulty identifying cognitive distortions. Furthermore, given that direct coping (as opposed to acceptance coping) is more esteemed and is linked to improved mental health for European Americans (Lazarus & Folkman, 1984), it is important for clinicians to understand fatalismo and thus why acceptance might be a method of coping linked to well-being among Latino clients in particular. Regarding clients with robust religious beliefs, it may be worthwhile for clinicians to work within Latino clients' beliefs that God's will determines what will occur in order to motivate more direct coping among religiously devout clients (Organista, 2000). In particular, dichos are a particularly salient method of motivating clients.

As noted in Chapter 4 of this volume, *dichos* or *refranes* are proverbs in Latino culture to exhibit cultural beliefs and ideals to describe the human condition (Cobos, 1985); these proverbs teach and counsel younger generations into their ascribed roles in a tradition-based culture (Newton & Ruiz, 1981). Dichos are not only used in everyday language among Latinos to aid daily coping (Castellanos & Gloria, Chapter 4, this volume) but also offer clinicians culturally viable tools with which to mitigate any resistance from clients, to enhance motivation, or to reframe problems (Zuniga, 1992). Clinicians should become knowledgeable about various types of dichos so as to discern the clinical situations in which each type may prove useful. For instance, when clinicians sense strong feelings of despair or hopelessness in their clients, especially in initial sessions, a dicho that offers hope and acknowledges the client's feelings can be used (e.g., *No hay mal que por bien no venga;* There is nothing bad from which good does not come/It's a blessing in disguise; Galvan & Teschner, 1985). In another example, when clinicians have a resistant client who tends to repeatedly obsess over a past scenario, a dicho that pushes for movement may be *Lo que paso volo* (There's no use crying over spilled milk.). With many immigrants being at increased risk of poor mental health adjustment, clinicians can offer recognition of the experience of entering new social and occupational situations by using a dicho such as *Estabas como perro en barrio ajeno* (He/she is a fish out of water). Thus, the clinician who uses such proverbs not only offers hope but also contributes to relationship building. Although this technique may positively engage the client, it must be carefully considered to avoid potential pitfalls. Consultation with colleagues on their use should be sought among non-Spanish speaking clinicians, and English-only clinicians should attempt such cultural techniques with great modesty and humor. For example, the clinician may allow the client to be the expert on the pronunciation and meaning of such sayings, opening up a dialogue on the origins and personal meaning the saying may hold for the client. Doing so may allow for therapeutic impact, but also may serve as a manner in which the clinician can demonstrate deference to the client.

DEVELOPING AN INTEGRATIVE MODEL OF POSITIVE PRACTICE IN WORKING WITH LATIN AMERICANS: GUIDELINES AND SUGGESTIONS

As Latino mental health research has improved over recent decades, practice with such clients should improve accordingly. In particular, our understanding of Latin Americans as a resilient population is advancing, providing practitioners and educators with a number of tools and techniques to implement when working with Latino clients. Here we suggest an integrative and comprehensive model of positive practice for professionals working with Latin American clients that encompass the facilitation of positive affects, positive behaviors, and positive cognitions.

The implementation of a culturally competent practice with Latino clients calls for a clinician–client interaction that is not entirely guided by Western norms, especially in facilitating positive affects with these individuals. For example, rather than delving into mental health issues immediately during therapy sessions, clinicians should first work to establish and maintain a positive therapeutic alliance with the Latino client. Using techniques such as platicando to communicate with clients, while also fostering a warm and welcoming ambiente, clinicians can use cariño and simpatía to develop a trusting and meaningful relation with the client. Moreover, because Latinos are most likely to disclose personal information to trusted family and friends, forming a warm ambiente and taking added time to develop a trusting relationship are of considerable importance. In addition, clinicians should be cognizant that Latinos are generally an emotionally expressive group; this may affect diagnosis rates of affective issues.

After establishing a positive therapeutic alliance with the client, the clinician may select from a number of behavioral and cognitive techniques and therapies. Latino clients typically experience added barriers to effective treatment, such as multiple psychosocial stressors, difficulty understanding the rationale for behavioral strategies due to limited educational background (Organista, 2000), and less access to costly behavioral treatments because of lower socioeconomic status; as a result, these clients may benefit from a thorough guiding through the rationale for behavioral strategies. This would ensure that clinician and client achieve a mutual understanding of the strategy and are able to shape it together. It may also be worthwhile to discuss the range of adaptiveness of behavioral responses to a stressor, to facilitate understanding of a mood–behavior connection. For instance, the clinician and client could work collaboratively to generate cognitions that are increasingly maladaptive, to allow the client to recognize his or her reactions to increasingly maladaptive behaviors, and ultimately to understand that he or she has control over behaviors.

With regard to cognitive techniques, strategies similar to those used with behavioral techniques are recommended. That is, given clients' potential difficulty understanding cognitive principles (e.g., cognitive distortion, validity of cognitions) as a result of a limited educational background (Beck, Rush, Shaw, & Emery, 1979; Ramirez & De La Cruz, 2002), clinicians should give their Latino clients opportunities to explore and understand the reasoning and methods of cognitive restructuring (Bernal, Bonilla, Padilla-Cotto, & Pérez-Prado, 1998). In addition, understanding the challenges of cognitive restructuring would likely translate to better clinical judgment and thus lead to better implementation of the technique. For clinicians working with clients with a high sense of fatalismo (i.e., clients who believe that they lack control over their own moods and cognitions), clinicians should be attuned to natural variations in the intensity of cognitions to understand how different thoughts are associated with varying levels of distress. Moreover, doing this may highlight for clients the utility of cognitive restructuring. For instance, when a client reports a slight improvement or a slight decrease in mood, clinicians can inquire about the cognitions accompanying that mood. This may be an especially useful technique when working with Latino clients with a high sense of emotional expressiveness. In addition, it is worthwhile for clinicians to capture these techniques with culturally relevant language, or dichos.

Latino culture, especially as compared with Western cultures, places heavy emphasis on the family. Indeed, embracing familismo has been linked to better psychological health and physical health behaviors and lower perceived burden of stress (Gallo et al., 2009). Assessing for family strengths has even been found salient for children coping with a parent's depression, highlighting the importance of family-centered, strength-based approaches (Zhou et al., 2002). Hence, clinicians should seek to understand the client's interactions with his or her family and to bring the family unit into therapy sessions as necessary. Furthermore, it may be important for clinicians to ask about the family's immigration/migration narrative, their hopes for their new life, and their current circumstances (Bermudez & Mancini, 2013). Accordingly, family-focused interventions have been found to support and foster positive functioning for Latino clients (Cannon & Levy, 2008; Weisman et al., 2005; Willerton, Dankoski, & Martir, 2008). One particular family-based therapy, brief strategic family therapy (BFST; Muir, Schwartz, & Szapocznik, 2004; Santisteban, Suarez-Morales, Robbins, & Szapocznik, 2006), focuses on within-family dynamics to assist families with recovery from substance use among Latino adolescents. BFST engages all family members in the process and progress of therapy to improve interactional patterns between family members, rather than targeting only one member. Another example, filial therapy (Garza & Watts, 2010), is based on the notion that children in families affected by mental illness are much more likely to trust and interact in spontaneous emotional ways with their parents rather than with their clinicians or therapists. Hence, groups of parents are trained to therapeutically respond to their children during play sessions. Filial therapy is well-suited to Latino American families, given strong cultural respect for parental figures and elders as well as strengths such as warmth, trust, and interdependence.

In keeping with the increased role that somatic symptoms may play in psychopathology among Latinos, interventions that target physical functioning can also be used as necessary. For instance, relaxation techniques, physical exercise, or distraction may help to reduce physical distress and cope with problems of *nervios* (nerves). Although a great deal is understood about barriers Latinos face in improving mental health and accessing mental health care, we are still beginning to understand manners in which to effectively overcome these barriers. Given the considerable barriers to access to mental health care services, as well as related challenges, it would be worthwhile to understand the efficacy of an approach to treating mental health within the medical system (Downey & Chang, 2012). In particular, therapy in a medical context may be especially effective when a family-based approach is used, because this is consistent with culturally competent care. Not only would mental health diagnosis and treatment in a medical context be more time-efficient, but it may also target mental and related physical issues simultaneously and eliminate issues of stigma for receiving mental health issues.

FUTURE DIRECTIONS IN POSITIVE PRACTICE

Regarding potential future directions in positive practice research with Latino American clients, it is useful to refer to Figure 12.1. In addition, it is especially important to conduct future studies that are empirically based, with the ability to replicate empirical understanding of assessment tools used with Latino clients in practice. It is likewise necessary to design and test interventions that are linguistically suited—in other words, to consider factors such as language barriers, acculturative differences, and generational differences. In addition, future research may benefit from looking more closely at the mind-set of the therapist working with Latino clients to foster positive well-being and resilience. For instance, is it sufficient for a therapist working with Latino clients to have been immersed in the culture of the clients, or is it sufficient for therapists to simply be culturally aware? Given considerable challenges stemming from socioeconomic status, language barriers, and lack of education, future research should seek to inform meaningful education of alternative pathways and resources to enable Latino clients to increase and maintain positive well-being.

REFERENCES

Acevedo, V. (2008). Cultural competence in a group intervention designed for Latino patients living with HIV/AIDS. *Health & Social Work, 33,* 111–120. http://dx.doi.org/10.1093/hsw/33.2.111

Ai, A. L., Pappas, C., & Simonsen, E. (2015). Risk and protective factors for three major mental health problems among Latino American men nationwide. *American Journal of Men's Health, 9,* 64–75.

Alegría, M., Canino, G., Ríos, R., Vera, M., Calderón, J., Rusch, D., & Ortega, A. N. (2002). Inequalities in use of specialty mental health services among Latinos, African Americans, and non-Latino whites. *Psychiatric Services, 53,* 1547–1555. http://dx.doi.org/10.1176/appi.ps.53.12.1547

Alegría, M., Cao, Z., McGuire, T. G., Ojeda, V. D., Sribney, B., Woo, M., & Takeuchi, D. (2006). Health insurance coverage for vulnerable populations: Contrasting Asian Americans and Latinos in the United States. *Inquiry, 43,* 231–254. http://dx.doi.org/10.5034/inquiryjrnl_43.3.231

Alegría, M., Mulvaney-Day, N., Woo, M., Torres, M., Gao, S., & Oddo, V. (2007). Correlates of past-year mental health service use among Latinos: Results from the National Latino and Asian American Study. *American Journal of Public Health, 97,* 76–83. http://dx.doi.org/10.2105/AJPH.2006.087197

Alegría, M., Takeuchi, D., Canino, G., Duan, N., Shrout, P., Meng, X., . . . Gong, F. (2004). Considering context, place and culture: The National Latino and Asian

American Study. *International Journal of Methods in Psychiatric Research, 13*, 208–220. http://dx.doi.org/10.1002/mpr.178

Alvidrez, J. (1999). Ethnic variations in mental health attitudes and service use among low-income African American, Latina, and European American young women. *Community Mental Health Journal, 35*, 515–530. http://dx.doi.org/10.1023/A:1018759201290

Añez, L. M., Paris, M. J., Bedregal, L. E., Davidson, L., & Grilo, C. M. (2005). Application of cultural constructs in the care of first generation Latino clients in a community mental health setting. *Journal of Psychiatric Practice, 11*, 221–230. http://dx.doi.org/10.1097/00131746-200507000-00002

Bachman, J. G., O'Malley, P. M., Freedman-Doan, P., Trzesniewski, K. H., & Donnellan, M. B. (2011). Adolescent self-esteem: Differences by race/ethnicity, gender, and age. *Self and Identity, 10*, 445–473. http://dx.doi.org/10.1080/15298861003794538

Beck, A. T., Rush, A. J., Shaw, B. F., & Emery, G. (1979). *Cognitive therapy of depression.* New York, NY: Guilford Press.

Bermudez, J., & Mancini, J. A. (2013). Familias fuertes: Family resilience among Latinos. In D. S. Becvar (Ed.), *Handbook of family resilience* (pp. 215–227). New York, NY: Springer Science + Business Media.

Bernal, G., Bonilla, J., Padilla-Cotto, L., & Pérez-Prado, E. M. (1998). Factors associated to outcome in psychotherapy: An effectiveness study in Puerto Rico. *Journal of Clinical Psychology, 54*, 329–342. http://dx.doi.org/10.1002/(SICI)1097-4679(199804)54:3<329::AID-JCLP4>3.0.CO;2-K

Burnam, M., Telles, C. A., Karno, M., Hough, R. L., & Escobar, J. I. (1987). Measurement of acculturation in a community population of Mexican Americans. *Hispanic Journal of Behavioral Sciences, 9*, 105–130. http://dx.doi.org/10.1177/07399863870092002

Campbell, W. (2008). Lessons in resilience: Undocumented Mexican women in South Carolina. *Affilia, 23*, 231–241. http://dx.doi.org/10.1177/0886109908319172

Cannon, E., & Levy, M. (2008). Substance-using Hispanic youth and their families: Review of engagement and treatment strategies. *The Family Journal, 16*, 199–203. http://dx.doi.org/10.1177/1066480708317496

Catanzarite, L. (2002). Dynamics of segregation and earnings in brown-collar occupations. *Work and Occupations, 29*, 300–345. http://dx.doi.org/10.1177/0730888402029003003

Chang, E. C., Yu, E. A., & Hirsch, J. K. (2013). On the confluence of optimism and hope on depressive symptoms in primary care patients: Does doubling up on *bonum futurun* proffer any added benefits? *The Journal of Positive Psychology, 8*, 404–411. http://dx.doi.org/10.1080/17439760.2013.818163

Chang, E. C., Yu, E. A., Kahle, E. R., Jeglic, E. L., & Hirsch, J. K. (2013). Is doubling up on positive future cognitions associated with lower suicidal risk in

Latinos?: A look at hope and positive problem orientation. *Cognitive Therapy and Research, 37,* 1285–1293. http://dx.doi.org/10.1007/s10608-013-9572-x

Cheavens, J. S., Feldman, D. B., Gum, A., Michael, S. T., & Snyder, C. R. (2006). Hope therapy in a community sample: A pilot investigation. *Social Indicators Research, 77,* 61–78. http://dx.doi.org/10.1007/s11205-005-5553-0

Cobos, R. (1985). *Refranes: Southwestern Spanish proverbs.* Santa Fe: Museum of New Mexico Press.

Comas-Díaz, L. (2006). Latino healing: The integration of ethnic psychology into psychotherapy. *Psychotherapy: Theory, Research, Practice, Training, 43,* 436–453. http://dx.doi.org/10.1037/0033-3204.43.4.436

Comas-Díaz, L., & Duncan, J. W. (1985). The cultural context: A factor in assertiveness training with mainland Puerto Rican women. *Psychology of Women Quarterly, 9,* 463–476. http://dx.doi.org/10.1111/j.1471-6402.1985.tb00896.x

Comas-Díaz, L., & Griffith, E. H. (1988). *Clinical guidelines in cross-cultural mental health.* Oxford, England: John Wiley & Sons.

Cuéllar, I., & Roberts, R. E. (1997). Relations of depression, acculturation, and socioeconomic status in a Latino sample. *Hispanic Journal of Behavioral Sciences, 19,* 230–238. http://dx.doi.org/10.1177/07399863970192009

Daviglus, M. L., Talavera, G. A., Avilés-Santa, M. L., Allison, M., Cai, J., Criqui, M. H., . . . Stamler, J. (2012). Prevalence of major cardiovascular risk factors and cardiovascular diseases among Hispanic/Latino individuals of diverse backgrounds in the United States. *JAMA, 308,* 1775–1784. http://dx.doi.org/10.1001/jama.2012.14517

Diener, E. (2000). Subjective well-being. The science of happiness and a proposal for a national index. *American Psychologist, 55,* 34–43. http://dx.doi.org/10.1037/0003-066X.55.1.34

Downey, C. A., & Chang, E. C. (2012). Multidimensional clinical competence: Considering racial group, development, and the positive psychology movement in clinical practice. In E. C. Chang & C. A. Downey (Eds.), *Handbook of race and development in mental health* (pp. 355–382). New York, NY: Springer Science + Business Media. http://dx.doi.org/10.1007/978-1-4614-0424-8_19

Duarté-Vélez, Y. M., & Bernal, G. (2008). Suicide risk in Latino and Latina adolescents. In F. L. Leong & M. M. Leach (Eds.), *Suicide among racial and ethnic minority groups: Theory, research, and practice* (pp. 81–115). New York, NY: Routledge/Taylor & Francis Group.

D'Zurilla, T. J., & Nezu, A. M. (2010). Problem-solving therapy. In K. S. Dobson (Ed.), *Handbook of cognitive-behavioral therapies* (3rd ed., pp. 197–225). New York, NY: Guilford Press.

Edgerton, R. B., & Karno, M. (1971). Mexican-American bilingualism and the perception of mental illness. *Archives of General Psychiatry, 24,* 286–290. http://dx.doi.org/10.1001/archpsyc.1971.01750090092014

Erol, R. Y., & Orth, U. (2011). Self-esteem development from age 14 to 30 years: A longitudinal study. *Journal of Personality and Social Psychology, 101*, 607–619. http://dx.doi.org/10.1037/a0024299

Everson, S. A., Maty, S. C., Lynch, J. W., & Kaplan, G. A. (2002). Epidemiologic evidence for the relation between socioeconomic status and depression, obesity, and diabetes. *Journal of Psychosomatic Research, 53*, 891–895. http://dx.doi.org/10.1016/S0022-3999(02)00303-3

Flores, J. (2000). *From bomba to hip-hop: Puerto Rican culture and Latino identity.* New York, NY: Columbia University Press.

French, S., & Chavez, N. R. (2010). The relationship of ethnicity-related stressors and Latino ethnic identity to well-being. *Hispanic Journal of Behavioral Sciences, 32*, 410–428. http://dx.doi.org/10.1177/0739986310374716

Galanti, G. A. (2003). The Hispanic family and male-female relationships: An overview. *Journal of Transcultural Nursing, 14*, 180–185. http://dx.doi.org/10.1177/1043659603014003004

Gallo, L. C., de los Monteros, K. E., Allison, M., Roux, A. D., Polak, J. F., Watson, K. E., & Morales, L. S. (2009). Do socioeconomic gradients in subclinical atherosclerosis vary according to acculturation level? Analyses of Mexican-Americans in the multi-ethnic study of atherosclerosis. *Psychosomatic Medicine, 71*, 756–762. http://dx.doi.org/10.1097/PSY.0b013e3181b0d2b4

Galvan, R. A., & Teschner, R. V. (1985). *El diccionario del Español Chicano* [The dictionary of Chicano Spanish]. Lincolnwood, IL: National Textbook Company.

Garcia, J. G., & Zea, M. C. (Eds.). (1997). *Psychological interventions and research with Latino populations.* Upper Saddle River, NJ: Prentice Hall.

Garfield, S. (1994). Research on client variables in psychotherapy. In A. E. Bergin & S. Garfield (Eds.), *Handbook of psychotherapy and behavior change* (4th ed., pp. 190–228). Oxford, England: John Wiley & Sons.

Garza, Y., & Watts, R. E. (2010). Filial therapy and Hispanic values: Common ground for culturally sensitive helping. *Journal of Counseling & Development, 88*, 108–113. http://dx.doi.org/10.1002/j.1556-6678.2010.tb00157.x

Golash-Boza, T., & Hondagneu-Sotelo, P. (2013). Latino immigrant men and the deportation crisis: A gendered racial removal program. *Latino Studies, 11*, 271–292. http://dx.doi.org/10.1057/lst.2013.14

Gomez, E., & Cook, K. (1978). *Chicano culture and mental health* (No. 1). San Antonio, TX: Centro del Barrio, Worden School of Social Services.

Guttfreund, D. G. (1990). Effects of language usage on the emotional experience of Spanish-English and English-Spanish bilinguals. *Journal of Consulting and Clinical Psychology, 58*, 604–607. http://dx.doi.org/10.1037/0022-006X.58.5.604

Hernandez, A. M., & Curiel, Y. S. (2012). Entre nosotros: Exploring Latino diversity in family therapy literature. *Contemporary Family Therapy, 34*, 516–533. http://dx.doi.org/10.1007/s10591-012-9208-4

Hernandez, A., & Sachs-Ericsson, N. (2006). Ethnic differences in pain reports and the moderating role of depression in a community sample of Hispanic and Caucasian participants with serious health problems. *Psychosomatic Medicine*, 68, 121–128. http://dx.doi.org/10.1097/01.psy.0000197673.29650.8e

Holleran, L. K., & Jung, S. (2005). Acculturative stress, violence, and resilience in the lives of Mexican-American youth. *Stress, Trauma and Crisis: An International Journal*, 8, 107–130. http://dx.doi.org/10.1080/15434610590956895

Husain, M. M., Rush, A. J., Trivedi, M. H., McClintock, S. M., Wisniewski, S. R., Davis, L., . . . Fava, M. (2007). Pain in depression: STAR*D study findings. *Journal of Psychosomatic Research*, 63, 113–122. http://dx.doi.org/10.1016/j.jpsychores.2007.02.009

Interian, A., & Díaz-Martínez, A. M. (2007). Considerations for culturally competent cognitive-behavioral therapy for depression with Hispanic patients. *Cognitive and Behavioral Practice*, 14, 84–97. http://dx.doi.org/10.1016/j.cbpra.2006.01.006

Kandula, N. R., Kersey, M., & Lurie, N. (2004). Assuring the health of immigrants: What the leading health indicators tell us. *Annual Review of Public Health*, 25, 357–376. http://dx.doi.org/10.1146/annurev.publhealth.25.101802.123107

Kim, G., Aguado Loi, C. X., Chiriboga, D. A., Jang, Y., Parmelee, P., & Allen, R. S. (2011). Limited English proficiency as a barrier to mental health service use: A study of Latino and Asian immigrants with psychiatric disorders. *Journal of Psychiatric Research*, 45, 104–110. http://dx.doi.org/10.1016/j.jpsychires.2010.04.031

Lambert, D., Agger, M., & Hartley, D. (1999). Service use of rural and urban Medicaid beneficiaries suffering from depression: The role of supply. *The Journal of Rural Health*, 15, 344–355. http://dx.doi.org/10.1111/j.1748-0361.1999.tb00756.x

Lau, A. S., Tsai, W., Shih, J., Liu, L. L., Hwang, W. C., & Takeuchi, D. T. (2013). The immigrant paradox among Asian American women: Are disparities in the burden of depression and anxiety paradoxical or explicable? *Journal of Consulting and Clinical Psychology*, 81, 901–911. http://dx.doi.org/10.1037/a0032105

Lazarus, R. S., & Folkman, S. (1984). *Stress, appraisal, and coping.* New York, NY: Springer.

Malgady, R. G., & Zayas, L. H. (2001). Cultural and linguistic considerations in psychodiagnosis with Hispanics: The need for an empirically informed process model. *Social Work*, 46, 39–49. http://dx.doi.org/10.1093/sw/46.1.39

Martinez, O., Roth, A. M., Kelle, G., Downs, M., & Rhodes, S. D. (2014). Adaptation and implementation of HoMBReS: A community-level, evidence-based HIV behavioral intervention for heterosexual Latino men in the midwestern United States. *AIDS Education and Prevention*, 26, 68–80. http://dx.doi.org/10.1521/aeap.2014.26.1.68

Martínez Pincay, I. E., & Guarnaccia, P. J. (2006). "It's like going through an earthquake": Anthropological perspectives on depression among Latino immigrants. *Journal of Immigrant and Minority Health*, 9, 17–28. http://dx.doi.org/10.1007/s10903-006-9011-0

Mechanic, D. (2012). Review of "Public mental health." *Journal of Sociology and Social Welfare, 39,* 183–185.

Muir, J. A., Schwartz, S. J., & Szapocznik, J. (2004). A program of research with Hispanic and African American families: Three decades of intervention development and testing influenced by the changing cultural context of Miami. *Journal of Marital and Family Therapy, 30,* 285–303. http://dx.doi.org/10.1111/j.1752-0606.2004.tb01241.x

Nadeem, E., Lange, J. M., Edge, D., Fongwa, M., Belin, T., & Miranda, J. (2007). Does stigma keep poor young immigrant and U.S.-born Black and Latina women from seeking mental health care? *Psychiatric Services, 58,* 1547–1554. http://dx.doi.org/10.1176/ps.2007.58.12.1547

National Center for Health Statistics. (1985). Plan and operation of the Hispanic Health and Nutrition Examination Survey, 1982–1984. *Vital Health Statistics* (DHHS No. (PHS) 85-1321).

Newton, F. C., & Ruiz, R. A. (1981). Chicano culture and mental health among the elderly. In M. Miranda & R. Ruiz (Eds.), *Chicano aging and mental health* (pp. 38–62). Rockville, MD: Department of Health and Human Services.

Nezu, A. M., Nezu, C., & Lombardo, E. (2004). *Cognitive-behavioral case formulation and treatment design: A problem-solving approach.* New York, NY: Springer.

Organista, K. C. (2000). Latinos. In J. R. White & A. S. Freeman (Eds.), *Cognitive-behavioral group therapy: For specific problems and populations* (pp. 281–303). Washington, DC: American Psychological Association. http://dx.doi.org/10.1037/10352-011

Ortega, A. N., & Alegría, M. (2002). Self-reliance, mental health need, and the use of mental healthcare among island Puerto Ricans. *Mental Health Services Research, 4,* 131–140. http://dx.doi.org/10.1023/A:1019707012403

Padilla, A. M., & De Snyder, V. N. S. (1988). Psychology in pre-Columbian Mexico. *Hispanic Journal of Behavioral Sciences, 10,* 55–66. http://dx.doi.org/10.1177/07399863880101004

Paniagua, F. A., & Yamada, A. (2013). *Handbook of multicultural mental health: Assessment and treatment of diverse populations* (2nd ed.). San Diego, CA: Elsevier Academic Press.

Patient Protection and Affordable Care Act of 2010, Pub.L. No. 111-148, 124 Stat. 119-1025 (2010).

Personal Responsibility and Work Opportunity Reconciliation Act of 1996, Pub.L. No. 104-193, 110 Stat. 2015 (1996).

Pescosolido, B. A., Wright, E. R., Alegría, M., & Vera, M. (1998). Social networks and patterns of use among the poor with mental health problems in Puerto Rico. *Medical Care, 36,* 1057–1072. http://dx.doi.org/10.1097/00005650-199807000-00012

Portes, A., & Sensenbrenner, J. (1993). Embeddedness and immigration: Notes on the social determinants of economic action. *American Journal of Sociology, 98,* 1320–1350.

Prieto, L. R., McNeill, B. W., Walls, R. G., & Gómez, S. P. (2001). Chicanas/os and mental health services: An overview of utilization, counselor preference, and assessment issues. *The Counseling Psychologist, 29,* 18–54. http://dx.doi.org/10.1177/0011000001291002

Ramirez, R. R., & De La Cruz, G. P. (2002). *The Hispanic population in the United States.* Washington, DC: U.S. Census Bureau.

Reyes, J. A., & Elias, M. J. (2011). Fostering social–emotional resilience among Latino youth. *Psychology in the Schools, 48,* 723–737. http://dx.doi.org/10.1002/pits.20580

Rosenthal, C. (2000). Latino practice outcome research: A review of the literature. *Smith College Studies in Social Work, 70,* 217–238. http://dx.doi.org/10.1080/00377310009517589

Sabogal, F., Marin, G., Otero-Sabogal, R., Marin, B. V., & Perez-Stable, E. J. (1987). Hispanic familism and acculturation: What changes and what doesn't? *Hispanic Journal of Behavioral Sciences, 9,* 397–412. http://dx.doi.org/10.1177/07399863870094003

Samaan, R. A. (2000). The influences of race, ethnicity, and poverty on the mental health of children. *Journal of Health Care for the Poor and Underserved, 11,* 100–110. http://dx.doi.org/10.1353/hpu.2010.0557

Santisteban, D. A., Suarez-Morales, L., Robbins, M. S., & Szapocznik, J. (2006). Brief strategic family therapy: Lessons learned in efficacy research and challenges to blending research and practice. *Family Process, 45,* 259–271. http://dx.doi.org/10.1111/j.1545-5300.2006.00094.x

Schwartz, A. L., Galliher, R. V., & Domenech Rodríguez, M. M. (2011). Self-disclosure in Latinos' intercultural and intracultural friendships and acquaintanceships: Links with collectivism, ethnic identity, and acculturation. *Cultural Diversity & Ethnic Minority Psychology, 17,* 116–121. http://dx.doi.org/10.1037/a0021824

Seligman, M. P. (2002). *Authentic happiness: Using the new positive psychology to realize your potential for lasting fulfillment.* New York, NY: Free Press.

Stevens, E. P. (1973). The prospect for a women's liberation movement in Latin America. *Journal of Marriage and the Family, 35,* 313–331. http://dx.doi.org/10.2307/350661

Sullivan, G., Jackson, C. A., & Spritzer, K. L. (1996). Characteristics and service use of seriously mentally ill persons living in rural areas. *Psychiatric Services, 47,* 57–61. http://dx.doi.org/10.1176/ps.47.1.57

Telzer, E. H., & Fuligni, A. J. (2009). Daily family assistance and the psychological well-being of adolescents from Latin American, Asian, and European backgrounds. *Developmental Psychology, 45,* 1177–1189. http://dx.doi.org/10.1037/a0014728

Torres, V. (2004). The diversity among us: Puerto Ricans, Cuban Americans, Caribbean Americans, and Central and South Americans. *New Directions for Student Services, 2004,* 5–16. http://dx.doi.org/10.1002/ss.112

U.S. Census Bureau. (2010). *The Hispanic population: 2010*. Retrieved from http://www.census.gov/prod/cen2010/briefs/c2010br-04.pdf

U.S. Department of Health and Human Services. (2001). *Mental health: Culture, race, and ethnicity—a supplement to mental health: A report of the surgeon general*. Rockville, MD: U.S. Department of Health and Human Services, Substance Abuse and Mental Health Services Administration, Center for Mental Health Services.

Van Voorhees, B. W., Walters, A. E., Prochaska, M., & Quinn, M. T. (2007). Reducing health disparities in depressive disorders outcomes between non-Hispanic Whites and ethnic minorities: A call for pragmatic strategies over the life course. *Medical Care Research and Review, 64*(Suppl.), 157S–194S. http://dx.doi.org/10.1177/1077558707305424

Vega, W. A., & Alegría, M. (2001). Latino mental health and treatment in the United States. In M. Aguirre, C. W. Molina, & R. E. Zambrana (Eds.), *Health issues in the Latino community* (pp. 179–201). Oxford, England: John Wiley & Sons.

Vega, W. A., Gil, A. G., & Kolody, B. (2002). What do we know about Latino drug use? Methodological evaluation of state databases. *Hispanic Journal of Behavioral Sciences, 24*, 395–408. http://dx.doi.org/10.1177/0739986302238211

Vega, W. A., Kolody, B., Aguilar-Gaxiola, S., & Catalano, R. (1999). Gaps in service utilization by Mexican Americans with mental health problems. *The American Journal of Psychiatry, 156*, 928–934. http://dx.doi.org/10.1176/ajp.156.6.928

Weech-Maldonado, R., Morales, L. S., Elliott, M., Spritzer, K., Marshall, G., & Hays, R. D. (2003). Race/ethnicity, language, and patients' assessments of care in Medicaid managed care. *Health Services Research, 38*, 789–808. http://dx.doi.org/10.1111/1475-6773.00147

Weisman, A., Feldman, G., Gruman, C., Rosenberg, R., Chamorro, R., & Belozersky, I. (2005). Improving mental health services for Latino and Asian immigrant elders. *Professional Psychology: Research and Practice, 36*, 642–648. http://dx.doi.org/10.1037/0735-7028.36.6.642

Willerton, E., Dankoski, M. E., & Martir, J. (2008). Medical family therapy: A model for addressing mental health disparities among Latinos. *Families, Systems, & Health, 26*, 196–206. http://dx.doi.org/10.1037/1091-7527.26.2.196

Zhou, Q., Eisenberg, N., Losoya, S. H., Fabes, R. A., Reiser, M., Guthrie, I. K., . . . Shepard, S. A. (2002). The relations of parental warmth and positive expressiveness to children's empathy-related responding and social functioning: A longitudinal study. *Child Development, 73*, 893–915. http://dx.doi.org/10.1111/1467-8624.00446

Zuniga, M. E. (1992). Families with Latino roots. In E. W. Lynch & M. J. Hanson (Eds.), *Developing cross-cultural competence: A guide for working with children and their families* (pp. 151–179). Baltimore, MD: Paul H Brookes.

13

POSITIVE PSYCHOLOGY PRACTICE WITH AFRICAN AMERICANS: MENTAL HEALTH CHALLENGES AND TREATMENT

SUSSIE ESHUN AND ESTHER MORTIMER PACKER

Mental illness among African Americans must be considered in the light of past and current discrimination and other negative experiences as well as the impact of personally mediated, internalized, and institutionalized racism. The effect of these experiences manifests as cultural distrust and subsequent poor mental health treatment seeking, which in turn affect the health, well-being, and optimal functioning of African Americans. Despite well-documented challenges, African Americans have developed strengths, including Africentric values, that are consistent with, and could therefore be applied to, the basic principles underlying positive psychology. However, the influence of unique historical, spiritual, and cultural factors must not be ignored. In this chapter, we present an integrative model, including treatment suggestions, for effectively applying positive psychology to practice with African Americans.

http://dx.doi.org/10.1037/14799-013
Positive Psychology in Racial and Ethnic Groups: Theory, Research, and Practice, E. C. Chang, C. A. Downey, J. K. Hirsch, and N. J. Lin (Editors)

Ethnic minorities, particularly African Americans, have a long history of racism, prejudice, and discrimination, which influences their perception of themselves, their perception of others, and how others perceive them (Ayalon & Young, 2005; Mills & Edwards, 2002; D. R. Williams & Williams-Morris, 2000), as well as their health and well-being. Jones (2000) identified three levels of racism:

- *personally mediated racism*, which "includes acts of commission as well as acts of omission . . . and manifests as lack of respect, . . . suspicion, . . . devaluation, . . . scapegoating, . . . and dehumanization" (Jones, 2000, p. 1213);
- *internalized racism*, or "acceptance by members of the stigmatized races of negative messages about their own abilities and intrinsic worth . . . which involves embracing *whiteness*, . . . self-devaluation, . . . and resignation, helplessness, and hopelessness" (p. 1213); and
- *institutionalized racism*, or "differential access to the goods, services, and opportunities of society by race." (p. 1212)

Most African Americans face racism and prejudice on a daily basis and in almost all aspects of their lives.

African Americans have routinely been exposed to institutional racism even in scientific endeavors, which have often resulted in portrayals of African Americans as racially inferior (Guthrie, 2004). This exposure has fostered a pattern of cultural mistrust, such that African Americans tend to exhibit a generalized distrust of Western worldviews or Whites and may, therefore, be hesitant to share information or interact with them for fear of being exploited (Caldwell-Colbert, Parks, & Eshun, 2009; Terrell, Taylor, Menzise, & Barrett, 2009). This same mistrust is often extended to health care professionals, including mental health practitioners (Hatcher, 2012; Whaley, 2001). Terrell et al. (2009) illustrated this by recounting an incident involving an African American client who "blurted out: 'I don't even trust White people enough to tell them that I don't trust them'" (p. 300). This perceived lack of cultural understanding from the predominantly White majority may have a negative impact on the mental health of African Americans.

Data from a recent population census indicate that African Americans make up a significant proportion of the U.S. population, approximately 13.6% or 41.8 million persons, constituting the second largest ethnic minority group (Rastogi, Johnson, Hoeffel, & Drewery, 2011). Although they make up a notable proportion of the U.S. population, significant factors in our society directly and indirectly force ethnic minorities to fit in with the norms of the majority culture, with little regard for their own ethnic or cultural values and norms. These influences exert unnecessary strain on (and ultimately affect) the mental health of, African Americans (Menke & Flynn, 2009) and may result in higher rates of certain psychological disorders among African Americans and other ethnic minorities than among Whites. For instance, Gonzalez et al. (2010) found that compared with non-Hispanic Whites, non-Hispanic African Americans, Hispanics, and other minority races reported higher levels of major depression. Similar findings were reported among African American, Black Caribbean, and non-Hispanic White mothers (Boyd, Joe, Michalopoulos, Davis, & Jackson, 2011). Other studies imply that past chronic oppression and atrocities as well as cultural mistrust have negatively influenced psychological well-being and the mental health status of African Americans (Suite, La Bril, Primm, & Harrison-Ross, 2007).

Although prevalence rates for mood disorders among African Americans are lower than among Whites, it is important to note that chronicity and severity are often higher for African American and Caribbean Blacks (D. R. Williams et al., 2007). African Americans and Hispanics may also tend to report more somatic symptoms than non-Hispanic Whites (Ayalon & Young, 2003); however, among some ethnic minority groups, somatization of depression is a more acceptable way of presenting one's stress (Nadeem, Lange, & Miranda, 2009) because it avoids negative stigma. In other words, African Americans may have lower rates of mood disorders, but they may endure more chronic and severe forms of the illness, and they may manifest psychological symptoms somatically. The picture is equally unclear for prevalence rates of anxiety disorders among African Americans, who tend to report lower rates of anxiety disorders, with the exception of posttraumatic stress disorder (Earl & Williams, 2009). In a study of posttraumatic stress disorder prevalence, African Americans and Hispanics were more likely to have experienced child maltreatment and witnessed domestic violence than Whites, and Asians, African American men, and Hispanic women were more likely to have experienced war-related trauma than Whites (Roberts, Gilman, Breslau, Breslau, & Koenen, 2011). Such findings indicate a need to focus on the unique experiences and prevalence rates of specific disorders for African Americans, shifting away from generic information underscoring lower rates without thoroughly considering their unique cultural experiences.

Prevalence rates for psychotic disorders among African Americans have always been known to be high. Higher rates of psychotic disorders, particularly schizophrenia, among African Americans than Whites have been consistently reported (Strakowski et al., 1996), and more recent studies suggest African Americans are 4 times as likely to be diagnosed with schizophrenia than Whites, regardless of setting (Barnes, 2004; Blow et al., 2004). However, such reports must be interpreted in light of diagnostic bias. For example, using traditional psychiatric diagnostic interviews and semi-structured interviews, African Americans tend to be diagnosed more often with schizophrenia than other ethnicities (Neighbors, Trierweiler, Ford, & Muroff, 2003; Strakowski et al., 2003).

Given these higher rates of serious mental illness for African Americans yet relatively lower rates of certain common psychological disorders, African Americans continue to report lower or worse levels of life satisfaction and psychological well-being than Whites (Earl & Williams, 2009). Such differences may be related to past and present challenges created by different forms of racism (Suite et al., 2007; Whaley, 2001). In summary, African Americans may continue to demonstrate cultural mistrust because racism, prejudice, and discrimination are still present in their daily lives. Such experiences can negatively influence attitudes about many socially constructed institutions, including health care, which, in turn, may reduce their likelihood of reporting mental illness or seeking appropriate help (Terrell et al., 2009). The continued experience of racial discrimination, individually or as a group, deepens wounds and contributes to greater cultural mistrust, and the experience of being treated unfairly regardless of personal efforts may promote a sense of ambivalence, feelings of poor self-worth and group worth, learned helplessness, and ultimately poor psychological health. Furthermore, socioeconomic factors, including lower educational levels, higher unemployment rates, and lack of access to quality mental health care, are significant issues to be considered (Gary, 2005; Hines-Martin, Malone, Kim, & Brown-Piper, 2003) and are known to contribute additional risk for African Americans.

VALUE OF POSITIVE PSYCHOLOGY PRACTICE WITH AFRICAN AMERICANS

The historical impact of slavery and continued, persistent experiences of racism, prejudice, and discrimination have negatively influenced views of the health system and perceptions about mental illness, as well as health-seeking behaviors of African Americans (Ayalon & Young, 2005; Benkert, Peters, Clark, & Keves-Foster, 2006; Mills & Edwards, 2002). Faced with seemingly insurmountable obstacles, African Americans have developed strengths crucial to their survival (Caldwell-Colbert et al., 2009), suggesting that the basic principles underlying positive psychology may be applicable and effective in clinical interventions and psychological practice with African American clients.

Positive psychology has been described as "a science of positive subjective experience, positive individual traits, and positive institutions [that] promises to improve quality of life and prevent pathologies that arise when life is barren and meaningless" (Seligman & Csikszentmihalyi, 2000, p. 5). An important tenet of positive psychology is that "treatment is not just fixing what is wrong; it is also building what is right" (Seligman, 2005, p. 4). This idea may be attractive to a people who have endured oppression and have been made to feel less ideal than the norm or majority group. Positive psychology's advantage in applicability to African Americans stems from the assumption that they possess strengths that could be fostered through empowerment, promotion of hopefulness, and sense of control over their success. In other words, positive psychology may make psychotherapy less intimidating by emphasizing strengths, perhaps reducing some degree of stigma typically associated with seeking help for mental illness (Thompson, Bazile, & Akbar, 2004). It is important, therefore, to consider the various ways in which positive psychology can inform mental health interventions targeted at African Americans.

As summarized by Caldwell-Colbert et al. (2009), "Positive psychology conveys a message of optimism, hope, and survival . . . [a] message that is easily applicable to the cultural values of African Americans" (p. 377). Many of the strengths recognized in positive psychology such as optimism, hope, well-being, courage, forgiveness, and benevolence are also emphasized as core African American values. The basic tenets of positive psychology are compatible with Africentric cultural values (most of which originate from the principles of Kwanzaa), namely, (a) unity, (b) self-determination, (c) collective work and responsibility, (d) cooperative economies, (e) purpose, (f) creativity, and (g) faith (Caldwell-Colbert et al., 2009). Core protective factors, including resiliency, wisdom, hope, support from the community and extended family, and spirituality, have helped African Americans overcome oppression, which seems to suggest that positive psychology would be a good fit for psychological treatment when working with African Americans. Furthermore, adherence to such Africentric cultural values is associated with good mental health (Constantine, Alleyne, Wallace, & Franklin-Jackson, 2006; Neblett, Seaton, Hammond, & Townsend, 2010), suggesting that if applied appropriately and contextually, positive psychology principles may inform the development of mental health interventions for African Americans.

Effective application of positive psychology practice with African American clients means that practitioners must be willing to incorporate important systems or structures, including extended family, church or clergy, and other community resources in treatment planning. In an article that attracted much criticism, McNulty and Fincham (2012) questioned the assumption that positive psychology processes are fundamentally effective for improving functioning and well-being. Although their review focused on longitudinal studies of married couples, and not necessarily on African American samples, they pointed out that positive psychology constructs such as "optimistic expectation, positive thoughts . . . can either benefit or harm well-being depending on the context in which they operate" (p. 101). It could be argued that encouraging optimism in the face of chronic racism and discrimination could have harmful effects for African Americans if there is no hope that the conditions that encourage injustice and prejudice will change.

Despite the good arguments for applying positive psychology in practice, no studies have focused on its effectiveness with African Americans. A review of the literature yielded no empirical studies in the past 10 years focused on Africentric, positive psychology interventions, which suggests that mixed-method research studies are needed on possible interactive influences of race, ethnicity, culture, and socioeconomic factors on mental health and well-being. Lyubomirsky (2012) responded to McNulty and Fincham (2012) as follows: "If optimism, happiness, kindness, or forgiveness have deleterious effects for certain individuals, under specific conditions, or when practiced or expressed in particular ways, then the results are all the more interesting, challenging common assumptions and calling for more research" (p. 2). We echo her sentiment and hope to see more research focused on the unique experiences of African Americans.

FACILITATING POSITIVE AFFECT IN AFRICAN AMERICANS

Non-African Americans often assume that African Americans possess more negative than positive affect because of their long history of discrimination and social injustice. This may not be true. Any discussion of mental health interventions for African Americans would be deficient if it did not consider their history; mistrust of Whites or Westernized health systems; and socioeconomic status, low educational level, and access to health care.

Positive affect involves expressed emotions such as joy, contentment, interest, and pride. Such emotions positively influence attention, curiosity, and creativity and, in turn, positive behaviors and optimal functioning over time (Fredrickson, 2001; Kobau et al., 2011). As summarized by Fredrickson (2001), "positive affect prompts individuals to engage with their environments and partake in activities, many of which are adaptive for the individual" (p. 219). Positive affect fosters flourishing or optimal functioning in diverse life spheres, including job performance, creativity, marital satisfaction, social relationships, and general physical health (Layous, Chancellor, Lyubomirsky, Wang, & Doraiswamy, 2011).

Facilitating positive affect in African Americans is compatible with philosophical views proposed by proponents of Black identity development, many of which stem from Tajfel's (1979) social identity theory, which emphasizes the importance of positive affect toward one's group. Social identity theory is extended in models such as Phinney's (1992), which posits that individuals who view their ethnic group positively and develop a sense of belonging tend to adapt to stressors more readily, experience better psychosocial functioning, and develop a stronger personal identity (J. L. Williams, Tolan, Durkee, Francois, & Anderson, 2012). In a meta-analysis of 46 studies, "positive ethnic–racial affect was positively and significantly related to positive adjustment" (Rivas-Drake et al., 2014, p. 77). Specifically, positive affective characteristics such as love, joy, and peace are associated with well-being, positive identity development, and optimal functioning (Caldwell-Colbert, et al., 2009; Myers et al., 1991). Positive affect is also related to engagement in activities that promote positive coping skills (Taylor, Kemeny, Reed, Bower, & Gruenewald, 2000) and, for African Americans, such adaptive skills may include resilience (APA Task Force on Resilience and Strength in Black Children and Adolescents, 2008; Johnson-Garner & Meyers, 2003), a character strength they are likely to be familiar with from childhood because of generalized ethnic-related discrimination (Hopps, Tourse, & Christian, 2002). These findings suggest that a sense of ethnic identity, belonging, and incorporating core African values are important in developing and maintaining positive affect.

Historically, African Americans have overcome oppression by holding on to spirituality and strong religious beliefs as crucial protective factors (Chatters, Taylor, Jackson, & Lincoln, 2008; Ward & Heidrich, 2009). Thus, one potential way to facilitate positive affect in this group is to highlight specific types of affect that are part of spiritual growth while also providing information about research linking spiritually sanctioned positive affects with physical and psychological well-being. For instance, a biblical concept that is commonly discussed is "fruits of the spirit," which include "love, joy, peace, long-suffering, goodness and faith" (Galatians 5:22, The Holy Bible, King James Version), and which are similar to the aforementioned components of positive affect. Thus, spiritually based positive psychology interventions or activities, such as counting one's blessings (Emmons & McCullough, 2003; Froh, Sefick, & Emmons, 2008; Lyubomirsky, Sheldon, & Schkade, 2005) and performing acts of kindness (Dunn, Aknin, & Norton, 2008; Sheldon, Boehm, & Lyubomirsky, 2013), could be used to initiate and maintain positive affect, given that such efforts would be supportive of the basic core values of spirituality, Africentric norms and expectations, and feelings of interconnectedness associated with collectivism, that are valued by many African Americans.

Other practical ways to facilitate positive affect or emotions in African Americans include introducing specific coping methods such as problem-focused coping and incorporating meaningful positive experiences (Folkman & Moskowitz, 2000). Positive psychology exercises are practical ways of enabling positive affect (Gander, Proyer, Ruch, & Wyss, 2013). For example, in one exercise (One Door Closes, Another Door Opens) the individual is encouraged to remember a moment when a negative event led to unexpected positive consequences; another exercise (Three Good Things) has the individual write down three things that went well for him or her each day and explain why they went well. These exercises (and there are others) can be easily adapted to address the daily stresses associated with the prejudice and discrimination experienced by ethnic minority groups.

A note of caution: When attempting to facilitate positive affect in African Americans, one must bear in mind the context within which events occur, as well as the interpretation of those events; both are important to any successful intervention. Furthermore, even when considering cultural context, practitioners must be careful not to overgeneralize core values such as spirituality; not all African Americans may view spiritual growth or belief in God as crucial to their well-being. When examining expression of affect, one should try to find out how that individual typically expresses joy, interest, or even love, so as to avoid erroneous assumptions that might have a negative effect on treatment. Facilitating positive affect in African Americans encourages resilience and better coping skills, nullifies negative emotions, and improves psychological well-being (Fredrickson, 2001).

FACILITATING POSITIVE BEHAVIORS IN AFRICAN AMERICANS

Effective facilitation of positive behaviors calls for a true understanding and appreciation of the African American experience. Both the media and society at large have tended to focus on behaviors of African Americans that are considered wrong, or as character flaws or weaknesses, while neglecting appropriate or even extraordinarily positive behaviors. This unfair and inaccurate portrayal, stemming primarily from personally mediated racism, could result in feelings of helplessness in which individuals believe that they will inevitably be treated unfairly and thus have no incentive to show their strengths (Terrell et al., 2009). Mental health practitioners who want to successfully facilitate positive behaviors in African Americans should consider "that an African American client might be mistrustful of Whites [or white-institutionalized practices] and, when attempting to interpret test results or conducting therapy, to understand that this may have influenced the client's performance or behavior" (Terrell et al., 2009, p. 306). This comment focuses on interactions between ethnic minority (African American) clients and majority (White) practitioners, but it could be expanded to include all therapists (regardless of ethnicity) who by virtue of their professional training are perceived to belong to the general Westernized- or White-institutionalized system (Obasi & Leong, 2009).

For the purpose of this chapter, *positive behaviors* are defined as overt actions or covert considerations that are geared toward helping the individual succeed or flourish in life, by building specific strengths that ultimately translate into virtues (Peterson & Seligman, 2004). Thus, it could be argued that given the level of continued adversity experienced by some African Americans, it would be beneficial to facilitate behaviors that build character strengths such as persistence, curiosity, forgiveness, self-control, kindness, hope or optimism, and spirituality. African Americans have demonstrated the courage to face overwhelming challenges and a capacity for resilience (APA Task Force on Resilience and Strength in Black Children, 2008). Practitioners and other responsible adults could help African American youth as they go through identity, social, cognitive, emotional, and physical growth; the active involvement of adults during these times could help youth build their resilience and ability to persevere. These personal characteristics ultimately help develop courage, an important trait when one faces systemic disadvantages and barriers in life. In practice, the character strengths of resilience and persistence, and the virtue of courage, may be facilitated by training and encouraging parents to provide their African American children with a realistic expectation about ethnic-related oppression and prejudice that they might face. Positive interventions to promote perseverance could involve exercises such as the activity mentioned above. By writing about an experience in which positive consequences unexpectedly follow from a negative event (Niemiec, 2012a), clients can identify and acknowledge obstacles that may be unique to them, but they may also see positive elements in the situation.

Another positive behavior to be encouraged in African Americans is journaling. This technique provides an opportunity for individuals to reflect on events that occur and to gain insight into alternate perspectives. For example, the use of "gratitude journals," or keeping nightly journals of positive events that occurred during the day, has been reported to increase happiness and sense of well-being (Parks, Schueller, & Tasimi, 2013; Seligman, Steen, Park, & Peterson, 2005). Gratitude journaling may help develop the character strength of gratitude as well as the virtue of transcendence, which enhance optimal functioning. The cultural norms of African Americans—respect, collectivism, and openly showing appreciation—seem conducive to developing the virtues of humanity (strengths of love, kindness, compassion) as well as transcendence (strengths of gratitude, hope, and spirituality or faith). Although no studies have focused solely on African American samples in this regard, some study results have suggested that gratitude as an intervention seems to work best for people who believe, from the onset, that such a technique would be helpful (Sin, Della Porta, & Lyubomirsky, 2011).

For African Americans who abide by Africentric values of respect, spirituality, forgiveness, and collectivism, positive interventions that help develop similar strengths could be facilitated. Given continued prejudice toward African Americans, it may be beneficial to facilitate the strength of forgiveness as a way of symbolically freeing themselves from hurtful and offensive acts. In fact, beyond the affective or internal aspects of forgiveness, African Americans may appreciate the behavioral manifestation of forgiveness, perhaps some form of peaceful interaction with the offender, because of their collectivistic sense of community (Hook, Worthington, & Utsey, 2009). The collectivistic value of social harmony, which has its roots in traditional African culture, suggests that facilitating positive social behaviors, such as acts of kindness, would be appropriate and beneficial to African Americans (Otake, Shimai, Tanaka-Matsumi, Otsui, & Fredrickson, 2006). Therapeutic exercises encouraging African American clients to engage in acts of generosity (to the extent that they feel comfortable), even toward individuals who they perceive to be prejudiced, and keeping a log or count of such acts could help develop the strengths of kindness and compassion and build the virtue of humanity. In fact, engaging in acts of kindness and volunteerism is related to positive mental and physical health (Van Willigen, 2000).

Another strength that could be facilitated in psychotherapy with African Americans is humor, which has been an important part of telling the story about a history of oppression (Gordon, 1998; Smith, 2010). Furthermore, there is credible support that a positive association exists between humor and optimal functioning or coping with stress (Niemiec & Wedding, 2008). A commonly used intervention is to have the individual write down a number of funny experiences he or she had during the course of the day and review why and how it happened (Niemiec, 2012b). The client may also be assigned to watch a comedy show and later reflect on what was funny. Although it may be an effective intervention, the practitioner needs to be aware that humor is subjective and must, therefore, be flexible enough to allow for varying interpretations of why an experience is funny (or not).

FACILITATING POSITIVE COGNITIONS IN AFRICAN AMERICANS

African Americans are bombarded with ongoing negative messages about their abilities and self-worth, and over time they may begin to doubt themselves, a condition that connotes internalized racism (Jones, 2000). If we were to predict cognitions or thoughts based solely on the negativity experienced over the course of a lifetime, African Americans would be expected to have more negative cognitions and be more pessimistic than other ethnic groups in the United States; however, numerous studies have linked African American strengths of resiliency to optimism (Baldwin, Jackson, Okoh, & Cannon, 2011). Positive cognitions are crucial to the flourishing of African Americans because of the established relationship between thoughts, affect, and behavior; our cognitions strongly contribute to the way we feel and motivate many of our behaviors (Fishman, 2013).

Practical ways to facilitate positive cognitions in African Americans may include taking advantage of and building on resilience and strengths (optimism, hope, and faith) associated with positive thoughts about the future (Seligman, 2005). For instance, encouraging a person to identify or remember past experiences during which he or she, or even relevant ancestors or historical figures, demonstrated resilience amidst persistent stigmatization, may bolster optimism and hope. Positive interventions such as writing about one's best possible self or imagining one's positive future have been found to encourage meaning in life (Sheldon & Lyubomirsky, 2006). We acknowledge that these interventions may not work for some African Americans who have been bombarded with excessive negativity; they may have difficulty being hopeful about the future (Parks & Biswas-Diener, 2013).

Positive cognitions in African Americans might be facilitated through religiosity, a core value associated with self-discipline and positive mental health and self-discipline (Barbarin, 1993; Christian & Barbarin, 2001). Certain actions, including prayer and participation in religious services, have helped African Americans endure racism, oppression, and general injustice and successfully navigate and persist in life. Thus, a positive intervention (e.g., counting your blessings) could help keep a focus on strengths and gains instead of perceived weaknesses and life losses and, ultimately, facilitate positive cognitions about one's self and experiences. Similarly, *personal affirmation* is another positive intervention that may be used to enable positive cognitions in African American clients who value religion. Common religious activities, such as encouraging the client to focus on God's view of humankind as opposed to generalized negative views from society, and their value to members of their religious group, could facilitate coping and promote hope and optimism about the future.

Positive cognitions can be facilitated by guiding clients to reevaluate perceived negative events in a manner that decreases negative self-talk and mind-sets (Fishman, 2013). For instance, a therapist may enable positive cognitions in African American clients suffering from depression by first acknowledging the reality of their specific situation (e.g., symbolic racism or prejudice) and then guiding them to identify and rectify negative mind-sets and self-talk (e.g., polarizing, filtering, catastrophizing). Positive reappraisal (e.g., reappraising a negative situation to change the emotional impact) may be a useful tool in this regard, to establish and maintain positive cognitions and indirectly enhance resilience (Garland, Gaylord, & Fredrickson, 2011), given its contribution to adaptive coping and its stress-reductive effects. Finally, building social support and meaningful relationships within (as well as outside) one's ethnic group is crucial for the development of positive cognitions; the relation between social support and positive mental health has been demonstrated in African American adolescents (Lindsey, Joe, & Nebbitt, 2010), women (van Olphen et al., 2003), and men (Watkins & Jefferson, 2013). In summary, meaningful social support may help facilitate positive cognitions and ultimately promote optimal mental health in African Americans.

DEVELOPING AN INTEGRATIVE MODEL OF POSITIVE PRACTICE IN WORKING WITH AFRICAN AMERICANS: SOME GUIDELINES AND SUGGESTIONS FOR PRACTITIONERS AND EDUCATORS

We have addressed the application of positive psychological concepts and interventions to African Americans, with much-needed attention to historical and cultural contexts. Such influences are noted in the Cultural Formulation section of the *Diagnostic and Statistical Manual of Mental Disorders* (5th ed., American Psychiatric Association, 2013), suggesting that an understanding of an individual's self-perception and ethnic identity is crucial to the process of assessment, diagnosis, treatment planning, and compliance. Clinicians are encouraged to consider (a) cultural identity of the individual, such as ethnic–cultural reference group and level of acculturation; (b) cultural explanations of the individual's illness, including common symptoms or expressions of distress and severity of illness as well as beliefs about the cause of illness; (c) cultural factors related to psychosocial environment and levels of functioning such as role of religion and the extended family and other forms of social support or resources; and (d) cultural elements of the relationship between the individual and the clinician, including differences in social status, communication problems related to differences in spoken and expressed language, and lack of equivalence or difference in the meaning of behaviors and concepts discussed (American Psychiatric Association, pp. 749–750).

Developing an integrative model of positive practice for working with African Americans requires a comprehensive view of the biological and genetic, sociocultural, and psychological backgrounds of that specific individual within the context of the general group and individual experiences. Such a biopsychosocial view must be the underlying consideration for applying basic tenets of positive psychology to the individual; a one-size-fits-all approach should not be used for ethnic minority groups. Practitioners should begin by developing an understanding of what flourishing means to the individual client. For instance, for an African American client who believes his problems are due, in part, to prejudice, a definition of flourishing would be an ability to move forward psychologically, socially, and economically in the midst of daily challenges of discrimination. It is important not to avoid difficult topics (the proverbial "elephant in the room") because that discussion may increase trust, an important component of an effective therapeutic intervention. However, it is equally important to help clients who may not view prejudice and lack of resources as crucial to their problems (e.g., marital problem, parent–child problem); they too should be encouraged to provide their own perspectives on flourishing, based on cultural norms and expectations. In summary, eliciting a client-generated definition of what it means to flourish is crucial to conceptualizing the problem and developing an effective treatment plan that incorporates context and cultural values.

Because positive psychology interventions involve engagement in actions and behaviors that are self-monitored, they may provide a sense of empowerment for African American clients by minimizing total dependency on the practitioner. Positive activities or interventions involve "brief, self-administered, and non-stigmatizing exercises that promote positive feelings, positive thoughts, and/or positive behaviors, rather than directly aiming to fix negative or pathological feelings, thoughts, and behaviors" (Layous et al., 2011, p. 677). For any group with a history of oppression and cultural mistrust, such exercises limit dependency on a health system that some African Americans may have difficulty or ambivalence about trusting. Development of cognitive and emotional strengths may increase motivation for African Americans to engage in psychological interventions, especially if strength-promoting interventions are collaboratively selected.

In essence, an integrative model of positive practice working with African Americans requires a biopsychosocial approach with interventions that acknowledge the dual role of the cultural history of the client as a potential part of the problem, but also crucial to the solution, and promotes wellness by highlighting and improving existing strengths and not merely addressing weaknesses. Figure 13.1 summarizes important steps toward achieving such an integrative model.

Because personally mediated racism is real, it is crucial that mental health practitioners critically examine their own unintentional acts of racial bias by openly discussing concerns that their African American clients may have. Failure to do so may negatively influence the extent to which the client engages in and trusts the therapeutic relationship. Below are guidelines and suggestions to help promote positive therapeutic practice with African Americans:

1. Practitioners must acknowledge and confront their own assumptions about African Americans, which may be based on generalizations and stereotypes that are mostly negative. It is also crucial to avoid the assumption that an individual possesses cultural strengths (e.g., music, athletic, social abilities), or weaknesses (e.g., poverty, less education) without a thorough assessment; unfounded assumptions are likely to undermine trust. This is crucial even for ethnic minority practitioners.

2. To the best of their abilities, practitioners must develop partnerships with relevant religious institutions to build trust and gain practical insights about contemporary, practical, African

Step 1. Identify presenting problem or condition to be improved.

Step 2. Solicit background information. Identify strengths through a biopsychosocial approach.

Step 3. Ask the client about his or her experience of prejudice and level of cultural identity.

Step 4. Generate a generalized, empirically supported theoretical basis for positive interventions.

Step 5. Collaborate with the client to select appropriate positive interventions.

Step 6. Implement the positive interventions and then evaluate them.

Step 7. Decide whether to continue the existing intervention or to consider alternate approaches (**back to Step 5**).

Figure 13.1. Process derived from an integrative model of positive practice.

American norms and values. Because culture is dynamic, changes in acceptable norms within a given culture may occur quickly; thus, there is a need to keep abreast with changes in real life.
3. When selecting positive psychological interventions, approaches that are solution focused and practical (e.g., weekly homework) and that incorporate cultural or contextual factors should be given priority; they tend to be more effective for African Americans (Talleyrand, 2012).
4. Serious consideration ought to be given to implementing empirically supported interventions in African American samples. Unfortunately, such efforts are almost non-existent, which suggests the need for more research in the area of applying positive psychological principles adapted to the cultural context of African Americans, not studies that that merely use and compare them with other ethnic groups.

We end with words of wisdom eloquently expressed by the late Toy Caldwell-Colbert: "From their African roots, traditional African American culture is filled with messages of encouragement, optimism, community support, and resilience: That is the more reason why positive psychology [in practice] is ripe and needs to be embraced with a passion" (Caldwell-Colbert et al., 2009, p. 381).

REFERENCES

American Psychiatric Association. (2013). *Diagnostic and statistical manual of mental disorders* (5th ed.). Arlington, VA: Author.

APA Task Force on Resilience and Strength in Black Children and Adolescents. (2008). *Resilience in African American children and adolescents: A vision for optimal development.* Retrieved from http://www.apa.org/pi/families/resources/resiliencerpt.pdf

Ayalon, L., & Young, M. A. (2003). A comparison of depressive symptoms in African Americans and Caucasian Americans. *Journal of Cross-Cultural Psychology, 34,* 111–124. http://dx.doi.org/10.1177/0022022102239158

Ayalon, L., & Young, M. A. (2005). Racial group differences in help-seeking behaviors. *The Journal of Social Psychology, 145,* 391–403. http://dx.doi.org/10.3200/SOCP.145.4.391-404

Baldwin, D. R., Jackson, D., III, Okoh, I., & Cannon, R. L. (2011). Resiliency and optimism: An African American senior citizen's perspectives. *Journal of Black Psychology, 37,* 24–41. http://dx.doi.org/10.1177/0095798410364394

Barbarin, O. A. (1993). Coping resilience: Exploring the inner lives of African American children. *Journal of Black Psychology, 19,* 478–492. http://dx.doi.org/10.1177/00957984930194007

Barnes, A. (2004). Race, schizophrenia, and admission to state psychiatric hospitals. *Administration and Policy in Mental Health, 31,* 241–252. http://dx.doi.org/10.1023/B:APIH.0000018832.73673.54

Benkert, R., Peters, R. M., Clark, R., & Keves-Foster, K. (2006). Effects of perceived racism, cultural mistrust and trust in providers on satisfaction with care. *Journal of the National Medical Association, 98,* 1532–1540.

Blow, F. C., Zeber, J. E., McCarthy, J. F., Valenstein, M., Gillon, L., & Bingham, C. R. (2004). Ethnicity and diagnostic patterns in veterans with psychoses. *Social Psychiatry and Psychiatric Epidemiology, 39,* 841–851.

Boyd, R. C., Joe, S., Michalopoulos, L., Davis, E., & Jackson, J. S. (2011). Prevalence of mood disorders and service use among US mothers by race and ethnicity: Results from the National Survey of American Life. *The Journal of Clinical Psychiatry, 72,* 1538–1545. http://dx.doi.org/10.4088/JCP.10m06468

Caldwell-Colbert, A. T., Parks, F. M., & Eshun, S. (2009). Positive psychology: African American strengths, resilience, and protective factors. In H. A. Neville, B. M. Tynes, & S. O. Utsey (Eds.), *Handbook of African American psychology* (pp. 375–384). Thousand Oaks, CA: Sage.

Chatters, M. C., Taylor, R. J., Jackson, J. S., & Lincoln, K. D. (2008). Religious coping among African Americans, Caribbean Blacks and non-Hispanics whites. *Journal of Community Psychology, 36,* 371–386. http://dx.doi.org/10.1002/jcop.20202.

Christian, M. D., & Barbarin, O. A. (2001). Cultural resources and psychological adjustment of African American children: Effects of spirituality and racial attribution. *Journal of Black Psychology, 27,* 43–63. http://dx.doi.org/10.1177/0095798401027001003

Constantine, M. G., Alleyne, V. L., Wallace, B. C., & Franklin-Jackson, D. C. (2006). Africentric cultural values: The relation to positive mental health in African American adolescent girls. *Journal of Black Psychology, 32,* 141–154. http://dx.doi.org/10.1177/0095798406286801

Dunn, E. W., Aknin, L. B., & Norton, M. I. (2008). Spending money on others promotes happiness. *Science, 319,* 1687–1688. http://dx.doi.org/10.1126/science.1150952

Earl, T. R., & Williams, D. R. (2009). Black Americans and mental health status: Complexities and new developments. In H. A. Neville, B. M. Tynes, & S. O. Utsey (Eds.), *Handbook of African American psychology* (pp. 335–350). Thousand Oaks, CA: Sage Publications.

Emmons, R. A., & McCullough, M. E. (2003). Counting blessings versus burdens: An experimental investigation of gratitude and subjective well-being in daily life. *Journal of Personality and Social Psychology, 84,* 377–389. http://dx.doi.org/10.1037/0022-3514.84.2.377

Fishman, J. (2013). *Positive psychology: The benefits of living positively.* Retrieved from http://psychcentral.com/blog/archives/2013/03/11/positive-psychology-the-benefits-of-living-positively/

Folkman, S., & Moskowitz, J. T. (2000). Positive affect and the other side of coping. *American Psychologist, 55,* 647–654. http://dx.doi.org/10.1037/0003-066X.55.6.647

Fredrickson, B. L. (2001). The role of positive emotions in positive psychology. The broaden-and-build theory of positive emotions. *American Psychologist, 56,* 218–226.

Froh, J. J., Sefick, W. J., & Emmons, R. A. (2008). Counting blessings in early adolescents: An experimental study of gratitude and subjective well-being. *Journal of School Psychology, 46,* 213–233. http://dx.doi.org/10.1016/j.jsp.2007.03.005

Gander, F., Proyer, R. T., Ruch, W., & Wyss, T. (2013). Strength-based positive intervention: Further evidence for their potential in enhancing well-being and alleviating depression. *Journal of Happiness Studies, 14,* 1241–1259. http://dx.doi.org/10.1007/s10902-012-9380-0

Garland, E. L., Gaylord, S. A., & Fredrickson, B. L. (2011). Positive reappraisal mediates the stress-reductive effects of mindfulness: An upward spiral process. *Mindfulness, 2,* 59–67. http://dx.doi.org/10.1007/s12671-011-0043-8

Gary, F. A. (2005). Stigma: Barrier to mental health care among ethnic minorities. *Issues in Mental Health Nursing, 26,* 979–999. http://dx.doi.org/10.1080/01612840500280638

Gonzalez, O., Berry, J. T., McKnight-Eily, L. R., Strine, T., Edwards, V. J., Lu, H., & Croft, J. B. (2010). Current depression among adult, United States 2006 and 2008, *Morbidity and Mortality Weekly Report, 59,* 1229–1235.

Gordon, D. B. (1998). Humor in African American discourse: Speaking of oppression. *Journal of Black Studies, 29,* 254–276. http://dx.doi.org/10.1177/002193479802900207

Guthrie, R. L. (2004). *Even the rat was white: A historical view of psychology* (2nd ed.). Boston, MA: Allyn & Bacon.

Hatcher, L. S. (2012). African-Americans are less likely to seek mental health treatment. *HIV Clinician, 24*(4), 11.

Hines-Martin, V., Malone, M., Kim, S., & Brown-Piper, A. (2003). Barriers to mental health care access in an African American population. *Issues in Mental Health Nursing, 24,* 237–256. http://dx.doi.org/10.1080/01612840305281

Hook, J. N., Worthington, E. L., & Utsey, S. O. (2009). Collectivism, forgiveness, and social harmony. *The Counseling Psychologist, 37,* 821–847. http://dx.doi.org/10.1177/0011000008326546

Hopps, J. G., Tourse, R. W. C., & Christian, O. (2002). From problems to personal resilience: Challenges and opportunities with African American youth. *Journal of Ethnic & Cultural Diversity in Social Work, 11*(1-2), 55–77. http://dx.doi.org/10.1300/J051v11n01_03

Johnson-Garner, M. Y., & Meyers, S. A. (2003). What factors contribute to the resilience of African American children within kinship care? *Child & Youth Care Forum, 32,* 255–269. http://dx.doi.org/10.1023/A:1025883726991

Jones, C. P. (2000). Levels of racism: A theoretic framework and a gardener's tale. *American Journal of Public Health, 90,* 1212–1215. http://dx.doi.org/10.2105/AJPH.90.8.1212

Kobau, R., Seligman, M. E. P., Peterson, C., Diener, E., Zack, M. M., Chapman, D., & Thompson, W. (2011). Mental health promotion in public health: Perspectives and strategies from positive psychology. *American Journal of Public Health, 101*(8), e1–e9. http://dx.doi.org/10.2105/AJPH.2010.300083

Layous, K., Chancellor, J., Lyubomirsky, S., Wang, L., & Doraiswamy, P. M. (2011). Delivering happiness: Translating positive psychology intervention research for treating major and minor depressive disorders. *The Journal of Alternative and Complementary Medicine, 17,* 675–683. http://dx.doi.org/10.1089/acm.2011.0139

Lindsey, M. A., Joe, S., & Nebbitt, V. (2010). Family matters: The role of mental health stigma and social support on depressive symptoms and subsequent help seeking among African American boys. *Journal of Black Psychology, 36,* 458–482. http://dx.doi.org/10.1177/0095798409355796

Lyubomirsky, S. (2012). Positive psychologists on positive constructs. *American Psychologist, 67,* 574. http://dx.doi.org/10.1037/a0029957

Lyubomirsky, S., Sheldon, K. M., & Schkade, D. (2005). Pursuing happiness: The architecture of sustainable change. *Review of General Psychology, 9,* 111–131. http://dx.doi.org/10.1037/1089-2680.9.2.111

McNulty, J. K., & Fincham, F. D. (2012). Beyond positive psychology? Toward a contextual view of psychological processes and well-being. *American Psychologist, 67,* 101–110. http://dx.doi.org/10.1037/a0024572

Menke, R., & Flynn, H. (2009). Relationships between stigma, depression, and treatment in White and African American primary care patients. *Journal of Nervous and Mental Disease, 197,* 407–411. http://dx.doi.org/10.1097/NMD. 0b013e3181a6162e

Mills, T. L., & Edwards, C. A. (2002). A critical review of research on the mental health status of older African Africans. *Ageing & Society, 22,* 273–304. http://dx.doi.org/10.1017/S0144686X0200867X

Myers, J., Speight, S. L., Highlen, P. S., Cox, C. I., Reynolds, A. L., Adams, E. M., & Hanley, P. (1991). Identity development and worldview: Toward an optimal conceptualization. *Journal of Counseling & Development, 70,* 54–63. http://dx.doi.org/10.1002/j.1556-6676.1991.tb01561.x

Nadeem, E., Lange, J. M., & Miranda, J. (2009). Perceived need for care among low-income immigrant and U.S.-born black and Latina women with depression. *Journal of Women's Health, 18,* 369–375. http://dx.doi.org/10.1089/jwh.2008.0898

Neblett, E. W., Jr., Seaton, E. K., Hammond, W. P., & Townsend, T. G. (2010). Underlying mechanisms in the relationship between Africentric worldview and depressive symptoms. *Journal of Counseling Psychology, 57,* 105–113. http://dx.doi.org/10.1037/a0017710

Neighbors, H. W., Trierweiler, S. J., Ford, B. C., & Muroff, J. R. (2003). Racial differences in DSM diagnosis using a semi-structured instrument: The importance of clinical judgment in the diagnosis of African Americans. *Journal of Health and Social Behavior, 44,* 237–256. http://dx.doi.org/10.2307/1519777

Niemiec, R. (2012a). *New ways to happiness with strengths.* Retrieved from http://blogs.psychcentral.com/character-strengths/2012/04/new-ways-to-happiness-with-strengths/

Niemiec, R. M. (2012b). *7 new exercises to boost happiness.* Retrieved from http://www.psychologytoday.com/blog/what-matters-most/201212/7-new-exercises-boost-happiness/

Niemiec, R. M., & Wedding, D. (2008). *Positive psychology at the movies: Using films to build virtues and character strengths.* Cambridge, MA: Hogrefe.

Obasi, E. M., & Leong, F. T. L. (2009). Psychological distress, acculturation, and mental health-seeking attitudes with people of African descent in the United States:

A preliminary investigation. *Journal of Counseling Psychology, 56,* 227–238. http://dx.doi.org/10.1037/a0014865

Otake, K., Shimai, S., Tanaka-Matsumi, J., Otsui, K., & Fredrickson, B. L. (2006). Happy people become happier through kindness: A counting kindnesses intervention. *Journal of Happiness Studies, 7,* 361–375. http://dx.doi.org/10.1007/s10902-005-3650-z

Parks, A. C., & Biswas-Diener, R. (2013). Positive interventions: Past, present and future. In T. Kashdan & J. Ciarrochi (Eds.), *Mindfulness, acceptance, and positive psychology: The seven foundations of well-being* (pp. 140–165). Oakland, CA: Harbinger.

Parks, A. C., Schueller, S., & Tasimi, A. (2013). Increasing happiness in the general population: Empirically supported self-help? In I. Boniwell & S. David (Eds.), *Oxford handbook of happiness* (pp. 962–977). Oxford, England: Oxford University Press. http://dx.doi.org/10.1093/oxfordhb/9780199557257.013.0072

Peterson, C., & Seligman, M. E. P. (2004). *Character strengths and virtues: A handbook and classification.* Washington, DC: American Psychological Association and Oxford University Press.

Phinney, J. S. (1992). The multigroup ethnic identity measure: A new scale for use with diverse groups. *Journal of Adolescent Research, 7,* 156–176. http://dx.doi.org/10.1177/074355489272003

Rastogi, S., Johnson, T. D., Hoeffel, E. M., & Drewery, M. P. (2011). *The Black population: 2010 Census Briefs.* Retrieved from http://www.census.gov/prod/cen2010/briefs/c2010br-06.pdf

Rivas-Drake, D., Syed, M., Umaña-Taylor, A., Markstrom, C., French, S., Schwartz, S. J., & Lee, R., & the Ethnic and Racial Identity in the 21st Century Study Group. (2014). Feeling good, happy, and proud: A meta-analysis of positive ethnic-racial affect and adjustment. *Child Development, 85,* 77–102. http://dx.doi.org/10.1111/cdev.12175

Roberts, A. L., Gilman, S. E., Breslau, J., Breslau, N., & Koenen, K. C. (2011). Race/ethnic differences in exposure to traumatic events, development of post-traumatic stress disorder, and treatment-seeking for post-traumatic stress disorder in the United States. *Psychological Medicine, 41*(1), 71–83. http://dx.doi.org/10.1017/S0033291710000401

Seligman, M. E. P. (2005). Positive psychology, positive prevention, and positive therapy. In C. R. Snyder & S. J. Lopez (Eds.), *Handbook of positive psychology* (pp. 3–9). New York, NY: Oxford University Press.

Seligman, M. E. P., & Csikszentmihalyi, M. (Eds.). (2000). Positive psychology [Special issue]. *American Psychologists, 55*(1).

Seligman, M. E. P., Steen, T. A., Park, N., & Peterson, C. (2005). Positive psychology progress: Empirical validation of interventions. *American Psychologist, 60,* 410–421. http://dx.doi.org/10.1037/0003-066X.60.5.410

Sheldon, K. M., Boehm, J. K., & Lyubomirsky, S. (2013). Variety is the spice of happiness: The hedonic adaptation prevention (HAP) model. In J. Boniwell

& S. David (Eds.), *Oxford handbook of happiness* (pp. 901–914). Oxford, UK: Oxford University Press.

Sheldon, K. M., & Lyubomirsky, S. (2006). How to increase and sustain positive emotion: The effects of expressing gratitude and visualizing best possible selves. *The Journal of Positive Psychology, 1,* 73–82. http://dx.doi.org/10.1080/17439760500510676

Sin, N. L., Della Porta, M. D., & Lyubomirsky, S. (2011). Tailoring positive psychology intervention to treat depressed individuals. In S. I. Donaldson, M. Csikszentmihalyi, & J. Nakamura (Eds.), *Applied positive psychology: Improving everyday life, health, schools, work, and society* (pp. 79–96). New York, NY: Routledge.

Smith, J. C. (Ed.). (2010). *Encyclopedia of African American popular culture.* Santa Barbara, CA: ABC-CLIO.

Strakowski, S. M., Flaum, M., Amador, X., Bracha, H. S., Pandurangi, A. K., Robinson, D., & Tohen, M. (1996). Racial differences in the diagnosis of psychosis. *Schizophrenia Research, 21,* 117–124. http://dx.doi.org/10.1016/0920-9964(96)00041-2

Strakowski, S. M., Keck, P. E., Jr., Arnold, L. M., Collins, J., Wilson, R. M., Fleck, D. E., . . . Adebimpe, V. R. (2003). Ethnicity and diagnosis in patients with affective disorders. *Journal of Clinical Psychiatry, 64,* 747–754. http://dx.doi.org/10.4088/JCP.v64n0702

Suite, D. H., La Bril, R., Primm, A., & Harrison-Ross, P. (2007). Beyond misdiagnosis, misunderstanding and mistrust: Relevance of the historical perspective in the medical and mental health treatment of people of color. *Journal of the National Medical Association, 99,* 879–885.

Tajfel, H. (1979). Individuals and groups in social psychology. *British Journal of Social and Clinical Psychology, 18,* 183–190. http://dx.doi.org/10.1111/j.2044-8260.1979.tb00324.x

Talleyrand, R. M. (2012). Disordered eating in women of color: Some counseling considerations. *Journal of Counseling & Development, 90,* 271–280. http://dx.doi.org/10.1002/j.1556-6676.2012.00035.x

Taylor, S. E., Kemeny, M. E., Reed, G. M., Bower, J. E., & Gruenewald, T. L. (2000). Psychological resources, positive illusions, and health. *American Psychologist, 55,* 99–109. http://dx.doi.org/10.1037/0003-066X.55.1.99

Terrell, F., Taylor, J., Menzise, J., & Barrett, R. K. (2009). Cultural mistrust: A core component of African American consciousness. In H. A. Neville, B. M. Tynes, & S. O. Utsey (Eds.), *Handbook of African American psychology* (pp. 299–310). Thousand Oaks, CA: Sage.

Thompson, V. L., Bazile, A., & Akbar, M. (2004). African Americans' perceptions of psychotherapy and psychotherapists. *Professional Psychology: Research and Practice, 35,* 19–26. http://dx.doi.org/10.1037/0735-7028.35.1.19

van Olphen, J., Schulz, A., Israel, B., Chatters, L., Klem, L., Parker, E., & Williams, D. (2003). Religious involvement, social support, and health among African-

American women on the east side of Detroit. *Journal of General Internal Medicine, 18*, 549–557. http://dx.doi.org/10.1046/j.1525-1497.2003.21031.x

Van Willigen, M. (2000). Differential benefits of volunteering over the life course. *Journal of Gerontology B: Psychological Sciences and Social Sciences, 55B*, S308–S318. http://dx.doi.org/10.1093/geronb/55.5.S308

Ward, E. C., & Heidrich, S. M. (2009). African American women's beliefs about mental illness, stigma, and preferred coping behaviors. *Research in Nursing & Health, 32*, 480–492, http://dx.doi.org/10.1002/nur.20344

Watkins, D. C., & Jefferson, S. O. (2013). Recommendations for the use of online social support for African American men. *Psychological Services, 10*, 323–332. http://dx.doi.org/10.1037/a0027904

Whaley, A. (2001). Cultural mistrust: An important psychological construct for diagnosis and treatment of African Americans. *Professional Psychology: Research and Practice, 32*, 555–562. http://dx.doi.org/10.1037/0735-7028.32.6.555

Williams, D. R., González, H. M., Neighbors, H., Nesse, R., Abelson, J. M., Sweetman, J., & Jackson, J. S. (2007). Prevalence and distribution of major depressive disorder in African Americans, Caribbean blacks, and non-Hispanic whites: Results from the National Survey of American Life. *Archives of General Psychiatry, 64*, 305–315. http://dx.doi.org/10.1001/archpsyc.64.3.305

Williams, D. R., & Williams-Morris, R. (2000). Racism and mental health: The African American experience. *Ethnicity & Health, 5*(3-4), 243–268. http://dx.doi.org/10.1080/713667453

Williams, J. L., Tolan, P. H., Durkee, M. I., Francois, A. G., & Anderson, R. E. (2012). integrating racial and ethnic identity research into developmental understanding of adolescents. *Child Development Perspectives, 6*, 304–311. http://dx.doi.org/10.1111/j.1750-8606.2012.00235.x

14

POSITIVE PSYCHOLOGY PRACTICE WITH NATIVE AMERICANS

MICHAEL T. GARRETT, J. T. GARRETT, RUSS CURTIS,
MARK PARRISH, TARRELL AWE AGAHE PORTMAN,
LISA GRAYSHIELD, AND CYRUS WILLIAMS

The Native American Hoop Dance shows the movement, stamina, and skill of the hoop dancer, and is considered by many to be one of the most difficult and most revered of the Native dance styles on the powwow circuit. The Hoop Dance is a form of storytelling generally performed by a single dancer who can incorporate up to 30 or more hoops used to create both static and dynamic shapes, or formations, representing various animals, symbols, and storytelling elements. Part of the difficulty involved with the dance comes from the focus on very rapid moves and the construction of hoop formations around and about the body while it is in constant motion. In elaborate sequences of moves, the dancer extends the hoops from the body to form symbolic representations.

The Hoop Dance illustrates a number of concepts central to the experience of Native people in general, with an extraordinary emphasis on the harmony and balance required to survive and thrive. For Native

http://dx.doi.org/10.1037/14799-014
Positive Psychology in Racial and Ethnic Groups: Theory, Research, and Practice, E. C. Chang, C. A. Downey, J. K. Hirsch, and N. J. Lin (Editors)

people, the need to balance several identities, pressures, and expectations can take on a new meaning as it relates to the metaphorical movements of the hoop dancer. To better understand the lives and worldviews of these people in the context of positive psychology, it is important to hear their voices, their stories, and their experiences. To facilitate culturally sensitive and competent therapeutic practice with Native people through a positive psychology approach, we discuss the value of positive psychology practice with Native Americans and ways for facilitating positive affect, behaviors, and cognitions from a strength-based perspective to promote resilience and foster positive development and healing with this population.

VALUE OF POSITIVE PSYCHOLOGY PRACTICES WITH NATIVE AMERICANS

As a general theoretical orientation, positive psychology overlaps with indigenous ways of knowing and corresponding approaches to health and wellness (D. Dell & Hopkins, 2011). As a central concept in positive psychology, some authors have defined *resilience* as "a balance between individual strategies of coping with adversity and the availability of community support" (cited in D. Dell & Hopkins, 2011, p. 109), reflecting an emphasis that also is central to an indigenous worldview and ways of knowing. C. Dell, Hopkins, and Dell (2004) explained that

> traditional Native world view highlights one's spirit as the core of one's self—the motivator and animator of one's life . . . the spirit is what gives one the ability to bounce back . . . the spirit is not a material form, so it is indestructible . . . (cited in D. Dell & Hopkins, 2011, p. 109)

From a Native perspective, spirit is central to one's resiliency as a life force connected to all other life forces across time and space, and thus, one also has to be attuned to aspects of transcending historical oppression; current adversity that spans generations in spiritual, mental, and physical effects; and pathways for healing. Therefore, from a societal perspective, a sense of community and one's intentionality toward respecting and maintaining that sense of community become paramount to understanding the indigenous experience through a positive psychology lens. D. Dell and Hopkins (2011) expanded on this notion:

> From an Indigenous cultural worldview, knowing oneself comes from a connection to the universal family of creation, one's biological and extended family, and community. It is through this connection that one is nurtured in awareness of self in relation to others. Choosing self and acting with intention from a cultural perspective is about choosing a

life path that is reflective of cultural identity, intrinsically motivated by one's spirit and one's spiritual connection to family and community. Cultural knowledge facilitates an understanding about the "truth," purpose, and meaning of one's life, which sets the foundation for "giving self." (p. 110)

Cultural knowledge and practices form the basis for indigenous resilience rooted in family and community strength. Although Native Americans face many obstacles, members of this population also possess strengths that have helped them survive racism, forced relocation, and genocide (Brave Heart & DeBruyn, 1998). From a historical perspective, the Native American population is not just surviving—it is thriving in many areas: Nearly 55% of all Native Americans own their own home, 75% age 25 and older have at least a high school diploma, and 14% have a bachelor's degree (Goodluck, 2002). In 2003, Goodluck conducted a meta-analysis that focused on identifying the strengths of Native Americans. Results of the analysis yielded 42 specific strengths of Native Americans that were grouped into three categories: extended family, spirituality, and social connections. These strengths are important to acknowledge within a body of literature about Native people that tends to focus on struggles and obstacles rather than cultural strength and resilience.

To that end, helping professionals can integrate positive psychology strategies with Native people that have been shown to increase well-being in the general population (Seligman, Steen, Park, & Peterson, 2005). First, however, it is helpful for practitioners to understand some basics of what it takes to produce lasting happiness. Three overarching domains have been identified as creating sustained happiness: (a) increasing competence (e.g., learning a new skill strictly for enjoyment), (b) increasing relatedness (e.g., building and strengthening relationships), and (c) increasing autonomy (e.g., learning a new skill that reduces one's dependence upon others; Lyubomirsky, 2013). Many of these domains appear in the specific positive psychology strategies that are discussed in the next section.

When working with clients it is important for practitioners to understand the *Zeigarnik effect* (cited in Lyubomirsky, 2013), which states that people remember inactivity and unfinished ventures more than they do completed tasks, even when the result of the completed task is negative. The Zeigarnik effect is pertinent to positive psychology because many activities require action or behavior change, and when practitioners discuss this effect up-front, clients' awareness increases, which can increase their motivation to complete activities. In this section, we discuss the following positive psychology strategies: signature strengths, mindfulness, service, genogram of family strengths, gratitude, forgiveness, and meaning-making.

Signature Strengths

One promising positive psychology strategy is to help people recognize and use their unique personal strengths (commonly referred to as *signature strengths*; Schueller, 2010; Seligman et al., 2005). Native people have always believed in and encouraged their own gifts and potential, thereby demonstrating resilience long before it was identified (HeavyRunner & Morris, 1997; Kirmayer, Dandeneau, Marshall, Phillips, & Williamson, 2011). Resilience theory with a strength-based perspective can be used by helping professionals when working with this population.

A strength-based perspective is not a model or theory, but rather a collection of principles, ideas, and techniques that are evolving (Saleebey, 1996). This perspective honors the power of the self to heal and right itself with the help of the environment, recognizes the need for healthy alliances, and offers hope that life can get better. Unfortunately, clients who have experienced the types of abuse and subsequent multigenerational trauma faced by all Native people may find hope rather elusive. Helping Native people remember their innate strengths can be the starting point for healing and growth. With their inherent natural ability for introspection, Native people can often self-identify their signature strengths when asked by a trusted practitioner. Those who struggle, however, may find the signature strengths test (located at http://www.authentichappiness.com) to be a useful tool in contemplating and remembering their unique personal qualities. As with any assessment instrument, skilled practitioners collaborate with clients in making meaning of, and validating, the results.

When clients reidentify their signature strengths, skilled practitioners help them recognize how often they have used these strengths and how they might use them in novel ways. A practitioner may ask, for instance, "Between now and our next session, how could you use one of the strengths you identified in a meaningful way?"

We acknowledge the prevalence of generational poverty and other risk factors (to be discussed in a subsequent section), but we maintain that the strengths and resources of this client population must be identified. As HeavyRunner and Morris (1997) asserted,

> Cultural resilience is a relatively new term, but it is a concept that predates the so-called "discovery" of our people. The elders teach us that our children are gifts from the Creator and it is the family, community, school and tribe's responsibility to nurture, protect and guide them. This traditional process is what contemporary researchers, educators and social service providers are now calling resilience. Thus resilience is not new in our people; it is a concept that has been taught for centuries. The word is new but the meaning is old. (p. 28)

Several authors have described common core values that characterize Native traditionalism across tribal nations as a source of strengths and protective resources. One of these greatest strengths lies in the diversity among Native American groups. Contrary to the stereotypical image that Native Americans live exclusively or mostly on reservations, approximately 78% of the Native American population reside in urban areas; only 22% of the total population of Native people live on a reservation or other typically rural area. Native Americans come from different tribal groups with different customs, traditions, and beliefs; they live in a variety of settings (rural, urban, or reservation; M. T. Garrett & Pichette, 2000). Native Americans are also linguistically diverse, with more than 150 different languages (Russell, 2004). Despite this obvious diversity of tribal identities, a prevailing sense of "Indianness" based on a common worldview and a common history—what Grayshield and Mihecoby (2010) referred to as *Indigenous ways of knowing* (IWOK)—seems to bind Native Americans together as a people of many peoples (M. T. Garrett & Portman, 2011).

Although acculturation plays a major factor in the Native American worldview, there tends to be a high degree of psychological homogeneity and a certain degree of shared cultural standards and meanings based on core values that are common across tribal groups. Several authors have described common core values that characterize Native traditionalism across tribal nations: the importance of community contribution, sharing, acceptance, cooperation, harmony and balance, noninterference, extended family, attention to nature, immediacy of time, awareness of the relationship, and a deep respect for elders (M. T. Garrett, 1996, 1999). These traditional values show the importance of honoring, through harmony and balance, what Native people believe to be a very sacred connection with the energy of life and the whole of biodiversity. This provides the basis for a traditional Native worldview and spirituality across tribal nations that have served as the foundation for strength and resilience in the face of adversity over many generations.

Mindfulness and Indigenous Ways of Knowing

It is important to understand the multifaceted experiences of Native people in contemporary society. Anyone working in Native American communities must be aware of a deep sense of cultural loss that has resulted from the historical colonial era in American history. They should not, however, make any assumptions regarding clients' tribal or indigenous identities and experiences. It is more important to recognize that cultural sources of strength exist within tribal, communal, and familial entities as valuable resources in a Native American understanding of how to navigate one's life journey. To apply many of the most common theories and models of counseling without consideration of cultural constructs would be counterproductive in promoting optimal well-being for Native Americans. Moreover, an indigenous epistemology in our understanding of health and well-being may promote helping processes that are more sustainable and respectful for all individuals.

The attitudes, values, and beliefs of a group of people whose subsistence has largely relied on their relationship with their natural environment for thousands of years have something to teach the rest of us about balance and harmony in today's world. Indigenous knowledge forms have allowed indigenous and tribal groups to maintain their existences in specific geographic locations over time. Their epistemologies, ontologies, and cosmologies construct ways of being and experiencing in relationship to their physical surroundings (Grayshield & Mihecoby, 2010). Unfortunately, continuous exposure to the incongruent ways in which American culture attempts to manipulate and control all aspects of life can make it difficult for even the most assured and secure Native people to become unbalanced and therefore, disharmonious. Indigenous ways of knowing, like a boat at sea, can be easily rocked and even capsized by the waves of fear-based dominant cultural beliefs and behaviors. Fortunately, Native people, like Buddhists, have for generations recognized that all knowledge and healing come from within and can be more easily known and deciphered when one engages in a regular mindfulness practice.

Mindfulness quietly boasts one of the most robust bodies of research of all healing practices (Curtis & Robertson, 2009). In essence, mindfulness is the recognition that thoughts, emotions, and sensations, are *just* thoughts, emotions, and sensations. Referring to the boat analogy, which is a derivative of Kabat-Zinn's (1994) lake meditation, Native people recognize (although they may need help remembering at times) that they are not only the boat but also the sea, and when the surface is tumultuous and the boat is rocking, there is always calm below the surface. Practitioners, then, can best help Native people remember by taking time every day to look within, using a mindfulness practice congruent with their traditions and beliefs (e.g., walking in nature, drumming, dancing, sitting contemplatively in front of a fire).

Another salient point to keep in mind related to mindfulness is the inherent mistrust Native people have for non-Native people. To earn respect and trust, non-Native practitioners working with Native people must be perceived as being congruent and genuine. In other words, the practitioner as a person is far more important than the techniques used. Fortunately, recent counseling research indicates that practitioners who regularly practice mindfulness (e.g., meditation) are perceived by clients as more empathic, congruent, and able to maintain a stronger working alliance than those who do not practice mindfulness (Greason & Welfare, 2013). Thus, mindfulness practices can benefit both clients and practitioners on many levels, all of which increase personal awareness, intentionality, and personal connection.

Indigenous ways of knowing (IWOK) have been defined by Grayshield and Mihecoby (2010) as "a multidimensional body of lived experiences that informs and sustains people who make their homes in a local area and always takes into account the current socio-political colonial power dimensions of the Western world" (p. 6). They added,

> the literature identifies three central features within Indigenous knowledge forms that have both political and curricular implications: many Indigenous/tribal cultures related harmoniously to their environment; experienced colonization, and provided an alternative perspective on human experience that differed from Western empirical science. (p. 6)

According to Deloria (cited in Grayshield & Mihecoby, 2010), indigenous forms of knowledge are "the result of keen observations in the experience of daily life and in the interpretive messages received from spirits in ceremonies, visions and dreams" that coincide with a reality for tribal people based on "the experience of the moment coupled with the interpretive scheme that had been woven together over the generations" (p. 5). From this perspective, the true purpose of the helping process would be to promote engagement in activities that increase one's awareness of nature as a basic and fundamental construct of health and being well.

Service, Cultural Identity, and the Tribal Nation

For most Native people, cultural identity is rooted in tribal membership, community, and culture rather than in personal achievements, social or financial status, or acquired possessions. In this light, service to one's family and tribal community can be a significant source of growth and healing for Native people. The research is clear that engaging in meaningful service that builds and strengthens relationships is one of the most promising ways people can increase their happiness levels (Cheung & Kwan, 2006). It should be mentioned that this type of service, when engaged in a way without expectation for reward, can produce lasting intrapersonal well-being (Lyubomirsky, 2013). Many Native nations, such as the Cherokee, are traditionally matriarchal–matrilineal wherein children trace their heritage through the mother or grandmother, and the social structure of the tribe may place more emphasis on power held by women (Portman, 2001; Portman & Garrett, 2005). Many tribes, however, have taken on values that were forced through processes of colonization (assimilation) and imposed through the dominant value structures of church and state (Portman, 2001). Even so, for most Native Americans the extended family (at least three generations) and tribal group take precedence over all other affiliations.

The *tribe* is an interdependent system of people who are connected members of the greater whole (i.e., the tribe), which has an ancestral heritage intricately interconnected with the surrounding natural environment. Thus, the interconnectedness of relationships on numerous levels including those that extend beyond human-to-human interactions have typically defined indigenous thought and identity. This principle is expressed when traditional Native people judge themselves and their actions according to how connected they are with (and to what extent they benefit) their family, clan, and community.

Genogram of Family Strengths

It has been said that "about the most unfavorable moral judgment an Indian can pass on another person is to say 'He acts as if he didn't have any relatives'" (DuBray, 1985, p. 36). Whereas members of mainstream culture may ask, "What do you do?" when meeting for the first time, many Native people may ask, "Where do you come from? Who is your family? To whom do you belong? Who are your people?" The speaker's intent is to find out where she or he stands in relation to this new person and what commonality exists. This is a simple way of building bridges or recognizing bridges that already exist but are as yet unknown. Family may or may not consist of blood relatives. It is common practice in the Native American way, for instance, to claim a non-blood-related person as a relative, thereby welcoming him or her as a legitimate family member. Family can be a matter of both blood and spirit.

Respect for one's family, of course, can be easily diminished when faced with the effects of generational trauma (e.g., alcoholism, suicide, unemployment). Practitioners working with Native people can use a popular positive psychology strategy of having clients create genograms to reidentify with their inherent family strengths (Seligman, Rashid, & Parks, 2006). In creating a genogram of family strengths, clients are asked to list three generations of their family (e.g., grandparents, parents, siblings, cousins), and then beside each person list at least one strength each member possesses. Processing this genogram with Native people can help strengthen their innate respect for family and traditions.

In the traditional way, cooperation and sharing in the spirit of community is essential for harmony and balance. It is not unusual for a Native child to be raised in several different households over time. This is generally not due to a lack of caring or responsibility, but because it is both an obligation and a pleasure to share in raising and caring for the children in one's family

(Harper, 2011; Hunter & Sawyer, 2006). Grandparents, aunts, uncles, and other members of the community are all responsible for the raising of children, and they take this responsibility very seriously (BigFoot & Funderburk, 2011).

Gratitude for Wisdom Keepers

Native elders are the keepers of the sacred ways. They are protectors, mentors, teachers, and support givers. Native communities honor their elders as the "keepers of the wisdom," recognizing their lifetime's worth of knowledge and experience. Elders have always played an important part in the sustenance of the tribal community by functioning in the role of parent, teacher, community leader, and spiritual guide (Harper, 2011; Red Horse, 1980). To refer to an elder as *Grandmother, Grandfather, Uncle, Aunt, Old Woman,* or *Old Man* is to refer to a very special relationship that exists with that elder, characterized by deep respect and admiration. There is a very special kind of relationship based on mutual respect and caring between Native American elders and Native American children as one moves through the Life Circle, from birth to old age, from "being cared for" to "caring for" (Red Horse, 1980, 1997).

Building upon Native people's inherent respect for elders, practitioners can strengthen relationships and change negative thinking patterns by encouraging clients to either write a letter of gratitude to one of their elders or having them pay a gratitude visit in which they share their appreciation and respect (Seligman et al., 2006). As with all positive psychology strategies, the regular use of gratitude, whether keeping a journal of daily gratitude moments, or visiting an elder with whom one has not adequately expressed their appreciation, can change pessimistic views of the world, which can enhance clients' level of hope and optimism (Chen & Kee, 2008; Tucker, 2007).

With advancing age comes an increase in the sacred obligation to family, clan, and tribe. Native American elders pass on to children the notion that their own life force carries the spirits of their ancestors (Hunter & Sawyer, 2006). The following anecdote from Brendtro, Brokenleg, and Van Bockern (1990) illustrates the importance of being a caretaker within Native culture as a manifestation of family:

> In a conversation with his aging grandfather, a young Indian man asked, "Grandfather, what is the purpose of life?" After a long time in thought, the old man looked up and said, "Grandson, children are the purpose of life. We were once children and someone cared for us, and now it is our time to care." (p. 45)

With such an emphasis on connectedness, Native traditions revere children not only as ones who will carry on the wisdom and traditions but also as "little people" who are still close to the spirit world and from whom adults have much to learn.

Forgiveness and Meaning-Making

Forgiveness has little to do with reconciliation and everything to do with making the commitment to begin letting go of anger (Enright & North, 1998). Forgiveness is not forgetting, nor should it diminish the need to work toward correcting societal injustices; instead, it is an act by which the offended can move beyond the offense in healthy and productive ways. Clearly, for Native people and many other minority groups, terrible injustices have been perpetrated by the dominant culture, but it is rarely helpful to remain in the "victim" mind-set. Making clients aware of this is the first step in the forgiveness process: Clients might not ever forget the offense, nor should they cease from advocating for their rights, but forgiveness can help decrease anger so that their thoughts and energy can be directed to more productive endeavors. When helping clients with the forgiveness process, it is important to emphasize that forgiveness is a nonlinear process filled with peaks and valleys and that immediate relief is not common, but that over time, anger toward the offender can lessen. When realistic expectations about forgiveness are made clear, clients can find meaning in navigating the forgiveness process (Fitzgibbons, 1998).

Meaning-making is the process by which clients begin to identify how surviving an offense, while hurtful at the time, enabled them to recognize personal strengths and reformulate limited cognitive perceptions that may have never happened otherwise (Taylor, Kemeny, Reed, Bower, & Gruenewald, 2000). The meaning-making stage takes time, but practitioners can facilitate the process by asking clients to consider the ways in which they might have grown as a result of having gone through their ordeal. Practitioners need not force meaning-making, but they can plant the seed that can serve as a catalyst for eventual cognitive restructuring, so that clients transition from victims to survivors.

Living Spiritual Ways

Native Americans may ascribe to and practice any number of religious belief systems, in place of or even along with traditional tribal systems. Overall, however, it is important to understand traditional Native spirituality as a basic frame of reference (Hunter & Sawyer, 2006). Different tribal languages have different words or ways of referring to one's sense of connection. Honoring connection is valued across Native groups; a shared belief is that human beings exist on Mother Earth to be helpers and protectors of life. In Native communities, it is not uncommon, for example, to hear people use the term *caretaking* to refer to that which is a desired way of life. From the perspective of a traditionalist, being a caretaker is to accept responsibility for the gift of life by taking good care of that gift, the gift of life that others have received, and the surrounding beauty of the world in which one lives (M. T. Garrett et al., 2011).

The spiritual beliefs of any individual Native person depend on a number of factors, including her or his level of acculturation (traditional, marginal, bicultural, assimilated, pantraditional); geographic region; family structure; religious influences; and tribally specific traditions (M. T. Garrett & Pichette, 2000; LaFromboise, Coleman, & Gerton, 1993). However, it is possible to generalize, to some extent, about a number of basic beliefs characterizing Native American traditionalism and spirituality across tribal nations. The following list, adapted from Locust (1988, pp. 317–318), describes a number of basic Native American spiritual and traditional beliefs. This list of beliefs (by no means comprehensive) crosses tribal boundaries and provides insight into some of the assumptions that may be held by a "traditional" Native client.

- There is a single higher power known as Creator, Great Creator, Great Spirit, or Great One, among other names (this being is sometimes referred to in gender form but does not necessarily exist as one particular gender or another). There are also lesser beings known as "spirit beings" or "spirit helpers."
- Plants, animals, and inanimate beings such as rocks, like humans, are also part of the spirit world. The spirit world exists side by side with, and intermingles with, the physical world. Moreover, the spirit existed in the spirit world before it came into a physical body and will exist after the body dies.
- Human beings are described as having a body, mind, soul, and spirit. All of these facets (body, mind, soul, and spirit) of the human experience are interconnected; therefore, illness affects the mind and spirit as well as the body.
- Wellness is indicated through the experience of balance and harmony at the physical (body), mental (mind), soul (emotional), and spiritual levels of human existence. Likewise, unwellness or disease is a result of imbalance.
- Natural unwellness is caused by the violation of a sacred social or natural law of Creation (e.g., participating in a sacred ceremony while under the influence of alcohol, drugs, or having had sex within 4 days of the ceremony).
- Unnatural unwellness is caused by conjuring (witchcraft) from those with destructive intentions.
- Each of us is responsible for our own wellness by keeping ourselves attuned to self, relations, environment, and universe.

The most common way to conceptualize Native spirituality is in a basic holistic directions frame (see Figure 14.1). This forms the basis for an understanding of a wellness/strength-based approach to life from an indigenous worldview, as well as an approach to healing through harmony and balance.

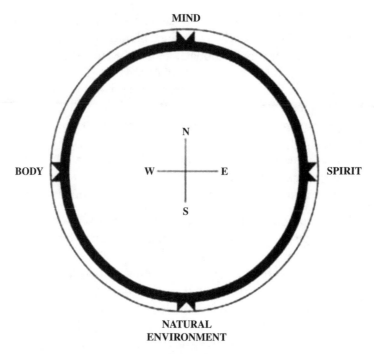

Figure 14.1. Medicine Circle representing the four directions.

Eagle Feather and Symbolism

Eagle feathers are considered to be infinitely sacred among Native Americans. These feathers are used for a variety of purposes, including ceremonial healing and purification. Native traditionalists refer to "Eagle Medicine," which represents a state of being achieved through diligence, understanding, awareness, and completion of initiation tests such as the Vision Quest or other demanding life experiences (Deloria, 2006; M. T. Garrett, 1998). Highly respected elder status is associated with Eagle Medicine and the power of connectedness and truth. It is through experience and patience that this Medicine is earned over a lifetime. And it is through understanding and choice that it is honored. There is an old anecdote that probably best illustrates the lessons of the Eagle feather by reminding us about the power of perspective: Once while acting as a guide for a hunting expedition, an Indian had lost the way home. One of the men with him said, "You're lost, chief." The Indian guide replied, "I'm not lost, my tipi is lost."

The Eagle feather represents duality in existence. It tells the story of life by symbolizing harmony and balance through which life has been able to persist. It tells of the many dualities or opposites that exist in the Life Circle, such as light and dark, male and female, substance and shadow, summer and winter, life and death, peace and war (M. T. Garrett & Myers, 1996; M. T. Garrett & Portman, 2011). The Eagle feather has both light and dark colors, dualities and opposites. Though one can make make the case that one color is more beautiful or more valuable, the truth is that both colors come from the same feather, both are true, both are connected, and it takes both to fly (J. T. Garrett & Garrett, 1996; M. T. Garrett & Portman, 2011). As one elder put it:

> The Eagle feather teaches about the Rule of Opposites, about everything being divided into two ways. The more one is caught up in the physical, or the West, then the more one has to go in the opposite direction, the East, or the spiritual, to get balance. And it works the other way too—you can't just focus on the spiritual to the exclusion of the physical. You need harmony in all Four Directions. (J. T. Garrett, 1991, p. 173)

Therefore, the colors of the Eagle feather could be perceived as opposite, but they are part of the same truth. The importance of the feather lies not in which color is most beautiful but in finding out and accepting what the purpose of the feather as a whole may be. In other words, there is no such thing as keeping the mountains and getting rid of the valleys; they are one and the same, and one exists because the other one does.

FACILITATING POSITIVE AFFECT, BEHAVIORS, AND COGNITIONS IN NATIVE AMERICANS

To work most effectively with members of the Native American population to facilitate positive affect, behaviors, and cognitions, it is important to understand the nature of their cultural experience, but it is also crucial to see the uniqueness of each and every client. The cultural dimension, which is emphasized here, allows the practitioner to better conceptualize current issues in a cultural context and select methods of approaching that client and issue(s) so that cultural values, beliefs, practices, and experiences are used as strengths and valuable resources for the client. In working with most Native American clients, practitioners should attend to two early-assessment factors: (a) assessing the extent to which the process of acculturation has affected the client's cultural identity and (b) understanding the influence of oppression on her or his experience and current presenting issues. We begin this section with a description of common presenting issues and recommendations, followed by a discussion of issues around identity and oppression, traditions, spirituality, and reconciling opposites for balance.

Common Presenting Issues and Recommendations

A summary of common presenting problems for Native Americans in school and mental health settings (see Table 14.1) was provided by Herring

TABLE 14.1
Common Presenting Problems for Native Americans by Age Group

Children	Adolescents	Adults
Failure to develop a strong ethnic identity and self-identity	Difficulty developing a positive self- and ethnic identity	Difficulties stemming from overcoming myths and stereotypes that the Native culture is evil, savage, and inferior
Adverse effects of misperceptions about Native peoples in general	Reactions to stereotypical misperceptions of Native peoples	Negative effects of injustice, discrimination, hardship, and degradation
Adverse effects of discrimination and hatred toward Native peoples, both generally and specifically	Communication difficulties (e.g., for those for whom English is a second language) or a preference for nonverbal communication	Negative effects of poverty
Distrust of European American school and helping professionals based on historical and contemporary negative interactions	Conflicts between family loyalty and peer pressures	Diverse cultural characteristics
Limited standard English skills or limited use of English	Effects of misunderstandings and misperceptions of school personnel	High suicide rate and low life expectancy
Nonverbal communication style conflicting with European American verbal expectations	Low academic achievement	Language difficulties and nonverbal communication misunderstandings
Difficulty reconciling Native cultural values and mainstream values	Substance use and abuse	Midlife crises
Lower academic achievements after the fourth grade	Adverse effects of discrimination and bias	Substance use and abuse
Conflicts resulting from changing from an extended family-centered world to a peer-centered one	Generational conflicts resulting from varying degrees of acculturation	Low self-concept and feelings of inferiority or rejection
Differences in physical appearance and psychosocial status; possible intellectual differences (including learning style differentiations)		Low educational attainment

Note. Data from Herring (1999), pp. 59, 76.

(1999, pp. 59, 76). While this list is not all-inclusive, it represents common themes or issues that seem to emerge for Native clients at various age levels. Recognizing common presenting issues across age groups and areas of attention for cultural responsiveness in therapeutic intervention, Herring (1999, pp. 56–57, 76) summarized specific recommendations that are pertinent to working with Native Americans (see Table 14.2). Each recommendation is intended to assist helping professionals in becoming more effective with Native clients from a variety of backgrounds and with a variety of presenting issues. However, beyond the logistics of working in one-on-one or group contexts, one must consider systemic, environmental, and other contextual factors that influence the health and well-being of Native clients in the context of issues related to identity, family, and acculturation.

Identity, Family, and Acculturation

As a first step in the counseling relationship, the practitioner should find out from which tribe the client comes and possibly whether that person is directly affiliated with that tribe (e.g., federal, state, or community recognition). Identifying the client in this way is a sign of respect. It

TABLE 14.2
Therapeutic Recommendations for Working With Native Americans

Awareness	Knowledge	Skills
Address openly the issue of dissimilar ethnic relationships rather than pretending that no differences exist. Respect the use of silence. Demonstrate honor and respect for the client's culture and show interest without being intrusive or presumptuous; with openness, be willing to admit your ignorance. Listen with your heart and your mind.	Evaluate the client's degree of acculturation. Be open to allowing the extended family or other valued persons (such as indigenous or faith-based healers) from the community to participate in the session as needed or requested by the client. Provide assistance to Native clients in exploring ethnic identity issues as needed.	Schedule appointments to allow for flexibility in ending the session as needed. Allow time for trust to develop before focusing on the problem. Use strategies that elicit practical solutions to problems, and focus on the positives/strengths as a rule with a coinciding potential for change. Establish sufficient eye contact to subtly match the client and create comfort nonverbally. Maintain the highest level of confidentiality.

Note. Data from Herring (1999), pp. 59, 76.

is not the job of practitioners to pass judgment on who is Native American and who is not, and thus one should never ask a Native client "how much Native American" they are or relate personal stories of Native American heritage in his or her family as a way of connecting with that client. That is often a quick way to lose a Native person's receptivity and trust. If a client says that he or she is Native, then a practitioner must assume that it is so. This acceptance of client self-report is a way to understand that client without having to get into the painful (and sometimes irrelevant) politics of categorization. More important, it gives the practitioner insight into that person's perception of his or her experience and place in the world.

When working with a Native American client, it is important to get a sense of that person's level of acculturation. The practitioner can informally assess the client's (a) values (traditional, marginal, bicultural, assimilated, pan-traditional); (b) geographic origin/residence (reservation, rural, urban); and (c) tribal affiliation (tribal structure, customs, beliefs; for further discussion of formal and informal assessment of Native American acculturation, see M. T. Garrett & Pichette, 2000). Both verbal and non-verbal cues give practitioners a good sense of a Native American client's level of acculturation (M. T. Garrett & Pichette, 2000). If questions remain, it is important to pose them in a respectful, unobtrusive way. The following general leads are intended to respectfully elicit important culturally relevant information:

- Tell me about your family, clan, tribe/nation, and/or community.
- Tell me about you as a person, culturally and spiritually, and how you identify yourself in those ways.
- Tell me how your culture/spirituality plays into how you live your life.
- Tell me about your life as you see it, past, present, or future.

To further determine acculturation and subsequent worldview, the practitioner should gather information about family history and structure, community of origin, and community of choice. Practitioners must avoid making assumptions about the cultural identity of Native American clients without first gathering information about both the internal and external experience of that person.

Healing From Historical Trauma and the Impact of Oppression

Given the historical and current contexts of social and political issues facing Native people, a major underlying, and ongoing, issue in counseling most Native clients is trust, as it is with many oppressed peoples

(Grayshield & Mihecoby, 2010). The question that the practitioner must ask herself- or himself is, "What can I do to create and maintain trust with a Native client?" It may be time well-spent to bring up the topic of oppression; the practitioner can ask the client to relate experiences that have had an impact on his or her life for better or for worse. Practitioners might further ask about some of the experiences across generations that have impacted the client and helped to shape how he or she sees the world. Specifically, practitioners should ask about the ways in which family and intergenerational history might be playing into what has brought the client in for services.

Brave Heart (2003, 2005) argued that both prevention and treatment should focus on ameliorating the historical trauma response and fostering a reattachment to traditional Native values, which can serve as protective factors to limit or prevent both substance abuse as well as further transmission of trauma across generations. Rekindling or imparting traditional cultural values through intervention and prevention activities might promote improved parenting skills and parent–child relationships (Brokenleg, 2012). Improved relationships across generations might serve as protection against both substance abuse and the transfer of the historical trauma response (Gone, 2009). The focus on helping parents heal from historical trauma and improving parenting skills is one type of intervention. An emphasis on traditional culture might also mitigate substance abuse (Brave Heart, 2003, 2005). The extensive familial and social support networks in Native culture also offer protection against substance abuse. Native ceremonies often require discipline and commitment, delaying gratification, and they provide Native children with healthy role models of refusal behavior and healthy defenses against substance use and other risk factors.

One model that is useful in both prevention and intervention programs is the historical trauma and unresolved grief intervention, which addresses risk and protective factors for substance abuse through group trauma and psychoeducational interventions that seek to restore attachment to traditional values (Brave Heart, 2000, 2003, 2005; Brave Heart & DeBruyn, 1998; Crazy Thunder & Brave Heart, 2005). Intervention goals are congruent with posttraumatic stress disorder treatment, where a sense of mastery and control are transmitted (Brave Heart, 2003) within a traditional retreatlike setting, providing a safe, affectively containing milieu. Participants in the historical trauma and unresolved grief model are exposed to content through audiovisual materials that stimulate historically traumatic memories; this is done in order to provide opportunities for cognitive integration of the trauma as well as affective cathartic working through, necessary for healing (Brave Heart, 2003). Small- and large-group processing provide occasions for increasing capacity to tolerate and regulate emotions, trauma mastery, and at least short-term amelioration of historical trauma response. Traditional prayer and ceremonies, incorporated throughout the intervention as feasible, afford emotional containment and increased connection to indigenous values and a pretraumatic tribal past. Purification ceremonies have been observed as having a curative effect in posttraumatic stress disorder treatment (Brave Heart, 2003, 2005).

Preliminary research on the historical trauma and unresolved grief model and its integration into parenting sessions indicated that there was (a) a beginning trauma and grief resolution, including a decrease in hopelessness as well as an increase in joy; (b) an increase in positive tribal identity; (c) an increase in protective factors and a decrease in risk factors for substance abuse; (d) perceived improved parental relationships with children and family relationships across generations; and (e) perceived improvement in parenting skills, family connections, and sensitivity to one's children (Brave Heart, 2000). By educating themselves about the history of tribes from which Native clients come and forward thinking treatment modalities based on the historical trauma and unresolved grief model, practitioners can better understand the impact of institutional racism and acculturation, as well as the meaning of the Native American experience, for any given client and begin the process of healing in a way that incorporates culture as a central focus.

Drawing on Traditions

For Native people, there is great potential for cultural conflicts because their values clash with those of the larger society, which tends to emphasize self-promotion, saving for the future, domination of others, accomplishment, competition and aggression, individualism and the nuclear family, mastery over nature, a time orientation toward living for the future, a preference for scientific explanations, time-consciousness, winning, and reverence for youth (M. T. Garrett & Garrett, 2012). Therefore, exploration of cultural conflicts might be an important goal for counseling. Native clients can be encouraged to talk about the meaning that family, clan, or tribe holds for them as a way of exploring worldview, especially in light of intergenerational differences or the effects of oppression or presenting issues. Practitioners must ask themselves, "What can I do to create and maintain trust with a Native client and create a deeper understanding of his or her individual needs?" Practitioners should think about some of the traditional Native values, beliefs, experiences, and traditions related so far in this chapter. They should ask themselves which of these their client holds and in what ways they are played out in his or her life. Furthermore, practitioners should consider how to build on their knowledge of these values, beliefs, experiences, and traditions to show understanding and to develop rapport and matching interventions.

Integrating Spirituality

A practitioner must recognize the vast diversity of spiritual traditions and customs that can be tribally specific and ones that may also have been influenced or replaced by forms of Christianity or other belief systems. It may be important to let the client tell you what she or he needs in terms of spiritual support or ceremony and how that might be best achieved within the context of counseling. Native spirituality manifests itself in many different forms, such as traditional tribal ways, Christian traditions, or attending a Native American church. With a client who seems to have more traditional values and beliefs, it may be particularly helpful to suggest that the family or a Medicine person participate in the process to support the client as he or she moves through important personal transitions and subsequent personal cleansing. It should be noted that having a general understanding of Native American spirituality does not prepare practitioners to participate in or conduct Native ceremonies as part of the counseling process (M. T. Garrett et al., 2011). That is the responsibility of those who are trained as Native Medicine persons; they can serve as an important resource to practitioners working with Native clients.

Bringing Opposites to Balance

An understanding of an indigenous worldview and approach to contrasting opposites is essential for working with Native American clients who may be experiencing dissonance in their lives, but who perceive this in a much different way than someone within the majority culture. Asking the right questions and being open to what practitioners do not readily perceive bridges the gap between what practitioners see and what exists underneath perceived facades. Within the context that everything has meaning and purpose (a Native worldview), one goal of counseling is to help Native clients discover their purpose, examine their assumptions, seek an awareness of universal and personal truths, and make choices that allow them to exist in a state of harmony and balance within the Life Circle. Talking with the client about his or her powerful cultural symbols, such as the Eagle feather, and what they represent to that particular client may help facilitate an opening to a dialogue that will give much insight into current issues, internal and external resources, and needed approaches. Cultural symbols provide insight into potential therapeutic goals for achieving harmony and balance among the four directions— mind, body, spirit, and natural environment.

CONCLUSION: CIRCLES WITHIN AND CIRCLE WITHOUT

Native Americans face many difficult challenges that include being at greater risk than other populations for substance abuse, suicide, accidental death, violence, and mental health problems, as well as contextual factors that include living in communities characterized by high rates of unemployment, poverty, physical and mental health disparities, violence, and lower levels of educational achievement. At the same time, many positive efforts throughout the country are directed at fostering resilience among Native Americans and promoting positive growth and development. The overall purpose of this chapter was to offer a comprehensive overview and understanding for researchers, educators, and practitioners working with Native Americans from a positive psychology approach based on current research and practice. We discussed the value of positive psychology practice with Native Americans and ways for facilitating positive affect, behaviors, and cognitions with members of this population to promote resilience and foster positive development and healing.

We return once again to the image with which this chapter began: the sound of the drum rumbling low, the sharp, impassioned cries of the singers. The vibration moves through you like a storm that rises in the distance, building slowly in the azure sky, then unloading in a rhythmic yet gentle pounding of the soil. Anyone, Native or non-Native, who has ever had the opportunity to experience the colors, movement, sounds, tastes, and smells of the powwow understands the feeling that passes through you. It is different for every person, but if you really experience the feeling, you know that it is connection. For some, it is a matter of seeing old friends or making new ones. For some, it is the image of the dancers moving in seemingly infinite poses of unity and airy smoothness to every flowing pound of the drum. For some, it is the laughter and exchange of words and gestures. For some, it is silent inner prayer giving thanks for another day of life. For some, it is the delicious taste of your second helping of that piping hot fry-bread, corn, or beans. It may be the sound of children playing, or families and friends talking and laughing together. Whatever it is, in the end, it is coming together in one way or another, and walking in step with the Greater Circle. And just when you think you have seen all there is to see, the hoop dancer quietly emerges from the crowd and enters the Circle.

REFERENCES

BigFoot, D. S., & Funderburk, B. W. (2011). Honoring children, making relatives: The cultural translation of parent–child interaction therapy for American Indian and Alaska Native families. *Journal of Psychoactive Drugs, 43*, 309–318. http://dx.doi.org/10.1080/02791072.2011.628924

Brave Heart, M. Y. H. (2000). Wakiksuyapi: Carrying the historical trauma of the Lakota. *Tulane Studies in Social Welfare, 21–22*, 245–266.

Brave Heart, M. Y. H. (2003). The historical trauma response among natives and its relationship with substance abuse: A Lakota illustration. *Journal of Psychoactive Drugs, 35*, 7–13. http://dx.doi.org/10.1080/02791072.2003.10399988

Brave Heart, M. Y. H. (2005). *Substance abuse, co-occurring mental health disorders, and the historical trauma response among American Indians/Alaska Natives* (Research Monograph). Washington, DC: Bureau of Indian Affairs, DASAP.

Brave Heart, M. Y., & DeBruyn, L. M. (1998). The American Indian Holocaust: Healing historical unresolved grief. *American Indian and Alaska Native Mental Health Research, 8*(2), 56–78.

Brendtro, L. K., Brokenleg, M., & Van Bockern, S. (1990). *Reclaiming youth at risk: Our hope for the future.* Bloomington, IN: National Education Service.

Brokenleg, M. (2012). Transforming cultural trauma into resilience. *Reclaiming Children and Youth, 21*, 9–13.

Chen, L. H., & Kee, Y. H. (2008). Gratitude and adolescent athletes' well-being. *Social Indicators Research, 89*, 361–373. http://dx.doi.org/10.1007/s11205-008-9237-4

Cheung, C., & Kwan, A. Y.-H. (2006). Inducting older adults into volunteer work to sustain their psychological wellbeing. *Ageing International, 31*(1), 44–58. http://dx.doi.org/10.1007/s12126-006-1003-9

Crazy Thunder, D., & Brave Heart, M. Y. H. (2005). *Cumulative trauma among tribal law enforcement officers: Search, rescue, & recovery at Ground Zero and on the reservation* (Research Monograph). Washington, DC: Bureau of Indian Affairs, DASAP.

Curtis, R., & Robertson, P. (2009). Prayer and meditation: A review of research. *Counselling and Values, 28*(2), 11–32.

Dell, C., Hopkins, C., & Dell, D. (2004). Resiliency and holistic inhalant abuse treatment. *Journal of Aboriginal Health, 1*, 4–12.

Dell, D., & Hopkins, C. (2011). Residential volatile substance misuse treatment for indigenous youth in Canada. *Substance Use & Misuse, 46*(Suppl. 1), 107–113. http://dx.doi.org/10.3109/10826084.2011.580225

Deloria, V., Jr. (2006). *The world we used to live in: Remembering the powers of the medicine men.* Golden, CO: Fulcrum.

DuBray, W. H. (1985). American Indian values: Critical factor in casework. *Social Casework, 66*, 30–37.

Enright, R. D., & North, J. (Eds.). (1998). *Exploring forgiveness.* Madison: The University of Wisconsin Press.

Fitzgibbons, R. (1998). Anger and the healing power of forgiveness: A psychiatrist's view. In R. D. Enright & J. North (Eds.), *Exploring forgiveness* (pp. 63–74). Madison: The University of Wisconsin Press.

Garrett, J. T. (1991). Where the medicine wheel meets medical science. In S. McFadden (Ed.), *Profiles in wisdom: Native elders speak about the earth* (pp. 167–179). Santa Fe, NM: Bear & Company.

Garrett, J. T., & Garrett, M. T. (1996). *Medicine of the Cherokee: The way of right relationship*. Santa Fe, NM: Bear & Company.

Garrett, M. T. (1996). Reflection by the riverside: The traditional education of Native American children. *The Journal of Humanistic Education and Development, 35*, 12–28. http://dx.doi.org/10.1002/j.2164-4683.1996.tb00349.x

Garrett, M. T. (1998). *Walking on the wind: Cherokee teachings for harmony and balance*. Santa Fe, NM: Bear & Company.

Garrett, M. T. (1999). Understanding the "medicine" of Native American traditional values: An integrative review. *Counseling and Values, 43*, 84–98. http://dx.doi.org/10.1002/j.2161-007X.1999.tb00131.x

Garrett, M. T., & Garrett, J. T. (2012). *Native American faith in America* (2nd ed.). New York, NY: Facts on File.

Garrett, M. T., & Myers, J. E. (1996). The rule of opposites: A paradigm for counseling Native Americans. *Journal of Multicultural Counseling and Development, 24*, 89–104. http://dx.doi.org/10.1002/j.2161-1912.1996.tb00292.x

Garrett, M. T., & Pichette, E. F. (2000). Red as an apple: Native American acculturation and counseling with or without reservation. *Journal of Counseling and Development, 78*, 3–13. http://dx.doi.org/10.1002/j.1556-6676.2000.tb02554.x

Garrett, M. T., & Portman, T. A. A. (2011). *Counseling and diversity: Counseling Native Americans*. Boston, MA: Cengage/Lahaska Press.

Garrett, M. T., Torres-Rivera, E., Brubaker, M., Portman, T. A. A., Brotherton, D., West-Olatunji, C., . . . Grayshield, L. (2011). Crying for a vision: The Native American sweat lodge ceremony as therapeutic intervention. *Journal of Counseling and Development, 89*, 318–325. http://dx.doi.org/10.1002/j.1556-6678.2011.tb00096.x

Gone, J. P. (2009). A community-based treatment for Native American historical trauma: Prospects for evidence-based practice. *Journal of Consulting and Clinical Psychology, 77*, 751–762. http://dx.doi.org/10.1037/a0015390

Goodluck, C. (2002). *Native American children and youth well-being indicators: A strengths perspective*. Portland, OR: National Indian Child Welfare Association. Retrieved from http://www.nicwa.org/research/03.Well-Being02.rpt.pdf

Grayshield, L., & Mihecoby, A. (2010). Indigenous ways of knowing as a philosophical base for the promotion of peace and justice in counseling education and psychology. *Journal for Social Action in Counseling and Psychology, 2*(2), 1–16.

Greason, P. B., & Welfare, L. E. (2013). The impact of mindfulness and meditation practice on client perceptions of common therapeutic factors. *Journal of Humanistic Counseling, 52*, 235–253.

Harper, F. G. (2011). With all my relations: Counseling American Indians and Alaska Natives within a familial context. *The Family Journal, 19*, 434–442. http://dx.doi.org/10.1177/1066480711419818

HeavyRunner, I. & Morris, J. S. (1997). *Traditional Native culture and resilience.* Retrieved from http://purl.umn.edu/145989.

Herring, R. D. (1999). *Counseling with Native American Indians and Alaska Natives: Strategies for helping professionals.* Thousand Oaks, CA: Sage.

Hunter, D., & Sawyer, C. (2006). Blending Native American spirituality with individual psychology in work with children. *The Journal of Individual Psychology, 62*, 234–250.

Kabat-Zinn, J. (1994). *Wherever you go there you are.* New York, NY: Hyperion.

Kirmayer, L. J., Dandeneau, S., Marshall, E., Phillips, M. K., & Williamson, K. J. (2011). Rethinking resilience from indigenous perspectives. *Canadian Journal of Psychiatry, 56*, 84–91.

LaFromboise, T., Coleman, H. L. K., & Gerton, J. (1993). Psychological impact of biculturalism: Evidence and theory. *Psychological Bulletin, 114*, 395–412. http://dx.doi.org/10.1037/0033-2909.114.3.395

Locust, C. (1988). Wounding the spirit: Discrimination and traditional American Indian belief systems. *Harvard Educational Review, 58*, 315–331. http://dx.doi.org/10.17763/haer.58.3.e0r224774008738p

Lyubomirsky, S. (2013). *The myths of happiness: What should make you happy, but doesn't. What shouldn't make you happy, but does.* New York, NY: Penguin Press.

Portman, T. (2001). American Indian women sex role attributions. *Journal of Mental Health Counseling, 23*, 72–84.

Portman, T., & Garrett, M. T. (2005). Beloved women: Nurturing the sacred fire leadership from an American Indian perspective. *Journal of Counseling & Development, 83*, 284–291.

Red Horse, J. G. (1980). Indian elders: Unifiers of families. *Social Casework, 61*, 490–493.

Red Horse, J. G. (1997). Traditional American Indian family systems. *Families, Systems, & Health, 15*, 243–250. http://dx.doi.org/10.1037/h0089828

Russell, G. (2004). *American Indian facts of life: A profile of today's tribes and reservations.* Phoenix, AZ: Native Data Network.

Saleebey, D. (1996). The strengths perspective in social work practice: Extensions and cautions. *Social Work, 41*, 296–305.

Schueller, S. M. (2010). Preferences for positive psychology exercises. *The Journal of Positive Psychology, 5*(3), 192–203. http://dx.doi.org/10.1080/17439761003790948

Seligman, M. E. P., Rashid, T., & Parks, A. C. (2006). Positive psychotherapy. *American Psychologist, 61*, 774–788. http://dx.doi.org/10.1037/0003-066X.61.8.774

Seligman, M. E. P., Steen, T. A., Park, N., & Peterson, C. (2005). Positive psychology progress: Empirical validation of interventions. *American Psychologist, 60,* 410–421. http://dx.doi.org/10.1037/0003-066X.60.5.410

Taylor, S. E., Kemeny, M. E., Reed, G. M., Bower, J. E., & Gruenewald, T. L. (2000). Psychological resources, positive illusions, and health. *American Psychologist, 55,* 99–109. http://dx.doi.org/10.1037/0003-066X.55.1.99

Tucker, K. (2007). Getting the most out of life: An examination of appreciation, targets of appreciation, and sensitivity to reward in happier and less happy individuals. *Journal of Social and Clinical Psychology, 26,* 791–825. http://dx.doi.org/10.1521/jscp.2007.26.7.791

V
CONCLUSION

V

CONCLUSION

15

CHALLENGES AND PROSPECTS FOR POSITIVE PSYCHOLOGY RESEARCH, THEORY, ASSESSMENT, AND PRACTICE IN A MULTIRACIAL AND MULTIETHNIC WORLD

CHRISTINA A. DOWNEY, EDWARD C. CHANG,
JAMESON K. HIRSCH, AND NATALIE J. LIN

Like most scholarly texts in this rapidly growing field, the present volume was designed to accomplish a lofty goal: to review and critique a broad body of work associated with positive psychology research, assessment, and practice, with specific attention to the American racial/ethnic minority experience. This required our contributors—a diverse group of scholars—to maintain a fine balance between questioning the assumptions upon which positive psychology is founded and offering conclusions and recommendations that researchers and practitioners will find useful. These scholars responded to this call with enthusiasm and sophistication, filling in important "gaps" in the empirical literature with knowledge and wisdom from fields as varied as philosophy, religion, anthropology, sociology, and the oral traditions. We are grateful for their work and hope that readers value their contributions as much as we do.

A main conclusion that must be drawn from the efforts of these scholars is that building and disseminating knowledge in multicultural positive

http://dx.doi.org/10.1037/14799-015
Positive Psychology in Racial and Ethnic Groups: Theory, Research, and Practice, E. C. Chang, C. A. Downey, J. K. Hirsch, and N. J. Lin (Editors)

psychology is—to put it mildly—very tricky. The scholar who claims to be equally committed to the values of science and multiculturalism faces an ultimate epistemological quandary: Scientific ideals of empiricism, operationalization of variables, reliability and validity of measurement, and replication may not mesh easily with a full awareness of how culture shapes individual and collective perception, cognition, affective response, problem solving, and moral and ethical orientation at the most fundamental level. How does one acquire belief that can be trusted as factual, when one is aware that there are culturally driven limitations on one's own rational perspective? It is akin to trying to identify the bluest color possible—is blue defined as a specific, objective wavelength of light, or as a perceptive experience prone to individual and contextual alteration? The consequences of misunderstanding a psychological construct are arguably far greater than those resulting from misunderstanding a color tone, leaving the scholar of multicultural positive psychology with a serious set of responsibilities to consider.

The contributors to this volume understood and appreciated this quandary but (thankfully) were not paralyzed by it. How can that be? We would argue that to a large degree, scholars fortify their resolve to push the field forward through reliance on a set of core principles. An examination of the chapters herein makes it clear that these scholars are committed to some important ideas:

- *Demographic and social pragmatism.* Contributors noted how changes in the U.S. population through shifting birth patterns and immigration necessitate a broader and deeper understanding of various racial, ethnic, and cultural group experiences and values. This includes considerations of how race and ethnicity are defined in the United States—for example, appreciation of subgroups by national origin, religion, and historical cohort—and the process and impact of acculturation to American society. The multicultural positive psychology of the future is one that is vibrant and penetrating, and it reaches out to other fields in full acknowledgement of these demographic trends.

- *Embrace of the intent of positive psychology while cautioning against past cultural bias.* Contributors voiced a common appreciation for what seems to have been a main goal of positive psychology—understanding the nature and promotion of well-being from a psychological perspective—but also shared concerns that too much past research, assessment, and practice identified with this discipline has been insufficiently sensitive to cultural issues. For example, defining, measuring, and promoting autonomy as a positive human characteristic may have worked consistently well for some cultural groups (e.g., White middle- and upper-class male Americans) but has worked less well for various other cultural groups. A multicultural positive psychology of the future digs into the history of the discipline to reconsider such biases and forms new questions to address them.

- *Emphasis on the value of understanding indigenous belief systems and practices relevant to positive psychology.* Contributors made clear that investigating different levels of cultural group endorsement of a single set of culturally defined positive characteristics, and then aligning cultural groups along some kind of endorsement continuum, is not compatible with demonstrating true respect for difference (the appropriate approach to take in the field). Likewise, indigenous healing practices should not be attempted only when they can be incorporated into (or, some would say, co-opted by) predominant psychotherapeutic practice. Contributors to this volume have made the case for more nuanced, indigenous understandings of phenomena that White Western psychologists might blithely refer to as *love, well-being,* and *helping,* an approach that should continue as part of a multicultural positive psychology of the future.

- *Awareness of how multiculturalism is no longer mainly a societal-level phenomenon but increasingly occurs at the family and individual levels.* Contributors noted that bicultural and multicultural individuals and families face particular challenges and opportunities related to their well-being. More than at any time in the past, the U.S. population has come to accept romantic relationships and families across previously rigid racial, ethnic, and cultural lines. However, one's social status, geographic location, and individual circumstances affect the unique experiences that bicultural and multicultural populations have in navigating life choices and challenges. A multicultural positive psychology of the future affords these unique individuals, families, and groups their due attention in regards to research, assessment, and practice.

- *Appreciation of different group histories and how that awareness places the notion of resilience at the center of multicultural positive psychology.* Contributors affirmed that the well-being of individuals, families, and cultural groups does not develop in a vacuum. Instead, members of different groups have faced vastly different historical psychological and social pressures, to which each group has been forced to adapt. Some individuals or groups, such as racial/ethnic minorities who have been able to manifest strong ties to their cultural values and practices, seem to have been largely successful at this adaptation. Some individuals and groups, particularly racial/ethnic minorities who have been faced with discrimination within their communities, seem to have been largely unsuccessful. It must be noted, however, that judging the success (or lack thereof) of these individuals and groups is itself problematic because determining one's success in a life domain seems to depend in large part on where one started out. *Resilience*, or the ability to rebound to a homeostatic level of function and achieve positive life outcomes despite adversity (e.g., Harvey & Delfabbro, 2004; Hawley & DeHaan, 1996; Masten, 2001; Rutter, 2006), is one of relatively few psychological constructs that by its nature can accommodate contextual factors such as cultural history. Though not all scholars have applied the concept in this way, we feel that its implicit inclusion of context is an important factor in understanding positive functioning and well-being through a multicultural lens. Therefore, we are convinced that a multicultural positive psychology of the future must embrace an advanced understanding of resilience.

In this chapter, we review the scholarship on resilience. In response to calls for stronger theoretical frameworks for future resilience research (Harvey & Delfabbro, 2004; Howard, Dryden, & Johnson, 1999; Luthar, Cicchetti, & Becker, 2000), we present a two-dimensional model of experiences of adversity and then discuss the model in terms of multicultural positive psychology research, assessment, and practice. We then offer recommendations for future research in this area.

RESILIENCE: DEFINITIONS AND CHALLENGES

To clarify our definition of *resilience* as a two-dimensional construct before expanding on its necessity, let us explain each dimension briefly in turn. Dimension 1 is theorized as representing the relative safety of coping approaches and strategies that might be used in response to stressful situations. Such coping might be undertaken by individuals, families, or groups, and it is identified along a continuum that ranges from what is anticipated to be *safe* (having a high probability of bringing positive outcomes in most similar circumstances) to that which is *risky* (having a high probability of bringing negative outcomes in most similar circumstances). Dimension 2 is theorized as representing the relative positivity of the actual life outcomes that follow from the use of these coping strategies. These outcomes would vary from *positive* (increasing well-being) for the self, family, or group, to *negative* (decreasing well-being). In this model, there may or may not be a direct causal connection between Dimension 1 and Dimension 2 in every case, even though Dimension 2 life outcomes would temporally follow Dimension 1 coping. This distinction is crucial to our model in specific reference to multicultural positive psychology, because the diverse factors that may or may not relate one's coping to subsequent life outcomes are assumed to vary significantly with cultural factors.

In most previous research, *resilience* has been defined as positive functioning despite adversity. However, specific definitions of resilience have varied considerably over time and among scholars, with the result that an exceptionally wide range of ideas and variables have been explored as indicative of, or bringing about, resilience (Arrington & Wilson, 2000; Barbarin, 1993; Waller, 2001). Research on resilience originally began with the recognition that ecological factors seemed to put specific populations in a position of risk and disadvantage to their psychological and social well-being—that environmental influences outside of individual control consistently led to greater incidence of a variety of types of distress and dysfunction among certain groups. However, interest soon developed in understanding why such influences did not affect all members of at-risk groups equally. Researchers wished to know what characteristics or practices allowed some members of disadvantaged groups to emerge relatively unscathed (Barbarin, 1993; Harvey & Delfabbro, 2004; Howard et al., 1999; Luthar et al., 2000; Tusaie & Dyer, 2004).

Despite rapid growth in the number of studies published on resilience since the 1970s, the continuing lack of agreement regarding how best to conceptualize resilience for research and practice makes findings from various studies difficult to understand and compare (Ahern, Kiehl, Sole, & Byers, 2006; Windle, Bennett, & Noyes, 2011). For example, many researchers who study the factors that keep dysfunction at bay have attempted to identify personal characteristics that distinguish resilient from nonresilient individuals. Traits such as optimism, creativity, intelligence, humor, good social skills (Tusaie & Dyer, 2004), hardiness, tenacity, personal competence (Clauss-Ehlers, 2008), extraversion, conscientiousness (Campbell-Sills, Cohan, & Stein, 2006; Davey, Eaker, & Walters, 2003), self-efficacy, religious involvement, and positive racial/ethnic identity (Waller, 2001) are among the many individual-level variables that have been described as indicative or leading to resilience. However, concerns have been raised that the individual level of analysis can lead to unfair "victim blaming" if people do not prevail above their circumstances—that is, people who succumb to adversity are lacking in desirable personal qualities (Waller, 2001). In response, others have worked to identify environmental factors that seem to make success despite adversity more or less likely to occur (Davey et al., 2003; Smith & Carlson, 1997). In these studies, protective factors such as access to good education, positive mentoring, high-quality employment opportunities (Waller, 2001), community networks, civic engagement, norms of cooperation, tolerance of diversity (Ledogar & Fleming, 2008), cultural values, cultural assets, and sociocultural support (Clauss-Ehlers, 2008) have received attention. In this view, resilience still implies triumph over adversity; however, it is having the correct set of contextual resources to balance against life's challenges that make triumph possible. Simply listing resources, though, does not specify how they are used to bring about well-being despite adversity.

Acknowledging this shortcoming, many authors have argued that resilience is neither a personal trait nor a feature of the environment but rather a dynamic, transactional process where adversity, protective environmental factors, and personal tendencies interact (Agaibi & Wilson, 2005; Ahern et al., 2006; Arrington & Wilson, 2000; Luthar et al., 2000; Rutter, 2006; Smith & Carlson, 1997). That is, the specific ways that people respond to adversity, and do or do not take advantage of protective factors available to them, are significantly influenced by individual characteristics. Effective coping has been identified as one mechanism through which personal characteristics thought to be related to resilience can lead to beneficial life outcomes (Davey et al., 2003; Harvey & Delfabbro, 2004; Luthar et al., 2000). Effective coping can be thought of as applying one's internal and external resources appropriately to resolve stress (Smith & Carlson, 1997). The literature on coping is vast (Skinner, Edge, Altman, & Sherwood, 2003), and a number of specific coping methods and styles have been identified that tend to result in better or worse outcomes; the methods that tend to result in positive outcomes would be considered more effective. Therefore, resilient individuals would be those whose particular traits make them more likely to apply their resources well, to achieve positive outcomes despite adversity.

Many of the most frequently used self-report measures of resilience have been applied as if resilience were a trait; however, examination of these measures reveals that they generally conceptualize resilience as "bouncing back" from adversity. This is more aligned with the process view or, in essence, a response to stress that achieves a positive outcome. These measures include items assessing behaviors similar to effective coping, and many imply or state in their verbiage that some desired outcome resulted from that coping (Ahern et al., 2006; Windle et al., 2011). Some research using such measures has found that coping styles predict variance in resilience above and beyond personality traits and, in some cases, rendering the effects of personality on resilience nonsignificant (Campbell-Sills et al., 2006); what such research may actually be indicating is that resilience is not a trait (like personality) but, rather, a process (like coping). We agree with Rutter (2006) that resilience involves "relative resistance to environmental risk experiences, or the overcoming of stress or adversity" (p. 2; see also Waller, 2001)—that is, resilience is an active, goal-directed reaction to difficult circumstances. However, there is also evidence in the literature that "resistance" alone is not sufficient to capture resilience. How one resists, and what one experiences following resistance, are also key to the concept of resilience.

INTRODUCTION OF A TWO-DIMENSIONAL MODEL OF EXPERIENCES OF ADVERSITY

We believe we can offer a broader view of adversity, coping, and outcomes that resolves the circularity and culturally problematic person-focus of past resilience work (Leipold & Greve, 2009; Rutter, 2006). We define *resilience* as a response to significant adversity involving safe coping approaches, with a subsequent experience of positive life outcomes. What this implies is that resilience per se is not a personal quality, nor an environmental factor; it is an outcome with specific antecedents (some of which are person-centered, and some of which are situation-centered; Cicchetti & Rogosch, 2009). Although some scholars have spoken of resilience as an outcome (e.g., Bonanno, 2004, 2005), others (e.g., Leipold & Greve, 2009) have argued against considering resilience an outcome and have suggested that resilience is the "conceptual bridge" between coping and the outcome of healthy development (Leipold & Greve, 2009, p. 40). However, we feel that explicitly identifying specific combinations of coping and outcomes that do or do not represent a resilient experience of adversity is more useful for future research and practice in supporting well-being across various groups.

To return, then, to our model (see Figure 15.1): We conceptualize resilience in the context of adversity as two-dimensional and temporally based, involving the examination of three key elements in human experience that cycle and transact repeatedly through the life span. The first element involves external *stressors*. Perception of stressors varies with regard to personal vulnerability factors, individual concepts of health (see Downey & Chang, 2013, for further discussion), other cognitive appraisals, and life circumstances (e.g., risk and protective factors), which themselves are affected by culture (Arrington & Wilson, 2000; Barbarin, 1993; Fleming & Ledogar, 2008; Kuperminc, Wilkins, Roche, & Alvarez-Jimenez, 2009; Tummala-Narra, 2007; Ungar, 2008). The greater the stressor, the greater the impetus for a response.

When an individual (or family, or group) identifies a situation as a stressor, *coping* is triggered (the second element of the model). As noted above, we theorize a continuum of coping methods available for use in response to any given stressor, from those that are probably most safe to those that are more risky. Safe coping methods are those that would generally be expected to result in positive outcomes, such as removal of the stressor and

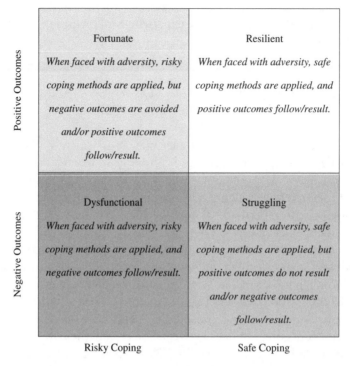

Experiences of Adversity

	Risky Coping	Safe Coping
Positive Outcomes	**Fortunate** — *When faced with adversity, risky coping methods are applied, but negative outcomes are avoided and/or positive outcomes follow/result.*	**Resilient** — *When faced with adversity, safe coping methods are applied, and positive outcomes follow/result.*
Negative Outcomes	**Dysfunctional** — *When faced with adversity, risky coping methods are applied, and negative outcomes follow/result.*	**Struggling** — *When faced with adversity, safe coping methods are applied, but positive outcomes do not result and/or negative outcomes follow/result.*

Figure 15.1. Two-dimensional model of experiences of adversity.

emotional fortification. Risky coping methods are those that would generally be expected to result in negative outcomes, such as maintenance or worsening of the stressor and emotional fatigue or upheaval. The determination of whether a coping method is safe or risky would depend not only on general anticipated outcome, but also on the specific individual's past experience with that method and his or her cultural context (Barbarin, 1993; Kuperminc et al., 2009; Tummala-Narra, 2007; Ungar, 2008; Ungar et al., 2007). For example, past exposure to a stressor may have strengthened an individual's ability to marshal resources to deal effectively with the situation (Rutter, 2006), and his or her cultural background might provide a strong push toward a particular coping choice (Arrington & Wilson, 2000; Fleming & Ledogar, 2008; Ungar, 2008; Ungar et al., 2007). Thus, for that person, a certain coping method might be quite safe, whereas it might be only slightly safe or even risky for another person.

Safe coping often seems to lead to positive outcomes, or at least avoidance of negative outcomes. However, even the safest, most well-practiced, and culturally congruent coping method does not always result in positive outcomes. It has been noted how many of those who enjoy so-called protective factors for resilience do not necessarily exhibit corresponding benefits (Harvey & Delfabbro, 2004). We would argue that this is because many stressors are not under personal control. Indeed, events that are under less personal influence are actually more likely to cause stress in the first place (Maier & Watkins, 2005). If the stressor is severe, pervasive, unexpected, novel, or inescapable, there may be no coping approach safe enough to reduce or remove the stressor. Conversely, there are times when even very unsafe coping responses to stressors do not lead to reductions in well-being. That is, some individuals may be so protected in their well-being that even a risky coping approach to stressors does not result in negative life outcomes. Although these individuals seem to maintain their well-being, these cases also would not fit the concept of resilience as traditionally defined because their actions should have been followed by continuation or worsening of the stressor.

Life outcomes, we believe, are the third element to examine when deciding whether resilience is present. Life outcomes are best seen as a related but not fully determined factor in one's experience of adversity. The life outcomes that follow or result from coping would themselves fall on a continuum (from positive to negative), our second theorized dimension of experiences of adversity. Positive outcomes might range from benign (e.g., not harmful) to extremely positive (e.g., greatly improving well-being), and negative outcomes might range from slightly negative (e.g., not helpful) to extremely negative (e.g., greatly reducing well-being). The positive or negative valence of outcomes would be determined by various factors, such as the individual's desires and values, the situation, and the cultural context (Kuperminc et al., 2009; Leipold & Greve, 2009; Tummala-Narra, 2007; Ungar, 2008). It would also be important to maintain a transactional perspective on outcomes, in that the "outcome" of one coping cycle may itself become a stressor in the next coping cycle.

Assuming these dimensions to be valid, experiences of stress and adversity would divide into four basic types. The first, already noted above, is *resilient*. This would be the case of a safe coping response to adversity being followed by, or contributing to, some positive life outcome, including a return to a previous level of successful functioning. However, an individual may also function better after an adverse event, such as in the case of thriving or posttraumatic growth (Sirois & Hirsch, 2013). Take the case of a child who faces parental neglect (the stressor) by attaching to another trusted, positive adult role model (safe coping) and eventually goes on to grow and flourish psychologically and socially (positive life outcome). This is the prototypical case of resilience that has long held the attention of researchers in this area. Adversity was clearly present, but the individual "found a way" to overcome it. One's safe coping approach probably should receive at least some credit in the positive outcome; thus, it is important, in future research, to determine the interrelationships between type of stressor encountered, method of coping used (i.e., safe vs. risky), and the valence of the outcome, whether positive or negative. It would also be very important to consider the cultural context at hand. For instance, some cultural groups, such as Whites or acculturated minority groups, may have greater access to education, resources, or role models that make safe coping responses and resilience in the face of adversity more likely.

The second type of experience of stress and adversity, which we call *fortunate*, would be the case of a risky coping response to adversity being followed by, or contributing to, some positive life outcome. For example, imagine a college student who overdraws his bank account (the stressor) but ignores the situation (risky coping). When a parent is notified of the empty account and associated fees, the fund is replenished (positive life outcome). Although the student may get a stern warning about such behavior in the future, the long-term impact of the coping behavior is minimal (and in fact might even be taken as a "lesson learned" to "develop character"). We would argue that although the outcome was positive, this kind of reaction to adversity should not be classified as resilient, because the coping approach adopted by the individual should have been expected to worsen, not ameliorate, the stressor. Classifying this experience of adversity as "fortunate" does not negate the potential for it to serve as a learning experience, but does acknowledge that the individual (or family, or group) was protected by a contextual factor. For members of some cultural groups, there may be more, or less, such contextual protective factors available. For instance, members of ethnic groups that endorse a collectivistic social perspective may be more able to absorb the consequences of risky coping, perhaps as a result of the availability of assistance from others or diffusion of potential deleterious consequences across a group of individuals, rather than a sole individual bearing the burden of the stressor sequelae.

The third type of experience of stress and adversity, which we call *struggling*, would be the case of a safe coping response to adversity being followed by, or contributing to, some negative life outcome. For example, imagine that a family is served with an eviction notice (the stressor) so the two adolescent children get part-time jobs to help the family improve their financial security (safe coping). However, the amount of money they contribute to the family income is insufficient to halt their eviction, and they experience anxiety and depression (negative life outcome). Such a case would not typically be identified as resilient according to past definitions (in this case, because the outcome was negative); yet, as resilience has been described as a resource that is not an unlimited, persistent or insurmountable adverse circumstances may deplete even the most robust efforts to overcome stressors (Rutter, 2006). That these youth attempted to cope actively to improve their circumstances seems to merit some consideration despite the poor outcome. The stressor was too great to overcome, but focusing on a "lack of resilience" does not capture possible strengths of these youth. It may be that significant proportions of individuals from particular racial/ethnic minority groups fall into this category at some point in their lives, as a result of either overt or institutionalized discrimination. As but one example, consider the recent economic crisis in America paired with the well-documented discrimination that occurs during the hiring process for non-White individuals. Thus, an African American or Latino American may exhibit the safe coping response of applying for jobs but may be overlooked as a result of his or her ethnicity, resulting in consequent despair and continuing financial distress.

The fourth type of experience of stress and adversity, which we call *dysfunctional*, would be the case of a risky coping response to adversity being followed by, or contributing to, some negative life outcome. An example might be that of a mother whose job is eliminated (the stressor) who begins drinking heavily to escape her feelings of anxiety and worthlessness (risky coping). The drinking then impairs her ability to seek and retain employment quickly, and her financial situation becomes worse (negative life outcome). Although it is true that anyone having a dysfunctional experience of adversity would feel some suffering, it is still crucial to consider how cultural differences might make the stressor more or less likely to happen to various people or groups, might moderate (increase or decrease) the harm resulting from risky coping, and/or might impact social perceptions of the individuals involved. Might more blame or stigma be assigned to a non-White person coping in this manner than to a White person making the same choice, for example? Or might a less acculturated minority immigrant face more negative views than a more acculturated one would? Social condemnation versus forgiveness of unsafe coping methods might vary with culture, which would then translate into different degrees of dysfunction under adversity.

RESEARCH QUESTIONS IMPLIED BY THE EXPERIENCES OF ADVERSITY MODEL

We hope that by clearly distinguishing between three temporally sequenced elements of experiences of adversity—stressor, safe–risky coping, and positive–negative outcome—many of the past theoretical and methodological difficulties plaguing progress in the resilience literature can be curtailed (Harvey & Delfabbro, 2004). For example, traits found to be associated with resilience could be examined as moderators of stress and of coping—that is, individuals with varying levels of these traits would be theorized to appraise stressors and coping methods differently and to engage in safe or risky coping with greater or lesser frequency. Therefore, individuals falling into the four different types probably differ in these traits; for example, conscientiousness is probably highest among those with resilient experiences of adversity and lowest among those with dysfunctional experiences of adversity. External factors associated with resilience, such as socioeconomic status, would not only affect stress appraisal and coping, but would also affect the actual stressors encountered. Past experience of stress and coping would also be an important factor to assess, as an individual with little exposure to or success with safe coping may be unlikely to attempt such methods when encountering a stressor.

It should also be clear to the reader that this model is intended to represent (in admittedly simple terms) a phenomenon that is culturally very complex. What is a stressor, and which stressors can people expect to face over the course of development? Race, ethnicity, and other aspects of culture are clearly factors in definitions of, and exposure to, stress, and thus must be accounted for in research and intervention design. Will people cope in safe or risky ways with those stressors? Again, race, ethnicity, and culture are factors in defining safe versus risky coping, as well as whether individuals can engage in coping methods that they deem safe. Therefore, there must be consideration of culture in study and intervention with safe and risky coping. Will people's attempts to cope result in positive or negative outcomes? Yet again, race, ethnicity, and culture help determine what kinds of outcomes follow coping and thus are factors in shaping a lifelong developmental trajectory toward or away from well-being. In short, researchers seeking to examine our model must keep multiculturalism in mind when developing research questions and measurement tools, interpreting study results, and applying results through interventions.

Over time, individual categorization into these four types would likely be fairly consistent. However, these four types of experiences should not be viewed as static. Individuals may shift between types, depending on the results of past coping shaping future coping (Tusaie & Dyer, 2004). In addition, the same individual might fit two different types at one point in time, in different life domains (e.g., an adolescent might be resilient at home, but struggling at school; Fraser, Galinsky, & Richman, 1999; Luthar et al., 2000). Researchers of the model must clearly specify what variables they are investigating as the stressor(s) and outcome(s) of a coping cycle. In addition, stressors must be considered carefully for their complexity (in that some aspects of certain stressors are more stressful and difficult to cope with than others) to prevent past methodological problems in resilience research from being repeated (Luthar & Zigler, 1991). Understanding what may lead to shifts between types, and how to intervene to create shifts away from dysfunction and toward resilience, would be key to future work with the model. In addition, attention should be paid to the three quadrants of the model besides resilience, particularly to the struggling population (who would seem most at risk of descending into the dysfunctional quadrant if continued frustration and lack of progress dominates their experience).

FINAL CONCLUSION

It has been heartening to see the wealth of information and issues that our contributors brought forth when given the opportunity to write on the topic of multiculturalism and positive psychology. No contributor shied away from acknowledging the challenges that various groups face, and there was also a great deal of pride that came through in their reviews and testimonies. To return to our earlier question regarding the intersection of science and a multicultural perspective, and how a scholar can be equally committed to two philosophies with opposing aims, we observe that both endeavors are based on a willingness to explore truth, to question assumptions, and to assess the value of assuming various perspectives. Therefore, as long as scholars remain committed to reconsider (and reconsider, and reconsider) the facts, our shared understanding will grow and continue to influence the positive psychology movement.

REFERENCES

Agaibi, C. E., & Wilson, J. P. (2005). Trauma, PTSD, and resilience: A review of the literature. *Trauma, Violence, & Abuse, 6,* 195–216. http://dx.doi.org/10.1177/1524838005277438

Ahern, N. R., Kiehl, E. M., Sole, M. L., & Byers, J. (2006). A review of instruments measuring resilience. *Issues in Comprehensive Pediatric Nursing, 29,* 103–125. http://dx.doi.org/10.1080/01460860600677643

Arrington, E. G., & Wilson, M. N. (2000). A re-examination of risk and resilience during adolescence: Incorporating culture and diversity. *Journal of Child and Family Studies, 9,* 221–230. http://dx.doi.org/10.1023/A:1009423106045

Barbarin, O. A. (1993). Coping and resilience: Exploring the inner lives of African American children. *Journal of Black Psychology, 19,* 478–492. http://dx.doi.org/10.1177/00957984930194007

Bonanno, G. A. (2004). Loss, trauma, and human resilience: Have we underestimated the human capacity to thrive after extremely aversive events? *American Psychologist, 59,* 20–28. http://dx.doi.org/10.1037/0003-066X.59.1.20

Bonanno, G. A. (2005). Resilience in the face of potential trauma. *Current Directions in Psychological Science, 14,* 135–138. http://dx.doi.org/10.1111/j.0963-7214.2005.00347.x

Campbell-Sills, L., Cohan, S. L., & Stein, M. B. (2006). Relationship of resilience to personality, coping, and psychiatric symptoms in young adults. *Behaviour Research and Therapy, 44,* 585–599. http://dx.doi.org/10.1016/j.brat.2005.05.001

Cicchetti, D., & Rogosch, F. A. (2009). Adaptive coping under conditions of extreme stress: Multilevel influences on the determinants of resilience in maltreated children. *New Directions for Child and Adolescent Development, 2009,* 47–59. http://dx.doi.org/10.1002/cd.242

Clauss-Ehlers, C. S. (2008). Sociocultural factors, resilience, and coping: Support for a culturally sensitive measure of resilience. *Journal of Applied Developmental Psychology, 29,* 197–212. http://dx.doi.org/10.1016/j.appdev.2008.02.004

Davey, M., Eaker, D. G., & Walters, L. H. (2003). Resilience processes in adolescents: Personality profiles, self-worth, and coping. *Journal of Adolescent Research, 18,* 347–362. http://dx.doi.org/10.1177/0743558403018004002

Downey, C. A., & Chang, E. C. (2013). Assessment of everyday beliefs about health: The Lay Concepts of Health Inventory, college student version. *Psychology & Health, 28,* 818–832. http://dx.doi.org/10.1080/08870446.2012.762099

Fleming, J., & Ledogar, R. J. (2008). Resilience, an evolving concept: A review of literature relevant to Aboriginal research. *Pimatisiwin, 6,* 7–23. Retrieved from http://www.pimatisiwin.com/uploads/834803515.pdf

Fraser, M. W., Galinsky, M. J., & Richman, J. M. (1999). Risk, protection, and resilience: Toward a conceptual framework for social work practice. *Social Work Research, 23,* 131–143. http://dx.doi.org/10.1093/swr/23.3.131

Harvey, J., & Delfabbro, P. H. (2004). Psychological resilience in disadvantaged youth: A critical overview. *Australian Psychologist, 39,* 3–13. http://dx.doi.org/10.1080/00050060410001660281

Hawley, D. R., & DeHaan, L. (1996). Toward a definition of family resilience: Integrating life-span and family perspectives. *Family Process, 35,* 283–298. http://dx.doi.org/10.1111/j.1545-5300.1996.00283.x

Howard, S., Dryden, J., & Johnson, B. (1999). Childhood resilience: Review and critique of literature. *Oxford Review of Education, 25,* 307–323. http://dx.doi.org/10.1080/030549899104008

Kuperminc, G., Wilkins, N., Roche, C., & Alvarez-Jimenez, A. (2009). Risk, resilience, and positive development among Latino youth. In F. A. Villarruel, G. Carlo, J. M. Grau, M. Azmitia, N. J. Cabrera, & T. J. Chahin (Eds.), *Handbook of U.S. Latino psychology: Developmental and community-based perspectives* (pp. 213–233). Thousand Oaks, CA: Sage.

Ledogar, R. J., & Fleming, J. (2008). Social capital and resilience: A review of concepts and selected literature relevant to Aboriginal Youth resilience research. *Pimatisiwin, 6,* 25–46. Retreived from http://www.pimatisiwin.com/uploads/492281261.pdf

Leipold, B., & Greve, W. (2009). Resilience: A conceptual bridge between coping and development. *European Psychologist, 14,* 40–50. http://dx.doi.org/10.1027/1016-9040.14.1.40

Luthar, S. S., Cicchetti, D., & Becker, B. (2000). The construct of resilience: A critical evaluation and guidelines for future work. *Child Development, 71*, 543–562. http://dx.doi.org/10.1111/1467-8624.00164

Luthar, S. S., & Zigler, E. (1991). Vulnerability and competence: A review of research on resilience in childhood. *American Journal of Orthopsychiatry, 61*, 6–22. http://dx.doi.org/10.1037/h0079218

Maier, S. F., & Watkins, L. R. (2005). Stressor controllability and learned helplessness: The roles of the dorsal raphe nucleus, serotonin, and corticotropin-releasing factor. *Neuroscience and Biobehavioral Reviews, 29*, 829–841. http://dx.doi.org/10.1016/j.neubiorev.2005.03.021

Masten, A. S. (2001). Ordinary magic. Resilience processes in development. *American Psychologist, 56*, 227–238. http://dx.doi.org/10.1037/0003-066X.56.3.227

Rutter, M. (2006). Implications of resilience concepts for scientific understanding. *Annals of the New York Academy of Sciences, 1094*, 1–12. http://dx.doi.org/10.1196/annals.1376.002

Sirois, F. M., & Hirsch, J. K. (2013). Associations of psychological thriving with coping efficacy, expectations for future growth, and depressive symptoms over time in people with arthritis. *Journal of Psychosomatic Research, 75*, 279–286. http://dx.doi.org/10.1016/j.jpsychores.2013.06.004

Skinner, E. A., Edge, K., Altman, J., & Sherwood, H. (2003). Searching for the structure of coping: A review and critique of category systems for classifying ways of coping. *Psychological Bulletin, 129*, 216–269. http://dx.doi.org/10.1037/0033-2909.129.2.216

Smith, C., & Carlson, B. E. (1997). Stress, coping, and resilience in children and youth. *The Social Service Review, 71*, 231–256. http://dx.doi.org/10.1086/604249

Tummala-Narra, P. (2007). Conceptualizing trauma and resilience across diverse contexts: A multicultural perspective. *Journal of Aggression, Maltreatment & Trauma, 14*(1-2), 33–53. http://dx.doi.org/10.1300/J146v14n01_03

Tusaie, K., & Dyer, J. (2004). Resilience: A historical review of the construct. *Holistic Nursing Practice, 18*(1), 3–10. http://dx.doi.org/10.1097/00004650-200401000-00002

Ungar, M. (2008). Resilience across cultures. *British Journal of Social Work, 38*, 218–235. http://dx.doi.org/10.1093/bjsw/bcl343

Ungar, M., Brown, M., Liebenberg, L., Othman, R., Kwong, W. M., Armstrong, M., & Gilgun, J. (2007). Unique pathways to resilience across cultures. *Adolescence, 42*, 287–310.

Waller, M. A. (2001). Resilience in ecosystemic context: Evolution of the concept. *American Journal of Orthopsychiatry, 71*, 290–297. http://dx.doi.org/10.1037/0002-9432.71.3.290

Windle, G., Bennett, K. M., & Noyes, J. (2011). A methodological review of resilience measurement scales. *Health and Quality of Life Outcomes, 9*(8), 1–18. http://dx.doi.org/10.1186/1477-7525-9-8

INDEX

Acceptance
  as positive cognition, 139
  in positive practice with Latinas/
    os, 246
Acceptance and Action
    Questionnaire-II, 139
Acculturation
  of American Indians/Alaska Natives,
    203
  of Asian Americans, 38, 52, 227
  and biculturalism, 21
  of Latinas/os, 63
  of Native Americans, 285, 295–296
  and positive emotions, 222
  stress due to, 222–223
  of values vs. behaviors, 142
Acculturation gap distress, 51
Aceptación, 70
Adjustment, as trait, 42
Adversity, two-dimensional model of
    experiences of, 313–319
Adversity paradox, 89
Affective states
  positive and negative, 41
  and positive emotion, 173–175
"African American humor," 99
African Americans, 83–100, 171–186,
    259–273
  and communalism, 11
  demographics of, 84–85
  developing assessment tools for, 186
  developing positive psychology for,
    99–100
  facilitating positive affect in,
    264–266
  facilitating positive behaviors in,
    266–268
  facilitating positive cognitions in,
    268–270
  and hope, 17
  integrative model of positive practice
    with, 270–273
  measures of positive affect in,
    172–176
  measures of positive behaviors in,
    177–181

  measures of positive cognitions in,
    181–185
  mental health of, 259–262
  theory and research on positive
    affect in, 87–88
  theory and research on positive
    behaviors in, 88–91
  theory and research on positive
    cognitions in, 91–99
  value of assessing positive strengths
    in, 172
  value of positive psychology for,
    85–87
  value of positive psychology practice
    with, 262–264
Africentric cultural values, 263,
    267–268
Africentric psychology, 85–86
Africultural Coping Systems Inventory,
    180
Afrocultural ethos, 86–87
AI/ANs. *See* American Indians/Alaska
    Natives
AI-SUPERPFP (American Indian
    Service Utilization, Psychiatric
    Epidemiology, Risk and Protec-
    tive Factors Project), 207
Allery, A., 122
Altarriba, J., 70
Altruistic engagement, 89–91
American Indian Community Center
    (New York City), 118–119
American Indians/Alaska Natives
    (AI/ANs), 109–122, 195–209.
    See also Native Americans
  assessment of well-being in, 199–202
  cultural differences in assessment of,
    202–203
  current approaches to assessment of,
    207–208
  demographics of, 110–112
  developing positive psychology for,
    121–122
  emic assessment methods for,
    204–205
  ideal assessment for, 205–206

theory and research on positive
affect of, 113–117

theory and research on positive
cognitions of, 117–121

transitional assessment models for,
206–207

value of assessing positive strengths
in, 196–198

value of positive psychology for,
112–113

American Indian Service Utilization,
Psychiatric Epidemiology, Risk
and Protective Factors Project
(AI-SUPERPFP), 207

American Psychological Association
(APA), 15, 24, 26

Andersson, G., 162

Andrews, K., 136

Anxiety disorders, 261

APA (American Psychological
Association), 15, 24, 26

Armoring (strategy), 181

Arousal, 41

Artistic expression, 154–155

Asian Americans, 37–52, 131–143,
217–231

case studies of positive psychology
interventions with, 228–230

and cultural models of the self,
38–40

demographics of, 38, 218

developing assessment tools for,
140–143

developing positive psychology for,
48–52

facilitating positive affect in,
220–222

facilitating positive behaviors in,
222–223

facilitating positive cognitions in,
223–224

familism in, 22

integrative model of positive practice
with, 224–226

measures of positive affect in,
132–134

measures of positive behaviors in,
134–137

measures of positive cognitions in,
138–140

and model minority stereotype,
218–219

optimism and pessimism of, 16–17

positive psychology practice guidelines for, 226–228

theory and research on positive
affect in, 40–42

theory and research on positive
behaviors in, 45–47

theory and research on positive cognitions in, 42–45

value of positive psychology practice
with, 219–220

Asian American Values Scale, 136,
139–140

Asian Canadians, 41

Assessment(s). See also specific assessments
cultural differences in assessment
of American Indians/Alaska
Natives, 202–203

current approaches to assessment
of American Indians/Alaska
Natives, 207–208

developing, for African Americans,
186

developing, for Asian Americans,
140–143

developing, for Latinas/os, 162–164

emic methods for American Indians/
Alaska Natives, 204–205

ideal, for American Indians/Alaska
Natives, 205–206

measures of positive affect in African
Americans, 172–176

measures of positive affect in Asian
Americans, 132–134

measures of positive affect in Latinas/
os, 153–155

measures of positive behaviors in
African Americans, 177–181

measures of positive behaviors in
Asian Americans, 134–137

measures of positive behaviors in
Latinas/os, 155–159

measures of positive cognitions in
African Americans, 181–185

measures of positive cognitions in
Asian Americans, 138–140

measures of positive cognitions in
Latinas/os, 159–162

traditional, 197, 204–206
transitional assessment models, 206–207
value of assessing positive strengths in African Americans, 172
value of assessing positive strengths in American Indians/Alaska Natives, 196–198
value of assessing positive strengths in Latinas/os, 152–153
of well-being in American Indians/ Alaska Natives, 199–202
Authenticity, 45
Awareness, and well-being, 74–75
Awareness of Connectedness Scale, 207
Ayalong, L., 173

Bagley, C. A., 89
Baker, A. M., 223
Baldwin, J. A., 89
Barr, A., 175
Beck Depression Inventory–Second Edition, 174
Behavioral integrity, 96–97
Bendiciónes, 70
Bergman, Robert, 196
Bermúdez, J. M., 72
Bermúdez, S., 72
Berry, J. W., 21
BFST (brief strategic family therapy), 249
Bias(es)
    in assessment of American Indians/ Alaska Natives, 198
    cultural, 308–309
    optimism, 16–17
    pessimistic, 17
    self-enhancement, 19
Biculturalism, 51–52
    awareness of, 309
    as culture-specific strength, 21–22
    and well-being, 223–224
Bilingualism
    among clinicians, 237–238
    and flexible thinking, 159–160
Boehm, J. K., 221
Bowman, P. J., 89
Boykins, A. W., 94
Brave Heart, M. Y. H., 112, 297
Brendtro, L. K., 289
Brief RCOPE, 179

Brief strategic family therapy (BFST), 249
Brockmeier, J., 115
Brokenleg, M., 289
Brooks, R. B., 121

Calderón-Tena, C. O., 156
Caldwell-Colbert, A. T., 186, 263, 273
Campa, B., 156
Campesino, M., 161
Carbaugh, D. A., 115
Cariño, 242
Carlo, G., 156
Carroll, J., 89
Castellanos, J., 68
Cervantes, J. M., 68
Chancellor, J., 119
Chang, E. C., 17, 132, 133, 185, 221
Character Strengths and Virtues (Peterson and Seligman), 4
Chavez, Cesar, 72
Chavez, N. R., 240
Children's Hope Scale, 184
Chin, J. L., 136
Choice behaviors, 45–46
Christopher, J .C., 25–26
Church
    activities of, 95
    development of African American, 95–96
Cochran, S. D., 88
Cognitive disputation, 246
Cognitive flexibility, 22
Cognitive reframing, 71
Coles, Robert, 196
Collaborative religious coping, 179
Collective identity
    of American Indians/Alaska Natives, 113
    of Latinas/os, 65
Collective self-esteem, 133
Collective Self-Esteem Scale, 133
Communalism
    in positive practice with African Americans, 268
    and racial socialization, 94
Communities
    importance of, for American Indians/ Alaska Natives, 118–119
    importance of, for Latinas/os, 65, 66

Community-defined evidence, 203
Community-derived assessments,
    205–206
Community resilience, 120
Compadrazgo, 66
Concern for face, 139
Constantine, M. G., 153
Contreras, J. M., 22
Cook, D., 139
Coparentage, in Latin American
    communities, 66
Coping
    among American Indians/Alaska
        Natives, 118
    culturally specific, by African
        Americans, 179–181
    and culture, 318
    as positive behavior, 134
    in positive practice with African
        Americans, 265–266
    and religion, 94, 178–179
    and resilience, 120–121, 310, 312
    safe vs. risky, 313–317
Coping Strategies Inventory, 134–135
Coresearcher methodology, 163
Crazy Horse (Tasunka Witko), 115, 201
Crocker, J., 155
Cross-Cultural (Chinese) Personality
    Assessment Inventory, 137
Cross-Cultural Personality Assessment
    Inventory-2, 134
Csikszentmihalyi, M., 15, 20, 24,
    224, 262
Cultural bias, 308–309
Cultural competence, 26
Cultural frame switching, 22
Cultural identity, 287–288
Cultural integration, 24–25
Culturally relevant assessments, 154
Cultural mistrust, 260
    of African Americans, 97
    of Native Americans, 286–287,
        296–297
Cultural models of the self, 38–40
Cultural resilience, 120–121
Cultural socialization, 92–93
Cultural stigma, regarding mental
    illness, 236–237
Cultural strengths, 227–228
Cultural transcendence, 24

Culture
    and coping, 318
    importance of, to Latinas/os, 63
    and optimism, 15–17
    positive psychology in changing,
        14–15
    priming of, 40
Culture-specific strengths, 20–23
Curanderismo, 67

Dana, R. H., 206
Dandeneau, S. F., 120
Dantley, M. E., 95
Davidson, C. L., 17
Davis, D. E., 157
Deferred religious coping, 179
Defining Issues Test, 96
Dell, C., 282
Dell, D., 282–283
Deloria, V., Jr., 287
Depression
    among African Americans, 261
    among Asian Americans, 221–222
Destino, 70–71, 244
Diagnoses, and culture, 243
Diagnostic and Statistical Manual of
    Mental Disorders (American
    Psychiatric Association), 4
Diagnostic and Statistical Manual of
    Mental Disorders, 5th ed.
    (American Psychiatric
    Association), 270
Dialectical thinking, 44
Dichos, 73–74, 246–247
Diener, E., 154
Discrimination
    addressing, in positive practice with
        Latinas/os, 240
    negative effects of, 152
    positive behaviors to mitigate, 156
    and subjective well-being, 18–19
Diversity, in psychological studies, 5–6
Dixon, A., 87
Donahue, D. M., 154
Dornbusch, S. M., 156
Dreams, as inspiration, 204
DuBray, W. H., 288
Dumka, L., 157
Duran, B., 112
Duran, E., 112

Duran, Phillip, 195
Durkheim, E., 23
Dweck, C. S., 160

Eagle feathers, 292–293
"Eagle Medicine," 292–293
East Asians
    low arousal positive states in, 41–42
    mixed emotions in, 41
    world view of, 44–45
Edwards, K. J., 161
Elders, respect for, 289
Ellsworth, P. C., 221
Emic approach
    to Latina/o values, 68–69
    to well-being, 73, 75
Emotional intelligence, 6–7
Emotional suppression, 47
Emotion regulation
    as Asian and Asian American
        value, 140
    in Asians, 47
    cultural differences in, 174
Emotions
    mixed, 41
    positive. See Positive emotions
    social context of, 42
Emotion socialization behavior, 174
Enculturation
    of Asian Americans, 38, 52
    of Latinas/os, 71
Engagement, 271
Erdrich, Louise, 116
Eshun, S., 186
Ethnic gloss, 121
Ethnic groups
    among African Americans, 84,
        91–92
    among American Indians/Alaska
        Natives, 110–111
    among Asian Americans, 38, 52
    among Latinas/os, 62–63
Ethnic identity
    as culture-specific strength, 20–21
    of Latinas/os, 155, 240
Ethnocentric criticism, of positive psy-
    chology, 25–26
Evans-Campbell, T., 118
Evidence-based practice, 202
Exline, J. J., 158

Explicit social support, 51
Ey, S., 182

Face
    concern for, 139
    loss of, 219
Fairness, 96–97
Faith, 160–161
Falicov, C. J., 70
Familism
    as cultural value, 156–157
    as culture-specific strength, 22
    in positive practice with Latinas/os,
        240, 242
Familismo, 65–66, 156–157, 248–249
Family(-ies)
    dealing with mental illnesses within,
        236–237
    importance of, for Latinas/os, 65–66,
        71–72
    positive behaviors stemming from,
        136
    in positive practice with Latinas/os,
        244–245, 248–249
    in positive practice with Native
        Americans, 295–296
    resilience in African American,
        88–89
    resilience in Asian American, 223
Family genograms, 288–289
Family growth initiative, 142
Family obligation, 136
Family Recognition through Achieve-
    ment subscale, 136
Fatalismo, 70, 244, 246, 248
Filial piety, 136
Filial Piety Scale, 136
Filial therapy, 249
Fincham, F. D., 263
Fixed mind-set, 160
Fixico, D. L., 196–197
Fleming, J., 120
Flórez, K. R., 70
Flourishing, defining, 270–271
Forgiveness
    among Native Americans, 290–293
    in Asian context, 50–51
    as positive behavior, 177–178
    in positive practice with African
        Americans, 267–268

Fredrickson, B., 164
Fredrickson, B. L., 116, 117, 153, 155, 264
French, S., 240
"Fruits of the spirit," 265
Fuligni, A. J., 156

Gamst, G., 63
Garrett, J. T., 293
Garrett, M. T., 116
Germán, M., 157
Gloria, A. M., 68
Goldstein, S., 121
Gomez, M. A., 91–92
Gonzalez, L. M., 136
Gonzalez, N. A., 157
Gonzalez, O., 261
Goodluck, C., 283
Gopalan, H., 222
Gordon, D. B., 99
Graham, S., 5
Gratitude
    of African Americans, 98
    and Asian Americans, 224, 226–227
Gray-Little, B., 175
Grayshield, L., 285, 287
Gregory, W. H., Jr., 89
Griddine, K., 87
Group level (positive psychological
        approach), 319
Growth mind-set, 160
Guanxi Behaviors Scale, 137
Guanxi Favors subscale, 137
Guanxi Friends subscale, 137
Guanxi use, 137

Haciendo tiempo, 69
Hafdahl, A. R., 175
Hall, M. E., 153
Hall, T. W., 161
Happiness
    in Asian American culture, 220
    as component of positive psychol-
        ogy, 222
    and depression, 221–222
    in different cultures, 222
    life satisfaction vs., 138
    measures of, 132–133
Harmony, 134
Harmony subscale, 134
Harrell, J. P., 180

Harter Self-Perception Profile for
        Children, 175–176
Hayes, S. C., 139
Health outcomes, 16
Health Psychology, 110
Healy, S., 120–121
Heatheron, T. F., 155
HeavyHead, R., 200
HeavyRunner, I., 284
Heine, S. J., 5
Henrich, J., 5
Herring, R. D., 293–295
Herringshaw, A. J., 133, 221
Hickinbottom, S., 25–26
High arousal positive states, 41–42
Hirsch, J. K., 17, 177–178, 185
Historical trauma
    defined, 112
    healing from, 296–298
Historical trauma and unresolved grief
        intervention, 297–298
Hodge, D. R., 206–208
Hook, J. N., 157
Hoop Dance, 281
Hope
    assessment of, 138, 183–185
    as predictor, 17
Hopelessness Scale, 182
Hope Scale, 138, 184
Hopkins, C., 282–283
Horse Spirit Society (Sung Nagi
        Okolakiciye), 205
Humilidad, 158
Humility
    as American Indian value, 119
    measures of, 157–159
    as positive cognition, 139–140
    relational, 157–158
Humility Inventory, 140
Humility Subscale, 139–140
Humor
    and American Indians/Alaska
        Natives, 116–117
    as coping strategy, 98–99
    in positive practice with African
        Americans, 268

Ideal affect, 41–42, 50
Identifying Signature Strengths
        exercise, 225

Identity development theory, 20
Immigration, 38
Implicit social support, 51
Income, and subjective well-being, 18, 245
Independent view of self, 39–40
Index of Family Obligation, 136
Indian Relocation Act of 1956, 111
Indians, choice behavior of, 46
Indigenous ways of knowing (IWOK), 285–287
Individual level (positive psychological approach), 319
Influence, as trait, 42
Injustice, 89–91
Institutionalized racism, 260
Insurance coverage, 238
Integra/o, 153
Integrative model
    of positive practice with African Americans, 270–273
    of positive practice with Asian Americans, 224–226
    of positive practice with Latinas/os, 247–249
Intelligence
    beliefs about, 160
    emotional, 6–7
Intent, 76
Intention, 76
Intentional behavior (Personal Growth Initiative Scale-II), 135
Interconnectedness
    of American Indians/Alaska Natives, 112, 115, 117
    of Latinas/os, 64–69
    in Native American spirituality, 290
Interdependent view of self, 39–40
Internalized racism, 260
Interpersonal relationships, 47
Interventions, culturally consistent, 50–52
Isaac, C., 120
IWOK (Indigenous ways of knowing), 285–287

Japanese
    choice behavior of, 46
    mixed emotions of, 221
    social context of emotions in, 42

Jeglic, E. L., 17, 177–178
Jones, C. P., 260
Journaling, 267
Justice, 96–97

Kahle, E. R., 17
Kawahara, D. M., 136
Keyes, C. L., 117
Kiang, L., 136
Kim, B. K., 136, 140, 141
Kim, J., 222–223
Kim, S., 222
King, J., 118–120
Kirmayer, L. J., 120
Kitayama, S., 155
Kliewer, W., 93
Knight, G. P., 156, 175
Knox, P. L., 96
Koo, K., 24–25, 220
Koreans
    acculurative stress among, 222–223
    and authenticity, 45
Koshares, 116–117
Krumrei, E. J., 162
Kruse, E., 119
Kubokawa, A., 222

LaFromboise, T. D., 121
Lakota, world view of, 200–201
Lakota Oyate Wakanyeja Owicakiyapi (LOWO), 205
Langer, R., 153
Language
    and assessment tools, 154
    as barrier to mental health services, 237–238
    native, 69–70
Larsen, R. J., 154
Latinas/os, 61–76, 151–164, 235–250
    demographics of, 62–63, 152
    developing assessment tools for, 162–164
    facilitating positive affect in, 69–71, 242–244
    facilitating positive behaviors in, 71–72, 244–245
    facilitating positive cognitions in, 72–74, 245–247
    and hope, 17

Latinas/os, *continued*
   integrative model of positive practice with, 247–249
   interconnectedness among, 64–69
   and *latinidad*, 63–64
   measures of positive affect in, 153–155
   measures of positive behaviors in, 155–159
   measures of positive cognitions in, 159–162
   mental health challenges of, 236–239
   value of assessing positive strengths in, 152–153
   value of positive psychology practice with, 239–242
   well-being of, 74–76
Latinidad, 63–64
Latino Spiritual Perspectives Scale (LSPS), 161
Layous, K., 271
Ledogar, R. J., 120
Lee, E. A., 223
Lee, Y., 134
Leu, J., 24–25, 220, 227
Lewis, M., 89
Lewis, R., 87
Life Orientation Test–Revised (LOT-R), 183
Life outcomes, 315
Life satisfaction, 18, 138
Life Satisfaction Index A, 174
Limb, G. E., 206–208
Lin, Y., 134
Little Bear, Leroy, 200
Lopez, S. J., 163, 197–198
Loss of face, 219
Loss of Face scale, 139
LOT-R (Life Orientation Test–Revised), 183
Love
   in Africentric psychology, 87–88
   and positive psychology, 164
Low arousal positive states, 41–42
LOWO (Lakota Oyate Wakanyeja Owicakiyapi), 205
LSPS (Latino Spiritual Perspectives Scale), 161
Lucas, R. E., 154

Luhtanen, R., 155
Lyubomirsky, S., 119, 221, 264

Mackinnon, C., 68
Macquez, Gabriel García, 235
Major, B., 180
Markus, H. R., 155
Martínez, K. J., 202, 203
Maslow, Abraham, 200
Mattering, in Africentric psychology, 87
Mattis, J. S., 90, 91, 94
Mays, V. M., 88
McAdams, D. P., 89
McMartin, J., 153
McNulty, J. K., 263
Meaningful activities, 223
Meaning-making, 114–115, 290–293
Medicaid, access to, 238
Medicine Wheel, 112
Mental health challenges
   of African Americans, 259–262
   of Latinas/os, 236–239
Mental health services
   language as barrier to, 237
   socio-economic factors in utilization of, 238–239
   underuse of, by Asian Americans, 219
   underuse of, by Latinas/os, 236–237
Mestizo spirituality, 68
Mexican American Cultural Values Scale, 157, 161
Michaels, M. L., 175
Mickelson, K. D., 23
Microaggressions, racial, 141
Middle Passage, 84
Mihecoby, A., 285, 287
Mindful Attention Awareness Scale, 138–139
Mindfulness
   and Asian Americans, 227
   and Native Americans, 285–287
   as positive cognition, 138–139
Mistrust, 260
   of African Americans, 97
   of Native Americans, 286–287, 296–297
Mixed emotions, 41, 221
Miyamoto, Y., 221
Model minority stereotype, 218–219

Mohatt, N. V., 122
Mood disorders, 261
Morality, 96–97
Moral motives, of altruism, 90
Moral Orientation Scale, 96
Morris, J. S., 284
Motivational interviewing, 122, 163
Multi-Axial Model of Coping, 181
Multidimensional Students' Life Satis-
    faction Scale, 174
Myers, L. J., 86

Narratives, 114
National Health and Nutrition
    Examination Survey, 111
Native Americans, 281–300. *See also*
    American Indians/Alaska Natives
    common presenting issues of,
        293–295
    cultural identity of, 287–288,
        295–296
    family genograms of, 288–289
    forgiveness and meaning-making
        among, 290–293
    healing from historical trauma by,
        296–298
    and Indigenous ways of knowing,
        285–287
    signature strengths of, 284–285
    spirituality in treatment of, 299
    traditions in treatment of, 298–299
    value of positive psychology prac-
        tices with, 282–283
    and wisdom keepers, 289
Native language, 69–70
Need-based motives, of altruism, 90
Negative affective states, 41
Nobles, W. W., 86
Norenzayan, A., 5
Norton, N. E. L., 163

Oishi, S., 18
Optimal functioning
    and Africentric psychology, 86
    in different cultures, 48–49
Optimism
    of African Americans, 97–98
    of American Indians/Alaska Natives,
        117–118
    of Asian Americans, 44–45

assessment of, 181–183
as component of positive psychol-
    ogy, 222
and culture, 15–17
Optimism bias, 16–17
Ottaway, A., 222

Pace, T. M., 207
Pal, M. S., 136
Parental pressure, 52
Parks, F. M., 186
Pathways thinking, 184, 185
Patient Protection and Affordable Care
    Act (2010), 238
Patrón, 64
Patten, A. H., 89
Pavlenko, A., 154
Peace of mind, 134
Peace of Mind Scale, 134
Penn Resiliency Program, 182
Perez, C. R., 223
Perreira, K. M., 156
Personal affirmation, 269
Personal growth initiative
    defined, 135
    family vs., 142
Personal Growth Initiative Scale-II
    (PGIS-II), 135
Personalismo, 69, 242
Personally mediated racism, 260, 271
Personal Responsibility and Work
    Opportunity Reconciliation Act
    (1996), 238
Pessimism
    of Asian Americans, 44–45
    and Asians and Asian Americans, 16
Pessimistic bias, 17
Peterson, C., 4, 24, 25
PGIS-II (Personal Growth Initiative
    Scale-II), 135
Phinney, J. S., 20
Physical health, 111. *See also* Somatic
    symptoms
Ping chang xin, 141
Planfulness (Personal Growth Initiative
    Scale-II), 135
Positive affect
    in African Americans, 87–88
    in American Indians/Alaska Natives,
        113–117

Positive affect, *continued*
  in Asian Americans, 40–42
  facilitating, in African Americans,
    264–266
  facilitating, in Asian Americans,
    220–222
  facilitating, in Latinas/os, 242–244
  high vs. low arousal, 41–42
  in Latinas/os, 69–71
  measures of, in African Americans,
    172–176
  measures of, in Asian Americans,
    132–134
  measures of, in Latinas/os,
    153–155
  and negative, 41
Positive affectivity, 132
Positive Affectivity subscale, 132
Positive and Negative Affect
    Schedule, 132
Positive and Negative Affect
    Schedule—Expanded, 174
Positive behaviors
  in African Americans, 88–91
  in Asian Americans, 45–47
  defining, 266–267
  facilitating, in African Americans,
    266–268
  facilitating, in Asian Americans,
    222–223
  facilitating, in Latinas/os, 244–245
  in Latinas/os, 71–72
  measures of, in African Americans,
    177–181
  measures of, in Asian Americans,
    134–137
  measures of, in Latinas/os, 155–159
Positive cognitions
  in African Americans, 91–99
  in American Indians/Alaska Natives,
    117–121
  in Asian Americans, 42–45
  facilitating, in African Americans,
    268–270
  facilitating, in Asian Americans,
    223–224
  facilitating, in Latinas/os, 245–247
  in Latinas/os, 72–74
  measures of, in African Americans,
    181–185

  measures of, in Asian Americans,
    138–140
  measures of, in Latinas/os, 159–162
Positive emotions
  in different cultures, 24–25
  in positive practice with Asian
    Americans, 220, 227
Positive psychological approach, 319
Positive psychology, 13–27
  in a changing culture, 14–15
  and changing demographics, 14
  components of, 222
  cultural competence in, 26
  and culture-specific strengths, 20–23
  debate within field of, 23–26
  developing, for African Americans,
    99–100
  developing, for American Indians/
    Alaska Natives, 121–122
  developing, for Asian Americans,
    48–52
  emergence of, 3–4
  optimism and culture in, 15–17
  self-esteem in, 19–20
  subjective well-being in, 18–19
  universal applicability of, 6–7
  value of, for African Americans,
    85–87
  value of, for American Indians/
    Alaska Natives, 112–113
Positive Psychology Center, 4
Positive psychology practice
  case studies of positive psychology
    interventions with Asian
    Americans, 228–230
  facilitating positive affect in African
    Americans, 264–266
  facilitating positive affect in Asian
    Americans, 220–222
  facilitating positive affect in Latinas/
    os, 242–244
  facilitating positive behaviors in
    African Americans,
    266–268
  facilitating positive behaviors in
    Asian Americans, 222–223
  facilitating positive behaviors in
    Latinas/os, 244–245
  facilitating positive cognitions in
    African Americans, 268–270

facilitating positive cognitions in Asian Americans, 223–224

facilitating positive cognitions in Latinas/os, 245–247

genograms in, 288–289

guidelines for, 226–228

integrative model of, with African Americans, 270–273

integrative model of, with Asian Americans, 224–226

integrative model of, with Latinas/os, 247–249

value of, with African Americans, 262–264

value of, with Asian Americans, 219–220

value of, with Latinas/os, 239–242

value of, with Native Americans, 282–283

Positive reappraisal, 269

Positive strengths
value of assessing, in African Americans, 172

value of assessing, in American Indians/Alaska Natives, 196–198

value of assessing, in Latinas/os, 152–153

Posttraumatic growth, 153–154

Posttraumatic stress disorder (PTSD), 261, 298

Practice-based evidence, 202, 203

Presenting issues, of Native Americans, 293–295

Prilleltensky, I., 6

Priming, of culture, 40

Problem-solving behavior, 21–22

Proctor, Sam, 196

Protective factors, 311–312

Psychological disengagement, 180

Psychotic disorders, 261–262

PTSD (posttraumatic stress disorder), 261, 298

Raboteau, A. J., 95

Racial identity, 91–92

Racial microaggressions, 141

Racial socialization, 92–94

Racism, 260

Rashid, T., 164

Readiness for change (Personal Growth Initiative Scale-II), 135

Reframing, 71, 245–246

Relational humility, 157–158

Relationships
in American Indians/Alaska Natives world view, 199–200

interpersonal, 47

and positive affect, 69

and positive behaviors, 137, 155–156

in positive practice with African Americans, 269–270

in positive practice with Latinas/os, 242–243

Religion
and African Americans, 94–96, 178–179, 269

as culture-specific strength, 23

and hope, 184

and Latinas/os, 66–67

and well-being, 161–162

Religious coping, 179

Ren, 140–141

Ren qing, 137

Ren Qing scale, 137

Resilience
of African Americans, 88–89, 265

of American Indians/Alaska Natives, 120–121

of Asian Americans, 131, 223

as collection of protective factors, 311–312

as collection of traits, 311

differing conceptualizations of, 310–313

of Latinas/os, 240

in multicultural positive psychology, 309–310

of Native Americans, 282–283

as process, 312

two-dimensional model of, 313–319

Revised Trait Hope Scale, 185

Reynolds, J., 89

Rhue, S., 88

Richardson, F. C., 25

Risky coping, 313–317

Rivas-Drake, D., 265

Roosa, M. W., 175

Rosenberg Self-Esteem Scale, 133, 175, 176

Rosmarin, D. H., 162
Ruberton, P. M., 119
Ruthig, J. C., 122
Rutter, M., 312

Safe coping, 313–317
Sakokwenionkwas, 116, 117
Sánchez, George I., 63–64
Sandage, S. J., 118
Sanna, L. J., 133, 221
Santiago-Rivera, A. L., 65, 70
Satisfaction with Life Scale, 138
Schizophrenia, 261–262
Schmader, T., 180
School Domain subscale, 174
Schwartz, S. J., 11
Sears, D. O., 5
Sehdev, M., 120
Self
    American Indian/Alaska Native
        concept of, 200–201
    cultural models of, 38–40
    development of, as basis of positive
        psychology, 25
    self-esteem across cultures, 43
    views of, in different populations,
        5–6
Self-determination, 222
Self-directed religious coping, 179
Self-disclosure, 243–244
Self Domain subscale, 174–175
Self-enhancement
    of Asians, 46–47
    in different cultures, 19–20
Self-enhancement biases, 19
Self-esteem
    and American Indians/Alaska
        Natives, 200
    of Asian Americans, 133
    assessment of, 175–176
    collective, 133
    and different views of self, 43
    of Latinas/os, 155
    in positive psychology, 19–20
Self-esteem formation theory, 179–180
Self-regulation, 93
Self-report measures, of resilience, 312
Seligman, M. E. P., 3, 4, 15, 20, 24, 25,
        109, 153, 224, 262–263
Sellers, R. M., 92

Seneca (Iroquois prophet), 119
Service, in positive practice, 287–288
Shamanism, 67–68
Sheldon, K. M., 221
Sherman, D. K., 110
Shults, F. L., 118
Signature strengths, 284–285
Silva, L., 21
Simoni, J. M., 118
Simpatía, 242
Sims, T., 41, 50
Slavery, 84
Slife, B. S., 25
Smith, T. B., 21
Snyder, C. R., 197–198
Social class, and cultural differences, 52
Social context, of emotions, 42
Social identity, and altruism, 91
Social identity theory
    and ethnic identity, 20
    positive affect in, 264–265
    and self-esteem, 175
Socially disengaging emotions, 42
Socially engaging emotions, 42
Social support
    in Asian context, 51
    and biculturalism, 22
    as buffer against acculturative stress,
        223
    in positive practice with African
        Americans, 269–270
    racial microaggressions mitigated
        with, 141
Socio-economic factors, 238–239
Socio-political motives, of altruism, 90
Somatic symptoms
    in positive practice with Latinas/
        os, 249
    psychological distress expressed as,
        237
    reported by African Americans, 261
Soto, J. A., 223
Sotomayor, Sonia, 72
"Spanglish," 69
Spirituality
    and African Americans, 94–96, 265
    and American Indians/Alaska
        Natives, 118
    as culture-specific strength, 23
    defined, among Latinas/os, 67

and Native Americans, 290–293, 299

and well-being, 161–162

The Spiritual Life of Children (Coles), 196

Steidel, A. G. L., 22

Stein, G. L., 136

Storytelling, as coping strategy, 98, 114

Strength-based perspective, 284

Strengths

cultural, 227–228

culture-specific, 20–23

positive. *See* Positive strengths

signature, 284–285

Stressors, 313

Subjective Happiness Scale, 132–133

Subjective level (positive psychological approach), 319

Subjective well-being, 18–19, 222

Substance abuse, 297

Sue, D. W., 153

Suh, W., 222

Sung Nagi Okolakiciye (Horse Spirit Society), 205

Supple, A. J., 136

Swamp, J., 114

Tabak, M. A., 23

Tasunka Witko (Crazy Horse), 115, 201

Taylor, J., 87

Taylor, S. E., 110

Technical Assistance Partnership for Child and Mental Health, 203

Terrell, F., 260, 266

Therapeutic alliance

with African Americans, 271–272

with Latinas/os, 247

Thomason, T., 207–208

Three Good Things exercise, 224–225

Toltec teachings, 67–68, 76

Tomasulo, D. J., 164

Traditional assessments, 197, 204–206

Traditions, in treatment of Native Americans, 298–299

Trait Hope Scale, 185

Transformation, and well-being, 75

Transitional assessment models, 206–207

Trauma, as growth agent, 153

Tribal groups, 287–288

Trimble, J. E., 118, 119, 121

TRIOS model, 180–181

Tsai, W., 133, 221

Tucker, C., 87

Two-dimensional model of experiences of adversity, 313–319

Uba, L., 134, 140

Uchida, Y., 221

Using resources (Personal Growth Initiative Scale-II), 135

Using Signature Strengths exercise, 225–226

Valence, 41

Valenzuela, A., 156

Values

Africentric cultural, 263, 267–268

in different cultures, 25–26

and intent, 76

of Latinas/os, 64, 68–69, 73–74, 244–245

Native American, 285, 297

Van Bockern, S., 289

Verghese, A., 118

Visser, P. L., 185

Waller, M .A., 113

Walters, K. L., 118

Wang, J., 24–25, 220

Ward, J. V., 96

Watters, E., 7

Ways of Coping measure, 181

Webb, J. R., 177–178

WEIRD characteristics, 5–6

Weisskirch, R. S., 11

Well-being

American Indian/Alaska Native definitions of, 119–120

in American Indian/Alaska Native world view, 113

assessment of, in American Indians/Alaska Natives, 199–202

Well-being, *continued*
    defining, for Asian Americans, 48
    and happiness, 132
    of Latinas/os, 72–76
    and religion/spirituality, 161–162
    subjective, 18–19, 222
Will, as Latina/o value, 72
Wisdom keepers, 289
Worldviews
    of American Indians/Alaska Natives,
        111–112, 114–116, 119–120,
        196–197
    of Asian Americans, 44–45
    emphasis on different, 309

of Latinas/os, 63–64
of Native Americans, 282–283
Wright, B. A., 163
Wyland, C. L., 155

Yahirun, J. J., 156
You at Your Best exercise, 225
Young, M. A., 173
Youth Life Orientation Test, 182
Yu, E. A., 17

Zeigarnik effect, 283
Zeigler-Hill, V., 176
Zuniga, M. E., 73

ABOUT THE EDITORS

Edward C. Chang, PhD, is a professor of psychology and social work, and a faculty associate in Asian/Pacific Islander American Studies, at the University of Michigan, Ann Arbor. He is a fellow of the Asian American Psychological Association. Dr. Chang received his BA in psychology and philosophy from the State University of New York at Buffalo, and his MA and PhD degrees from the State University of New York at Stony Brook. He completed his American Psychological Association (APA)–accredited clinical internship at Bellevue Hospital Center–New York University Medical Center. Dr. Chang serves as a program evaluator for the Michigan Department of Community Health–Social Determinants of Health, working with the Asian Center Southeast Michigan. He also serves as an associate editor of *American Psychologist* and *Cognitive Therapy and Research*. Dr. Chang has published more than 100 works on optimism and pessimism, perfectionism, social problem solving, and cultural influences on behavior. He is the editor of *Optimism and Pessimism: Implications for Theory, Research, and Practice* (2001); *Self-Criticism and Self-Enhancement: Theory, Research, and Clinical Implications* (2006); *Handbook of Adult Psychopathology in Asians: Diagnosis, Etiology, and Treatment* (2012); and is a coeditor of *Virtue, Vice, and Personality: The*

Complexity of Behavior (2003); *Social Problem Solving: Theory, Research, and Training* (2004); *Judgments Over Time: The Interplay of Thoughts, Feelings, and Behaviors* (2006); *Handbook of Race and Development in Mental Health* (2012); and *Biopsychosocial Approaches to Understanding Health in South Asian Americans* (forthcoming). Along with other honors and awards, Dr. Chang was the recipient of the 2012 Theodore Millon Award in Personality Psychology sponsored by the American Psychological Foundation and the Society of Clinical Psychology.

Christina A. Downey, PhD, is an associate professor and chair of psychology at Indiana University Kokomo. She received her BA in psychology from Purdue University in West Lafayette, Indiana, and her MS and PhD degrees in clinical psychology from the University of Michigan, Ann Arbor. Dr. Downey completed her APA-accredited clinical internship at the University of Michigan Center for the Child and Family, and the University of Michigan Psychological Clinic. She has published articles on various topics related to lay concepts of health, eating disorder symptoms and perfectionism, perceptions of online versus face-to-face social interactions, and effective college teaching methods in journals such as *Eating Behaviors*, *Psychology and Health*, the *Scandinavian Journal of Psychology*, and the *Journal of Effective Teaching*. She also serves on the editorial board of *Cognitive Therapy and Research*, and is a reviewer for several scholarly journals. Dr. Downey was coeditor of the *Handbook of Race and Development in Mental Health* (2012) and has published several chapters on racial and ethnic factors in positive and negative mental health.

Jameson K. Hirsch, PhD, is an associate professor of clinical psychology and assistant chair at East Tennessee State University, and maintains faculty appointments in the Department of Psychiatry, University of Rochester Medical Center, the Department of Public Health, East Tennessee State University, and as a research scientist at the Mountain Home VAMC. Dr. Hirsch received his PhD from the University of Wyoming, completed his APA-accredited internship at SUNY Upstate Medical Center, and his National Institute on Mental Health postdoctoral fellowship at the University of Rochester School of Medicine and Dentistry. Dr. Hirsch's research focuses on protective, positive psychological characteristics that buffer against psychopathology, particularly depression and suicidal behavior, occurring in the context of stressors such as medical illness and impairment and in underserved and under-represented groups, including rural, elderly, and ethnic minority individuals. Dr. Hirsch has published over 75 peer-reviewed articles on protective factors, including positive affect, happiness, optimism, forgiveness, hopefulness, and future orientation, as they relate to physical and mental health. He currently serves as a member of the APA Committee on Rural Health and on numerous editorial boards, including those of *Cognitive Therapy and Research* and *Suicide and Life Threatening Behavior*.

Natalie J. Lin, MHSA, is a postgraduate fellow in health care administration at Kaiser Permanente, Southern California. She received her MHSA degree from the School of Public Health at the University of Michigan, Ann Arbor. Ms. Lin received her BA in psychology and a BMA in piano performance, both achieved with honors distinction, from the University of Michigan, Ann Arbor. She has conducted, presented, and published research on a wide range of topics, including perfectionism, rumination, optimism, motivation, well-being, suicide-risk, and multicultural psychology. In addition to conducting research in these areas, Ms. Lin has also previously served as a research associate of the Asian Center Southeast Michigan, a nonprofit community-based organization focusing on the diverse health needs of Asians and Asian Americans living in Southeast Michigan.